Nature and Lifeworld

Theoretical and practical Metaphysics

Odense University Studies in Philosophy vol. 15

Nature and Lifeworld

Theoretical and practical Metaphysics

Edited by Carsten Bengt-Pedersen
and Niels Thomassen

Odense University Press

Nature and Lifeworld is published with the generous support of Odense University

Anbefalet til udgivelse af professor, dr.phil. David Favrholdt, lektor, dr.phil. Erich G. Klawonn og professor, mag.art. Jørgen Dines Johansen

Cover illustration: Henrik Thomassen

© The authors and Odense University Press 1998
Printed in Denmark by Narayana Press

ISBN 87-7838-311-0
ISSN 0107 7384

Odense University Press
Campusvej 55
DK-5230 Odense M

Phone +45 66 15 79 99
Fax. +45 66 15 81 26
E-mail: Press@forlag.ou.dk
www-location:http//www.ou.dk/press

Distribution in The United States and Canada

International Specialized Book Services
5804 NE Hassolo Street
Portland, OR 97213-3644
USA

Phone +1 503 287 303
Fax +1 503 287 3093

Contents

Preface 7

I

Robin Attfield
Progress, Nature and Metaphysics 11

Carsten Bengt-Pedersen
Man and his Knowledge of Nature 27

Ragnar Fjelland
From Evolutionary Epistemology to the Life World A Priori 39

Róbert H. Haraldsson
From Metaphysical Subjects to Naturalized Selves 59

Vittorio Hösle
Sein und Subjektivität. Zur Metaphysik der ökologischen Krise 87

Ingvar Johansson
Perception as the Bridge between Nature and Life-World 113

Simo Knuuttila
Plenitude, Reason and Value:
Old and New in the Metaphysics of Nature 139

II

*Britt D. Andresen, Helle Balsby, Cathrine Egeland,
Mette Richter, Henriette Vognsgaard and
Ulla Wiborg Johansen*
Identity and Ethics 155

Henrik Bruun
Nature as a Symbol of Identity 167

Dan Egonsson
Man's Place in Nature 191

Martin Ishøy
Kants Critique of Judgement, the Inherent Ethics 203

Jonas Nilsson
Rationality, Substantive Belief, and the Metaphysical 209

Per Nilsson
Critical Theory and Nature 235

Sami Pihlström
The Pragmatist Critique of Metaphysics and the Nature of Man 249

Toni Rønnow-Rasmussen
Moral Realists and Moral Experts 281

Pär Sundström
Historicism and the Study of Human Nature
or does Philosophical Anthropology have a Subject Matter? 299

Merete Sørensen
Environmental Ethics and/or Environmental Aesthetics? 313

Tommi Vehkavaara
A Metaontology and the Metaphysics of *Différance* 321

Peter Wolsing
Nature and Life Practice in the Epistemology of the Young Hegel 339

Preface

In August 1995, the XI Internordic Philosophy Symposium was held at Odense University. The theme of the meeting was *Nature and Lifeworld. Theoretical and practical Metaphysics*, which was described in the following way:

A persistent theme of the philosophy of the 20th century has been a critique of metaphysics. It has taken its point of departure either in the scientific-technological project, in historization of man or in modern forms of enlightenment. But the limitations of these forms of thought are manifesting themselves more and more clearly. Among these limitations is the fact that both inner and outer nature have form and structure. Philosophy of nature becomes unavoidable. The lifeworld of man cannot be thoroughly understood without metaphysical reflection.

As long as man is seen as an expansive and creating being everything else can be seen as a means for its productive unfolding. History and progress constitute the totality. Whatever is wrong is largely interpreted as alienation. But when nature can no longer bear to be a means, it becomes clear that the historical unfolding of man is not all. The metaphysical questions return. The relationship between nature and history becomes a problem once again, moreover a practical-philosophical problem.

Nature has always challenged human understanding. But we have nearly forgotten that nature as the strange and enigmatic has thrown man into contemplative wonder. The metaphysical problems are as before also theoretical and aesthetical problems.

The theme of the conference thus is the metaphysical questions about man and nature and the relationship between them, as these questions emerge in the human lifeworld beyond the critique of metaphysics of our century.

The meeting adopted the structure of the Nordic philosopy symposia, grouped round seven main lectures and four workshops. The lectures were given by the two specially invited philosphers Robin Attfield and Vittorio Hösle, plus one lecturer from each of the five Nordic countries.

There were four workshops with the following topics: *Technology and Assessment of Technology, Fundamental Metaphysical Problems, Nature, Ethics and Aesthetics* and *Philosophy and Gender*.

Section I of the present book comprises the seven main lectures of the meeting, while Section II consists of a number of the workshop contributions. Each article is preceded by an abstract and concludes with information about the author.

We would like to take this opportunity of thanking the authors for the willingness with which they have placed their manuscripts at the disposal of this book.

Funding from the Philosophy Department at Odense University enabled the meeting to take place; this publication has been made possible thanks to the Odense University Publication Fund. We would like to express our gratitude to them for their support.

Carsten Bengt-Pedersen and Niels Thomassen

I

Robin Attfield

Progress, Nature and Metaphysics

Abstract
Respecting nature appears incompatible with belief in progress. But there are diverse concepts of progress and of nature. First I scrutinize Robert Nisbet's concept of progress, which incorporates belief that social improvement is possible. I argue that believers in progress need not accept Nisbet's five presuppositions as they stand. I next consider Nicholas Lasch's rejection of progress because of its implication of ever-increasing consumption. I argue that Lasch's belief in limits to growth could be combined with Nisbet's concept of progress.

Two approaches to nature are discussed which claim to ensure its protection, Deep Ecology, and nature as Natural Capital. But Deep Ecology generates problems in metaphysics and axiology, whilst the Natural Capital approach treats nature as resource only.

I conclude that a model of nature is needed which recognises nature's otherness as well as its use-value. The best model is perhaps nature as both resource and enigma.

Progress, Nature and Metaphysics

The concepts of progress and of nature seem to be coupled in an inverse manner. Thus believers in a metaphysic of perpetual progress fuelled by unlimited desires and in an ethic of desire-satisfaction, consumerism and growth are likely to regard the natural environment either as a dispensable externality or as an unlimited sink for absorbing pollution. There again, people like Deep Ecologists who believe in identification with nature and all its species and ecosystems are highly unlikely to believe that progress is either inevitable or desirable, or, when the laws of thermodynamics have been taken into account, even possible. The mythological counterpart of this inverse relation consists in the warfare between Prometheus, who stole fire from heaven for the forges of human technology and, on the other side, the gods from whom he stole it, including Demeter the Earth-mother and her ancestor Gaia, the Earth itself.

Clearly several concepts both of progress and of nature are here in play. Thus different concepts of progress are used when we speak of progress sometimes as desirable and sometimes as inevitable; and different concepts of nature are present when we contrast nature with humanity and think of it as, for example, a sink to absorb pollution, and when we instead contemplate identification with nature or take the view that we are part of nature already. Suitable distinctions will be drawn in due course, but cannot be drawn at the outset in view of the tangled notions which we inherit from history. This is rather the place to explain that my project is to investigate whether we can adhere to some recognisable form of belief in progress and some defensible concept of nature at the same time, without abandoning either our own identity, or hope for the future, or that acceptance of nature's otherness without which we might easily lose our sense of proportion.

I begin with the notions of progress of Robert Nisbet[1], a believer in progress, and of Christopher Lasch[2], who claims to reject this belief. Nisbet's concept of progress is in some ways a moderate one; in order to stress continuity between post-Renaissance belief in progress and ancient beliefs, he does not require belief in progress to involve belief that either scientific or social improvement is perpetual or inevitable. For Nisbet, belief in progress means that social improvement is possible and that there are grounds to look for it. Such being progress, he manages to identify many believers in progress through the centuries, finding traces of this belief in Sophocles[3], despite his belief in cosmic nemesis, and even in Augustine[4], despite his belief in the Fall.

Nisbet also makes explicit five premises or presuppositions of progressive belief, which jointly comprise a metaphysic, and which, according to Nisbet, are in danger of rejection in the twentieth century. They are as follows: "belief in the value of the past; conviction of the nobility, even superiority of Western civilization; acceptance of the worth of economic and technological growth; faith in reason and in the kind of scientific and scholarly knowledge that can come from reason alone; and, finally, belief in the intrinsic importance, the ineffaceable *worth* of life on this earth."[5]

All these presuppositions have a bearing on nature, whether understood as the entire material universe or, to borrow John Stuart Mill's second definition, as "what takes place without … the voluntary and intentional agency of man [sic]"[6]. For belief in the value of the human past and in Western civilization imply affirmation both of technological modifications of nature and of Western efforts to enhance nature through art, architecture, and the building of cities with their parks and gardens. Acceptance of economic and technological growth implies that nature may rightly be subjected to constantly increasing use and, if necessary, disruption. Faith in scientific reason and in scholarship implies that nature can be sufficiently comprehended by human efforts at understanding for related action to be well-grounded. And belief in the intrinsic value of life on earth concerns partly the worthwhileness of the lives of human agents and partly, and perhaps unintentionally, the value of biotic nature as found on our planet.

Some might suggest at this point that nothing has a bearing on nature, as nowhere on our planet is left unaffected by human agency, as was recently argued by Bill McKibben[7], and thus nature has ceased to exist. But Mill's second definition, which represents nature as what is unaffected by voluntary and intentional agency, still has an application even if McKibben is right about this; and in any case nature in the form of most of the solar system and the entire universe outside it has not been significantly affected by humanity, at least so far.

Clearly there are some tensions between Nisbet's presuppositions as applied to nature. But, sooner than explore them, I want to point out that believers in progress need not be committed to all these presuppositions in any case, at least in this form.

Take belief in the value of the past and of Western civilisation. While believers in progress must find something of value in the past and in their own civilisation if they are to have inherited values and a sense of identity and belonging, they do not need to believe in the value of the entire past, or that Western civilisation has been wholly admirable. If they have any sense of values, they will rather reject these inflated views, and recognise that, for example, the imperialism, the speciesism and the patriarchy of the Western past are nothing to be proud of. Belief in progress requires rather some received standards, such as possibly the beliefs of the Enlightenment in reason, humanitarianism and tolerance, plus an awareness that the past leaves plenty of room for improvement in terms of these standards. While postmodernist approaches seek to problematise even these values, and thus belief in progress too, adherents of progress need not adopt the entire package of technological optimism or of uninhibited modernism.

As for belief in the supposed worth of economic and technological growth, a belief which Nisbet believes to have almost invariably accompanied belief in progress from the Greeks to the Victorians, I shall later be arguing that belief in progress does not depend on it, at least in the form of belief in the growth of goods as opposed to services. For example, supporters of progress such as J. S. Mill have also advocated conservation of nature and a steady-state economy, which he held to be compatible with artistic and cultural development. Although there would be strains in such a society, the scenario of a society with such strains is, apparently, a genuine possibility and not a contradiction. I will be returning to this subject in view of the claim of Christopher Lasch, which in some ways echoes Nisbet, that progress involves perennially increasing consumption, a claim which leads Lasch to reject progress altogether.

What of faith in reason and in scientific and scholarly knowledge? In part, the situation parallels that already discussed concerning the value of the past. Nisbet, however, is right to claim that belief in progress involves belief in the cumulative nature of human knowledge and culture, and also to point out that scientists are currently under attack as never before. But the very criticisms of science, the arts and the social sciences usually themselves depend on new theory, and on the possibility of newer perceptions being more profound than old ones. While some of the criticisms seek to undermine the very possibility of scientific explanations, most concern either shortcomings in understanding nature, as among geologists, who used until recent decades to reject continental drift, and biologists who used to be reluctant to adopt a holistic approach to biotic systems, or alternatively defects in science as a working practice, as when it is maintained that there are no moral limits to scientific inquiry. So most of the criticisms of science presuppose the value of reason and the possibility of better theories or better practice; and this Nisbet should welcome. Belief in progress does not involve admiration for scientists or for scholars across the board, but only belief in the attainability of improved theories and understandings, for example through sciences such as the science of ecology.

Nisbet's final presupposition concerns belief in the intrinsic value of life on earth. Here I think that he is right, in that every endeavour, including efforts to understand nature, depends on a sense of its own worthwhileness; while efforts to enhance society depend also on belief in the value of at least some if not all human life. Nisbet's difficulty here concerns twentieth-century boredom and disillusionment, which for him preclude these beliefs. To the extent that he traces much of this to expanded leisure, his position is implausible, since leisure facilitates richer lives as well as emptier ones; maybe his complaint should be directed instead at unemployment, which often undermines morale as well as supplying leisure. But even disillusionment with past achievements, art-forms and technology often expresses not a nihilism inimical to progress but a rejection of past philistinism and past certainties, and a sense of the need to be more honest and to make a new and humbler start; and all this coheres with belief in progress. If Nisbet's objection were to the perception of both good and evils as illusory or insignificant, there would be room to sympathise with this objection; but this perception would not seem integral to twentieth-century disillusion, or indeed to taking nature seriously. Actually the ecological movement, strongly influential as it is within Western counter-cultures, is prone to stress the independent value of nature, a value firmly, if accidentally, included in Nisbet's advocacy of belief in the value of life on earth.

So my interim conclusion is that the presuppositions of progress do not conflict with characteristic twentieth-century beliefs and attitudes, or with an affirmation of the natural world as unmodified by humanity. They do, no doubt, conflict with the postmodernist beliefs that norms and values arise only within different, incommensurable cultures, and have no universal or objective validity, and that universally valid principles do not exist. But these beliefs, as we have seen, are not mandated by twentieth-century scepticism about traditions, received disciplines, authority and the past, or by twentieth-century apathy and disillusion. And this is just as well, since, if we disavow universally valid principles, we cannot appeal to or reason about consistency, and no possible opportunity would remain for us either for affirming or for denying the consistency of belief in progress with characteristic twentieth-century beliefs and attitudes, or with beliefs about the value of nature either.

But this interim survey omits the role in belief in progress played, according to Christopher Lasch, by desire-satisfaction and by continually increasing consumption. In *The True and Only Heaven: Progress and Its Critics,* Lasch castigates believers in progress for holding that there are no limits to growth, that a perpetual expansion of industrial civilisation is in prospect[8], and that the ever-increasing satisfaction of consumers' unlimited desires is guaranteed by the inevitable processes of history[9]. Accordingly he is able to contrast belief in progress, which he also calls "conventional optimism", with the hopefulness of republican "populism"[10]. Believers in hopefulness, he affirms, are prepared for disappointments and for the worst, whereas believers in the inevitability of improvement have little need for hope, and little motivation to struggle to improve society or the world[11]. So belief in progress should be abandoned.

We should at once note that Lasch's rejection of belief in progress is not grounded in a postmodernist rejection of universal values. Lasch is committed to the goodness of life, despite its tragedies, to a more equitable human world society which would not overburden the nonhuman earth, to self-help and thus to a form of hope "more vigorous" than progressive ideologies[12]. He is thus committed to several of the values found in Nisbet's list of the presuppositions of progress, but is repelled by another value implicit there, the desirability of unlimited economic and technological progress. Here he agrees with Nisbet that this tenet is essential to belief in progress; but his rejection of the tenet prompts a rejection of that overall belief.

Now there is no doubt that Lasch can identify a number of advocates of progress who believed both in unlimited growth and in inevitable and perpetual progress. This is unsurprising, granted that the the older view of belief in progress, held by J. B. Bury and others[13], and challenged by Nisbet, defined the distinctively modern belief in progress as essentially involving perpetual and inevitable improvement, and granted that, as Nisbet argues, the characteristic message of the Enlightenment included an advocacy of untrammelled economic freedom at the same time. Yet Nisbet avoided building belief either in perpetual and inevitable improvement or in unlimited economic growth into his definition; if he had done so, he could not have found progressive beliefs either among pagan Greeks and Romans such as Sophocles and Lucretius, or among Church fathers such as Augustine, or among millenarians such as Joachim of Flora and many of Oliver Cromwell's Puritan supporters.

Lasch is consistent in criticising Nisbet for "throwing classical and Christian authors indiscriminately together into the progressive camp", and for marginalising the fact that both millenarianism and belief in perpetual progress have usually been regarded as heretical among Christians[14]. But one of Nisbet's main achievements is to discern a continuity between ancient and modern beliefs in progress; and this recognition itself requires an inclusive working definition of progress which incorporates believers in the possibility of gains in the course of time to knowledge, happiness, liberty and/or equality as well as believers in the inevitability of those gains. This inclusive concept is implicit in Nisbet's text, and enables him to include Francis Bacon (though with reservations)[15] and John Stuart Mill[16] in his *History,* as well as believers in inevitable social and economic improvement such as Condorcet, Marx, and Spencer. Among those he wrote of, some emphasised the unfolding of civilisation in the forms of literature or philosophy rather than of economics, while not all the progressivists who wrote about economics believed in unlimited material growth (as we have seen with Mill). Yet his decision to ascribe progressive beliefs to them all seems well justified.

Thus, without endorsing Nisbet's views e.g. on Bacon or on the twentieth century, there is good reason to follow him in adopting an inclusive rather than a narrow concept of progress, which applies to believers in the possibility of improvement as well as believers in its inevitability, and again to believers in unlimited economic and technological growth (such as we have seen Nisbet himself to be) and to those who regard change in the direction of a steady-state economy as progress (such as Lasch). And this leaves us free to concur with Lasch's rejection, as unfounded optimism, of the kind of belief in progress involving inevitable unlimited economic growth, without having to discard belief in progress altogether. (We are also free, with Clifford Cobb of the organisation "Redefining Progress", to discard GNP and GDP as measures of progress. Cobb replaces them with what he calls GPI, or the Genuine Progress Indicator, which takes environmental and other quality-of-life factors into account[17].) At the same time we can combine Lasch's belief in both limits to growth and in hope for the future with Nisbet's recognition and celebration of many believers in progress down the centuries, from (say) Lucretius to Mill. While I do not have space or time to discuss here the grounds of this combination of views as a whole, Lasch himself has made out a good case for the parts he would affirm; my earlier critique of Nisbet supplies further support; and Nisbet's argument for the historical continuity of progressive thought would also play a part.

But how far is all this consistent with an acceptable metaphysic of nature? I have suggested that this kind of belief in progress presupposes belief in the value of life on earth; but may it still fall victim to the charge of treating nature as dispensable, rather as belief in unlimited growth is often accused of doing? Such a position would, of course, be self-undermining, for humanity is dependent for survival on the intactness of many of the systems of nonhuman nature, and for individual health and flourishing on further such systems.

But the attitude which regards nature as dispensable corresponds to the kind of progressivism which upholds unlimited economic and technological growth, and treats nature as a bottomless mine for resource-depletion and a bottomless sink for pollution. Such growth could in principle dispossess any nonhuman species and obliterate any habitat. Believers in limits to growth, on the other hand, can square their belief with nature having intrinsic value; at the same time they are not necessarily committed to holding that it actually has such value, and their reason for belief in limits may consist in, for example, their interpretation of the relevance of the laws of thermodynamics, plus awareness of the scarcity of low-entropy resources[18]. However, unless the limits are supposed not to arise until the sun explodes or cools, believers in limits to growth are still plausibly immune from the charge of regarding nature as dispensable.

Yet it is sometimes held that nature will be inadequately appreciated and inadequately defended unless it is either understood as a seamless web or single system with which, as a totality, human individuals can identify, or unless at least we adopt an organismic model of nature, and discard the

Cartesian view of nature as a machine. A further, and apparently more moderate, suggestion is that, rather than regard nature as other than and external to our enterprises, we should regard it as natural capital, and that only if this is done will it be properly cherished. Before proceeding further, I should emphasise that I find the Cartesian view unappealing, if only because of the need for sensitivity to sentience. But it is one thing to disown the Cartesian metaphysic and another to adopt any of those just mentioned.

Consider the stance of the Deep Ecology movement. When Arne Naess first distinguished shallower and deeper ecology movements, his distinction turned partly on the anthropocentric value-theory of the former (which ascribed value to human beings and human interests only) and on the recognition of the latter of intrinsic value in nature[19]. But self-styled Deep Ecologists now, according to Warwick Fox, have no axiological theories (or value theories) at all, and instead teach psychological identification with nature[20]. They adopt a field theory of reality which takes relations to be essential; thus the identities of all individuals are interdependent, and no individual could exist without any of the others. Reality (or nature) is thus a single web. It is also, once we recognise this, the greater self of each of us; and self-defence at once becomes a defence of the whole. This is no static account of reality, for it is compatible with recognition of dynamic processes of change. But this just discloses that the entire array of reality spread out through time comprises the greater self with which, once enlightened, we identify.

But some relations are not essential to the items which they relate. Thus many future relations will depend on present actions, and may take one form or another accordingly, without this affecting the identities of all the items concerned. Certainly some identities do depend on present actions (such as those of children yet to be conceived). But many identities will remain intact from the present into at least the near future, such as the identities of current agents, and of many of the familiar features of our environment. There again, many present relations depend on actions of the recent past, and could have taken different forms if those actions had been different. But, once again, this does not mean that all the affected items, e.g. lakes and seas visited, or forests selectively felled or reprieved, have different identities in consequence, even though in some cases, as where a forest has been entirely felled, there may have been such a drastic change that there is no identity remaining.

If all relations *were* essential, then reality would comprise just one thing, as in the philosophy of Spinoza. Indeed there would be no problem about identification, as what are currently called human beings would already each be essential aspects of that one being. But there would also be no distinct identities, and distinctions between individuals would be illusory. So too would be the distinctions which we now draw between agents and the world around them. Such a philosophical system has no place for moral responsibility, since there is no such thing as agents having powers to act on anything independent of themselves, whether for better or for worse. I do not wish to deny that in many ways agents are interdependent with each other and with their environment; but this same partial interdependence presupposes the existence of distinct individuals, capable of genuine causal relations with other distinct individuals. Retaining belief in such distinctness means rejecting the kind of metaphysical holism under discussion.

Besides, there is room to doubt whether the world with which we are encouraged by Deep Ecologists to identify really is the world of wild nature. For the world's field of interdependence includes cities, with their streets and factories, and countryside with its villages and fields, as well as wilderness. So if our interdependence with this world somehow confers on us a motive to preserve it, then we shall thereby be motivated to preserve cities, countryside and all their artefacts just as much as forests, wetlands and tundra. Admittedly the total mass of nature (in Mill's second sense) is much greater than that of the sites of civilisation; but what makes this true is the vastness of abiotic nature, areas such as the earth's core and outer space, and these are once again not the locations which preservationists normally seek to preserve. Recently some of them have been campaigning against the possibility of introducing life to other planets[21]; but it is far from clear that preserving the lifelessness of lifeless places coheres with, or upholds, e.g. the preservation of *biospheric* integrity as commended by Aldo Leopold[22]. My conclusion here is that identification with reality as a whole would be a misguided kind of motivation.

There is a further problem for reconciling the philosophy of Deep Ecology with moral responsibility. For without belief in intrinsic value and in obligations, no one would have reasons for action. People might still have motives, such as love and loyalty, contempt and fear, but they would have no interpersonal grounds to present either to themselves or to others to justify either actions or policies or institutions. While action is often poorly guided as things now are, the prospect of it being intelligently directed in the absence of grounds and justifications is more slender by far. The prospect is also slight of rational criticism of actions, policies and institutions, with a view to redirecting them to what there is reason to do or to seek, whether that is the satisfaction of human needs, along the lines traditionally urged by advocates of progress, or the preservation or even the restoration of wilderness. Thus any philosophy which discards ethics and axiology needs to be replaced or at least supplemented by one which reinstates them.

I now turn to a consideration of whether we should adopt an organismic model of nature, as opposed to a mechanistic model, as is implicitly commended by Carolyn Merchant[23]. Organisms are widely regarded as embodying an inbuilt telos, and as having organs which function in a manner subservient to this telos, and a good largely determined by that telos. They are thus capable of good or bad health, and of well-being or ill-being[24], and can be respected as such. Accordingly if nature came to be understood in this way, it too could, and perhaps would be respected. If, by contrast, it is understood as a mechanism, consisting of inert matter slavishly complying with natural laws whether in the realms unaffected by humanity or as artefacts, gyrating as moving parts at the behest of civilisation, it will neither be appreciated nor respected.

Now, as I have already said, I find the Cartesian view of nature as simply a mechanism unattractive. For some of nature is animate, and some of animate nature consists of sentient and purposive creatures. Also, if the mechanistic view denies that biotic nature is significantly different from abiotic nature, this view seems inconsistent with proper recognition of the importance of irreducible and nonderivative teleological explanations for the behaviour of purposive creatures, and (as previously mentioned) of the need to be sensitive to creatures which are sentient. In some ways, then, we need an organismic approach to nature, which reintroduces teleological explanations and sensitivity to sentience.

But it may not make sense to adopt an organismic model of nature as a whole, or of large tracts of abiotic nature. We can recognise the glory of the stars without claiming that their behaviour is explained by inbuilt purposes, or that they have the kind of properties which would make this explanation even a possible one. Nor is it necessary to regard the Earth as our mother in order to have grounds to avoid despoiling it. Indeed what goes for the stars almost certainly goes for our planet too. The planetary biosphere is not such a clear case, as the Gaia hypothesis represents the biosphere as a self-regulating system comparable with a living organism. But it has not won majority support among scientists, and does not seem to demonstrate a sufficiently close similarity between biospheric components and organs to uphold organismic claims. So talk of the health and well-being of the biosphere remain metaphors. It remains true that apparently inert matter turns out to be capable of purposiveness in that most elements can enter into the tissues of purposive creatures. But this does not mean that non-living matter should be understood organismically as it is.

What surely remains important is to make distinctions between organisms and non-organismic matter. For the respect due in differing degrees to the former should not belong to the latter, on pain of incurring the charge of metaphysical idolatry. Metaphysical mistakes may seem insubstantial, and so they often are; but this one would have the practical implication that the abiotic world should be respected and left alone, not only where there are sites of natural beauty, but just because of its supposed organismic nature. If, however, the needs of living creatures can be best met or only met by extracting and processing abiotic minerals, then, other things being equal, this surely should be done. (Other things often will not be equal, as much extraction and processing is counterproductive, as the same resources are often needed for something else, and as there may be a greater need on the part of living creatures to be allowed to evolve without intervention and thus left alone. But other things are unlikely always to be unequal.) My suggestion is that the adoption of an organismic model of nature would distort our perceptions of nature by eliding salient distinctions between organisms and the rest of nature. It is far better to have a model which proportions attitudes to their objects, and thus understands biotic nature organismically, abiotic nature mechanistically, and ecosystems in a manner closer to the former than the latter, and which recognises that many organisms depend on them.

Should we also regard nature as natural capital, which as such should not be allowed to decline? This is the view of many environmental economists, who can argue in its favour that instead of being treated as an externality, nature is on this approach regarded as a valuable asset, not lightly to be squandered or degraded. In particular, this is the approach of David Pearce and the other authors of *Blueprint for A Green Economy*[25]. Examples of natural capital include resources such as genetic information and waste assimilation capacity[26].

On Alan Holland's interpretation, what these authors probably intend by "natural capital" is natural resources as "used or usable in human social or economic systems", and what is to be preserved is probably its economic value, reductions resulting from the use of natural resources being offset by increments from technological innovations[27]. Since the authors seem not to abandon the claim that nature as physical stock should also be preserved, Holland's suggestion is that they are unknowing subscribers to belief in the goodness of the natural world[28]. But their official position is that a "physical stock" interpretation of natural capital would rule out any human use whatever of nonrenewable resources, and is thus unworkable[29]. This position complies with their central concern for sustainable development, interpreted as "non-declining human welfare over time"[30], a choice of phrase which also confirms the progressive but anthropocentric nature of their approach.

Would an understanding of nature as natural capital conduce to improved practices? Such an approach might seem likely to reduce waste and pollution, and encourage better husbanding of nonrenewable resources; for even though it permits their consumption, it counts this as a cost to be minimised. Since the approach has these merits, we should recognise it as better than the kind of anthropocentric approach which, without respect for nature's intrinsic qualities, regards it as a cross between a limitless goldmine and a limitless sink. Further, its concern to provide for the sustainability of human society and not to preclude the consumption which this inevitably requires is surely to be applauded. Yet it has encountered a withering Marxist critique from Martin O'Connor, who regards it as an attempt to rescue capitalism by expanding its domain to encompass areas of life previously regarded as outside its balance-sheets and its grasp. These areas include the family, the non-industrialised economies of the Third World, and nature itself[31].

For O'Connor, global environmental problems represent a crisis of legitimation for capitalism. Its response is to devise a new legitimation for itself, in which the biophysical milieu in which capitalist production operates (nature) is represented as a stock of property with an economic value, and which is to be sustainably and rationally used. The same extended approach is taken to Third World economies and to the domestic sphere (households). Generally, instead of treating these spheres as an external and exploitable domain, capitalism hereby takes control of them, and thus of the reproduction of the conditions of production[32]. Evidence of all this is found in the 1992 Rio Conference and in the opening up of ailing economies to world trade, while local communities are enlisted in this cause through representing them as stewards of social and natural capital[33].

Even the "physical stock" interpretation of "natural capital" would fall victim to this critique, insofar as it represents nature as a stock of capital. This interpretation might have seemed immune through seeking to prohibit the consumption of nonrenewable resources. But, by regarding nature as a resource to be managed for the sake of the international economy, it remains in the firing-line. Only if management had been foresworn would this approach have been immune, but this retreat would also involve foregoing the language of "stock". In any case, as we have seen, this is not the interpretation endorsed by Pearce and his fellow-authors, and is in some ways an undesirable one.

Since, however, a prohibition of all use of nonrenewable resources would be misguided, is the model of nature as "natural capital" really as reprehensible as O'Connor represents it? Here my answer is both "no" and "yes". For there is a double ambivalence in coming to regard nature as manageable for the benefit of the global economy. One ambivalence concerns whether the global economy has to be a capitalist economy, and whether this capitalist aspect of the world economy is the source of the criticism. For a socialist global economy would *also* have problems of waste, pollution and resource depletion; and might operate better if nature were regarded as manageable than as an external domain. Plausibly any form of global economy would be in the same position, for even decentralised, anarchistic forms would need to regulate areas of nature shared between different local communities. If so, there are desirable aspects to proposals for nature to be managed, even if the management of nature within capitalism (like the related management of primitive peoples and of domestic households) is likely to be inequitable and to involve adverse impacts on vulnerable interests.

The second source of ambivalence implicit in regarding nature as manageable concerns whether management is regarded as our sole or dominant concern, or is instead liable to be overridden for the sake of other concerns. Parallel issues clearly arise for indigenous peoples and for households. If the model of natural capital means that in all circumstances nature has its price, or that peoples or households do, and may be exploited by parties willing to pay that price, then at least a balancing model is required, if not a conflicting one, to ensure that limits are observed. And since the model of natural capital is likely to be construed in just this manner by the economists of large corporations and by those working for the World Bank and the International Monetary Fund, it becomes unwise to endorse this model at all. This can be accepted even if we agree with Pearce and his colleagues that the domain of nature ought in general to be managed rather than limitlessly exploited.

The need for a different model should not entice us to adopt the model of nature as sanctuary, where use is prohibited. Sanctuaries sometimes have an important place, such as the whale sanctuary of the Antarctic Ocean. But to ban all use of nonrenewable resources would be to ensure that human needs cannot be met, whether sustainably or at all, and thus to preclude the desirable elements of belief in progress, including grounds for hope of fulfilling the needs of humanity.

The need is rather for a model which recognises nature's otherness as well as its use-value. For while we need at every breath to use nature as a resource, we also need nature as something alien, external and untameable, with which to compare ourselves – and by reference to which to understand ourselves. Nature in some of its manifestations is wonderful, and in some terrifying, and it is for our good if it remains so. Nor can this need be satisfied if we transform it into a pre-packaged resource for experiences of wonder or of terror. Besides, in some of its manifestations it has intrinsic value, as I have argued elsewhere[34], though value of this kind is the exception rather than the rule. If this is all granted, then to treat nature as if it were exclusively capital would be to diminish or (to use a paradoxical metaphor) to impoverish ourselves. Perhaps even Nisbet recognises this when he writes of belief in progress presupposing belief in the intrinsic importance, the ineffaceable *worth* of life on this earth[35].

What model is equal to these requirements? No single model passes this test. The model of treasure, for example, could cover alternatively nature's high value and its pricelessness, but not both in the same sense of treasure. The model of home covers both these aspects, but falls down over excessively domesticating nature and neglecting its untameable aspect; and the same applies to the models of nature as family, as neighbourhood or even as environment. While all these models could have a place in combination, the least misleading single model is, I suggest, the model of nature as enigma. This suggestion is intended to be reminiscent of nature's otherness, needed for our sense of belonging and of proportion, without ruling out use of nature, both consumptive and otherwise, so that a sustainable future for humanity and for other creatures may be found. Where nature is a resource, doubtless it should be regarded as capital rather than as interest, or, better still, as common inheritance, a concept which has broader roots than those of capitalism.

This combination of models is consistent with a moderate belief in progress, concerning the possibility of improvement in understanding, in social arrangements and in the satisfaction of needs. Belief in perpetual or inevitable progress, while consistent with a range of beliefs about nature, is likely to undermine those tracts of nature which form our environment, and thus to prove unstable (and disastrous). But belief in growth having limits need not extinguish belief in progress, as long as we do not define this belief as having unacceptable implications, as Lasch does, or supply it with unacceptable (and disproportionate) presuppositions, as Nisbet does. Once Nisbet's presuppositions have been trimmed and revised in the ways that I have already argued that they should be, they prove to be compatible with a full recognition of nature and its value.

Here is a summary of my revision of Nisbet's presuppositions. Belief in progress requires endorsement of some continuity with the past and of received standards, such as belief in reason, humanitarianism and tolerance, plus awareness that the past leaves room for improvement as measured by these standards. It does not presuppose belief in the worth of economic and technological growth, nor the related belief that nature is dispensable. But it does involve belief in the cumulative nature of human knowledge and culture, in the possibility of better theories, better understandings and better practice, and thus in hope for the future. It also involves belief in the value of at least some progressive endeavour, and thus of much if not all life on earth, and also in the need to be more honest and more modest than past certainties allowed of.

All these presuppositions can readily be claimed to be compatible with belief in there being limits to growth, with a recognition of the independent value of nature, as advocated by many of the ecological critics of progress, and with due sensitivity to the organismic and the sentient segments of nature, and due appreciation of its untamed, alien and enigmatic aspects. Progressive beliefs authorise some degree of management of natural resources, without driving us to believe that nature in its entirety is capital for our deployment and benefit. Thus an acceptable metaphysic of nature can cohere with belief in progress, or rather with the saner kinds of such belief[36].

Biography

Robin Attfield (born 1941) is Professor of Philosophy at University of Wales Cardiff, Britain. He is the author of *God and The Secular* (1978 and 1993), *The Ethics of Environmental Concern* (1983 and 1991), *A Theory of Value and Obligation* (1987), *Environmental Philosophy: Principles and Prospects* (1994), and *Value, Obligation and Meta-Ethics* (1995); and joint editor of *International Justice and the Third World* (1992), *Philosophy and the Natural Environment* (1994), and *Values, Conflict and The Environment* (1989 and 1996).

Notes

1. Robert Nisbet, *History of the Idea of Progress,* London: Heinemann, 1980.
2. Christopher Lasch, *The True and Only Heaven*: *Progress and Its Critics,* New York and London: W. W. Norton & Co., 1991.
3. Nisbet, p. 21.
4. Nisbet, pp. 54-76.
5. Nisbet, p. 317.
6. John Stuart Mill, 'Nature', in *Three Essays on Religion,* New York: Greenwood Press, 1969, pp. 3-65.
7. Bill McKibben, *The End of Nature* (1987), London: Viking, 1990 .
8. Christopher Lasch, *The True and Only Heaven*, pp. 22-24.
9. Lasch, pp. 81, 529-532.
10. Lasch, pp. 42, 81.

11. Lasch, p. 81.
12. Lasch, pp. 529f.
13. J. B. Bury, *The Idea of Progress: An Inquiry into its Origin and Grouwth* (1920), New York: Dover, 1955; also John Baillie, *The Relief in Progress,* London: Oxford U.P., 1950.
14. Lasch, p. 46.
15. Nisbet, pp. 112-115.
16. Nisbet, pp. 224-227.
17. Clifford Cobb, "A Call for New Measures of Progress" (pamphlet), San Francisco: Redefining Progress, 1994.
18. Thus Keekok Lee, *Social Philosophy and Ecological Scarcity,* London and New York: Routledge, 1989.
19. Arne Naess, "The Shallow and the Deep, Long-Range Ecology Movement: A Summary", *Inquiry,* 16, 1973, pp. 95-100.
20. Warwick Fox, *Toward a Transpersonal Ecology,* Boston and London: Shambala, 1990.
21. Thus Keekok Lee, "Awe and Humility: Intrinsic Value in Nature. Beyond an Earthbound Environmental Ethics", in Robin Attfield and Andrew Belsey (eds.), *Philosophy and the Natural Environment,* Cambridge: Cambridge University Press, 1994, pp. 89-101.
22. Aldo Leopold, *A Sand County Almanac,* New York: Oxford University Press, 1966.
23. Carolyn Merchant, *The Death of Nature* (1980), London: Wildwood House, 1982.
24. Georg Henrik Von Wright, *The Varieties of Goodness,* London: Routledge & Kegan Paul, 1963, p. 50.
25. David Pearce, Anil Markandya and Edward B. Barbier, *Blueprint for a Green Economy,* London: Earthscan, 1989.
26. Alan Holland, "Natural Capital", in Robin Attfield and Andrew Belsey (eds.), *Philosophy and the Natural Environment,* Cambridge: Cambridge University Press, 1994, pp. 169-182, at p. 169.
27. Holland, p. 171.
28. Holland, pp. 179, 180f.
29. Holland, p. 171.
30. Pearce *et al.*, p. 1.
31. Martin O'Connor, "On the Misadventures of Capitalist Nature", *Capitalism, Nature, Socialism,* 4 (3), 1993, pp. 7-40.
32. O'Connor, pp. 8f.
33. O'Connor, pp. 9, 11.
34. Robin Attfield, *The Ethics of Environmental Concern,* Athens and London: University of Georgia Press, 1991, ch. 8.
35. Nisbet, p. 317.
36. This paper was first presented at the XI Biennial Symposium of the Inter-Nordic Institute of Philosophy (Odense, 1995). I am grateful to participants for comments and criticisms.

Carsten Bengt-Pedersen

Man and his Knowledge of Nature

Abstract
In this paper I urge that science is based on an a priori in the praxis of the life-world. In a way somewhat parallel to the opinions of the German Erlanger-School of Philosophy of Science it is argued that Man's ability to act as a material body in an external world – and not just to perceive he is acting in his life-world – is a transcendental condition for any real knowledge at all. This is related to the fundamental questions of the relation between language and reality. Finally Niels Bohr's ideas of the necessity of the "common sense-language" (ordinary language) for the development of the language of classical physics and further that the language of classical physics is a precondition for modern physics (quantum mechanics and Einsteinian relativistic physics) are explicated.

Some time ago – as a member of the organizing comittee of this symposium – I had the opportunity to read professor Ragnar Fjelland's fine paper *From evolutionary epistemology to the life world a priori*, just given today as a lecture to this audience. (Printed in this book.)

I must admit that I at the same time felt both very satisfied and a little disappointed. Satisfied because it is a fine and interesting article, but on the other hand in some way disappointed because Ragnar Fjelland was more or less discussing the same subject matter and was partly advocating the same thesis and using the same arguments which I was actually doing in my own paper which I originally intended to give the subtitle *"Science is based on an a priori in the praxis of the life-world"*.

Then, I realized that in spite of the many changes I felt was now required in my paper, it was really a very lucky situation as I decided to regard it as a sign of the importance of our common field of work and the relevance of my own proposed solutions.

A little later that happy feeling increased, in spite of the further changes in my present paper that was made necessary, when I received professor Ingvar Johansson's highly interesting paper *Perception as the Bridge between Nature and Lifeworld,* delivered here yesterday as the opening lecture. (Printed in this book.) He was advocating a kind of direct realism, as I do.

All these remarks may be considered not only as statements of matters of fact in Hume's sense, but also as an act – in short a "performative" in J. L. Austin's sense – whereby I do apologize or excuse that you not in advance, as you rightfully might have expected, have been presented – not even in the form of an abstract, by this rather sketchy lecture.

Man, Nature and Life-World

In this lecture I shall deal with the relation between *man* as a subjective, rational and, not the least, an acting being and the rest of *nature* in the narrow, but basic sense of discussing some classical epistemological (and metaphysical) problems of man's possibility to obtain an objective and true knowledge of nature. As this knowledge becomes more and more articulated and sophisticated, we normally speak of science. The following remarks are then to be considered as belonging to epistemology in general and one of its special branches, the philosophy of science.

By *"nature"* I here – quite unsophisticatedly – understand what is totally independent of man's subjective mind or consciousness; or as Ingvar Johansson said it yesterday in his lecture: "By 'nature' I mean the world as it would be if man passed out of existence... Nature I here take for granted, exists independently of man, whereas, of course, our life-world does not."

By *"life-world"* I mean the world in which we by acting and perceiving in our everyday life – in a broad sense – experience this nature. This meaning of life-world might be a little different from its use in Edmund Husserl's philosophy. I am not denying that in many ways man is part of nature in the sense just explained, at least as man has a body – a material body, that is part of the objective nature – but I am not going to inquire further into this for my present purpose quite different and very complicated antropological problem of what it means, that man is a part of nature. What I am arguing is that man can and in fact does to a smaller or greater extent have some true knowledge of such an objective nature, because he as an acting subject is a part of the objective, material nature.

By *"truth"* I understand quite ordinarily, that if a proposition is true, then it is true independently of who (if any at all) advocates it and when and where (in time and space) it is advocated. What I am advocating is realism in all normal respects: There exists (ontologically) an objective or mind-independent reality, and man is by means of acting, sensing and thinking able to know (epistemologically) something about that reality. I am advocating a theory of perception that could be named *a direct and critical realism* which is not too far from the theory of perception presented by Ingvar Johansson yesterday.

Some in fact not too *trivial Remarks on Epistemology*

In his stimulating opening lecture professor Ingvar Johansson yesterday spoke of "The Cartesian-Lockean Heritage" and argued, that both classical and modern empiricism and rationalism – including both phenomenalism and phenomenology – by necessity implies an insurmountable ontological gulf between nature and life-world. To be consistent they are all bound to accept some kind of idealism. If our only access to reality, nature, is our senses, then we are forced by logic to accept a kind of idealism, which means that the classical problem of the external world becomes insoluble. But to paraphrase the point of discussion correctly, you have to say: If my only access to reality, nature, is my senses, then I am forced by logic to accept a special, subjective kind of idealism, known as solipsism. (Unless you believe in parapsychology, i.e. a telepathical mode of direct access to other minds.) This means that the two classical problems of other minds and of the external world become invincible.

Even to Husserl all possible human knowledge is restricted to the life-world; as Ingvar Johansson said: "The method of epoché (and similar procedures) gives us the nature of the life-world but not the real man-independent nature which natural scientists think they are studying." I do agree very firmly, but I am not – as Ingvar Johansson is not – willing to accept that this kind of life-world in any way can be conceived of as an intersubjective life-world as Husserl did. An *intersubjective* life-world presupposes the existence of other minds. The Husserlian life-world is perceived only by one individual, one subject, even if this individual wrongly conceives of it as something intersubjective and perceives something, he considers to be other minds in this life-world.

As Ingvar Johansson told us: "My life-world is only mine and your life-world is only yours; ... If life-world and nature is kept apart, the life-world breaks apart, too.". In my opinion it is even impossible to speak of another person as a subject and of his life-world as something different from a part of my solipsistic life-world.

It is very important to note in this quite fundamental issue as Ingvar Johansson stressed, that it is necessary for phenomenology to understand, that "Intentional acts presuppose for their existence something which is not part of themselves, namely a body with a nervous system and a brain." A modern version of the cartesian demon, a brain in the vat perceiving something, is absurd in this context as an epistemological argument, because it explicitely presupposes the existence of the brain and the vat as material things.

It is only possible (meaningful) to speak of any kind of intersubjectivity in distinction to subjective idealism (solipsism) if you accept the existence of an objective world inhabited by other subjects in blood and flesh, not just ghosts or something like Leibniz' monads. It means real persons existing in an objective and material nature. The epistemological problem of other minds is not an easy little obstacle that can be thrown away without at first or at least at the same time answering (solving) the much simpler problem of the existence of external world.

It is nowadays a common-place to postulate that any theory of knowledge that urges the possibility of man having a true and objective knowledge of nature as something mind-independent, will have to face the well-known friesian trilemma, also known as the Münchhausen-trilemma. This is the background of the great popularity of the late sir Karl R. Popper's evolutionary fallibilism (e.g. his *Objective Knowledge*, Oxford 1972) as one way of evading the horns of the trilemma. As might be evident from my former remarks I am going to take the bull directly by its horns in defending a position, that some philosophers would like to call dogmatism – trying to show that it is not in any way dogmatic.

You may have guessed that my way of arguing is in some ways close to the descriptive transcendentalism you may know from Peter F. Strawson in his *Individuals*, London 1959, but it was earlier proposed by the Danish philosopher Peter Zinkernagel (in *Omverdensproblemet* (The Problem of the External World), Copenhagen 1957, later published in a revised English edition as *Conditions for Description*, London 1962). Such modern forms of transcendentalism has quite a strong tradition in Danish philosophy in the last half of the 20.th century (To mention just a few more names: Niels Bohr, David Favrholdt, Justus Hartnack, Arne Thing Mortensen) and it is very much alive here in Odense.

Any theory of knowledge that postulates that some kind of knowledge of the external world (nature) is obtainable by a disembodied spirit, a mind – whether it be God or a res cogitans without a special relation to a res extensa, or even a mind in a totally paralyzed body – exclusively by the means of either reason or perception or by a combination of both, has forgotten that is it an indispensible condition for the acquiring of any knowledge, that you are able to act. I said to *act in a real nature* or in an objective world in addition to thinking and perceiving, not just to perceive or imagine that you are acting in a subjective life-world.

A British philosopher, Don Locke, absolutely not his famous pal of names, John Locke, has very convincingly nicknamed these purely subjective types of theory of knowledge as a paralytic or perhaps even better as a *paraplectic epistemology*.

1) Any scientific knowledge has its basis in the life-world
Husserl insisted – in The Crisis of the European Sciences (Die Krisis der europäischen Wissenschaften, Haag 1962, eng. tr. *The Crisis of European Sciences and Transcendental Phenomenology*, Evanston, IL, 1970) – that: The sciences are founded "… on the basis of the life-world a priori" as Ragnar Fjelland already has pointed out in his lecture. "… we must inquire back into its origin in pre-theoretical activity" as he explains Husserl's project. I agree with Fjelland in this statement, but I would also like to stress that an important part of the life-world consists of the relation between the ability to use the fundamental descriptive part of ordinary language and the ability to do simple, everyday actions in a practical, or if you prefer technical, relation to nature.

In my opinion the life-world is not just a perceived or perceptual world, but simply the battlefield where mans most fundamental interaction – and this interaction is much more than just a perception of mans interaction – with nature takes place. If the life-world is just a world of my own perceptions, we will end up in solipsism as I have already argued.

Ingvar Johansson said in his lecture, that "ordinary language philosophy is so close to the phenomenological philosophy of the life-world". I agree with Johansson to a certain extent. A central concept in Wittgenstein's later philosophy, namely that of "forms of life", has many similarities to Husserl's "life-world". But for my present purpose there is at least one very important difference: Husserl is looking for some universal structures common to mankind; in a sense according to Husserl we do all live *in the same life-world* – or at least partly congruent life-worlds – given the big cultural differences between the situations of a Danish philosopher today and a Chinese mandarine three thousands years ago. In contrast Wittgenstein seems to deny any common ground or basis for forms of life; there are only a lot of *varying forms of life* (and related language games); and they are so to speak incongruent or (absolutely) incommensurable.

This means, in my opinion, that Wittgenstein's forms of life– in contradistinction to Husserl's life-world in my understanding – cannot be *the priori basis for science* or for that matter of any kind of universal and objective knowledge; according to the later Wittgenstein science cannot be regarded as something quite different from other language games, say religion, mythology or whatever other ideological games man might like to play. Science is just a kind of language games inherent in the western forms of life.

According to the later Wittgenstein there does not exist an objective or even a universally intersubjective knowledge of nature. There are only different opinions of the reality of nature among different cultures (forms of life). Opinions are only common to groups of people sharing the same form of life. Black magic, say woo-doo woo-doo, is in every respect on a par with newtonian mechanics.

Thomas S. Kuhn's philosophy of science *(The Structure of Scientific Revolutions*, Chicago 1962, second enlarged ed., Chicago 1970) with its denial of the rationality of science and its relativistic thesis of the incommensurability of scientific paradigms, may be regarded as a consequent application of the later Wittgenstein's philosophy. My remarks about Kuhn can be applied equally well against other apologists of the later Wittgenstein, say Peter Winch's philosophy of the social sciences *(The Idea of a Social Science*, London 1958). Forms of life are totally enclosed in themselves and can only be understood from within; there are no common standards of any kind between forms of life that can be used to make comparisons. No universal standards of rationality can be found at all. This may (pejoratively) be characterized as the cultural relativism at its peak.

The idea of the life-world as an a priori of science so far advocated comes very close to the central viewpoints of the important, but still too neglected, German Erlanger-School of Philosophy (of Science); important members are Paul Lorenzen, Kuno Lorenz, Peter Janich, Wilhelm Kamlah and Jürgen Mittelstrass. (e.g. Mittelstrass: *Die Möglichkeit von Wissenschaft* (The Possibility of Science), Frankfurt a.M. 1974.) The members of the Erlanger-School regard the formation of what they call the proto-sciences, e.g. proto-geometry, proto-physics (which includes euclidean geometry), the only basis on which science can be constructed. According to the Erlanger-School the proto-sciences have developed in the inevitable praxis of man, man acting in his natural environment to survive and thereby learning to survive, in short: the everyday use of technology in his life-world.

As professor Fjelland already convincingly has demonstrated in his lecture – and I am not going to repeat it in my own words – the proto-geometry – inherently a very central part of the (or any possible kind of) life-world – will by necessity, if you try to theorize about it, end up in the euclidian geometry. The good oldfashioned euclidean geometry is not just a conventional game, that you can replace by another game, say a Lobatjevskij – or a Riemann-geometry. What I am saying is that the euclidean geometry with its special axiom of parallellity ("to any straight line can be drawn one but only one line through a given point parallel to the first") is both genetically, but more important also epistemologically, fundamental. This means that it is only on the basis of the euclidean geometry, that any generalization of geometry, e.g. in the form of an abstract or a Riemann type, but also as an analytical (cartesian) geometry, can be made. Man or any other rational being, say a martian, could not in principle have developed the Lobatjevskij-geometry before they had acquired an understanding of euclidean-geometry.

Once more I want to stress a most important point, which is clearly stated also in Ragnar Fjelland's lecture, namely that action, not perception of action, is an important part of this (non-husserlian) life-world and is a necessary prerequisite of acquiring even implicit knowledge of the proto-geometry. It is *by handling things in the external world* that *man is forced by nature to understand proto-geometry.*

The euclidean geometry is not just a game that you can choose to play as you like it or choose not to play at all. If you want to describe with some precision what is going on in the life-world, you have to – on the a priori basis of the proto-geometry – to develop and use euclidean geometry; this geometry is one of *many interdependent transcendental conditions* for any kind of descriptions at that level of precision. As such it is even an a priori precondition for the development of non-euclidean geometries.

Euclidean geometry is a precision of something implicite in the ordinary, descriptive language; a basic and universal language that is necessary in order to understand and describe any kind of life-worlds. It is the only possible way of such a precision; there is in a sense no alternative at all to an euclidean geometry. I am arguing that euclidean geometry is a transcendental condition for science as such. You may very well speak of a *synthetical a priori* if you like the kantian way of expression.

In reverse, it is also a fact that no scientific knowledge, if it really is knowledge and is correctly understood and interpreted, will be at odds or inconsistent with the basic knowledge of the life-world ("common-sense"). This is in part just the important, but obvious requirement of science as having an empirical foundation. Quantum mechanics, as strange as it might seem to people without an education in science, explains a lot of things in the life-world, for instance the fact that there exists stable objects at the macro-level. If there did not exist a universal quantum (Planck's famous constant: h) at the micro-level, that means that if matter and energy were distributed continously and not as is the case in small, non-divisible packets, then there could not be stable objects, say chairs and tables, at the macro-level.

This insistence of the necessary connection between theoretical scientific knowledge and empirical phenomena, which are related to common-sense facts of the life-world, is, as it were also the central issue of Carl G. Hempel's famous theory of "bridge-statement" (Vide: *Philosophy of Natural Science,* Englewood Cliffs, NJ, 1966). Science will allways explain some facts of the life-world; quantum mechanics say, explains why gold is very heavy and resistent to (most) acids.

2) Science as a more and more sophisticated form of precision, generalization, abstraction and idealization of the basic facts inherent im ordinary language
The concepts of classical *(newtonian) physics* is a *precision* of some basic concepts of the ordinary language (be it formulated in Danish, Chinese or Swahili) of any life-world. The newtonian concepts of, say velocity, acceleration and inertia are founded on some very fundamental, but imprecise concepts inherent in the language of any life-worlds. In this context I can give you only a sketch of the idea: From our everyday life we all experience some aspects of velocity and acceleration when we are running to catch something, or think of the experience of taking a sharp turn to the left on a bicycle. The newtonian concepts – and the whole theory, they are a part of – are the only possible way of a precision of the everyday concepts you use in describing these experiences; so I argue that there is no alternative to classical physics in exactly the same way as there is no alternative to euclidean geometry.

This is by the way also the basic position of Niels Bohr in his epistemology. Two of many quotations on this subject matter from the writings of Niels Bohr:

> "Notwithstanding refinements of terminology due to accumulation of experimental evidence and development of theoretical conceptions, all account of physical experience is, of course, ultimately based on common language, adapted to orientation in our surroundings and tracing of relationships between cause and effect."
> *(Quantum Physics and Biology,* p. 1, in S*ymposia of the Society for Experimental Biology,* no. XIV, Cambridge 1960.)

> "It is true that the imposing edifice of so-called classical physics, ... rests on principles representing the clarification and refinement of elementary concepts embodied in ordinary language adapted to orientation in our surroundings."
> *(Philosophical Lesson,* MSS, No. 23, 23.1.58)

In a way modern physics (in short: *relativity theories and quantum mechanics*) is – quite opposite the questionable view of Thomas S. Kuhn – just a *generalization of classical mechanics*; it is further in many respects the only possible way of a generalization. According to Niels Bohr the validity of classical physics (inside its boundaries of application) is a *sine qua non* (a fundamental or if you wish a *transcendental* condition) for modern physics. Without the knowledge and the use of classical (newtonian) physics it is totally impossible to describe (and perform, to act in) the experimental situations, that defines the phenomena modern physics is studying.

A single and very explicit quotation from Bohr's famous article *Discussion with Einstein on Epistemological Problems in Atomic Physics:*

> "For this purpose, it is decisive to recognize that, *however far the phenomena transcend the scope of classical explanation, the account of all evidence must be expressed in classical terms.* The argument is simply that by the word "experiment" we refer to a situation where we can tell others what we have done and what we have learned and that, therefore, the account of the experimental arrangement and of the results of the observations must be expressed in unambiguous language with suitable application of the terminology of classical physics."
>
> Bohr, Niels: *Essays 1932-1957 on Atomic Physics and Human Knowledge*, Ox Bow Press, Woodbridge, Connecticut 1958, p. 39.

(For a further elaboration of these arguments, vide: Favrholdt, David: *Fysik, Bevidsthed, Liv – Studier i Niels Bohrs filosofi*, (Physics, Consciousness, Life – Studies in the Philosophy of Niels Bohr), Odense University Press, Odense 1994, pp. 65-104, and Bengt-Pedersen, Carsten: *Natur og Erkendelse,* (Nature and Knowledge), Gyldendal, Copenhagen 1995, pp. 70-80 and 180-182).

3) Concluding and hopefully provocative remarks
Much of the subject matter discussed here are inspired by my cooperation with professor David Favrholdt for many years; I strongly recommend anyone able to understand Danish to read his recent book, *Erkendelsesteori* (Epistemology), Odense 1994. Written as it is in a plainforward language in the form of an introductory textbook, Favrholdt argues very forcefully for the kind of theory of knowledge presented here, and convincingly against most competing theories.

He is treating subjects, that includes discussions of the inevitability of the descriptive, ordinary language – a language describing a world of things in time and space – that cannot be "reduced" to a language of pure perception; a theory of the knowing subject (man) as having a body that mingles with reality as a necessity for knowledge at all; and a new and original theory of perception as direct, critical realism.

As should be clear from what I have said before, language is an indispensable part of any life-world, especially that kind of language I like to call the descriptive, ordinary language. There is only one such language, but many tongues (Danish, Hopi-indian, Finnish, English, Mandarine-chinese etc.).

Ordinary (aristotelean) divalent logic is a part of language in the sense explained, as is proto-euclidean geometry and proto-arithmetics. This means that the divalent logic is just as fundamental for the development of the polyvalent logics as is the euclidean geometry for the non-euclidean ones. There is an often quite complicated and implicit interdependence between a whole bunch of concepts from seemingly diffent parts of the descriptive language; especially is it impossible to understand logic and use the ordinary language of things independently of each other.

The mutual possibility of translation of language in this sense – the ordinary, descriptive language – is a fact; all fundamental knowledge inherent in all possible life-worlds can both be expressed in all existing (human) natural tongues and even in all possible non-human languages of possible rational alien beings.

The special language of physics can be expressed in any tongue, even Hopi-indian (as the Sapir-Whorff hypothesis in any interesting interpretation is basicly wrong.) Naturally, it will require some hard work to develop new Hopi-indian expressions for the newtonian or quantum mechanical concepts as it was for the scientific founders of these theories.

Noam Chomsky has argued that his transformational grammar can explain the possibility of translation of all the different *human* tongues to each other. Chomsky argues for an idea of the innateness of the depth structure of language, e.g. in *Cartesian Linguistics*, 1966. He considers the innateness as connected with the evolution of the human brain. But language, especially its most central part, which includes the "depth structure", in distinction to its tongue – is not something that is specifically *human in distinction to say martian.* Language is absolutely universal and even God or any kind of an intelligent being anywhere in the universe (on a planet in a distant galaxy) will fundamentally have that same language or will have to develop it, forced by the brute facts of nature.

Indeed, there is an important difference between the descriptive ordinary language of elementary facts of nature ("classificatory" language), and other specifically cultural-dependent uses of language, say artistic expressions. To understand a Japanese Haiku-poem you must have an intimate acquaintance with Japanese culture in all its aspects. If you try to translate such a poem from Japanese to Danish, you have two alternatives: You may try to create a new poem in Danish (which might evoke thoughts and feelings close to those the original Haiku-poem does to the Japanese reader) or you can translate it quite litterally, which means that the result is more or less without any serious meaning, or at least without much connection to the original meaning.

But language has its limits. When I am speaking with my nephew, who is born blind, he has learnt to call the grass "green", and he in a sense uses the language correctly when he speaks of the "red" mail-box. Given modern technology (an advanced spectrometer with sound signals) he might well be able to verify that grass is green and turns yellowish in a dry period and that a mail-box is red in Denmark and blue in the USA; but he has absolute no perceptions of colours and no conceptual (not to say experiental) understanding of colours except as a quantitative concept associated with an experiental perception of different sounds. He cannot discuss the artistic qualities of Raphael's wonderfull painting, "The School in Athens", in the Vatican.

Ladies and gentlemen!

"Whereof you cannot speak, thereof you must be silent."
I am silenced – at least for a moment.

Biography

Carsten Bengt-Pedersen, b. 1942, Associate Professor, mag.art., Chairman, Department of Philosophy, Odense University, and Reader in Philosophy of Science at the Royal Danish Veterinary and Agricultural College, Copenhagen. Has been Reader in Philosophy and Methodology of Social Anthropology at the Department of Anthropolgy and Etnology, University of Copenhagen, and Visiting professor at San Diego State University, California, USA, in 1978. Has published many papers on various philosophical subjects, and books in danish about conservative political philosophy, history and philosophy of science, most recently: "Natur og erkendelse" (Nature and Scientic Knowledge), Gyldendal, København 1995.

Ragnar Fjelland

From Evolutionary Epistemology to the Life World A Priori

Abstract
Stephen Toulmin and Karl Popper introduced evolutionary theory into the philosophy of science, partly as a response to Thomas Kuhn's theory of scientific revolutions. Popper's theory is especially interesting because he sees science – including scientific instruments – as being a product of an evolutionary process. However, in contrast to Popper, who stresses the importance of theory in the production of instruments, this present paper points to the intimate relationship between instruments and Euclidean geometry. This relationship has been pointed out by the late Edmund Husserl, the "Erlangen School", and more recently by the "father" of fractal geometry, Benoit Mandelbrot. Husserl specifically emphasized that Euclidean geometry is imperative to modern science, and he further argued that Euclidean geometry is founded in the life world. This paper eleborates upon this position, and concludes that an awareness of these relationships enables us to come to grips with aspects of modern science that have been largely ignored: idealization, the prevalence of the artificial over the natural, and the importance of symmetries.

Introduction

For two decades evolutionary epistemology has been in fashion. Two of the first to introduce evolutionary theory into the philosophy of science were Stephen Toulmin[1] and Karl Popper[2], at least partly as a reaction to Kuhn's theory of scientific revolutions. In particular Popper's theory is interesting because not only science, but technology is seen as a product of an evolutionary process. He advocates a prosthetic theory of technology, regarding technological devices as an extension of the human body.

Fundamental to Popper's theory is the evolution of a descriptive language. It establishes an autonomous world of theoretical entities. This is the world of science. In spite of the original evolutionary approach, science becomes fundamentally an ahistorical phenomenon. We learn more by studying the structures themselves than by studying the production of these structures. Hence, we learn more by studying theories than by studying the activities of the scientists.[3]

One of Popper's main examples is the Michelson-Morley experiment. It grew out of a theoretical problem, it refuted one theory, and it led to another. This is the special theory of relativity. However, contrary to Popper's view, we can learn something interesting from studying the activities of scientists, in this case Michelson's experiments. After all, he received the Nobel prize in physics for the development of his instruments and the precision of his measurements. In the production of these instruments Euclidean geometry played a fundamental part.

In contrast to Popper, who stressed the importance of theory in the production of instruments, the present paper points to the intimate relationship between Euclidean geometry and technology. This relationship has been pointed out by the late Edmund Husserl, the "Erlangen School", and more recently the "father" of fractal geometry, Benoit Mandelbrot.[4] In particular Husserl emphasized that the understanding of the intimate relationship between Euclidean geometry and technology was crucial to the understanding of modern science.

I try to show that awareness of this relationship enables us to come to grips with aspects of modern science that have been largely ignored: idealization, the prevalence of the artificial over the natural, and the importance of Euclidean geometry in the experimental situation.

Popper's evolutionary epistemology

The basis of all evolution is what Popper calls *objective problems*. That the problems are objective means that they need not be conscious or perceived as problems. For instance, the evolution of the eye solves the problem of giving a moving organism a warning to change its direction before it bumps into other objects. Evolution is "blind", using the method of trial and error-elimination. The mechanism of progress is the ability to eliminate unsuccessful trials. This method is the same at all levels of evolution.

Both Einstein and the amoeba used this method. The difference is, however, that in contrast to the amoeba, Einstein used the method consciously and systematically. The organism's ability to eliminate errors corresponds to the scientist's ability to reject false hypotheses. Popper quotes the physicist John Archibald Wheeler: "Our whole problem is to make the mistakes as fast as possible."[5] This is the Darwinian theory of evolution.

One contrast between evolution in the human world and biological evolution is that the first is mainly *exosomatic*, whereas the latter is mainly *endosomatic*. Exosomatic evolution takes place outside the organism, and endosomatic evolution inside the organism, by modifications of the organism's organs. Exosomatic evolution produces a world outside the individual. There are many examples of exosomatic evolution in animals. Spiders produce webs, which are analogous to human devices for catching animals, many birds build nests, which are analogous to human houses. Beavers are clever engineers, building dams, and so on.

Tools are outside our body, and may therefore be regarded as products of exosomatic evolution. Instead of growing better eyes and ears, man grows spectacles, microscopes, telescopes, telephones and hearing aids. Instead of growing better legs, man grows bicycles and automobiles, and instead of growing a better memory and brain, he grows paper, pens, typewriters, books and computers. Yet at the same time they can be regarded as an extension of our body. The Greek word for 'tool' is 'organon'. Popper attributes this theory to the English philosopher Samuel Butler. A similar theory was advocated by Arnold Gehlen as well, and we find the theory already in Aristotle.

Popper applies the concept of structure and function to organs and tools. As Aristotle pointed out, there is a close relationship between an organ's structure and its biological function. Therefore, the human eye can only fulfill its biological function if it has a certain structure, a lens, a retina etc. In the same way, an ax can only fulfill its function as an ax if it has a certain design.

According to Popper this theory of tools does not only apply to technology, but to theories as well: "Theories are organs." He distinguishes between three different worlds, or universes: World 1 is the world of physical objects and states. World 2 is the world of states of consciousness or mental states and World 3 is the world of objective contents of thought. Popper's World 3 is similar to Plato's world of ideas and Frege's world of *Gedanken*. The objects of World 3 are theoretical systems, problems, critical arguments and the contents of journals, books and libraries.

The precondition of the autonomy or objectivity of World 3 is the higher functions of language. The descriptive function of language is the fundamental precondition for the autonomy of World 3:

> Without the development of an exosomatic descriptive language – a language which, like a tool, develops outside the body – there can be *no object* for our critical discussion. But with the development of a descriptive language (and further, of a written language), a linguistic third world can emerge; and it is only in this way, and only in this third world, that the problems and standards of rational criticism can develop.[6]

According to Popper the descriptive function of language, in contrast to the lower functions, the signal and expressive function, introduces the notion of *truth*.

This is the basis of the autonomy of World 3. Although World 3 is the product of man, it transcends the subjective opinions of World 2. Among other reasons, Popper gives the following argument against the idea that World 3 should be subjective: Many may assert that a book is nothing without a reader. Only if a book is actually read and understood, it becomes a book. If not, it is only a physical object, a stack of papers with black spots on them. Popper disagrees with this view, and again he uses biological analogies. A bird's nest is a bird's nest after it has been deserted, and even if it has never been inhabited by birds. And a book remains a book even if it is never read. A book may not even have been written by a human being. Popper mentions a book containing tables of logarithms produced by a computer. Although it has not been produced by a human being and even if it is never read, it is still a book. It may one day be read, it has a potentiality for being read and understood. This potentiality makes it an object of World 3.

From theory to instruments

Popper is one of the modern philosophers who have put strongest emphasis on the theoretical aspects of science. But I think he jumps too hastily to the autonomous World 3. Although he refers to Butler's theory of technology, technological artefacts do not fit into any of his three "worlds". They obviously do not belong to World 3. There are several reasons for this. First, as already mentioned, Popper relates his World 3 to Plato's theory of forms and Frege's objective thought. For Plato and Frege evidently the objects are theoretical. A second reason is that the higher functions of language are a *necessary condition* for the autonomy of World 3. All the objects of World 3 are linguistic entities or abstracted from linguistic entities.

If technological artefacts cannot belong to World 3, they might belong to World 2. They are products of man, like the objects of World 2. But in a crucial sense they differ from the objects of World 2. An ax is an ax and a house is a house even if they have never been used. All the artefacts produced by man, machines, bridges, houses, books, would remain even if man ceased to exist. Therefore, although they are the products of man, their existence is objective. They have this in common with objects of World 3 and World 1.

The only alternative left then is World 1. But technological artefacts are not just physical objects, and from what has been said previously it is clear that Popper himself recognizes this fact. They may be regarded as extensions of the human body. Therefore it looks as if technological artefacts do not fit into any of Popper's "worlds". Therefore, in spite of his many interesting remarks about technology, Popper does not pursue this topic. Neither the body, nor technology, play any role in his theory of scientific knowledge.

In order to try to come to grips with the status of technology, I shall focus on a special kind of technology: measuring instruments. One reason for this is that Popper maintains that we "see" with theories. However, we "see" with measuring instruments as well. A large part of modern natural science is not built on simple sense perception, but on experiments and measurements. An important feature of the new science that emerged in the seventeenth and eighteenth century was the fact that experiments and measurements replaced simple observations. Therefore, not only theories, but scientific instruments are extensions of our sense organs. Measuring instruments in particular are important, and without measurements a large part of modern science would not have been possible.[7]

Popper would, of course not deny the importance of scientific instruments to the development of science. However, the instruments incorporate theoretical knowledge, and so nothing more than the theory-ladenness of observations is involved. Theory permeates scientific activity at all levels. Here is a typical quotation from Popper:

> What compels the theorist to search for a better theory, in these cases, is almost always the experimental *falsification* of a theory, so far accepted and corroborated: it is, again, the outcome of tests guided by theory. Famous examples are the Michelson-Morley experiment which led to the theory of relativity...[8]

However, it is interesting to see that Edmund Husserl, writing *The Crisis of the European Sciences and Transcendental Phenomenology* a few years after *The Logic of Scientific Discovery* had been published, emphasized the *pre-theoretical* elements of scientific activity in general and of scientific instruments in particular. Husserl argued that even the most theoretical sciences are founded in the "life world". This even applies to the most abstract theories. Husserl also refers to the relativity theory of Einstein:

> The sciences build upon the life-world as taken for granted in that they make use of whatever in it happens to be necessary for their particular ends... For example, Einstein uses the Michelson experiments and the corroboration of them by other researchers, with apparatus copied from Michelson's, with everything required in the way of scales of measurement, coincidences established, etc.[9]

The sciences are founded "...on the basis of the life-world a priori."[10]

From instruments to Euclidean geometry

Both Popper and Husserl refer to Michelson's experiments, and therefore I shall use them as a starting point.[11] These experiments were performed in the 1880s (partly with Morley, therefore the name 'Michelson-Morley experiment') to try to detect an ether. The theoretical background for these experiments is the following: Light is an electromagnetic phenomenon. It propagates as waves, like sound. However, sound needs a *medium* to propagate, for example air or water. It cannot propagate in a vacuum. In the same manner it was assumed that light needed a medium to propagate. This was called ether. If an ether existed, the velocity of light would be constant relative to this ether. But the earth would during its annual motion around the sun, move in different directions relative to the ether. Therefore it should be possible to show that the velocity of light measured from the earth, would vary according to the earth's motion.

The effect Michelson tried to detect are second-order effects. They might be detected, but it would require great precision. He developed an instrument, the interferometer, to measure these effects, and the experiment took almost ten years to carry out. Michelson and Morley did not detect an ether. Michelson received the Nobel prize in physics, though, and as Hacking has pointed out, he did not receive the Nobel prize for the negative results, but for his development of measuring instruments, which had an unequaled precision.[12]

When reading Michelson's own descriptions of his interferometer, one is struck by his diagrams based on geometrical optics (which is again based on Euclidean geometry). Therefore, one may argue that the observations made with the interferometer were based on Euclidean geometry, geometrical optics, and the wave theory of light as well, just to mention the most important theories involved. Even more striking is Michelson's description of how his mirrors were tested and improved. He claimed that the deviation from a plane surface in the mirrors was a twentieth of the wavelength of light, or less.

Michelson describes how the mirrors were tested. They were placed on the surface of a test plane, which was supposed to be plane to at least the same accuracy as the mirrors to be tested. We understand that the accuracy of the mirrors depended on the accuracy of the test plane. To manufacture the test plane Michelson needed three surfaces, A, B and C. A and B were polished to fit, and hence to have equal and opposite curvature. Then A and C were made to fit, and then B and C. The procedure was repeated until all the three surfaces fit exactly. Therefore, they must all be plane.[13] As we shall see later, this procedure uses the properties of translational and reflectional symmetry of a plane.

One might argue that Michelson used some fundamental properties of a plane surface, and therefore he presupposed Euclidean geometry. This argument would support the position that observations are theory-laden. However, the argument assumes that the fundamental forms and concepts of Euclidean geometry can be defined independently of the procedure described. Nevertheless, this assumption cannot be taken for granted. On the contrary, if one can show that this – or a similar – procedure is a prerequisite for the definition of the fundamental Euclidean concepts, then the situation is radically different.

This is the line of argument pursued by Husserl. He argued that to understand modern science properly, we must inquire into the meaning of (Euclidean) geometry. To understand the meaning of geometry, we must inquire back into its origin in pre-theoretical practical activity. The problem is according to Husserl that this has not been done. However, one might argue that this project is only of historical interest, and that our understanding of geometry has been greatly increased in this century. In particular the distinction between formal and empirical geometry has contributed to a better understanding of geometry. Husserl does not reject what has been accomplished by modern geometry, but it has not brought us closer to a fundamental understanding. The closest we come to the formation of elementary concepts is elementary geometrical instructions in textbooks. Yet the problem is that we learn to deal with *ready-made* concepts and sentences, and not with the formation of the concepts.

In "The Origin of Geometry"[14] Husserl sets out to trace the origin of

Euclidean geometry. He reconstructs the origin of geometry roughly as follows: The world consists of material bodies, with different shapes and 'material' qualities (colour, warmth, weight, hardness and so on). For technical praxis some particular shapes were preferred. These are partly selected, partly produced and improved according to certain directions of gradualness. Husserl describes how special forms are singled out: surfaces according to if they are more or less smooth, more or less perfect. Edges according to if they are more or less rough or even, for example more or less pure lines, angles, more or less perfect points. Among surfaces, even surfaces are preferred and among lines, straight lines are preferred, and so on. As technology makes progress, there is an increasing interest in what is technically more refined. The ideal of perfection is pushed further and further. So there is always an open horizon of *conceivable* improvements to be further pursued.

The ideal shapes of Euclidean geometry, like straight lines and planes, grew out of the praxis of technical perfecting. Husserl called them *limit-shapes* ("Limesgestalten"). These can be regarded as the pole that the process of perfection is approaching. When these ideal shapes are made our objects of investigation, when we are engaged in determining them and in constructing new shapes out of those already determined, we are "geometers". Therefore, the ideal geometrical figures are produced by the 'method of idealization'.

The technical foundation of Euclidean geometry

Euclidean geometry is grounded in the life world in the following way:

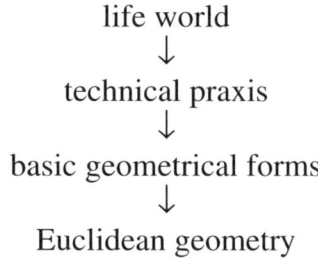

According to Husserl the intimate relationship between technical praxis and geometry had not been investigated before. This was not completely true. It had already been done in more detail by William Kingdon Clifford in 1885[15], and by Hugo Dingler in 1911[16]. Dingler had published continuously on the topic after that. However, Husserl refers neither to Clifford nor to Dingler. The work of Dingler has been carried on by Paul Lorenzen, Peter Janich and Rüdinger Inhetveen, sometimes called the "Erlangen School". In particular they have concentrated on the relationship between the second and the third level in the figure, demonstrating how the basic geometric forms can be constructed from a technical praxis. This field is called *proto-geometry* (from Greek: prōto = first[17]). They have carried out the program of founding Euclidean geometry in the life world with considerable detail and mathematical rigour.

I shall try to show how the basic forms of Euclidean geometry can be founded in a technical praxis, influenced by the work of the "Erlangen School". However, I shall not go into all the technical details, but concentrate on the principles of the construction.

It is a widely held view, which at least goes back to Herodotus, that the origin of geometry goes back to land surveying as performed in ancient Egypt. The word "geometry" means literally "earth measurement" (Greek: ge = earth, metron = measure), and the etymological link between geometry and land survey has allegedly established this link beyond doubt. However, it has been argued that the Greek word for geometry was not the same word as was used for land surveying[18]. Yet the strongest argument against land surveying as the origin of geometry is the fact that the "rope stretchers" took the concepts of 'area', 'straight line' and even 'right angle' for granted. So, they may be said to have *applied* the concepts rather than having created them.

A better candidate for the origin of geometry is the art of building. For instance, the Egyptian pyramids demonstrate that the methods of construction must have been highly developed in Egypt. Very important in this context is the fact that the pyramids are built of blocks that embody the basic Euclidean forms: plane surfaces, straight lines, parallel surfaces and lines, right angles.

Things made by man are *artefacts*. In the production of artefacts we can distinguish three different kinds:

1) Artefacts made by reshaping natural objects.
2) Compound artefacts, i.e. artefacts made by putting two or more objects together.
3) Compound artefacts consisting of like parts, "elements".

At the first stage there are no "theoretical" problems, but on the second stage one condition must be satisfied: The different parts might need to fit together. One way of ensuring this is to shape the one part after the other, but usually this will be a labourious task. A solution to the problem will be to use regular forms, forms that are easy to produce and reproduce. In that case we might even produce the parts independently of each other and then know that they would fit together afterwards.

These regular forms, like the cylinder, the sphere, the plane and so on, are the basic forms of Euclidean geometry. Fundamental in the production and identification of these regular forms is what is sometimes called the *principle of homogeneity*. "Homogeneous" means "consisting of parts all of the same kind" or "uniform", that is, you cannot separate one part and say that it is different from the other parts. Applied to surfaces this means that a homogeneous surface is a *smooth* surface. That a surface is smooth, means that when you touch it, you cannot distinguish one point or one part from other points or parts of the surface.[19]

The principle of homogeneity was first applied to the production of lenses. According to Paul Lorenzen this method is four thousand years old.[20] Lenses are produced by grinding two bodies composed of the required material against each other. The grinding takes place where the two surfaces are in contact, so that the unevenness will be ground away, and the two surfaces will progressively fit better together. It is important that the movements should be as irregular as possible. In this way one produces two spherical surfaces, one concave and one convex, and both have the same curvature. Therefore, the two surfaces have spherical symmetry.

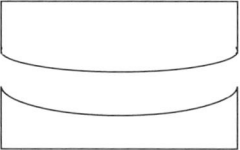

Figure 1. Production of two spherical surfaces.

This method produces two spherical surfaces, one concave and one convex. They are homogeneous, but not determinate, as they may have any curvature. Next we repeat the process, using three objects instead of two, grinding them alternately against each other. The result will be three surfaces that fit together. These surfaces can be neither concave nor convex. They cannot have any curvature; they must be *plane* surfaces. So, a homogeneous surface without curvature is a plane surface. As we have seen previously, this was the method used by Michelson.

Saying that a plane has the same shape all over is equivalent to saying that it has translational symmetry. What is valid for one part of the surface, is valid for any other part. For instance, if an object is placed on the surface, it can be moved to any other part of the surface, and it will make no difference as far as the relation between the object and the surface is concerned.

That it is the same shape on both sides is equivalent to saying that it has reflectional symmetry. I do not want to go into technical details, but it should at least be intuitively obvious to the reader that if the three surfaces mentioned above fit, they must have reflectional symmetry. Clifford proves that this procedure is unambiguous, which means that the outcome of the process in the ideal case is necessarily always the same. So, a third property of plane surfaces is that they all fit. This, of course, explains their importance to technology.

An example illustrating the function of the basic Euclidean forms

Now comes the third kind of artefact: artefacts composed of like parts. These parts can be called the "elements", or even the "atoms" of the objects. That man started to make objects composed of like parts is one of the greatest steps in the development of technology.

This development can be observed in Mesopotamia between 8000 and 3000 BC. The oldest dwellings found there consist of huts made directly of clay, without any planning. The walls were built by putting new clay on top of the clay that was already dry, thus building upwards. It is impossible to build more complicated buildings in this way.

So the invention of the brick is a fundamental step in the history of the art of building.[21] Here man for the first time learned to make compound objects from like parts. This was an important step towards a *formalization* of the operations. The bricks could be made completely independent of the building they were meant to be used in, and different buildings could be made of like elements, only in a different *order*.

Not just any material body can serve well as a brick. It is required that the brick be composed of the adequate material and that it has adequate spatial properties, such as adequate shape and size. The material of the brick does not concern us here. It is presupposed that the material is so hard that the brick can be called a rigid body in the ordinary sense of the word. So, apart from the question of the material, the spatial properties make the brick fill its function as a brick. The function of the shape and size of the brick is to fill a space. We can now define congruence for material bodies in the following way: two bodies are congruent when they fill the same space, and that is when they can take care of the same spatial function.[22]

The fact that bricks are congruent, makes it much easier to build in brick than to build with natural stones. Everybody knows the problems that arise when we build, for example, a wall of stones. We usually have to look carefully to find the right stone, and every stone thus gets its special place in the wall. Building a stable wall in this way is very labourious.

Yet building with congruent elements raises a new problem: the elements must have a special form to fit together. If for instance they had the form of a sphere, they would be congruent, but they would not fit together. So, not just *any* form can work. For the bricks to fit together they must have special symmetry properties.[23] These symmetry properties can be well shown by describing the various stages in the development of the brick. According to Lorenzen we find in Mesopotamia a gradual improvement of the form of the brick. This improvement means that more symmetries are realized in the brick. Let us take a closer look at the various stages (cf. fig. 2):

1) The brick is a lump of clay molded without any sort of tools and dried in the sun.

2) The brick is produced by putting a lump of clay on a plane surface, and then molded by hand. It has then one plane surface.

3) The next step is that a rectangular mould is used. This is placed on a plane surface, and then filled with clay, and the top is shaped by hand. In this brick all sides are plane, except the top. The brick has many symmetries. The sides stand at right angles to each other and to the bottom. The sides meet in edges that are straight lines, and the corners are points. The bricks fit perfectly well with one exception: When they are put on top of each other, they do not fit very well.

4) In the last step the top is made a plane surface, too.[24]

I have used the brick to show the significance of the fundamental Euclidean forms: plane surface, straight line, right angle and parallel planes and lines. However, anybody can convince himself of the significance of these forms to technology by looking at a modern house or the high-rise buildings of a big city.

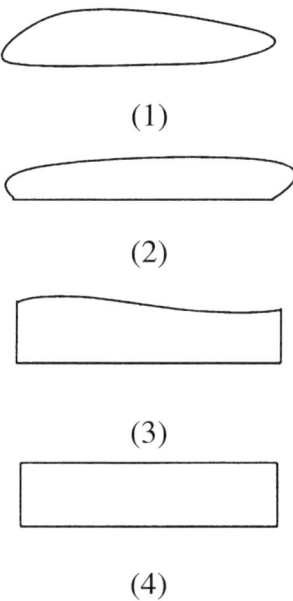

Figure 2. The development of the brick in Mesopotamia between 8000 and 3000 BC.

An example: length measurement

I shall use length measurements to illustrate the fundamental importance of Euclidean forms in the construction of instruments. One of the first to address the problem of geometrical measurements was Helmholtz. He argued that we are only entitled to talk about geometrical magnitudes if we have a way of measuring them. However, measurements in space "require that figures in space can be moved without any change in form or magnitude".[25] Figures in space that can be moved without deformation are what mathematicians call *rigid bodies*. So, the fundamental question is how rigid bodies can be defined.

Many of the fundamental questions in the philosophy of science of this century grew out of the problems of defining a rigid body. The general question is this: If I move an allegedly rigid body from place A to place B, how can I know that it has not been deformed? If the temperature in B is higher than in A it will expand. This deformation can be detected because bodies made of different material will expand differently. Therefore, heat can be called a *differential force*. However, if all material bodies expanded or contracted in the same way, i.e. the structure of space itself varied, we have *universal forces*.[26] One might try to make recourse to the concept of *congruence*, but one easily gets into vicious circles. The conventionalists concluded that universal forces can only be excluded by convention.

Clifford argued that the question of universal forces is meaningless. At least, when we take the life world as a starting point, the problem of universal forces does not arise. The only problem is to eliminate differential forces, and I shall demonstrate that the symmetry properties described previously, are important in the elimination of differential forces. We start with an everyday notion of rigidity. We say that a material body is rigid when it can withstand deformation, and by "deformation" I mean change in shape and size. We also know from everyday life that bodies are deformed by external forces, by heat and so on. The first step is choosing a suitable measuring rod. Let us, for example, try out four different measuring rods: a snake (proposed by Russell[27]), a rubber band (proposed by Carnap[28]), a wooden stick and a metal rod. We notice that the wooden stick and the metal rod will differ from the snake and the rubber band because they give approximately the same results. By repeated measurements on the same undeformed object (in the everyday notion of "undeformed"), the wooden stick and the metal rod will give approximately the same results, whereas the snake and the rubber band will give different results each time.

However, it is worth having in mind that what makes a measuring tool "good enough" is determined by the purpose of the measurements, which is again determined by the technical requirements. For example, the mechanical clocks existing at the time of Galileo were good enough for many purposes, but they were not good enough for Galileo to use them for time measurements in his experiments with bronze balls rolling on inclined planes. For many purposes and for a certain technological level, a wooden stick may be good enough as a measuring rod.

For tasks requiring great precision we will use a metal rod, but a metal rod is not a perfectly rigid body. In particular it expands when heated, and other physical phenomena may influence it as well. To control the effect of heat we have to determine the coefficient of expansion. One way of determining the coefficient of expansion is this: We have two bars of the same material. Initially they have the same temperature.[29] Then they are separated (or thermally insulated). One of the bars is heated, and the length is then compared with the length of the other bar. The expansion can be plotted as a function of temperature. However, for this to be possible, we have to solve a problem: How is it possible to compare the length of the two bars? Of course, they must be able to slide against each other. The obvious way of doing this is that the two bars have sides that are plane surfaces, and hence edges that are straight lines. Then they will have *translational sym-*

metry. If this had not been the case, comparing the two bars might have been possible, but measuring fractions of the bars would not have been possible. (See fig. 3)

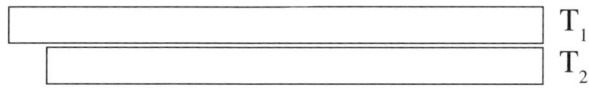

Figure 3.

Conclusion

One might argue that even if Euclidean geometry is important to the construction of scientific instruments, it does not imply that it is valid for the *objects* investigated with these instruments. I shall try to show in what sense it is valid, and point to two implications that I think are interesting.

The first is the importance of *idealization* in science. To see how it works I shall return to Popper. Popper himself regarded his own philosophy of science as a radical break with the prevailing view of the logical empiricists of the 1930s. However, although he shifted the emphasis from verification to falsification, he nevertheless retained the basic element of empiricism, "the principle of empiricism". It says "…that in science, only observation and experiment may decide upon the *acceptance or rejection* of scientific statements, including laws and theories".[30]

One theory is falsified and is succeeded by a better theory. Among others Popper uses the relation between Galileo's and Newton's theories of motion to illustrate this point. According to Galileo a thrown stone or a projectile moves in a parabola. Yet according to Newton this is false. A projectile on earth moves along an ellipse. For short throws a parabola is a very good approximation, but this approximation cannot be deduced from Newton's laws unless we add a false initial condition, to the effect that the radius of the earth is infinite.[31]

The curious thing is that Galileo said exactly the same as Popper. In *Dialogue Concerning Two New Sciences* he points out that his own results have been proved in the abstract, and when applied to concrete cases they will yield false results. The horizontal motion will not be uniform, a freely falling body will not move according to the law, and the path of a projectile will not be a parabola.³² Therefore, it looks as if Galileo himself did not regard his own laws as empirical.

However, how does Galileo himself defend his procedures? Speaking of the difficulties arising by these limitations, he immediately adds:

> ...in order to handle this matter in a scientific way, it is necessary to cut loose from these difficulties; and having discovered and demonstrated the theorems, in the case of no resistance, to use them and apply them with such limitations as experience will teach. And the advantage of this method will not be small; for the material and shape of the projectile may be chosen, as dense and round as possible, so that it will encounter the least resistance in the medium.

I will take this last sentence to indicate that Galileo was not only interested in investigating natural motion, but in *constructing* various kinds of artificial motion as well.

Here we face a problem. We know that Galileo made experiments, for instance with balls rolling down inclined planes, to investigate motion. What was the purpose of these experiments? Was the main purpose (1) to investigate natural motion, or was it (2) to construct various kinds of artificial motion?

In Galileo's texts we may find support for both views. He emphasizes the fact that the kinds of motion he investigated, are not artificial motion, but motion that occurs in nature. And he argues at length to demonstrate that results obtained from the investigation of balls rolling down inclined planes can be transferred to freely falling bodies. However, it is not difficult to find support for (2) either. Galileo was not only a natural scientist, but an engineer as well, and there are plenty of indications that Galileo was well aware of the technical aspects of his investigations of motion.

So, there is strong support for both (1) and (2). The solution of this apparent paradox is that Galileo did not see a crucial difference between the *artificial* and the *natural*. He regarded his own science not only as a natural science, but as a *science of the artificial* as well. Indeed, he regarded them as two sides of the same coin. In a letter he discusses various forms of artificial motion, and he continues:

> When experience has demonstrated that the motion of heavy bodies falling by nature [free fall, RF] have the same properties as artificial motion, we may confidently assert that the movement of the falling body is the same as we have assumed.³³

According to his contemporary Descartes "…the laws of Mechanics …are identical with those of Nature…"[34]

The second consequence is the importance of Euclidean geometry to the whole experimental situation. Ronald Giere tells how surprised he was when he noticed that the geometrical forms of a cyclotron facility were clearly visible in aerial photographs.[35] (Fig. 4 gives an illustration of an accelerator.[36]) As we see, the basic Euclidean forms, straight line, circle and right angle are evident.

According to Giere geometrical aspects also appear in formal and informal presentations. He seeks part of the explanation for this in cognitive patterns in our brains, making us predisposed to Euclidean geometry. He refers to experiments with rats that allegedly show that rats are also predisposed to Euclidean geometry. However, although I agree with Giere when he points to the significance of Euclidean geometry, I disagree with his explanation of its significance. I think he is wrong in suggesting that our perceived world is Euclidean.[37]

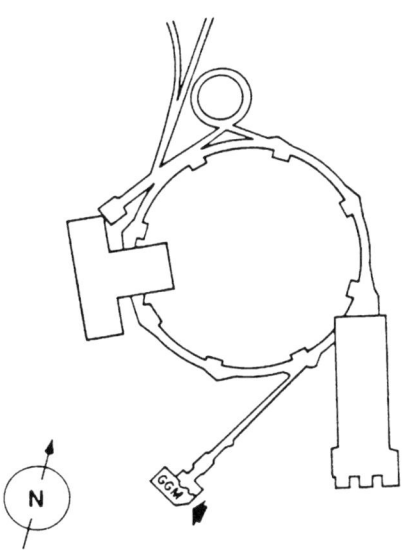

Figure 4. A diagram illustrating the Cern Proton Synchrotron 1967.

However, assuming that the perceived world is Euclidean to explain the significance of Euclidean geometry is not necessary. Giere himself suggests another reason why Euclidean geometry is important to science: the intimate relationship between geometry and technology.

From Evolutionary Epistemology to the Life World A Priori

Although few scientists today would share the metaphysical views of Galileo and Descartes, the view that there is no essential difference between the artificial and the natural has been dominating until this day. One implication has been that it has been generally overlooked that "traditional" science has mainly been limited to dealing with idealized, artificial situations.[38] However, it is an interesting fact that the emergence of theories of chaos and fractal geometry have reminded us of the very special assumptions of "traditional" science.

Biography

Ragnar Fjelland (born 1947) is professor of philosophy of science at the Center for the Study of the Sciences and the Humanities, University of Bergen. He is also affiliated with the Department of Physics. He has been a visiting scholar at Universität Konstanz, Germany (1976), Universiti Malaya, Kuala Lumpur, Malaysia (1984/85), University of Toronto, Canada (1988) and University of California /Berkeley, USA (1990). His current topics of interest include the significance of technology for the acquisition of scientific knowledge, philosophical implications of chaos theory and fractal geometry, ethical problems raised by modern science and technology, and the challenge of environmental problems to science. He is a member of the National Research Committee for Natural Science and Technology.

Notes

1. Stephen Toulmin: *Human Understanding*, Vol. 1, Princeton, New Jersey: Princeton University Press 1972.
2. Karl Popper: *Objective Knowledge*, London: Oxford University Press 1975, in particular pp. 206-255.
3. Ibid., p. 114.
4. Benoit Mandelbrot: *The Fractal Geometry of Nature*, 3. revised ed., New York: Freeman and Company 1983, p. 1.
5. John A. Wheeler: *American Scientist* 44/1956, p. 360, quoted in Popper, ibid, p. 247.
6. Ibid., p. 120.
7. Cf. Thomas Kuhn: "The Function of Measurement in Modern Physical Science", reprinted in Kuhn: *The Essential Tension*, Chicago and London: University of Chicago Press 1977.
8. Karl R. Popper: *The Logic of Scientific Discovery* (orig. 1934), London: Hutchinson & Co, 5. rev. ed. 1972, p. 108.

9. Edmund Husserl: *The Crisis of European Sciences and Transcendental Phenomenology*, Evanston: Northwestern University Press 1970, p. 125.
10. Ibid., p. 140.
11. We now know that both Popper and Husserl were historically wrong. The Michelson-Morley experiment probably played no part in the discovery of the special theory of relativity. In a letter to Michael Polanyi Einstein stated: "The Michelson-Morley experiment had no role in the foundation of the theory." (Michael Polanyi: *Personal Knowledge*, London: Routledge & Kegan Paul 1958, p. 11.) However, Einstein said different things on different occasions. There are reasons for believing that the Michelson-Morley experiment was not important, although he probably knew the experiment in 1905. (Abraham Pais: *'Subtle is the Lord...' The Science and Life of Albert Einstein*, Oxford: Oxford University Press 1982, pp. 502-519.) But this does not affect my argument. I use the experiment only to demonstrate the importance of technology and Euclidean geometry.
12. Ian Hacking: *Representing and Intervening*, Cambridge: Cambridge University Press 1983, p. 174.
13. A.A. Michelson: *Studies in Optics*, Chicago & London: The University of Chicago Press 1962, p. 73.
14. Written in 1936 and first published in 1939. Included as Appendix VI in the English translation of *Crisis* previously referred to.
15. William Kingdon Clifford: *The Common Sense of the Exact Sciences*, New York: Dover Publications 1955.
16. Hugo Dingler: *Die Grundlagen der angewandten Geometrie*, Leipzig: Akademische Verlagsgesellschaft 1911.
17. Rüdiger Inhetveen: *Konstruktive Geometrie*, Mannheim/Wien/Zürich: Bibliographisches Institut 1983, p. 10.
18. Ibid., p. 11-12.
19. We see here the origin of a principle that plays an important part in science. Benoit Mandelbrot has pointed to the importance of the principle:
    "...Euclid begins with the simplest shapes, such as lines, planes, or spaces. And the simplest physics arises when some quantity such as density, temperature, pressure, or velocity is distributed in a homogeneous manner." Benoit Mandelbrot: *The Fractal Geometry of Nature*, op.cit., p. 18
20. See Paul Lorenzen: "Das Begründungsproblem der Geometrie als Wissenschaft der räumlichen Ordnung", in Paul Lorenzen: *Methodisches Denken*, Frankfurt am Main: Suhrkamp Verlag 1968, p. 131.
21. Seton Lloyd: "Building in Brick ans Stone", in C. Singer, E. J. Holmyard and A. R. Hall: *A History of Technology*, New York and London: Oxford University Press 1954, Vol 1, pp. 456-494.
22. Inhetveen, op.cit., p. 26
23. Cf Philipp Frank: *Philosophy of Science*, Englewood Cliffs, N.J.: Prentice-Hall 1957, p. 54.
24. See Lorenzen, op.cit.
25. Hermann von Helmholtz: "Ueber den Ursprung und die Bedeutung der geometrischen Axiome", in Hermann von Helmholtz: *Vorträge und Reden*, 4. ed. Branschweig: F. Vieweg und Sohn 1896.
26. The distinction between differential and universal forces is due to Reichenbach. He

has an illuminatng discussion of the problems of defining a rigid body as well. See Hans Reichenbach: *The Philosophy of Space & Time*, New York: Dover Publications 1958, in particular §§ 3-5.
27. Bertrand Russell: *The ABC of Relativity*, New York: The New American Library, third rev. ed. 1959
28. Rudolf Carnap: *Philosophical Foundations of Physics*, ed. by Martin Gardner, New York: Basic Books 1966.
29. I shall not address the problems of temperature measurements. I just take it for granted that temperature can be measured independently of length measurements.
30. Karl Popper: *Conjectures and Refutations*, London: Routledge and Kegan Paul 1974, p. 54.
31. Karl Popper: *Objective Knowledge*, op.cit., p. 199.
32. Galileo Galilei: *Dialogue Concerning Two New Sciences*, translated by Henry Crew & Alfonso de Salvio (1914), New York: Dover Publications 1954, p. 251.
33. Quoted from Stillman Drake: *Galileo at Work*, Chicago: The University of Chicago Press 1978, p. 378.
34. René Descartes: *Discourse on Method*, in *The Philosophical Works of Descartes*, translated by Haldane and Ross, London: Cambridge University Press 1973, Vol 1, p. 115.
35. Ronald N. Giere: *Explaining Science. A Cognitive Approach*, Chicago and London: The University of Chicago Press 1988, p. 133.
36. The diagram is from Peter Galison: *How Experiments End*, Chicago and London: The University of Chicago Press 1987, p. 160.
37. See for example Patrick A. Heelan: *Space-perception and the Philosophy of Science*, Berkeley, Los Angeles, London: University of California Press 1988.
38. A few philosophers of science have pointed to this fact. I have already referred to Hacking's *Representing and Intervening*. I also want to mention Don Ihde: *Instrumental Realism. The Interface between Philosophy of Science and Philosophy of Technology*, Bloomington and Indianapolis: Indiana University Press 1991 and Alan Chalmers: *Science and Its Fabrication*, Minneapolis: University of Minnesota Press 1990.

Róbert H. Haraldsson

From Metaphysical Subjects to Naturalized Selves
– A Nietzschean Perspective on Pity –

Abstract
In the paper I consider whether a conception of the self as a fully natural entity – as opposed to a metaphysical soul or subject – should lead to a stronger emphasis on the importance of compassion for moral life. I argue that it should. My point of departure is Nietzsche's philosophy but some main themes in his philosophy seem at first glance to run counter to my argument. Nietzsche, who is one of the most outspoken proponent of the natural conception of the self, is widely reputed to have rejected compassion (Mitleid) as a morally harmful emotion. I argue that Nietzsche's critical evaluations of compassion have not been adequately understood by Nietzsche scholars. In particular I show how most Nietzsche sekolars have underestimated or simply ignored the important distinction Nietzsche draws between good and bad compassion. Once we properly understand this distinction we will se how Nietzsche's criticisms of (bad) compassion can be seen as criticisms of the conception of the human self (or soul) as a metaphysical subject, as something which is noncomposite, invisible, unchanging and divine. I also argue that Nietzsche articulates a new conception of compassion which fully recognizes the vulnerabilities of natural selves.

> More profoundly feeling people have at all times felt sympathy for the animals because they suffer from life and yet do not possess the power to turn the goad of life against themselves and understand their existence metaphysically; one is, indeed, profoundly indignant at the sight of senseless suffering. (Nietzsche)

I

Human beings are fragile and vulnerable creatures. They need to rely on others to thrive and flourish and they can come to harm through no faults of their own. Not only is human life precarious – it is almost a pessimistic platitude that a human life can be terminated without a warning and certainly without reason – human selves are so hard to create and sustain that one sometimes wonders how a self can survive – let alone thrive – in a world like ours marked by violence and senseless suffering. One certainly fails to see how a self could do so without the help and emotional support of other selves.

Given these obvious facts about human beings in nature one would expect that philosophers – throughout the ages – had spent a fair portion of their time discussing the role of sympathy and trust in the good life. Trust obviously merits such an attention since, in Sissela Bok's words, "whatever matters to human beings, trust is the atmosphere in which it thrives" (Bok 1978, 31n). And sympathy (or pity) as Aristotle pointed out is the appropriate emotional attitude towards someone who is experiencing suffering because of an evil he doesn't deserve, an evil that one might expect oneself, or some member of one's family, to suffer. However, with few well known exceptions, neither sympathy nor trust have been highly rated by moral philosophers. In Annette C. Baier's words "there has been a strange silence on the topic [of trust] in the tradition of moral philosophy..." (Baier 1994, 96). And although he overstates his case, Nietzsche makes a valid point about the philosophical tradition when he writes that: "hitherto philosophers have been at one as to the *worthlessness* of pity. I name only Plato, Spinoza, La Rochefoucauld and Kant – four spirits as different from one another as possible, but united in one thing: in their low estimation of pity" (GM, preface 5).[1]

In light of the vulnerability of human beings and the precarious nature of human selves one truly wonders why sympathy and trust have not received more attention from philosophers. It is of course difficult to determine the reasons for this conspicuous lack of attention but I would be willing to venture a small wager that the main reason is to be sought in the fact that the human species has been so inventive when it comes to applying religion, metaphysics and ethics to deny the vulnerabilities of human beings.[2] One needs only to consider the variety of ideas having to do with the immaterial nature of the soul and the immortality of the soul to gain a healthy, albeit a slightly ironic, respect for human inventiveness.

One ancient and particularly powerful idea which serves the purpose of denying the vulnerablities of human selves is the thesis that virtue is not only necessary but a *sufficient* condition of human happiness (or human flourishing).³ This idea – which originates with Socrates and becomes the dominant theory of happiness with the Stoics – immediately explains why we *need* not place much emphasis on trust and sympathy. To begin with it is clear – if Socrates and the Stoics are right – that no one but yourself can involve you in evil and misfortune. If a misfortune befalls you, you are either responsible for it yourself (it was in your control and should therefore not really be described as misfortune), or it should be of no concern to you (it was not in your control).

What needs to be explained, however, is how anyone could take this thesis seriously. Its strangeness is brought out in full by Epictetus when he teaches us to disregard the loss of reputation, a prized possession, a wife or a child.⁴ Such losses drive ordinary human beings to despair in part because they are unable to see the wisdom in one of Epictetus' favourite saying: my enemies have the power to put me to death, but not to harm me!⁵ It seems that Epictetus knew what he was talking about when he adviced his followers to prepare themselves to meet with ridicule and the jeers of ordinary mortals (Oates 1940, 437).

What makes this theory of happiness jar on our modern ears is that we do not generally accept Socrates' metaphysical assumptions regarding the soul and the rational order of things.⁶ Most of us today view the self as a natural entity that is subject to the same laws as other natural entities. Such a view is apparent in many modern theories of the self, whether they see the self as a social construct, as a bodily ego or as a complex set of natural beliefs and desires. A human being, or a human self, which has such a theory of itself (or such a self-consciousness) and cares about its destiny (and most selves do) will pay close attention to its relation to others. That includes paying attention to the emotional support it can give or gain from others and to the cooperative schemes which can help it to create and sustain a viable way of life.

This "natural" way of viewing the self seems to be in stark contrast to the way in which Socrates views the soul in *Phaedo*, a book much admired by the Stoics. The *Phaedo* describes how Socrates passed the last days of his life calmly discussing the nature of the soul – some would say inventing it – looking into the nature of generation and destruction and finding arguments for the immortality of the soul. His coolness did not fail to impress his friendly interlocutors nor subsequent generations of philosophers and other readers of *Phaedo*. In one of his arguments – the so-called argument from affinity – Socrates contrasts the soul with the body and describes the former as noncomposite, invisible, unchanging and divine (*Phaedo*, 78b-81e). The soul – and perhaps even something akin to the self⁷ – is thus saved from destruction. To view the soul as a metaphysical subject behind the everchanging world of appearances does, however, have its costs. The soul is separated from the body and the body – and even physical nature in general – is looked upon with scorn. The emotions are seen as an unruly lot – troublemakers in the soul – and the life of pleasure-seeking as something that is not fit for a human beings.

The teaching that virtue is sufficient for human flourishing becomes somewhat understandable in light of Socrates' conception of the soul.[8] At the same time it is understandable why Socrates and his followers should assign little importance to pity. Pity is not only unneccessary, it may even interfer with our quest for independence and rationality. In Martha C. Nussbaum's words: "Socratic thinking ... inaugurates a tradition of reflection that opposes pity as moral sentiment unworthy of the dignity of either the pitier or the recipient" (1994, 144).

In this paper I will focus on pity and related emotions. I want to consider the question whether a more natural conception of the self – which uses neither religion nor metaphysics to hide the vulnerabilities of human beings – ought not to reinstate sympathy or compassion as a fundamental concept in the ethics of nature. I use the word "reinstate" here because sympathy played a fundamental role in 18th century ethics. I will approach this topic indirectly by considering Nietzsche's criticisms of Mitleid (translated both as pity and compassion).[9] I have mainly two reasons for this approach.

Firstly, Nietzsche is a powerful critic of pity as a moral emotion. Philosophers commonly interpret Nietzsche's criticism as a fundamental attack on pity. "Fundamental" serves here to indicate that Nietzsche's attack is directed at all kinds of pity and related emotions such as sympathy and compassion. Philosophers like myself who want to emphasize the fundamental role of sympathy and compassion in the ethics of nature ought to have an answer to these criticisms. As I hope to show, we have a lot to learn from Nietzsche's criticisms.

Secondly, perhaps no philosopher has been as outspoken a proponent of the natural conception of the self as Nietzsche. He is tireless in his emphasis on both the bodily and the social nature of the self: of seeing the self as a social organization of drives and passions (BGE 12).[10] And no philosopher has been as relentless in his criticism of the metaphysical conception of the soul or the subject. How could Nietzsche, who has been so influential in forming our modern concept of the self, be so critical of pity and related emotions? Is he guilty of an inconsistency here?[11] Does he perhaps after all subscribe to a conception which assigns extra-natural qualities to the self, qualities which make it invulnerable to the violence and destructive powers we find at work in nature as well as in societies? Or was he simply insensitive to the sufferings of ordinary human beings?

II

In the preface to *On the Genealogy of Morals* Nietzsche maintains that whoever sticks with the problem of the value of pity and the morality of pity "will experience what I experienced – a tremendous new prospect opens up for him, a new possibility comes over him like a vertigo, every kind of mistrust, suspicion, fear leaps up, his belief in morality, in all morality, falters…" (6).[12] In Nietzsche's view, pity is clearly a central moral emotion and a critical examination of it will lead us to question not only pity but the whole of morality. Nietzsche himself certainly did not fail in that endeavour. We find critical comments about pity in nearly all of his works. Nussbaum has attempted to sum up those criticisms in her recent paper "Pity and Mercy: Nietzsche's Stoicism". According to Nussbaum, Nietzsche's criticisms of pity are fundamental, directed at compassion and sympathy as well as pity (1994, 140). She identifies six arguments against pity "that appear prominently in several texts" by Nietzsche:

> i) *Pity is an acknowledgment of weakness and insufficiency in the pitied.* ("To offer pity is as good as to offer contempt" (D 135)); ii) *Pity is an acknowledgment of weakness and insufficiency in the pitier.* (Pity is connected with a sense of our "impotence" and "human vulnerability and fragility in general" (D 132)); iii) *Pity is not really altruistic, but rather egoistic.* (The pitier is pained at the sight of the suffering of another, and his deed of pity is an attempt to get rid of his own pain. (D 133)); iv) *Pity does no good: it simply increases the amount of suffering.* (To give way to pity is to augment the number of sufferers, and thus to add to the total "amount of suffering in the world…" (D 134)); v) *The things for which we pity people are, on the whole, things that are not bad but good for them.* (External goods which we pity people for losing are actually bad for them, we should wish "suffering, desolation, sickness, ill-treatment" to those who are of any concern to us. (WP 910)); vi) *Pity is connected with revenge, and even with cruelty.* (…the "veiled glance" of pity, which looks inward on oneself with "a profound sadness," …is the basis of hatred, directed against a world that makes human beings suffer… (GM III:14)) (1994, 150-54)[13]

In the next section I will consider whether this is an adequate summary of Nietzsche's criticisms. If it is, and Nussbaum is certainly not alone in thinking that it is, it raises many questions. Perhaps the most serious question raised is how Nietzsche – who so often prides himself on being "a born and inevitable psychologist and unriddler of souls" – could have offered these as serious criticisms of pity and related emotions. These arguments, as reconstructed by Nussbaum, seem to overlook both obvious facts about the natural condition of human beings and what is morally valuable in some kinds of pity or fellow feelings. Pity only increases suffering in the world! One more person (the pitier) suffers! But if I pity someone I am inclined to alleviate his suffering and thus reduce the suffering in the world. And since as a bystander I rarely suffer as much as the person I pity (who may have just been hit by a motorcycle) I may be in a much better position to reduce his suffering than he is (he can't call the ambulance). It is easy to see the evolutionary value of pity for the human species. If we take the fourth argument seriously, we should conclude that one ought to take pleasure in viewing the agony of the motorcyclist (in that case something good comes out of the whole thing!).

The first argument implies that pitying someone is really a way of showing contempt for that person. But this too seems so obviously wrong. Clearly a case could be made for saying that when my *dominant* attitude towards someone is pity, I show – when expressing my pity – a contempt for that person. When we say of someone "what a pitiful *person*, I would not want to be that *person*" the contemptuous overtones are lost on no one. This is the kind of pity few people care to solicit directly. It sounds degrading to say: "Pity me!". But usually when I pity someone or show compassion for someone that's simply not the case. I might feel pity, compassion and sympathy for a violine player who had broken a finger on the night of his solo debut with the Pittsburgh Symphony Orchestra. Yet I might, in spite of his broken finger, admire the violine player, even envy him.

The second argument against pity, which states that pity is an acknowledgement of weakness and insufficiency in the pitier, is either wrong or shows pity in a favourable light. It is wrong if the weakness supposedly acknowledged has to do with my frail finger (I might have no reason to believe that my finger might be broken) or if it has to do with my present state of danger (I might be quite safe, sitting among the audience, listening). It speaks in favour of pity if it points to the simple fact that as a human being I am not immune from the "slings and arrows of outrageous fortune". Surely it is as *healthy* to acknowledge that fact from time to time as it is counterproductive to be obsessed with it. Regarding the third argument, it seems downright silly to say that my primary motive in helping the motorcyclist is to alleviate my own pain. That feat I could accomplish by simply looking away. Even if my conscience would not allow me to look away and if I were to realize that my only concern was to alleviate my own pain, I might still recognize that the best way – perhaps the only way for me as a civilized person – to alleviate my own pain was through alleviating the pains of the motorcyclist. Hence my pity would benefit the motorcyclist more than it would benefit me, since chances are my pains are miniscule compared to his. It is true, as argument number five points out, that we often pity people for losing things that are not really valuable, perhaps even harmful to them. I may pity a friend for losing a job even if I secretly think the job was no good and did not give him any opportunities to develop his talents. But in such cases I take into account what this job meant to my friend and how losing it would affect him.

Now it is of course possible that Nietzsche greatly overrated his ability to unriddle souls. He may have placed too much reliance on his keen eye to see a hidden text beneath the surface text. If these criticisms are to be taken at face value we are forced to conclude that Nietzsche was not even sensitive to the surface-text to say nothing of the nuances of the underlying text. If the above summary and explanation of Nietzsche's criticisms are correct we should not take them seriously. Instead we should look for an explanation of how Nietzsche could have been so wrong about pity. As it turns out there is no lack of such explanatory suggestions in the secondary literature on Nietzsche. Many of those explanations are interesting primarily because they reveal a common way of reading or, as it happens, misreading Nietzsche.

Nussbaum does think that Nietzsche's criticisms are weak, especially the fourth one, but she provides Nietzsche with a context which makes them understandable. She maintains that Nietzsche's project, when criticizing pity, makes him neither the "boot-in-the-face fascist" some claim he is nor the "noble and innocuous quasi-Christian moralist" Kaufmann saw in him. Rather, she argues, his project was "to bring about a revival of Stoic values of self-command and self-formation within a post-Christian and post-Romantic context" (Nussbaum 1994, 140). Nussbaum's interpretation is not only able to place Nietzsche in a respectable philosophical company – and there is some evidence that Nietzsche wanted somewhat uncharacteristically to advertise his union with the philosophical tradition when criticizing pity (GM preface 5 and HAH 103) – it also appears to be able to explain many of the counterintuitive criticisms of pity mentioned above. Arguments one and two become immediately understandable in light of the stoic theory that virtue is a sufficient condition for human flourishing (*eudaimonia*). The Stoic is in some sense invulnerable if he practices virtue and seeks wisdom. The Stoic emphasis on independence, self-sufficiency, freedom from the enslaving emotions (including pity and related emotions) does indeed create a context which makes most of the above criticisms understandable.

David E. Cartwright has offered an interpretation of Nietzsche that is in many ways similar to Nussbaum's. In his article "Kant, Schopenhauer, and Nietzsche on the Morality of Pity" he maintains that Nietzsche borrowed a page from Kant both in his conception and attack on pity. He argues that for both Nietzsche and Kant, pity leads to a loss of dignity (of the person pitied and the pitier), loss of autonomy and to a general loss of rationality; and pity unnecessarily increases the suffering in the world. It also leads to "undesirable forms of self-sacrifice, and/or pity may just wear one out – the suffering of others undermines one's own health" (Cartwright 1984, 91). Together, Cartwright and Nussbaum may offer an interesting genealogical account of Nietzsche's criticisms of pity. It is basically a Stoic criticism of pity, imported to Germany by Immanuel Kant!

One common assumption behind Nussbaum's and Cartwright's reading of Nietzsche is that Nietzsche does not distinguish between pity and compassion. Nussbaum does observe that Nietzsche recognizes that these words have different nuances but she maintains that it makes no difference for his attack. Cartwright maintains that Nietzsche's failure to distinguish between pity and compassion seriously undermines his attack on Schopenhauer since Schopenhauer wanted to base morality on compassion. Nietzsche's attack on the other hand is aimed only at pity (Cartwright 1988). In his essay "Compassion" Lawrence Blum also cites Nietzsche's failure to distinguish between pity and compassion to explain his criticism of pity (*Mitleid*):

> Nietzsche's use of the term *Mitleid* does not distinguish between compassion and pity. Because Mitleid is focused on the negative states of others, Nietzsche saw it as life-denying and without positive value. But insofar as compassion involves a genuine concern for the good of others and a "living sense of another's worth," it is unlike pity, fundamentally life-affirming and positive. (Blum 1980, 512)[14]

Like Nussbaum's and Cartright's explanations, the one offered by Blum does at first ring true. Many of Nietzsche's criticisms, at least as they are construed by Nussbaum, can be made against pity, which is a condescending emotion, but not against compassion which is a genuine concern for the good of others. "We can pity someone," Nancy E. Snow argues, "while maintaining a safe emotional distance from what he or she is undergoing. When we feel compassion this emotional distance is crossed... Central to compassion is the belief "that could happen to me"" (Snow 1991, 197). Did Nietzsche simply overlook the distinction between compassion and pity? Or is there perhaps no room for compassion in his philosophy?

III

Before we can answer that question we have to consider closer the interpretations offered by Blum, Cartwright and Nussbaum. It seems to me that they fail to capture both what is valuable and constructive in Nietzsche's criticisms of Mitleid and consequently fail to appreciate that Nietzsche might be articulating a new concept of compassion.[15] In the end their views are based on, and in turn reinforce, a familiar interpretation of Nietzsche. On this interpretation Nietzsche was an extreme elitist who did not care for the common man in the street and who was preoccupied with the rights of the strong, hard, non-vulnerable, self-formed, noble master. Such beings supposedly have no need for compassion from others and could even perish from pitying human beings.

To begin with Nussbaum's and Cartwright's interpretations leave many questions unanswered. Nussbaum, for example, does not attempt to explain obvious inconsistencies between her summary of Nietzsche's criticism of pity and some of Nietzsche's most deeply rooted convictions. The fourth argument, as reconstructed by Nussbaum, claims that pity only increases the suffering in the world. In light of Nietzsche's preoccupation with the educational role of suffering one might wonder why that is bad! Does suffering not help us to purify our metal – form ourselves into what we really are? Does Nietzsche perhaps, inconsistently, sympathize with the pitier and his pain (transferred from the pitied person)? Also, even if it could be shown that Nietzsche accepts Stoic psychology (at least parts of it), Nussbaum does not explain what difference it makes for Nietzsche's attack on pity that he accepts neither the Stoic theology nor their metaphysics. Futhermore, Nussbaum claims that Nietzsche – being a well-to-do academician preoccupied with self-formation – "assails [when criticizing pity] the roots of the deepest sorts of human love" (Nussbaum 1994, 140). He "really doesn't see what the life of a beggar is, what it is really like to lose your only child, what it is really like to love someone with all your heart and be betrayed" (Nussbaum 1994, 161). But Nussbaum fails to observe that for Nietzsche the process of self-formation fundamentally involves the deepest sort of human love.

Cartwright's account is also incomplete. He argues that Nietzsche takes over and extends Kant's attack on pity, sometimes even repeating verbatim Kant's warnings that pity leads to a loss of autonomy, dignity and rationality. But Cartwright only mentions in passing that Nietzsche's conception of autonomy, rationality and dignity is different from Kant's. He does not take into account how *radically* different it is from Kant's conception. Nietzsche simply does not share some of Kant's fundamental ethical, metaphysical and psychological insights; insights which seem necessary in order to adopt the Kantian perspective on pity. He often introduces his conception of these important moral phenomena in direct opposition to Kant (GM II: 2).[16]

More importantly the common assumption behind the interpretation offered by Nussbaum, Cartwright and Blum – that Nietzsche does not distinquish between positive and negative variants of pity (say between pity and compassion) – is wrong. One could only arrive at that assumption by ignoring the passages where Nietzsche speaks in favour of pity. In *The Will to Power* he speaks of his kind of pity (*Mitleid*):

> *My kind of "pity."* – This is a feeling for which I find no name adequte: I sense it when I see precious capabilites squandered, e.g., at the sight of Luther: what force and what insipid backwoodsman problems! (at a time when in France the bold and light-hearted skepticism of a Montaigne was already possible!) Or when I see anyone halted, *as a result of some stupid accident*, at something less than he might have become. Or *especially at the idea of the lot of mankind*, as when I observe with anguish and contempt the politics of present-day Europe, which is, under all circumstances, also working at the web of the future of *all* men. Yes, what could not become of "man," if –! This is a kind of "compassion" although there is really no "passion" I share. (WP 367, first and last italics are in the original)

This passage clearly shows that Nietzsche is aware of the positive role a feeling like compassion (a genuine concern for the good of others and a "living sense of another's worth") can play. He proudly describes it as his kind of pity. Interestingly enough Nietzsche's fellow feelings are directed at precisely those who have been halted by stupid accident at something less than they might have become. If Nietzsche is the modern Stoic Nussbaum claims he is, he ought not to accept the concept of "stupid accident." Luther ought to be the master of his own happiness, he should be in control of his own destiny – or at least he should acquiescence in it. It is even more interesting to see that Nietzsche is moved to sympathy – his kind of sympathy – with the "lot of mankind."

This passage is by no means unique in Nietzsche. Although it is traditional to turn a blind eye towards them, similar passages can be found in texts from all periods of his writing-career. In *Untimely Meditation* he speaks approvingly of "men who feel it as their *own* distress when they see the genius involved in toilsome struggle, or in danger of destroying himself, or when the shortsighted greed of the state, the superficiality of the moneymakers, the arid self-satisfaction of the scholars treat his work with indifference…" (UM 3:6). It is clear from the context that Nietzsche consider himself to be one of these men.[17] In *Beyond Good and Evil* he addresses directly the issue of the ambiguity of pity, where he contrast what we might, following Lester Hunt, call hedonistic pity (which seeks to abolish all suffering from the world) with what Nietzsche calls "our pity" which "is a higher and more farsighted pity…" (BGE 225). Nussbaum does recognize and acknowledge that Nietzsche points to conditions where pity does good. However, according to Nussbaum, these are rare cases of terrible condition of the spirit: "It does good, Nietzsche adds, only where, as in Indian philosophy, it functions as an antidote to suicidal disgust with existence, in the sense that it substitutes for that disgust the cognitive goal of knowing human misery as fully as possible" (Nussbaum 1994, 152). But in *Human, all to Human* written only two years before *Daybreak* which Nussbaum cites, Nietzsche had written:

> In very rare cases – when the genius of skill and understanding merges with the moral genius in the same individual – we have … those pains that must be seen as the exceptions in the world: the extra-personal, transpersonal feelings, in sympathy with a people, mankind, all civilization, or all suffering existence; these feelings acquire their value through association with especially difficult and remote perceptions (pity per se is not worth much). (HAH 157)

Pity per se is not worth much but it clearly can become so by association with remote and difficult perceptions. There is no indication here that these are gloomy perceptions resulting from suicidal disgust with existence. On the contrary it takes a genius of skill and understanding and a moral genius to arrive at these perceptions. Not only does Nietzsche distinguish between pity and pity, he concludes his powerful discussion of pity in section 225 of *Beyond Good and Evil* with the sentence: "Thus it is pity *versus* pity." Pity may be needed to overcome pity.[18]

Now it could of course still be argued that Nietzsche's criticisms of pity show that he was averse to pity in any shape or form. Thus someone might argue that we should – in light of Nietzsche's fundamental criticism of pity – simply ignore the passages where he speaks favourably of pity. We could write them off as sarcasms or inconsistencies on Nietzsche's part. But that would be a serious mistake. I acknowledge, however, that we need to square these gentle passages with his criticisms of pity. As it is impossible to consider all of Nietzsche's criticism here, I will mainly look at his book *Daybreak* written in 1881 and consider it in the light of other texts. It is from *Daybreak* that Nussbaum gets most of the material for her interpretation; it is here that we find one of Nietzsche's most extended critical discussion of pity.

Reading *Daybreak*, especially sections 131-146, one is struck by the wide variety of arguments against pity. More than one of these arguments could be construed as a fundamental criticism of pity. I will look at three main points Nietzsche offers in this context:[19]

1. Pity is impossibe because we can never understand (or empathize with) the suffering of others.
2. Pity involves sensitivity to suffering. A consistent pitier ought to be sensitive to all the suffering in the world. A person who strives to be sensitive to all the suffering in the world will immediately perish. Hence it is impossible to be a consistent pitier.
3. Pity is always egoistic and harmful. Its harmful effects may primarily be the result of the fact that the pitier always pretends to be altruistic. This deceitful nature of pity will harm both the pitier and the pitied person.

A recurrent theme in Nietzsche's criticism of pity is his claim that the pitier fails to understand (or empathize with) the situation and the plight of the person pitied. In some instances the pitier will incorrectly assume from facial expressions and the tone of voice that the person pitied is suffering. In other cases the pitier will greatly exaggerate the suffering the pitied person is undergoing (D 142). In still other cases the pitier may correctly identify the suffering but fail to understand its cause. "Magnificent characters" for example "suffer very differently from what their admirers imagine." They suffer from doubts about their own magnificence "not from the sacrifices and martyrdoms that their task demands of them" (GS 251). Those who pity may also interpret the suffering of others superficially stripping away what is distinctly personal in it and useful to those who suffer. Nietzsche identifies other reasons for this failure but he does not maintain that it is humanly impossible to understand (empathize with) the suffering of one's fellow creatures. Even our "personal and profoundest suffering is incomprehensible and inaccessible to *almost* everyone" (GS 338, italics are mine)[20]. And Nietzsche maintains that once you have understood his message you will wish to help "but only those *whose distress you understand entirely* because they share with you one suffering and one hope…" (GS 338, italics are mine). Nietzsche's criticism here are in perfect harmony with the passages where he speaks in favour of some kind of Mitleid (compassion). In both places he emphasizes how difficult it is to feel for others, how difficult it is to actively participate in the suffering of fellow human beings, but does not say that it is impossible to do so.

Regarding the second argument it is true that Nietzsche claims that almost "everywhere in Europe today we find a pathological sensitivity and receptivity to pain" (BGE 293). If such unmanly sensitivity, usually labeled as "pity", were "dominant even for a single day, mankind would immediately perish of it" (D 134). But it is difficult to argue that Nietzsche wants this to be taken as a fundamental criticism of pity since he does not believe that we ought to be equally sensitive to all the suffering in the world. Nietzsche does not subscribe to the egalitarian assumptions behind this fundamental criticism. He writes: ""Pity for all" – would be hardness and tyranny towards *you*, my dear neighbour!" (BGE 82). For him it is not a question of whether we should or should not be sensitive to pain and suffering. He clearly wants us to avoid some suffering (for example certain kinds of suffering with others) and welcome other kinds both in ourselves and others. Sensitivity to suffering can be a sign of weakness (an irritability) and it can be a sign of strength ("…it almost determines the order of rank *how* profoundly human beings can suffer…" (BGE 270).

But what about Nietzsche's charge that pity is always egoistic? Can that be reconstructed as a fundamental criticism of pity? For Nietzsche there is of course a sense in which every emotion – including pity – is egoistic. Emotions and, indeed, all human actions, are in some way connected to the self of that person. There is no selfless act, there is no selfless emotion. These familiar Nietzschean themes are direct consequences of his attack on rationalism and his denial that reason, pure reason, can be practical. Still, Nietzsche can make a valuable distinction between petty egoism and grand egoism. He is always against petty egoism but, of course, often in favour of grand egoism and self-assertiveness.[21]

In section 133 of *Daybreak* Nietzsche does indeed start with a little playful argument to show that pity is not really altruistic. He seems to argue that pity is always egoistic and that on the whole it does no good and that it is even essentially harmful. But it is very interesting that he says at the very start of his discussion: "The truth is: in the feeling of pity – *I mean in that which is usually and misleadingly called pity* – we, are to be sure, not consciously thinking of ourself but are doing so *very strongly unconsciously*…" (first italics are mine). Going by the English translation it is natural to assume that Nietzsche wants to make it known from the outset that there is a different kind of pity immune from the criticisms he is about to offer. But although that may indeed by the case, his immediate point is a different one. He argues that Mit-leid (suffering with) is a misleading name for the phenomena under discussion since when pitying we do not *participate* in the suffering of the pitied person. Nietzsche's point is that although we are suffering, it is "under all circumstances a suffering which he who is suffering in our presence is *free* of" (D 133). What is interesting here – and generally overlooked by the critics – is that Nietzsche emphasizes not only that

From Metaphysical Subjects to Naturalized Selves

we fail to participate in the plight of the pitied person (we may misrepresent his situation or fail to see it as he sees it) but also that we suffer and our suffering is something the pitied person is *free* of. In some sense the pitier is in a worse situation than the person he pities. To explain how that could be the case we need to take a look at the reasons for the suffering of the pitier. Why is the pitier suffering if he is not suffering with the pitied person?

Nietzsche gives a number of possible reasons. The pitier may be uncomfortably reminded that he is not invulnerable, he too could be harmed. He may feel anger toward the person (the motorcyclist to use our earlier example) for reminding him of this fact. Nietzsche is clearly criticizing the pitier for failing to come to terms with his own vulnerablities. The source of the suffering, Nietzsche maintains, could also be fear (the pitier might wonder whether he will rise to the occasion or whether he is a coward), disappointment (will my efforts be recognized, what will others think of me) or other thoughts about the pitier's impotence or likely diminution of honour in the eyes of others. The pitier's primary motive when helping the pitied person may also be a desire to avoid these dire consequences: his motive might be to seek or maintain recognition, honour and sense of power – to gain, in other words, a favourable view of himself.

It is tempting to read Nietzsche, in section 133, as saying that petty egoistic reasons always lie behind acts of pity and feelings of pity and thus to interpret his criticism of pity as fundamental. However, if we look at the reasons he gives for the suffering of the pitier and the motives the pitier acts on, we see that he clearly has a particular sort of pitier in mind. It is a pitier who is caught in a particular moral culture – a culture that resembles in many ways Rousseau's description of the bourgeois society where everyone lives only in the opinions of others, never acting on his or her own sentiments. Nietzsche explicitly calls the morality behind pity a "narrow and a petty bourgeois" one (D 146). He knows as well as anyone that this is not the only kind of morality that has existed on earth. There are other kinds of cultures where individuals are not as preoccupied with the impressions they make on others and where pity might not be contaminated in this way. Also, this bourgeois pitier is weak and even impotent. Nietzsche clearly indicates that if the person were stronger, and less prone to follow the opinions of others he might possess "an especially subtle, penetrating sense of suffering" which could lead him to do others good. The implied pitier makes it highly unlikely that Nietzsche intends section 133 as a fundamental attack on pity. Part of Nietzsche's argument in section 133 is to show that pity cannot solve the problem Rousseau identified as living in others. In *Emile* Rousseau had argued that the natural sentiment pity could ease Emile's transition from a quasi-natural state to a life in society (1979, 221-30). Through pitying others Emile would be able to relate to others in a positive way and escape the evil consequences of vanity (*amour propre*). Nietzsche's argument aims to show that pity, no less than pride, can be spoiled in a society where there is fierce competition for recognition.

Daybreak does contain the material for one *plausible* explanation of how pity increases the suffering in the world. It is not the simple – even simple minded – explanation that relies on the etymology of the words "compassion" and "Mitleid". Both words mean originally "to suffer with" and if one takes them literally one is forced to conclude that com-passion (*Mitleid*) increases suffering in the world as the new pain of the pitier is added to the original one.[22] As I see it pity does not simply augment the suffering in the world, it does not give us more of the same. At least, that is not the problem with pity, as I think Nietzsche is well aware of. The problem is that pity can, under certain social circumstances, change the nature of the original suffering. The pain of the pitier is often a moral or mental pain and as we know such pains can be more intense and more durable than physical pain. To fully appreciate this point it is helpful to recall Rousseau's description of the citizen. The citizen is "always active, sweats, agitates himself, torments himself incessantly in order to seek still more laborious occupations". He cares so strongly about his reputation – is so mortified by the mere thought that something might damage it – that he may even renounce his life in order to protect it (Rousseau 1964, 179). One should also recall Nietzsche's own account of moral guilt, shame and disgust to see how intense and durable he thinks moral pains can be: bad conscience eats into the guilty person "spreading within him like a polyp, until at last the irredeemable debt gives rise to the conception of irredeemable penance, the idea that it cannot be discharged ("*eternal* punishment")" (GM II: 21). Occasionally Nietzsche greatly overstates his point:

> …for my own part, I have no doubt that the combined suffering of all the animals ever subjected to the knife for scientific ends is utterly negligible compared with *one* painful night of a single hysteric bluestocking. (GM II: 7)[23]

It could of course be objected that the pitied person might be suffering because he had done something morally reprehensible or lost his reputation. But in such cases when the focus is moral suffering, Nietzsche points out that the pitier's suffering might still be greater than the original one: "When one of our friends is guilty of something ignominious, for example, we feel it more painfully than when we ourselves do it. For we believe in the purity of his character more than he does" (HAH 46).

Pity, or a peculiar bourgois kind of pity, is worthless, according to Nietzsche, because the pitier usually fails to grasp the situation of the pitied person adequately. The cause of the failure may be the fact that the pitier tries to "view and imbibe the experiences of others" as if they were his own (D 137). This ego standpoint involves "exaggeration and excess", like any ego-standpoint is apt to do, and it may lead to hyper-sensitivity. The criticisms mentioned above are therefore all closely connected. They enable Nietzsche to say both that we fail to suffer with others and that we tend to exaggerate the sufferings of others. None of these criticisms, however, show that Nietzsche is fundamentally opposed to pity, but only that he was aware of how difficult it is to feel properly for our fellow human beings.

We are apt to misunderstand many of Nietzsche's criticisms of pity unless we read them in the context of his discussion. He sometimes goes out of his way to make the context clear. When he claims, for example, that pity is essentially harmful he immediately adds: "In itself, it has as little a good character as any other drives: only where it is demanded and commended … does a good conscience adhere to it" (D 134). In some cases Nietzsche's criticisms should be read in the context of showing the limitations of Mitleid. Christian compassion can, for example, make one profoundly suspicious "of all the joy of one's neighbour, of the joy in all that he wants to do and can" (D 80). Nietzsche had stressed the same point in *Human, All Too Human*: "Sympathetic natures, always helpful in misfortune, are rarely the same ones who share our joy: when others are happy, they have nothing to do, become superfluous, do not feel in possession of their superiority…" (321). Interestingly enough, this is also the main limitation of compassion which Blum mentions in his essay "Compassion" which is cited above.[24]

Often Nietzsche simply assumes that his criticisms will be read in context. This, for example, is the case with his infamous sentence: "To offer pity is as good as to offer contempt." At the same place Nietzsche describes the call for pity as a cry out "for the most shameful and profoundest humiliation" (D 135). These are strong words, not likely to be used to describe what is involved in feeling compassion for someone who has, for example, lost a child or a spouse. What is "the most shameful and profoundest humiliation"? From section 135, which deals with relations between equals, it is clear that Nietzsche thinks it is to see oneself as fundamentally not equal to those *human beings* whom one solicits pity from. This is not the only place where Nietzsche argues that pity creates a fundamental gap between essentially similar beings. I think he has that argument in mind when he states that pity may "contain a subtle self-defence or even a piece of revenge" (D 133). He makes this claim when discussing the fact that pity may have a painful effect upon us as we are reminded of our own vulnerability and fragility when we see another human being suffer. "We repel this kind of pain and offence," Nietzsche argues, "and requite it through an act of pity." He does not explain how pity can be an act of self-defence and revenge at the same time. But the idea that pity creates a fundamental gap between essentially similar individuals gives him a plausible explanation. In that case pity is self-defense since the pitier is presumably immune from accidents that can happen to a being (the pitied person) who is fundamentally different from him. It is a revenge because it humiliates the suffering person. It is humiliating precisely because the person is not fundamentally different from the pitier. It could hardly be revenge unless the pitied individual were essentially similar to us and would recognize the humiliation. Nietzsche's criticism is similar to Blum's criticism of pity:

> Compassion ... involves a sense of shared humanity, of regarding the other as a fellow human being. This means that the other person's suffering (though not necessarily their particular afflicting condition) is seen as the kind of thing that could happen to anyone, including oneself insofar as one is a human being. This way of viewing the other person contrasts with the attitude characteristic of pity, in which one holds oneself apart from the afflicted person and from their suffering thinking of it as something that defines that person as fundamentally different from oneself. (Blum 1980, 511-12)

Few authors have noticed that if Nietzsche's arguments against pity can (at least partly) be explained as an argument against an emotion that creates a fundamental gap between individuals – defines the pitied person as fundamentally different from the pitier – then his argument can be construed as an argument against a particular invidious form of elitism.

IV

Whether we look at Nietzsche's criticisms of pity or the passages where he speaks in favour of pity we see that he makes a distinction between a positive and negative kinds of pity. This really ought not to surprise anyone since Nietzsche almost never missed a chance to emphasize the placticity of the emotions and their context-sensitivity. A life-denying emotion for a slave could be life-enhancing for a master and *vice versa*. A life-affirmative emotion in one culture, civilization or historical period could be life-denying at other times in other cultures. The "very same symptoms could point to *decline* and to *strength*," says Nietzsche when discussing "*the ambiguous character of our modern world*" and he prefaces this remark with the heading: "Overall insight" (WP 110). The claim that everything is ambiguous (*zweideutig*) could easily be seen as expressing Nietzsche's "overall insight". He makes much of the ambiguity of nihilism (WP 22), of calmness, of asceticism (of women, priests, philosophers, saints, artists) of egoism (of money-makers, artists, philosophers (UM and TI IX:33)), and of corruption ("corruption is something totally different depending on the organism in which it appears..." (BGE 258)). Here only a few examples are mentioned.

The thesis that emotions are context-dependent entails that we can change the emotions by influencing the context the emotion occurs in. In a simple case this might mean that we can change an emotion by influencing the ideas the individual has about the target of his emotions. More importantly we can change the nature of the given emotion by influencing – and if we are influential enough, changing – the culture we live in. In *Daybreak* Nietzsche talks about how emotions such as love can change with new cultural influences:

> *To think a thing evil means to make it evil.* The passions become evil and malicious if they are regarded as evil and malicious. Thus Christianity has succeeded in transforming Eros and Aphrodite – great powers capable of idealisation – into diabolical kobolds and phantoms... (D 76)

Nietzsche viewed himself as fighting – and changing – a culture that he characterized by a morality and religion of pity. His critics have failed to consider the possibility that Nietzsche viewed himself as struggling to change the way we experience pity. In my view that is precisely his project; it involve both the process of undermining the old concept of pity and articulating a new concept of pity.

Nietzsche tells us that he really does not have a name for this new concept of pity but following his lead I will call it Nietzschean compassion. A fairly comprehensive and consistent analysis of this concept can be pieced together from his works. He always emphasizes how difficult it is to experience his kind of compassion. It is based on hard and remote perception and is high and farsighted. It is a feeling that has been habitually sifted by reason.[25] We rarely come across this emotion, which acquires a value when experienced by a noble mind, in human beings:

> A man who says, "I like this, I take this for my own and want to protect it and defend it against anybody"; a man who is able to manage something, to carry out a resolution, to remain faithful to a thought,

to hold a woman ... when such a man has pity, well, *this* pity has value. (BGE 293)

A key to understanding Nietzschean compassion is to understand why it is so hard and rare. Some of the difficulties may be obvious in light of the discussion above, others might not become visible until we understand the central concerns of Nietzsche's philosophy.

It may strike some as strange to talk of an emotion as difficult or hard. Actions are said to be hard and difficult, emotions on the other hand are passions, they happen to us. But Nietzsche correctly maintains that emotions can be both active and passive. Nietzschean compassion is active and that is one of the reasons it is difficult. It does not involve a simple sharing or transfer of feelings. As we saw earlier Nietzsche does not believe that such transfer occurs successfully in ordinary cases of pity either. Although he does not share any passion in his compassion, it does not mean that his compassion is bereft of any feelings or emotions. Nietzsche's attitude towards the objects of his compassion is an emotional one. He does feel "anguish" and "contempt" at the sight of precious capabilities squandered. Nietzschean compassion allows for – even calls for – active participation in another's suffering. But such active participation is only possible for someone who recognizes how difficult it can be, not only because of how difficult it is to understand the suffering of others (and to appreciate the fact that people can benefit from facing and working on their suffering) but also because the pitier has to make sure that his compassion is not a bad love of himself, a way of losing himself: "there are a hundred decent and praiseworthy ways of losing *my own way*, and they are truly highly "moral"!" (GS 338).

Nietzschean compassion is also hard because it requires patience. One has to keep in check one's desire to help others since one might undermine their resourcefulness and also because one might have overlooked how their suffering could be useful to them. For Nietzsche the ability to wait is one of the hardest virtues and the inability to wait is the stuff tragedies are made of (HAH 61).

On Nietzsche's account it is difficult to show compassion because it is difficult to be the kind of person that can show compassion. It requires characteristics like forsight, patience, fairness, honesty and a peculiar mixture of sensitivity and hardness. These characteristics are not formed easily or quickly but there is nothing to indicate that they require natural talents only few people have. Anyone can cultivate these characteristics. It is true that we have not yet given a full account of why Nietzschean compassion is hard but I think that a closer examination of Nietzsche's view will show that he is not an extreme elitist.

Lester Hunt has given one explanation as to why Nietzschean compassion is hard. Hunt looks primarily to Nietzsche's discussion in *Beyond Good and Evil* where Nietzsche contrasts his (our) "higher and more farsighted pity" with hedonistic pity which aims at abolishing all human suffering. Hedonistic pity is a distress felt at

> injury to the feelings that we already possess, and is motivated by a desire to preserve this side of our nature [creature in us, as opposed to creator] from various assaults that life inevitably commits against it. Of course, this side of human nature should not be preserved at all, but transformed – in some cases pitilessly – in order to make better human beings of us. (Hunt 1991, 167)

There is certainly some truth to Hunt's interpretation. Nietzschean compassion is based on recognizing the importance of transforming oneself into a higher state of being than one has presently attained. Such a transformation inevitably involves suffering and pain which hedonistic pity cannot tolerate. Nietzschean compassion is the direct opposite of hedonistic pity. But like Nussbaum and Cartwright, Hunt is under the spell of the dominant view of Nietzsche as an extreme individualist who is preoccupied with the conditions of excellence for *isolated* individuals. Hunt writes:

> What is interesting for our purposes is the possiblitiy that, while he does not actually say so, he thinks that people who pursue a life of experimentation will tend to feel it too, that they too will be distressed by injuries suffered by the part of us that enables us to create virtue. Perhaps he thinks that a commitment to achieving excellence in one's own life naturally leads to this sort of concern for the conditions of excellence in others. (Hunt 1991, 167)

It is clear that Hunt believes that caring for others is something that could not come naturally to the Nietzschean. He allows for the possiblity that isolated Nietzscheans who strive to create themselves will somehow feel it when kindred spirits come to harm or fail to make the most of their lives. Nietzsche's theory, Hunt maintains, could at least conceivably be amended in such a way that it would explain why it is possible to feel for others (167).

But, I want to suggest, Nietzsche's theory does not have to be amended to account for how we can feel for others. If we understand his theory of the emotions and his philosophy of power relations we will learn to appreciate that point.

Power relations between individuals are of fundamental importance to Nietzsche. There is a sense in which Nietzsche views human life as a struggle between individuals who are trying to enhance their power or feeling of power. Human beings are not equally powerful. That fact, obvious even to a non-Nietzschean, is of enormous importance to Nietzsche. A human being will enter into three kinds of power relations when dealing with others. He will be dealing with those who are less, equal or more powerful than he is.

It is an important fact for our dealings with our fellow human beings that we keep track of these power relations. One needs to know who are one's equals, who are more powerful and who are less powerful. But keeping an accurate record of these power relations is difficult. It requires self-knowledge and a great deal of honesty. Rarely do we care to admit how power relations figure into our evaluations of others. Nietzsche illustrates that point with a perceptive aphorism in *Beyond Good and Evil*:

> "I don't like him." – Why? – "I am not equal to him." – Has any human being ever answered that way? (185)

Power relations are not fixed once and for all. They change as human beings gain or lose power. If it is difficult to admit that one dislikes someone because one is not equal to him, it is twice as difficult to admit that one dislikes someone because he used to be less powerful but is now more powerful than oneself in some respect. For these reasons it is not likely that people are fully aware of how they represent their relations to others or, in some cases, of what kind of relations they are forming with others. In *Thus Spoke Zarathustra* Nietzsche writes:

> And often love is only a device to overcome envy. And often one attacks and makes an enemy in order to conceal that one is open to attack. "At least be my enemy!" – thus speaks true reverence, which does not dare ask for friendship. (Z I: 14)

In my opinion it is through our emotions that we represent these power relations. Emotions are evaluations which usually are based on some comparison with others. In the case of pity, pride and envy this is obvious. In other cases, where it is not quite as obvious, a judgment about relative power positions may still determine precisely what emotion one is experiencing. Whether individuals hate, despise, or have contempt for each other may in part be determined by their relative power positions. Nietzsche is well aware of this fact: "One does not hate as long as one still despises, but only those whom one esteems equal or higher" (BGE 173).

Our power relations to other human beings are not only essential to how we conceive of ourselves: they are essential to who we are. The soul is a social structure of the drives and affects and there is no fundamental division in the soul between passions and desires on the one hand and reason on the other:

> The misunderstanding of passion and reason, as if the latter were an independent entity and not rather a system of relations between various passions and desires; and as if every passion did not possess its quantum of reason. (WP 387)

The process of self-formation is for Nietzsche a process that essentially involves working on one's relations to others. As an essentially emotional being a Nietzschean therefore has to care about his relations to other human beings.

The essential point of Nietzsche's criticisms of pity can now be restated. When I pity someone I show contempt for that person. I represent that person almost completely in terms of the misfortune (or negative condition) for which I pity that person. I act as if I had found the essential quality of that individual. I treat his suffering as the most important thing about him. This is an especially successful strategy in a powerstruggle since suffering tends to reduce the sufferer to despair. The sufferer often views himself almost exclusively in terms of his suffering and misfortune. Pitiers tend to reinforce that kind of self-description. Nietzsche maintains that when suffering awakens our lust for possession, pity may be the strategy we use to take possession of the sufferer:

> When we see somebody suffer, we like to exploit this opportunity to take possession of him; those who become his benefactors and pity him, for example, do this and call the lust for a new possession... "love"... (GS 14)

The fact that pity can be a strategy in a power struggle also gives Nietzsche an explanation of why it is seldom the same individuals who pity others and who share their joy when things are going well. When the pitied person experiences a reversal of fortune for the better the pitier may no longer "feel in possession of their superiority."

In *Untimely Meditations* Nietzsche makes a similar distinction between admiring a hero and attaching one's heart to a great human being as I am suggesting he makes between pity and compassion.[26] There he maintains that our admiration for the hero is our slander of the hero. This is so because in admiring the hero we elevate the hero "and believe that great men are great ... as it were through a gift... ...But being gifted or being compelled are contemptible words designed to enable one to ignore an inner admonition, slander on him who has paid heed to this admonition, that is to say on the great man... " (UM 3:4). Our admiration is slander since it strips the heroic from the heroic act. We refuse to admit that the hero is essentially like us even though he may be examplary in some ways. When we attach our heart to a great human being we affirm our essential similarity to the great human being. Thus Nietzsche stresses the same point when discussing our relation to those who are more powerful than we are as he does when he discusses our reltions to those who are less powerful than we are.

There is direct evidence that Nietzsche wanted his criticism of pity in *Daybreak* to be considered in light of his general theory of the emotions and also in light of his philosophy of power relations. As we have seen he emphasizes the context sensitivity of emotions in the earlier parts of the book and just before the main criticism of pity in sections 133-146 he offers the following passage:

> The "man who wants to be fair" is in constant need of the subtle tact of balance: he must be able to assess degrees of power and rights, which, given the transitory nature of human things, will never stay in equilibrium for very long but will usually be rising or sinking: – being fair is consequently difficult and demands much practice and good will, and very much very good *sense*. (D 112)

Nietzschean compassion requires fairness. It too demands much practice and good will and very good sense as human beings never stay in equilibrium but will usually be gaining or losing power. For the same reasons that it is hard to be considerate it is hard to be compassionate. It is difficult to be the kind of person who can show compassion not only because of the necessary characteristics but because of the attitude such a person needs to have towards life, culture and nature. That attitude is based on a full recognition of the uncertainties of one's own existence and of life in general. Nietzsche describes this attitude, this awareness of life, in a passage where he talks about the admonition of the great human being:

> ...he [the great human being] knows as well as any little man how to take life easily and how soft the bed is on which he could lie down if his attitude towards himself and his fellow men were that of the majority: for the objective of all human arrangements is through distracting one's thoughts to cease *to be aware* of life. Why does he desire the opposite – to be aware precisely of life, that is to say to

suffer from life – so strongly? Because he realizes that he is in danger of being cheated out of himself, and that a kind of agreement exists to kidnap him out of his own cave. Then he bestirs himself, picks up his ears, and resolves: "I will remain my own!" It is a dreadful resolve; only gradually does he grasp that fact. For now he will have to descend into the depths of existence with a string of curious questions on his lips: why do I live? what lesson have I to learn from life? how have I become what I am and why do I suffer from being what I am? (UM 3:4)

I my view Nietzsche sees this as an admonition to every human being. One does not need extraordinary natural characteristics to become aware of life. In the preface to *On the Genalogy of Morals* he wonders why we fail to experience life and asks "which of us has sufficient earnestness for [these experiences]? Or sufficient time? Present experience has, I am afraid, always found us "absent-minded" … " (1). It is not because we lack rare natural qualities that we fail to be aware of life but because we lack time and earnestness. It is because we are absent-minded.

V

We are now in a position to answer the two questions, or concerns, raised at the outset of this discussion. The first question was whether those of us who want to make sympathy a fundamental concept in ethics (especially in the ethics of nature) could answer Nietzsche's criticisms of Mitleid. The second question was whether there is an inconsistency between Nietzsche's criticisms of Mitleid and his conception of the self. Once we realize that Nietzsche makes a distincion between a positive and a negative variant of pity and that he articulates a new concept of compassion we see that his criticisms present no difficulty for those who want to make sympathy a fundamental concept in ethics and it is also clear that Nietzsche was not inconsistent or insensitive to human suffering. But I think this study shows more. It demonstrates, I think, that Nietzsche's main criticism of Mitleid is an extension of his criticism of the metaphysical subject. Furthermore, I think that his criticisms are useful for those who want to make compassion a fundamental concept in ethics of nature. I want to end this paper by considering these two points briefly.

There are clear similarities between Nietzsche's criticisms of Mitleid and his criticism of the metaphysical subject. The pitier and the metaphysician both assign permanence where there is only flux and ever going process of becoming and development. The pitier looks for a being, an agent who can be blamed, behind every suffering (painful events). The metaphysician in us also has a tendency to postulate a being, a subject, an actor behind every action. To some extent this strategy is necessary for survival:

> "The *real* and the *apparent* world" – I have traced this antithesis back to *value* relations. We have projected the conditions of *our* preservation as predicates of being in general. Because we have to be stable in our beliefs if we are to prosper, we have made "the real" world a world not of change and becoming, but one of being. (WP 507)

But like pity, this metaphysical tendency can be dangerous as Nietzsche points out in a powerful passage in *Beyond Good and Evil*. There he advices us not to remain stuck to a person, to a fatherland, to a science or to pity. He concludes the passage by saying: "Not to remain stuck to our own virtues and *become as a whole the victim of some detail in us…*" (BGE 41, italics are mine). Both the pitier and the metaphysician can make us less aware of life itself. In *The Will to Power*, Nietzsche addresses this point directly:

> This world is apparent: consequently there is a true world … this world is a world of becoming: consequently there is a world of being: – all false conclusions. …It is suffering that inspires these conclusions: fundamentally they are *desires* that such a world should exist; in the same way, to imagine another, more valuable world is an expression of hatred for a world that makes one suffer… (579)

Nietzsche's criticism of pity is a valuable contribution to the criticism of the metaphysical conception of the self and it can also be seen as a valuable contribution to the ethics of nature. It is often argued that sympathy or compassion cannot be a fundamental concept in the ethics of nature since we cannot feel with beings that do not have feelings or at least not our kind of feelings. But if Nietzsche's criticisms of Mitleid are correct they show that there is no simple sharing of feelings, not even in the human context. Whether we are "feeling with" human beings or non-humans it is an emotion we invent as much as we feel. It is a feeling we invent together as we create a common culture. "Feeling with" is either pity which should be avoided or compassion which should be cultivated with care. As pity it is a dishonest and ultimately unsuccessful strategy to enhance power. As compassion it is an active attitude which recognizes the conditions necessary for any given being to flourish and gain power.

Biography

Róbert H. Haraldsson (born 1959) has an M.A. in philosophy from the University of Pittsburgh and is working on his Ph.D. at the same university. He is a part-time teacher at the University of Iceland and editor of *Skírnir,* the Journal of the Icelandic Literary Society.

Notes

1. Nietzsche overlooks, or chooses not to mention, Aristotle and a host of eighteenth century philosophers including Hume and Rousseau. But he could claim these are the exceptions among philosophers.
2. Another plausible reason often mentioned is the fact that women have by and large been excluded from the philosophical tradition.
3. It should of course be stressed that this does not mean that this was the original purpose in putting forth the thesis.
4. In the following passages Epictetus seems to be saying that we should even despise such possessions: "Remember that you must behave in life as you would at a banquet. A dish is handed around and comes to you; put out your hand and take it politely. It passes you; do not stop it. It has not reached you; do not be impatient to get it, but wait till your turn comes. *Bear yourself thus towards children, wife*, office, wealth, and one day you will be worthy to banquet with the gods. But if when they are set before you, you do not take them *but despise them* then you shall not only share the gods' banquet, but shall share their rule" (Oates 1940, 471-71, italics are mine).
5. Epictetus rightly attributes this saying to Socrates. In his defense Socrates claims that although Anytus and Meletus could put him to death they could not harm him, since it "is not permitted that a better man be harmed by a worse" (*Apology*, 30c-d).
6. I leave it open to what extent the Stoics shared the assumptions about the soul which Socrates describes for example in *Phaedo*. They did believe in a rational principle that governs the universe and they do describe the governing principle as divine. The point I want to make here is that the sufficiency thesis and the criticism of pity become much more understandable if we assign extra-natural qualities to the soul and if we believe in some kind of divine guidance.
7. I do not want to get involved in the debate whether Socrates – or even the Ancient Greeks in general – did have a concept of the self. But the challenge Socrates accepts at the beginning of *Phaedo* is to show that "the soul exists after a man has died *and that it still possesses some capability and intelligence*" (*Phadeo*, 70b, italics are mine).

8. A vulgar version of that argument would simply be that virtue is sufficient for human flourishing since even if our efforts are not rewarded in this life we will get our pay in heaven or our comeuppance in hell.
9. "Mitleid" means literally to "suffer with" (Mit-leid). Since compassion is usually seen as a more positive feeling than pity, it may cause some confusion that the word "Mitleid" can be translated both as pity and compassion. Another problem is that we do not have a general name for this class of emotions. I use "pity" both as a general term referring to pity, compassion and sympathy and also sometimes for a negative fellow feeling. I use "compassion" for a positive fellow feeling.
10. The soul "is only a word for something about the body" (Z I:4).
11. Nussbaum does notice this apparent inconsistency. She maintains that it is a real one and that Nietzsche did not "grasp the simple fact that if our abilities are physical abilities they have physical necessary conditions..." (1994, 158).
12. It is interesting to compare this passage to a passage in *The Will to Power* where Nietzsche says: "It is not "pity" that opens the gates to the most distant and strange types of beings and culture to us, but rahter our accessibility and lack of partiality that does not empathize with or share suffering... " (119).
13. Some of Nussbaum's textual evidence is given in parentheses. The paraphrasing of Nietzsche's sentences is Nussbaum's.
14. Danto also thinks that Nietzsche fails to make a clear distinction between pity and compassion (Danto 1980, 184) and so does Robert Solomon (1983, 342).
15. It is only fair to point out that Blum criticizes Nietzsche only in passing in his penetrating analysis of compassion. As I will suggest below Nietzsche is fully aware of many of the valuable distinctions and fine points Blum makes when discussing pity.
16. Nietzsche, for example, maintains that ""autonomous" and "moral" are mutually exclusive."
17. Indeed, he seems to be describing his compassion for Schopenhauer in this passage.
18. This is in line with Nietzsche's view that the "will to overcome an affect is ultimately only the will of another, or several other, affects" (BGE 117).
19. It is interesting that Nussbaum only considers one of them in her summary.
20. "Fast allen" in German.
21. One thing that distinguishes petty egoism from grand egoism is the deceitfulness of petty egoism.
22. This is the argument Nussbaum understandably thinks is the weakest of Nietzsche's arguments.
23. The reference to a hysteric bluestocking (*hysterische Bildungs-Weibschens*) is particulary accurate when we come to realize that Nietzsche is developing arguments from *Daybreak*. And he clearly is. In section six of book two he refers explicitly to *Daybreak*. It is true that the sections Nietzsche refers to are not the same as are under discussion here but are earlier sections where he puts forth arguments developed in the section discussed here.
24. "A focus on misery and suffering in the absence of regard for others' joys and pleasures constitutes a limitation in the moral consciousness of the merely compassionate person" (Blum 1980, 509).
25. Compassion "must first be habitually sifted by reason; otherwise it is just as dangerous as any other affect" (WP 928).

26. The relevance of this distinction was brought to my attention by my teacher James Conant. I am indebted to him and to Tamara Horowitz. I would also like to thank the Icelandic Research Council for financial support.

Abbreviations to Nietzsche's works

BGE = *Beyond Good and Evil* (*Jenseits von Gut und Böse*). Trans. Walter Kaufmann, Vintage 1966.
D = *Daybreak: Thoughts on the Prejudices of Morality* (*Morganröthe*). Trans. R. J. Hollingdale, Cambridge University Press 1982.
GM = *On the Genealogy of Morals* (*Zur Genealogie der Moral*). Trans. Walter Kaufmann and R. J. Hollingdale, Penguin 1973.
GS = *The Gay Science* (*Die fröhliche Wissenschaft*). Trans. Walter Kaufmann, Vintage 1974.
HAH = *Human, All Too Human* (*Menschliches, Allzumenschliches*). Trans. Marion Faber, with Stephen Lehmann, University of Nebraska Press 1984 (first volume only).
TI = *Twilight of the Idols* (*Götzen-Dammerung*). Trans. Walter Kaufmann, in the Portable Nietzsche, Viking 1954.
UM = *Untimely Meditations* (*Unzeitgemässe Betrachtungen*). Trans. R. J. Hollingdale, Cambridge University Press, 1983.
WP = *Will to Power* (*Der Wille zur Macht*). Trans. Walter Kaufmann and R. J. Hollingdale, Vintage 1967.
Z = *Thus Spoke Zarathustra* (*Also Sprach Zarathustra*). Trans. Walter Kaufmann, in Portable Nietzsche, Viking 1954.

Other References

Baier, Annette C. 1994. *Moral Prejudices*. Harvard University Press.
Blum, Lawrence. 1980. "Compassion", in *Explaining Emotions*, A. O. Rorty (ed.), University of California Press.
Cartwright, David E. 1984. "Kant, Schopenhauer, and Nietzsche on the Morality of Pity," *Journal of the History of Ideas*. Volume XLV, Number 1.
Cartwright, David E. 1988. "Schopenhauer's Compassion and Nietzsche's Pity," *Schopenhauer Jahrbuch*, 69.
Danto, Arthur C. 1980. *Nietzsche as Philosopher*. Cambridge University Press Morningside Edition.
Nussbaum, Martha C. 1994. "Pity and Mercy: Nietzsche's Stoicism" in R. Schacht (ed.), *Nietzsche, Genealogy, Morality*, University of California Press.
Oates, W. J. 1940. *The Stoic and Epicurean Philosophers*. The Modern Library.
Plato. 1981. *Five Dialogues*. Trans. G.M.A. Grube, Hackett Publishing Company.
Rousseau, Jean-Jacques. 1965. *The First and the Second Discourse*. Trans. Roger D. and Judith R. Masters, St. Martin's Press.
Rousseau, Jean-Jacques. 1979. *Emile, or On Education*. Trans. Allan Bloom, Basic Books.
Snow, Nancy E. 1991. "Compassion," *American Philosophical Quarterly*, Volume 28, Number 3.
Solomon, Robert C. 1983. *The Passions*. University of Notre Dame Press Edition.

Vittorio Hösle

Sein und Subjektivität
Zur Metaphysik der ökologischen Krise

Abstract
Der Aufsatz versucht, Hegels udnd Heideggers metaphysische Konzeptionen zu kontrastieren und einen Mittelweg zwischen ihnen bei der Analyse der ökologischen Krise vorzuschlagen. Entscheidend ist die These, daß die ökologische Krise letztlich im Wesen des Organischen angelegt ist und ihre Verwirklichung in der Doppelnatur des Menschen als eines organischen Geistwesens begründet ist. Wichtig ist in dem Artikel der Einfluß von Hans Jonas' Biologiephilosophie.

Daß die ökologische Krise weitreichende Konsequenzen für Individualethik, Ökonomie und Politik hat, wird kaum ein Vernünftiger bezweifeln; und ebensowenig läßt sich bestreiten, daß sie tiefe Wurzeln in der europäischen Geistesgeschichte hat. Aber warum ist sie ein *metaphysisches* Problem? Und weshalb soll sie uns etwas gerade über das Verhältnis von Sein und Subjektivität sagen?

Da es sehr viele Metaphysikbegriffe gibt, will ich gleich zu Anfang den hier zugrundegelegten klären. Unter Metaphysik verstehe ich im folgenden die metaphysica generalis, also die Lehre vom Seienden als Seiendem; keineswegs ist damit schon die Annahme eines transzendenten Seienden impliziert. Dennoch drängt sich die Frage geradezu auf, warum die ökologische Krise mehr sei als ein regionalontologisches Problem. Denn daß die ökologische Krise, als anthropogenes Ereignis, über ein bestimmtes Seiendes, den Menschen, viel aussagt, ist offenkundig; aber wenn sie nur für die Lehre vom Menschen relevant ist, dann ist sie eben ein anthropologisches und kein metaphysisches Problem. Immerhin ließe sich hier schon entgegnen, daß der Mensch ein so besonderes Seiendes im Ganzen des Seins ist, daß er Licht wirft auf dieses Ganze: Während die Struktur des Seins als solchen nicht dadurch in Frage gestellt würde, daß etwa der Malachit nicht zu dem Seienden zählte, wäre das Wesen des Seins doch ein ganz anderes, wenn es nicht den Menschen hervorgebracht hätte, zumindest hätte hervorbringen können. Der alte Satz, daß der Mensch ein Mikrokosmos sei[1], besagt ja eben dies, daß in ihm das Ganze des Seins in konzentrierter Form präsent ist: Der einzelne Mensch ist ein physischer Gegenstand, der als solcher den Naturgesetzen unterworfen ist, er ist ein Organismus, in dem sich chemische Prozesse abspielen; er hat oder ist auch eine Innenseite, die in rätselhaftem Verhältnis zu seinem Leibe steht, jedenfalls einer eigenen, von der Psychologie zu ergründenden Logik gehorcht; er ist ein kulturschaffendes Wesen. Insofern führen Probleme der Anthropologie immer wieder zur Metaphysik: Das Rätsel des Menschen läßt sich ohne eine Theorie vom Ganzen des Seins nicht lösen; und eine allgemeine Ontologie wird nie befriedigen, aus der nicht er sichtlich ist, warum zum Sein dieses eigenwillige Wesen gehört, das alles Seiende gleichsam in sich zusammenfaßt und das allein die Frage nach dem Sein zu stellen vermag. Die eben gebrauchte Formulierung impliziert, daß realphilosophische Fragen aus der allgemeinen Ontologie zu begründen sind, und nicht umgekehrt; geltungstheoretisch ist an dieser Ordnung nicht zu rütteln. Und doch ist genetisch, im ordo cognoscendi, ein gleichsam induktiver Zugang durchaus sinnvoll: Aus der Analyse einzelner, besonders ausgezeichneter Seiender mag sich ein Weg finden zum Wesen des Seins[2].

Aber nicht nur ist der Mensch keineswegs bloß *ein* Seiendes neben anderen; auch die ökologische Krise ist nicht bloß *ein* Ereignis neben anderen in der Geschichte des Menschen. Im Menschen bildet sich das Ganze des Seins ab; in der ökologischen Krise, der ersten existenzgefährdenden Krise der Menschheit, geht es um das Ganze des Menschseins. Schon infolge des Mikrokosmoscharakters des Menschen ist diese Gefährdung des Menschen eine Gefährdung des Ganzen des Seins; sie ist darüber hinaus zweitens auch unmittelbar eine Gefährdung des restlichen Seienden: Bereits vor dem möglichen Verschwinden des Menschen wird die Ökosphäre in einer Weise geplündert und zerrüttet, die ein metaphysisches Ärgernis darstellt, weil sie die Welt zahlreicher in tierischen und pflanzlichen Arten verwirklichter Werte in einem naturgeschichtlich einzigartigen Ausmaße beraubt. Es ist in der Tat gerade diese Entgegensetzung des Menschen zur Natur, die eine besondere ontologische Bedeutung besitzt: Denn obgleich der Mensch sicher *auch* ein Naturwesen ist, besitzt er doch wie kein anderes Naturwesen die Fähigkeit, sich der ihn umgebenden Natur entgegenzusetzen und sie zu zerstören. Es ist diese Struktur, sich gegen das als ein Anderes zu wenden, was die eigene Grundlage ist, die uns einige Einsicht in das Wesen des Seins verspricht. Schon an dieser Stelle läßt sich sagen, daß diese

Struktur, die in der ökologischen Krise nur ihren sinnfälligsten Ausdruck erreicht, zwei entgegengesetzte Theorien vom Verhältnis von Natur und Geist als gleichermaßen einseitig erweist: Wäre der Geist der Natur nur entgegengesetzt, dann könnte er sich nicht mit der Gefährdung der Natur selbst in Gefahr bringen; wäre er nur ein Teil der Natur, dann wäre schwerlich zu erklären, wieso er dieses Gefährdungspotential gegenüber der Natur besitzt; jedenfalls wäre darin nichts Unnatürliches zu sehen, weil es außer der Natur nichts gäbe.

Die ökologische Krise ist, auch wenn im Wesen des Menschen angelegt, kein ewiges Strukturmerkmal des Geistes. Sie ist nur möglich in einem bestimmten geschichtlichen Moment des Menschen. Dies ist aus zwei Gründen hervorzuheben. Erstens ist diese historische Ortbarkeit der ökologischen Krise schon deswegen bemerkenswert, weil es sich nicht von selbst versteht, daß individuelle Ereignisse metaphysisch relevant sind. Die Metaphysik als allgemeine Ontologie handelt vom Seienden als Seiendem; und daß sich dieses Seiende als Seiendes nicht nur in einer Gattung wie dem Menschen, die ja immerhin noch etwas Allgemeines ist, sondern in einem geschichtlichen Vorgang gleichsam pointiert und in besonderer Intensität manifestiert, wäre für die griechische, vorchristliche Metaphysik geradezu eine contradictio in adiecto gewesen. In der Tat äußert sich in diesem am griechischen Seinsverständnis geschulten Einwurf durchaus ein gewichtiger Einwand, der ernst zu nehmen ist und auf den noch einzugehen sein wird. Immerhin kann jetzt schon darauf verwiesen werden, daß die zeitliche, ja geschichtliche Entfaltung des Seins in einer modernen Ontologie in anderer Form berücksichtigt werden muß, als es den Griechen noch möglich und notwendig war: Hegel und Heidegger sind zwei Beispiele für Metaphysiker, die Sein und Geschichte in einer Weise zusammendenken, die für die Griechen unvorstellbar gewesen wäre.

Allerdings sind die Unterschiede zwischen Hegel und Heidegger – und damit komme ich zum zweiten Punkt – nicht geringer als diejenigen zwischen griechischer und moderner Ontologie. Die Differenzen erhellen, wenn wir die Frage nach der Richtung der zeitlichen Entwicklung des Seins stellen. Für Hegel ist diese im wesentlichen Fortschritt: In der eidetischen Entwicklung der Kategorien ebenso wie in der zeitlichen Entfaltung der Welt stellt die spätere Stufe einen weiteren Schritt in der Selbsterkenntnis des dem Weltprozeß zugrundeliegenden Geistes dar. Geschichte ist insofern Fortschritt im Bewußtsein der Freiheit. Für den späten Heidegger hingegen ist zumindest die europäische Geistesgeschichte spätestens seit Platon von einer immer tiefergehenden Seinsvergessenheit bestimmt. Der Herrschaftswille des philosophischen Begreifens, der in der neuzeitlichen Subjektphilosophie gipfelt, führt im Programm der modernen

Sein und Subjektivität

Technik zu einer vollständigen Unterwerfung der Natur und damit zur ökologischen Krise, die eine notwendige Konsequenz der abendländischen Philosophie ist. Da diese Konsequenz die höchste Gefährdung des Menschen ist, läßt sich die abendländische Geschichte schwerlich anders denn als fortschreitender Verfall deuten, aus dem, wenn überhaupt, nur ein Gott noch retten könne.

Die Frage, ob die Entwicklung der letzten zweieinhalbtausend Jahre positiv oder negativ zu bewerten sei, ist für die Metaphysik insbesondere dann relevant, wenn, wie ich zu zeigen versuchen werde, deren Entwicklungsprinzip als Fortsetzung der vorangegangenen Geschichte des Seins gedeutet werden kann. Denn dann entscheidet man mit einem Urteil über die letzten zweieinhalbtausend Jahre zugleich über das Sein als Ganzes. Aber selbst wenn dies nicht der Fall ist, liegt es auf der Hand, daß ein Urteil über die europäische Zivilisation nicht ohne Konsequenzen für unser Selbstverständnis bleiben kann. Wie ein Mensch, dem die erkenntnis- und handlungsleitenden Prinzipien seines bisherigen Lebens zutiefst fragwürdig geworden sind, um eine Identitätskrise nicht herumkommt, so kann eine Kultur, die ihre eigene Geschichte als Verfall deutet, nicht so weitermachen wie bisher. Die schwere Identitätskrise, die seit einem Jahrhundert die europäische Kultur erschüttert, ist in den letzten zwanzig Jahren offenbar durch das Bewußtsein radikalisiert worden, die spezifisch abendländische Form der Rationalität sei mitverantwortlich für die existenzgefährdende ökologische Krise; und da das Identitätsbewußtsein einer Kultur *ein* Machtfaktor in der internationalen Ondnung ist, ist die philosophische Frage, ob es angesichts der ökologischen Krise noch Sinn macht, von Fortschritt zu reden, in hohem Maße ideologisiert, obgleich wir ihr hier sine ira et studio nachgehen wollen. Die Ideologisierung der Kategorie des Fortschritts resultiert auch daraus, daß seit dem 19. Jahrhundert die Geschichte immer mehr Gott oder die Gewissensautonomie als letzte Legitimationsinstanz für Ethik und Politik ersetzt hat. Wer den Fortschritt bestreitet, scheint daher sogar die Möglichkeit von Ethik zu zerstören.

Auch wenn in der abendländischen Geschichte, vielleicht sogar in der ganzen Entwicklung des Seins mehr Kontinuität walten dürfte, als auf den ersten Blick der Fall zu sein scheint, ist offenkundig, daß es ohne die neuzeitliche Subjektivität nicht zur ökologischen Krise gekommen wäre. Auch wenn Subjektivität jedem Menschen, ja schon Tieren und vielleicht selbst Pflanzen nicht abzusprechen ist, ist doch die neuzeitliche Subjektivität von den anderen geschichtlich verwirklichten Formen menschlicher Subjektivität·spezifisch unterschieden. Das richtige Verständnis ihrer Natur wird uns einer Beantwortung unserer Frage näherbringen, was denn die ökologische Krise für den Aufbau des Seins besage; die Kategorie »neuzeitliche

Subjektivität« wird uns ferner erlauben, die Identitätsprobleme der gegenwärtigen europäischen Kultur differenzierter zu analysieren.

Im folgenden will ich meinen Versuch einer Antwort auf die metaphysischen Implikationen der ökologischen Krise dadurch plausibler machen, daß ich sie über die Kritik an alternativen Konzeptionen vermittle. Die außerordentliche Schwierigkeit der Fragestellung mag es legitimieren, daß ich den Zugang zu der Sachfrage über den Umweg der bisherigen Lösungsvorschläge für unser Problem suche. Dabei will ich folgender maßen vorgehen: Zunächst will ich eine gewissermaßen triumphalistische Geistmetaphysik darstellen, die man vulgärhegelianisch bezeichnen könnte, auch wenn sie mit dem System Hegels nicht viel zu tun hat[3], und die den Hintergrund vieler Verharmloser des ökologischen Problems bildet (I). Alsdann will ich mich mit den zwei m.E. wichtigsten Kritiken der Geistmetaphysik auseinandersetzen: einerseits Heideggers Interpretation der Seinsgeschichte, andererseits dem ökologisch motivierten Naturpantheismus, als deren philosophisch anspruchsvollster Vertreter K. M. Meyer-Abich angesehen werden kann[4] (II), um schließlich meine eigene Lösung vorzuschlagen, die eine Synthese versucht (III)[5].

I

Hegels Überzeugung, in seinem System habe die abendländische Philosophie ihre Vollendung erreicht, ist aus verschiedenen Gründen keineswegs irrational zu nennen[6]. Erstens spricht der materiale Reichtum dieses Systems für einen derartigen Anspruch, zweitens seine außerordentliche begrundungstheoretische Leistung, der keine spätere Philosophie Vergleichbares an die Seite zu setzen hat. Schließlich kann Hegel beanspruchen, die innere Logik der vorangegangenen Philosophiegeschichte weiterzuführen – seine Philosophie der Geschichte der Philosophie holt die eigene Philosophie insofern wieder ein, als sie sie als folgerichtiges Resultat der bisherigen erweist. Es ist dieses »Selbsteinholungsprinzip«, das für Hegel extrem charakteristisch ist – sowohl für die Begründungsstrukturen seines Systems als auch für seine Philosophie der Gechichte. Hegel ist Transzendentalphilosoph in dem Sinne, daß er die Bedingungen der Möglichkeit des Geltungsanspruchs der eigenen Theorie rekonstruiert – seine »Wissenschaft der Logik« ist der Versuch einer zusammenhängenden Entwicklung all jener Kategorien, die in jeder Theorie, sei es über die Welt, sei es über jede mögliche Theorie über die Welt, immer schon vorausgesetzt werden. Die Entwicklung der Realphilosophie, die aus Natur- und Geistphilosophie besteht, zielt auf die Erreichung des Bewußtseins von den Kategorien, die der Entwicklung zugrunde liegen; und dieses Bewußtsein gipfelt in der Philosophie. Der Sinn der Welt liegt gleichsam darin, daß das, was an sich ist, für sich wird; in der zunehmenden Reflexivität besteht das entscheidende Kriterium für Fortschritt. Der Geist steht deswegen über der Natur, weil er die Natur erkennend übergreift, während die Natur weder um sich noch um den Geist weiß.

Die Entwicklungstendenz von der Natur zum Geist, das immer stärkere Hervortreten von Reflexivität, bestimmt nach Hegel auch die Natur, da der Übergang von der anorganischen zur organischen Welt ebenfalls als Prozeß der Reflexivisierung gedeutet werden kann. Sie bestimmt aber auch die Entwicklung des Geistes, und zwar sowohl die begriffliche des Systems seiner Kategorien als auch die zeitliche seiner Geschichte. In der Tat ist Hegel, nach Vico und Herder, einer der ersten großen Philosophen mit einem außerordentlichen Gespür für die Entwicklungsgesetze der menschlichen Geschichte. Selbst wer die ontologischen Prämissen seines Systems verwirft, kann schwerlich bestreiten, daß seine Analysen der Unterschiede etwa zwischen antiker und moderner Kunst oder zwischen antiker und moderner Philosophie gewöhnlich das Wesentliche treffen. Daß die europäische Geschichte durch das Christentum und den Aufgang der modernen Welt einem zunehmenden Prozeß der Subjektivierung unterworfen wurde, ist kaum zu leugnen, auch wenn die Bewertung dieses Prozesses noch offen bleiben mag.

Hegels Bewertung dieses Prozesses ist bekanntlich nahezu uneingeschränkt positiv. Während der junge Hegel den Entfremdungstendenzen seiner Gegenwart ein romantisch verklärtes Griechenland entgegensetzte, besteht die bewußtseinsgeschichtlich zentrale Idee der »Grundlinien der Philosophie des Rechts« in einer, wenn auch gebrochenen, so doch endgültigen Anerkennung der Unumgänglichkeit der Entzweiungen der modernen Welt – sosehr diese im Konzept der »Sittlichkeit« auch wieder aufgehoben werden sollen. Obgleich sich die moderne Industriegesellschaft zur Zeit Hegels gerade erst bildete, läßt sich doch sein rechts- und staatsphilosophisches Hauptwerk durchaus als eine Apologie der neuen politischen Ordnung lesen, die sich nach der Französischen Revolution und dem Wiener Kongreß in Westeuropa herausschälte und die mit erstaunlicher Kontinuität bis heute weiterwirkt. Insbesondere scheint Hegel, u.a. wegen seines Interesses an den begründungstheoretisch ausgezeichneten reflexiven Strukturen, die eigene Epoche für eine letztlich unüberbietbare gehalten zu haben: In seiner Philosophie, die das Absolute als Geist erfaßt, vollende sich die Geschichte der denkerischen Erfassung des Absoluten, die selbst Ausdruck des Absoluten sei. Weder auf dem Gebiet der politischen noch auf dem der Philosophiegeschichte scheint Hegel radikale Neuerungen mehr für möglich gehalten zu haben; zumindest hat ihn diese Frage nicht interessiert. Ein milder Fortschrittsoptimismus, der weitere Verbesserungen zwar nicht ausschließt, aber nicht mit einem Paradigmenwechsel rechnet: Auf diesen Begriff läßt sich seine Position wohl bringen.

Im vorigen habe ich Hegels Position in einer Weise vereinfacht, die ans Unverantwortliche grenzt. Dennoch mag das in diesem Kontext insofern gerechtfertigt werden, als an den derart verkürzten Hegel viele jener zeitgenössischen Philosophen anknüpfen, die die Dringlichkeit der ökologischen Krise bestreiten und jedenfalls als Abwiegler bezeichnet werden können – ich meine besonders die Ritterschule[7]. Stark beeinflußt von den wichtigen Arbeiten Joachim Ritters zur Rechtsphilosophie Hegels, erklären Autoren wie Herrmann Lübbe[8] oder Odo Marquard[9] die gegenwärtige Industriegesellschaft, von der Hegel nur die Keime sah, zu einer letztlich nicht sinnvoll hinterfragbaren Form institutionell geronnener Freiheit. Schon Ritter hatte in einer berühmten Interpretation von Hegels Eigentumslehre[10] dessen Auffassung, allein durch die Versachlichung der ihn umgebenden Welt erlange der Mensch Freiheit, verteidigt. Das volle, von Restriktionen befreite Eigentum der kapitalistischen Rechtsordnung wird bei Hegel geradezu als Ausdruck des Hoheitsrechtes des Geistes über die Natur gedeutet. Auch wenn die gegenwärtigen Neohegelianer der Ritterschule die Hegelsche Philosophie ihrer metaphysischen Grundlage berauben, führen sie mit ihrer affirmativen Einschätzung der gegenwärtigen Lage gewisse Momente des Hegelschen Denkens weiter. Erst indem er sich die Natur unterwirft, ist nach ihnen der Geist Geist; und auch wenn sie Korrekturen an einigen gegenwärtigen Tendenzen für erforderlich halten, geht es nach ihnen stets nur um technokratischen Fortschritt, auch und gerade in der Bewältigung der Techniknebenfolgen.

Wenn man die implizite Metaphysik dieses Vulgärhegelianismus (die im Grunde auch im Marxismus weiterwirkt) zusammenfassen möchte, lassen sich folgende Momente angeben: 1. Die Entwicklung der menschlichen Geschichte, vielleicht sogar der ganzen Seinsgeschichte ist durch ein immer stärkeres Hervordringen des Geistes gekennzeichnet. 2. Der Geist ist das eigentliche Telos des Seins; die Natur hat nur extrinsischen Wert, insofern sie eine Basis für den Geist ist. 3. Die Entwicklungstendenz »Von der Natur zum Geist« ist uneingeschränkt zu bejahen; insofern die moderne Industriegesellschaft den Rationalisierungsprozeß vollendet, ist sie die fortschrittlichste, ja die höchste uns bekannte Seinsform. 4. Auch wenn, wie gesagt, den zeitgenössischen Apologeten der Industriegesellschaft explizite metaphysische Reflexionen fernliegen, setzen ihre Wertungen voraus, daß der Geist entweder der eigentliche Seinsgrund der Natur ist (so

Sein und Subjektivität

lautet eine bestimmte, m.E. falsche Lesart Hegels) oder daß er zumindest eine eigene Substanz ist, die unabhängig von der Natur subsistiert (dies ist die Grundthese Descartes'). Daß der Marxismus die ersten drei Prinzipien akzeptiert, aber eine materialistische Ontologie vertritt, ist eine seiner vielen intellektuellen Schwächen.

Auch in der eben skizzierten, sehr verkürzten Form, die entscheidende Theoriebestandteile des Hegelschen Systems wie etwa die Dialektik und die Philosophie der Natur ausläßt, hat der Hegelianismus beachtliche intellektuelle Reize. Erstens ist seine Kohärenz zu bewundern – so sieht er in der Geschichte des Menschen, ja der Natur eine klare Entwicklungslinie. Positiv hervorzuheben ist insbesondere, daß er zwischen Natur- und Geistesgeschichte eine Kontinuität erblickt; auf diese Weise ist der abstrakte Dualismus zwischen Natur und Geist überwunden. Zweitens ist die Teleologisierung der Seinsentwicklung auf den Geist hin insofern unvermeidlich, als es ja der Geist ist, der eine philosophische Theorie entwickelt: wenn diese wahrheitsfähig sein soll, ist auf eine Auszeichnung des Geistes nicht zu verzichten, auch wenn sie keineswegs so ausfallen muß, wie sie der Vulgärhegelianismus ausarbeitet. Und drittens ist nicht ohne weiteres zu bestreiten, daß allein die moderne Welt seit der Industriellen Revolution Freiheit und Gleichheit in einem Maße garantiert, das in der Antike und im Mittelalter undenkbar gewesen wäre.

Und dennoch: Alle Argumente, die (neben, an Einfluß nicht zu unterschätzenden bildungsbürgerlichen Vorurteilen) für den Vulgärhegelianismus sprechen, können nichts an dem tiefsitzenden Unbehagen ändern, das immer mehr Menschen angesichts seiner empfinden. Er mag, zumindest auf den ersten Blick, von einer unerschütterlichen logischen Stringenz sein – den Phänomenen, deren Zeugen wir sind, ja deren Zeugen wir vielleicht erst zu sein vermögen, seit wir die geistigen Scheuklappen des Vulgärhegelianismus abgeworfen haben, wird er in manifester Weise nicht gerecht. Zu den Phänomenen, die ich im Auge habe, zähle ich an dieser Stelle nicht die unsäglichen politischen Verbrechen des 20. Jahrhunderts, die die Geschichtsphilosophie der Aufklärung einschließlich derjenigen Hegels so unwiderruflich desavouiert haben (auch wenn die Aufgabe bleibt, das, was in diesem Jahrhundert an Furchtbarem geschehen ist, zu begreifen und in seiner unheimlichen Logik geschichtsphilosophisch zu verstehen). Ich beschränke mich hier auf die ökologische Krise. Von einer solchen kann nach dem Vulgärhegelianismus im Grunde gar nicht die Rede sein, weil die Zerstörung der Natur, zumindest solange sie noch nicht für den Menschen bedrohlich ist, kein Übel dartellt, sondern, im Gegenteil, nur die Freiheit und Überlegenheit des Geistes manifestiert; und daß sie für den Menschen selbst bedrohlich werden könnte, wird deswegen nicht ernsthaft geglaubt, weil sie dem bisher bewährten Entwicklungsgesetz »Von der Natur zum Geiste« in unheimlicher Weise widerspräche: Der Geist verschwände in einem ökologischen Holozid, und nur die primitivsten Formen der Natur blieben übrig.

Aber die Tatsache, daß sich der Vulgärhegelianismus einschneidende ökologische Katastrophen nicht vorzustellen vermag, spricht mehr gegen ihn als gegen deren Wahrscheinlichkeit; und auch seine Unfähigkeit, angesichts des Massensterbens pflanzlicher und tierischer Arten zu trauern, ist, als Ausdruck einer fortgeschrittenen seelischen Verkümmerung, eher ein weiterer Grund zur Trauer als ein Argument gegen das Mißliche der gegenwärtigen Situation. Die Jahrzehnte lang andauernde kollektive Blindheit der sogenannten gebildeten Menschheit angesichts der drohenden Katastrophen läßt unsere Zweifel an der geistigen Kraft ihres Kategoriensystems wachsen, nicht schwinden. Wenn es dieses Ausmaßes an harten Fakten bedurfte, um den Abgrund zu sehen, auf den wir zutaumeln, dann muß die Philosophie, die für diese Begriffsstutzigkeit verantwortlich ist, in einem ganz fundamentalen Sinne falsch sein.

In der Tat ist nicht schwer zu sehen, daß der Vulgärhegelianismus auch rein logisch unhaltbar ist. Der entscheidende Einwand gegen ihn, der sich noch gar nicht auf externe Phänomene wie die ökologische Krise einläßt, lautet: Warum gibt es nach ihm überhaupt so etwas wie Natur? Ist diese nicht, wenn man seine Prämissen zugrundelegt, überflüssig wie ein Kropf? Wieso ist das Sein mehr als der Geist und seine Geschichte? Doch selbst wenn sich diese Frage beantworten ließe, müßte man weiterfragen: Wieso zerstört der Geist die Natur? Weshalb ist er an einer Herrschaft über sie interessiert? Ist der Geist eine selbständige Substanz, dann ist eine Interaktion mit der Natur schwer erklärbar, zumindest schwerlich sinnvoll; denn warum sollte sich etwas Höheres mit etwas Niedrigerem abgeben? Ferner: Wenn der Geist der Natur nicht bedarf, wieso kann er sich, mit der Vernichtung der Natur, selbst gefährden? Und wie kann man von einer linearen, kontinuierlichen Entwicklung von der Natur zum Geist reden, wenn doch offenbar gerade jene Epoche, die die bisher weitgehendste Herrschaft des Geistes über die Natur repräsentiert, auf dem Sprung ist, umzuschlagen in die Ära einer Natur, die wieder völlig geistlos geworden ist? Denn es ist allein die Macht der technologischen Zivilisation, die die Erde wieder wüst und leer werden lassen könnte; der archaische Mensch, gerade weil naturverbundener und an einem Triumph des Geistes über die Natur nicht interessiert, hätte diesen möglichen Triumph der Natur über den Geist nicht zu bewirken vermocht. Auch unabhängig von einer möglichen Apokalypse drängt sich die Frage auf, ob nicht schon das Maschinenmäßige der modernen Technik hinter das Lebendige regrediert und zur ersten Gestalt des Naturseins, dem anorganischen Sein, zurückkehrt.

Sein und Subjektivität

Schließlich: Was hilft der Sieg von Freiheit und Gleichheit in der Moderne, wenn er so ephemer ist, wie er zu werden droht? Ist sein Preis, also die Vernichtung unserer organischen Umwelt bzw. Mitwelt, nicht selbst dann zu hoch, wenn die Menschheit überleben sollte? Und macht sich jemand etwa wirklich vor, daß der Triumph der Industriegesellschaft die Menschen moralisch besser oder auch nur glücklicher gemacht hat? Wird nicht das ganze menschliche Streben nach Herrschaft über die Natur in furchbarer Weise durch die Erfahrung in Frage gestellt, daß die Zeit, während der man Hindernisse zu überwinden, mit der Natur zu kämpfen hatte, letztlich glücklicher war als diejenige errungener Saturiertheit, auch wenn diese damals als das Ziel jener galt? Wenig kann einem Menschen eher das Gefühl der letztlichen Vergeblichkeit unseres Daseins vermitteln als die Rückkehr aus einem armen Entwicklungsland mit seinen Leiden, aber auch seiner Freude und Vitalität, in den traurigen und lustlosen Konsumismus der Industriegesellschaften der Ersten Welt.

II

Es ist die Unbeantwortbarkeit dieser Fragen im vulgärhegelianischen Paradigma, die der Suche nach metaphysischen Alternativen einen rationalen Kern auch für den Fall verleiht, daß sie sich ausdrücklich zum Irrationalismus bekennt. Das Spektrum an metaphysischen Ansätzen, die von der ökologischen Krise ihren Ausgang nehmen, ist außerordentlich breit; am wirkungsmächtigsten ist dabei zweifelsohne der erste große Versuch einer »Verwindung« der bisherigen Tradition, die Spätphilosophie Heideggers[11]. So bizarr vieles an ihr auf den ersten Blick anmutet, sowenig kann doch zweierlei bestritten werden: Heidegger ist der erste Denker von Rang, der die moderne Technik in ihrer weltgeschichtlichen Bedeutung ebenso wie in ihrer Bedrohlichkeit erkannt hat; und er ist zweitens der erste, dem die Technik zum *metaphysischen* Problem geworden ist[12]. Sie ist ihm ein metaphysisches Problem einerseits deswegen, weil sie die letzte Konsequenz des Weltverständnisses der modernen Metaphysik ist, andererseits sind ihm die Seinslehre der neuzeitlichen Metaphysik ebenso wie die moderne Technik selbst eine Manifestation des Seins. Eben aus Heideggers tiefsitzendem Mißtrauen gegen die abendländische Philosophie, als deren notwendiges Resultat er die moderne Technik deutet, ergibt sich seine Ablehnung rationaler Methodik; seine Vorliebe für irrationales »Denken« ist daher von einer auch und gerade logisch durchaus beeindruckenden Schlüssigkeit.

Heidegger ist zwar nicht der erste, aber doch einer der ersten, der die

Erkenntnisse des Historismus auf die Wissenschaftsgeschichte anwendet. Für ihn ist der naturwissenschaftliche Naturbegriff keineswegs der einzig denkbare oder mögliche; er ist nur einer in einer langen Reihe von Naturkonzeptionen, die selbst wiederum stark abhängen vom jeweiligen Seinsverständnis. Die Idee einer »Kulturgeschichte der Natur«[13] ist daher bei ihm vorgeprägt. Es ist im Rahmen dieses Vortrags nicht möglich, Heideggers Analyse der Wandlungen im Naturbegriff, zumal derjenigen, die sich am Anfang der Neuzeit ereignen, genauer nachzuzeichnen; vieles an seinen historischen Rekonstruktionen ist ungenau und kritikwürdig, auch wenn dies nichts an seinem Verdienst ändert, bestimmte Fragestellungen an die Phlilosophie- und Wissenschaftsgeschichte überhaupt erst herangetragen zu haben: Heideggers Antworten sind oft falsch, aber die richtigen Fragen zu stellen, ist in der Philosophie durchaus eine nicht weniger wichtige Aufgabe als das Antworten. An Heideggers Rekonstruktion der abendländischen Geistesgeschichte bleibt unklar, ob nach ihm in der Entwicklung der verschiedenen Seinserfahrungen Kontinuität waltet oder nicht; manche Formulierungen lassen in der Tat den Eindruck aufkommen, als herrsche in der Geschichte der Seinsvorstellungen eine absolute Diskontinuität. Und doch ist eine Entwicklungslinie unübersehbar: Ähnlich Hegel nimmt auch Heidegger an, daß die Subjektivität in der Geschichte der Philosophie immer stärker hervortritt; anders als Hegel bedeutet das aber für Heidegger, daß sich das philosophierende Subjekt dem Sein immer mehr entfremdet. Platon zwingt das Sein unter das Joch der Idee[14]; mit Descartes' Metaphysik wird das Subjekt zur Grundlage aller Gewißheitsansprüche, das Sein wird zum Bild, gilt nur, soweit es dem Vorstellen verfügbar ist[15]. Der Wille zur Macht, der sich in diesem Seinsbegriff ausspricht, bringt die moderne Naturwissenschaft hervor; als eigenes metaphysisches Prinzip wird er in der Philosophie Nietzsches auf den Begriffgebracht. Der Kampf der Weltanschauungen, etwa von Nationalsozialismus und Bolschewismus, ist das letzte Resultat dieses Willens, der die höchste Gefahr für den Menschen darstellt.

In Anbetracht der eindeutig negativen Beurteilung der abendländischen Geistesgeschichte mag es zunächst überraschen, daß Heidegger in ihr dennoch die Manifestation eines Geschicks sieht – des absoluten Seins, das sich den Menschen in bestimmter Weise offenbart, indem es die Weise ihrer Welterfahrung festlegt. Allerdings ist diese Wendung von der Geistesgeschichte zur Metaphysik insofern konsequent, als Heidegger vom neuzeitlichen Subjektivismus Abschied nehmen will: Es kann daher nicht die Autonomie des Subjekts sein, die verschiedene Arten des Weltzugangs hervorbringt; die menschliche Autonomie ist vielmehr selbst eine Weise des Geschicks, und zwar jene allerunheimlichste, in der das Sein sich dadurch manifestiert, daß es sich am vollständigsten verbirgt. Weit davon entfernt, ein Triumph des Geistes über die Natur zu sein, ist die moderne Industriegesellschaft mit ihrer furchtbaren Sinnleere die heimtückischste Rache des Seins am autonomen Subjekt. Doch im Grunde ist auch diese Formulierung irreführend: Es ist nicht so, daß das Subjekt zuerst autonom wäre und dann dadurch »bestraft« würde, daß sich das Sein aus seiner Welt zurückzieht; seine Autonomie ist vielmehr selbst Ausdruck der Entgötterung, des Entzugs des Absoluten. Eben dieser Entzug ist freilich auch eine Manifestation des Absoluten, sein Sich-Verbergen eine Weise des Entbergens. Denn das Absolute könnte nicht absolut sein, wenn es nicht alles prinzipiieren wurde: »Nemo contra Deum nisi Deus ipse« scheint auch von Heideggers Sein zu gelten. Allein indem das Subjekt seine vermeintliche Autonomie und Allmacht als die grausamste Täuschung erkennt, in die ihn das Sein verstricken kann, erhält es eine Chance, einer neuen Manifestation des Seins teilhaftig zu werden. Erzwingen läßt sich eine solche freilich nicht; auf sie muß man in Gelassenheit und Demut warten.

Großartig an Heideggers metaphysischer Deutung des technischen Zeitalters ist sicher dies, daß er die geistesgeschichtlichen Wurzeln der modernen Technik wie kaum ein anderer gesehen hat. Auch wenn m.E. Platons Ideenlehre und die neuzeitliche Metaphysik keineswegs hinreichende, sondern nur notwendige Bedingungen des technischen Zeitalters sind, kann Heidegger durchaus beanspruchen, manche der Zusammenhänge durchschaut zu haben, die zwischen etwas so Abstraktem wie der Metaphysik und etwas so Konkretem wie der modernen Industriegesellschaft bestehen Auch daß sich in der modernen Technik ein Wille zur Macht ausspricht, der blind ist, weil er jeden Sinn für Grenze und Maß verloren hat, ist unbestreitbar. Daß das Programm der modernen Technik eine Struktur von Subjektivität voraussetzt, wie sie nur in der Neuzeit möglich geworden ist, läßt sich leicht einsehen: Nur wer in der Lage ist, sich selbst aus der Außenwelt zurückzuziehen und von ihrer Wirklichkeit zu abstrahieren, kann dem technischen Wunsch einer vollständigen Unterwerfung der Natur Sinn abgewinnen; die zweite Cartesianische Meditation mit ihrem Rückzug auf das cogito ist notwendige Voraussetzung des Lebensgefühls des Menschen des technischen Zeitalters. Man braucht nur dem Wagenlenker im Museum in Delphi in die Augen zu blicken, um zu wissen, daß eine Kultur, die aus derartigen Menschen bestand, zur Hervorbringung der modernen technologischen Zivilisation konstitutionell unfähig, ja unwillens gewesen sein muß.

Beeindruckend an Heideggers Theorie ist ferner die metaphysische Deutung der europäischen Geistesgeschichte. Wenn es ein Absolutes gibt, dann muß es in der menschlichen Suche nach dem Absoluten in besonderer

Weise präsent sein – dieser aus Hegel bekannten Implikation wird auch derjenige zustimmen müssen, der den Begriff des Absoluten aus der Philosophie verabschiedet. Denn zumindest unter der Voraussetzung, daß die Welt nicht ohne Zusammenhang mit dem Absoluten ist, muß die Weise, in der das Absolute in der Welt *für jemanden* ist, von dem Absoluten prinzipiiert sein: Nur so kann eine Theorie über das Absolute den eigenen Geltungsanspruch einholen. Auch Heideggers These, daß das Sich-Verbergen des Absoluten eine Weise seiner Präsenz ist, ist trotz ihrer Paradoxalität durchaus überzeugend. Wer verstummt, kann damit mehr mitteilen, als wenn er spricht; und die Abwesenheit etwa eines geliebten Menschen ist keineswegs ein Nichtseiendes, sondern etwas phänomenal Gegebenes, an dem man leiden kann, ja das uns manchmal erst die Bedeutung des Abwesenden ins Bewußtsein treten läßt. Faszinierend ist zumal Heideggers Interpretation des Autonomiewillens der neuzeitlichen Subjektivität als einer, wie man mit einer Metapher sagen könnte, heimtückischen Täuschung des Seins. Insofern der abstrakte Freiheits- und Emanzipationswille der Moderne (der als solcher notwendig Herrschaftswille ist) eine ganze Epoche bestimmt, kann er schwerlich auf einer freien Entscheidung beruhen; jene Freiheit ist vielmehr das *Schicksal* der Moderne. In der Abkopplung der Subjektivität vom Sein des Absoluten waltet das Sein selbst, also eine Macht, die die Subjektivität um so radikaler gerade dadurch transzendiert, daß sie von ihr verkannt, ja für überwunden gehalten wird. Heideggers Sein erinnert etwas an Julius Cäsar in Walter Jens' Fernsehspiel »Die Verschwörung«: Wie dieser es ist, der die Verschwörung gegen sich eingefädelt hat und im geheimen lenkt, so ist es bei Heidegger das Absolute, das seine eigene Entthronung durchsetzt; die neuzeitlichen Denker und Wissenschaftler, die die entgötterte moderne Industriegesellschaft vorbereiten, sind nur Marionetten in seiner Hand, um so bemitleidenswerter, für je autonomer sie sich halten. Ist schon Spinozas Substanzmetaphysik, die den Menschen zu einem vollständig determinierten Modus des Absoluten herabdrückt, eine der härtesten intellektuellen Zumutungen, die man sich überhaupt denken kann (zumal sie logisch so gut begründet ist), ist Heideggers metaphysischer Historismus ein noch größerer Affront, weil er eine Zeit herausfordert, die sich auf ihre vermeintliche Autonomie außerordentlich viel einbildet. Doch Philosophien werden nicht schon dadurch widerlegt, daß man sie als Provokation empfindet; es ist umgekehrt Stromlinienförmigkeit, die selten ein Kriterium für gute Philosophie ist.

Aber so durchdacht Heideggers Analyse und gnadenlose Ablehnung des modernen Subjektivismus auch ist, sowenig gibt sein Ansatz schon eine ausreichende Grundlage für eine logisch konsistente und mit den Phänomenen übereinstimmende Metaphysik der ökologischen Krise. So ist es kein Zufall, daß Heidegger nirgends von der ökologischen Krise spricht. Dies hat nicht nur damit zu tun, daß letztere zu seiner Zeit eine noch nicht absehbare Folge der Industriegesellschaft war. Der tiefste Grund liegt vielmehr darin, daß Heidegger über keinen Naturbegriff verfügt. Denn als radikaler Historist handelt Heidegger nur von den verschiedenen historisch realisierten Konzeptionen der Natur, nicht von der Natur als solcher. So wie in der analytischen Philosophie die Wissenschaftstheorie die Naturphilosophie verdrängt, so wird in Heideggers hermeneutischem Ansatz letztere durch die Philosophie der Geschichte der Wissenschaft ersetzt. Eben dieses Aufgehen der Naturphilosophie in Geschichtsphilosophie belegt nun aber, daß Heidegger selbst zur Epoche des »Gestells« gehört, wenn denn diese durch die Unmöglichkeit eines unmittelbaren Seins- und Naturbezugs gekennzeichnet ist. Auch Heidegger handelt nicht von der Natur, sondern nur von Vorstellungen der Natur; und an eine Metaphysik, die uns aus der ökologischen Krise hinausführen will, ist die Forderung zu stellen, daß sie eine eigene Naturphilosophie entwickelt.

Ohnehin ist ferner klar, daß der Nachweis, ein bestimmter Zugang zur Natur wie der einzelwissenschaftliche sei nur einer von den historisch verwirklichten Naturbegriffen, nichts beiträgt zur Lösung der Geltungsfrage, ob denn dieser Zugang das Wesen der Natur erfasse oder nicht. Alle Theorien sind historisch entstanden, wahre wie falsche, und um sich zur Wahrheitsfrage zu erheben, ist es unabdingbar, den Historismus hinter sich zu lassen. Dies gilt mit Bezug auf die Lehre nicht nur von der Natur, sondern auch vom Sein. In der Tat ist offenkundig, daß Heideggers Seinsmetaphysik nicht darauf Anspruch machen kann, in einer irgendwie nachvollziehbaren Weise begründet zu sein. Von einer Methode, die seine Einsichten über das Absolute generiere, kann nicht die Rede sein; und wenn Heidegger entgegnete, die Suche nach einer Methode sei selbst schon zutiefst fragwürdig, weil sie der Suche nach der Herrschaft über die Natur entstamme, so wäre dagegen zweierlei einzuwenden. Erstens wäre dies immer noch das kleinere Übel gegenüber der einzig bleibenden Alternative, die offenbar darin bestehen muß, sich den Versicherungen philosophischer Rauner auszuliefern; und zweitens ist es gar nicht wahr, daß der Wille nach Selbstvergewisserung, wie er für die moderne Metaphysik kennzeichnend ist, unvermeidlich zum »Gestell« führe. Erst die Abkopplung der modernen Wissenschaft von dem philosophischen Programm, Vernunft in der Wirklichkeit zu finden, bringt den Absolutismus der Technik hervor; zudem kennt die neuzeitliche Metaphysik schon vor Heidegger Denker, die den modernen Subjektivismus kritisieren, ohne doch deswegen die Idee rationaler Geltungsreflexion preiszugeben. Hier rächt sich, daß Heidegger nicht über eine differenzierte Rationalitätstheorie verfügt – die instrumentelle Rationalität der Technik wird bei ihm der philosophischen Vernunft gleichgesetzt, obgleich nur ihre Unterscheidung eine konsistente Kritik der modernen Industriegesellschaft ermöglicht. Auch wenn ferner das Verhältnis des Absoluten zur menschlichen Freiheit gewiß nicht einfach zu lösen ist, ist doch an jede Theorie, die einen Wahrheitsanspruch erhebt, die Forderung zu stellen, daß sie Platz für die Einsichtsfähigkeit des Menschen und damit für rationale Autonomie schafft. Eben das ist aber in Heideggers radikalem Historismus nicht mehr der Fall. Dies gilt besonders, da seine dysteleologische Geschichtskonzeption es als äußerst rätselhaft erscheinen läßt, warum nach einer mehrtausendjährigen Verfallsgeschichte überhaupt noch wahrheitsfähiges Denken möglich sein soll. Auch wenn negative Entwicklungen nicht auszuschließen sind – in der Blindheit für die Negativität der Moderne sahen wir ja einen der Hauptmängel des Vulgärhegelianismus –, ist ferner von einer Theorie der Geschichte, die sich wie die Heideggersche als metaphysische versteht, durchaus zu erwarten, daß sie eine rationale Erklärung für den Sinn dieses Verfalls gibt; ansonsten erscheint die Annahme, in diesem Verfall manifestiere sich das Absolute, als willkürliche Hypostasierung von Zufällen. Schließlich wird man nicht ohne großes Unbehagen monieren müssen, daß Heidegger die affirmativen Leistungen des modernen demokratischen Rechtsstaates philosophisch nie zu würdigen gewußt hat – sicher auch deswegen, weil er dem Prinzip der Autonomie, in seiner metaphysischen wie in einer politischen Form, mit großen Zweifeln gegenüberstand. Ethik und Politische Philosophie sind auf der Grundlage von Heideggers Metaphysik undenkbar.

Viele der Einwände gegen Heideggers Konzeption treffen nicht jene zweite Kritik am vulgärhegelianischen Paradigma, der ich mich jetzt zuwenden will – diejenige von Meyer-Abich. So ist zunächst hervorzuheben, daß Meyer-Abich durchaus über eine eigene Naturphilosophie verfügt – und nicht bloß über eine Theorie der geschichtlichen Entwicklung der verschiedenen Naturbegriffe. Zwar hat Meyer-Abich eine detaillierte Philosophie der einzelnen Formen der Natur nicht ausgearbeitet; von großer philosophischer Tragweite und Originalität sind freilich seine Überlegungen zum Verhältnis von Geist und Natur. Für Meyer-Abich ist der Mensch Teil der Natur: Während Hegel die Naturgeschichte als Vorspann zur Geschichte des Geistes versteht, ist für Meyer-Abich die Kultur der menschliche Beitrag zur Naturgeschichte. Der Einstellungswandel, den Meyer-Abich im modernen Menschen erzielen möchte, läßt sich in den Worten »Von der Umwelt zur Mitwelt« prägnant zusammenfassen: Nach ihm geht es darum, ein Gefühl der Empathie mit der organischen, ja selbst der anorganischen Natur zu entwickeln, diese eben als Mit-welt zu erleben. Es wird nicht geleugnet, daß der Mensch eine besondere Position innerhalb der Natur einnehme

Sein und Subjektivität

– aber eben *innerhalb* ihrer. »Natur« nennt Meyer-Abich das Ganze und Eine, das alles umfaßt; sie sei vollständig disjunkt zerlegbar in »Mensch« und »natürliche Mitwelt«. Der Grundgedanke seiner holistischen Ethik besteht gerade darin, den Kreis der Wesen, für die man Verantwortung wahrzunehmen hat, auf alles Natürliche auszuweiten: Über die Biozentrik Albert Schweitzers hinaus lehrt Meyer-Abich eine Physiozentrik, die die Werte auch des anorganischen Seins empfindet und bewahrt. Meyer-Abich bestreitet dabei nicht, daß mit der Ausweitung des Radius die Dringlichkeit der Pflicht abnimmt; seine Konzeption erinnert durchaus an die stoische Oikeiosislehre. Die Erweiterung der Mitwelt ist nach Meyer-Abich das eigentliche Kriterium für moralischen Fortschritt; geschichtsphilosophisch sieht er in der immer weitergehenden Überwindung des egozentrischen Partikularismus den Sinn der Moralentwicklung. Auch in der Politischen Philosophie fordert er einen Übergang vom Sozialstaat zum Naturstaat: Die Entwicklungsrichtung, die der moderne Staat mit dem Übergang vom liberalen Rechtsstaat zum Sozialstaat eingeschlagen habe und die in einer Übernahme von Verantwortung für die Schwächeren bestehe, werde im Naturstaat nur fortgesetzt. Gegen den Besitzindividualismus, den er witzig den Absolutismus des Kleinen Mannes nennt, fordert er nicht nur eine Sozial-, sondern auch eine Naturpflichtigkeit des Eigentums. Besonders wichtig ist, daß Meyer-Abich den Menschen als potentielle Bereicherung der Natur deutet. Nicht nur komme in ihm die Natur zur Sprache; durch den Menschen könne auch die Mitwelt eine Hege und Pflege erhalten, die sie ohne ihn nie hätte. Sosehr die gegenwärtige Industriegesellschaft Arten vernichte, sosehr sei zu bedenken, daß ohne die traditionelle Agrikultur die Artenvielfalt seit der letzten Eiszeit nicht so stark zugenommen hätte. Durch den Menschen könne die Natur durchaus besser und schöner werden als ohne ihn. Die ökologische Krise, die er als Krise des Verhältnisses des Menschen zu seiner Mitwelt deutet, versteht er als Antithese in einem Dreischritt der mit einer ursprünglichen Einheit mit der Mitwelt beginne und mit ihrer Wiedererringung ende.

Meyer-Abichs Kategorie der Mitwelt, seine Deutung der Kultur als menschlicher Forsetzung der Naturgeschichte, schließlich seine Anwendung der klassischen dialektischen Triade auf das Naturverhältnis des Menschen scheinen mir seine wichtigsten Beiträge zu einer Metaphysik der ökologischen Krise. Besonders hervorzuheben ist, daß Meyer-Abich dem Menschen im Ganzen der Natur eine potentiell positive Rolle zuschreibt. Wer dies nicht tut, aber trotzdem die Natur für den Inbegriff alles Werthaften hält, müßte im Grunde hoffen, daß sich der Mensch selbst zerstöre und die Welt von der Qual befreie, die er für sie darstellt; ja, wenn er konsequent ist, müßte er noch weitergehen und, da Zerstörung anderen

Lebens notwendig zumindest zu heterotrophen Organismen gehört, jenen Zustand der Welt herbeiwünschen, da es noch kein Leben gab[16]. Anders, wie gesagt Meyer-Abich, der dem Menschen die Fähigkeit zuspricht, die Natur schöner und besser zu machen. Aber genau hier setzt meine Frage ein. Wenn einiges Naturseiende besser und schöner ist als anderes, dann ist offenbar die Natürlichkeit nicht das Kriterium für Gutes und Schönes; denn natürlich ist alles Naturseiende gleichermaßen. Die Natur kann, scheint es, für normative Differenzen innerhalb des Natürlichen nicht aufkommen, auch wenn Meyer-Abich derartiger normativer Differenzierungen bedarf: Denn sonst könnte er nicht behaupten, daß die traditionelle Agrikultur eine bessere Natur hinterlassen habe als die moderne Agrochemie, ja er könnte nicht einmal sagen, daß eine Welt ohne Menschen schlechter wäre als eine mit Menschen. Eins nämlich ist klar: Selbst wenn die Menschheit sich und die meisten Arten zerstören sollte, die Natur würde übrigbleiben – es gäbe immer ein jeweiliges Ganzes von natürlich Seiendem. Kants Einsicht, daß normative Sätze sich nicht aus deskriptiven gewinnen lassen, scheint mir weiterhin gültig – sie wird auch nicht dadurch berührt, daß man mit Meyer-Abich gegen Kant anerkennt, in der belebten und unbelebten Natur seien Werte realisiert. Aber daß es sich dabei um Werte handelt, folgt nicht aus der Tatsache, daß sie in der Natur verwirklicht sind.

Auch wenn man eine unüberbrückbare Trennung von Sein und Sollen ablehnt, muß man doch an ihrem kategorialen Unterschied festhalten. Ähnliches gilt m.E. mit Bezug auf das Verhältnis von Innen- und Außenseite. Daß man zwischen beiden Aspekten differenzieren kann, ist eine unbestreitbare Tatsache, die nicht dadurch aus der Welt geschafft wird, daß man irgendwie auch an eine Einheit von Leib und Seele glaubt; die Vermittlung von Differenz und Einheit ist die eigentliche Aufgabe, die wohl noch von keinem Philosophen wirklich gelöst worden ist. Insbesondere bleibt die Begründung der Rationalität unseres Glaubens an eine Innenseite bei anderen Organismen ein Desiderat. Die von Meyer-Abich eindrucksvoll beschworene Einfühlung mit dem Kosmos[17] ist zweifelsohne eine beglückende und zu ökologischem Engagement motivierende Erfahrung, aber daß in ihr objektive Wirklichkeit erfaßt wird, bleibt noch zu zeigen. Auch die schwierige Frage, ob die lebensweltliche Naturerfahrung dem eigentlichen Sein der Natur näher komme als die wissenschaftliche Theoriebildung, wird von Meyer-Abich nicht wirklich beantwortet.

Ganz allgemein vermißt man bei Meyer-Abich begründungstheoretische Reflexionen. Was in der Philosophie wirklich als Argument gelten könne, wird nicht ausdrücklich geprüft. Dies ist nicht bloß eine Lücke in seinem beeindruckenden Entwurf – welche Philosophie hätte keine Lücken! –, sondern stellt auch seine zentrale ontologische Theorie in Frage, die Natur sei das Ganze. Denn offenbar ist auch die Kategorie der Wahrheit ebensowenig wie die des Guten ein Teil der Natur. Alle Theorien sind – bei Zugrundelegung von Meyer-Abichs Naturbegriff – Momente der Natur, aber nicht alle sind wahr: Also ist es nicht die Natur, die etwas wahr oder falsch macht. Gerade die Frage, warum die Natur erkennbar sei, führt über eine Ontologie hinaus, die die Natur zum eigentlichen Sein hypostasiert[18]. Denn erstens sind die Naturgesetze, ohne die die Natur nicht erfahrbar wäre, nichts Naturhaftes (sie sind etwa nicht zeitlich oder räumlich), und zweitens kommt mathematischen Entitäten, deren Erkenntnis in der Mathematik die wissenschaftliche Durchdringung der Natur erst möglich macht, ein ideales, kein natürliches Sein zu. (Immerhin muß man zugeben, daß Meyer-Abichs Naturbegriff nicht nur geistiges Sein übergreift, sondern möglicherweise auch ideales Sein – seine Natur ist, ähnlich Spinozas Substanz, zugleich Grund des empirisch Erfahrbaren.)

III

Versuchen wir das bisher in der Auseinandersetzung mit dem Vulgärhegelianismus und seinen Kritikern Gewonnene festzuhalten, so läß sich sagen, daß in Anbetracht der ökologischen Krise und der moralischen Konsequenzen, die wir aus ihr ziehen sollen, weder eine Metaphysik, die den Geist zur eigentlichen Substanz macht, noch eine Philosophie, die die Natur oder gar ein alogisches Absolutes nach Art Heideggers zum wahren Sein erhebt und Geltungsreflexionen verabschiedet, die angemessene Reaktion darstellt. Aber wenn weder die Natur noch der Geist als das grundlegende Sein angenommen werden dürfen, um die ökologische Krise zu begreifen, was bleibt dann noch übrig? Ich habe schon angedeutet, warum ich der Ansicht bin, daß man das ideale Sein als eine eigene Seinssphäre annehmen muß; und da ich diese Position, diejenige des objektiven Idealismus, an anderer Stelle und in einem anderen Zusammenhang ausführlich verteidigt habe[19], sei mir hier erlassen, die Argumente, die für sie sprechen, nochmals anzuführen. Der objektive Idealismus geht von dem Logischen, das Bedingung der Möglichkeit jeder Argumentation ist und hinter das nicht zurückgegangen werden kann, als Prinzip allen Erkennens, aber auch allen Seins aus; die logische, ideale Welt prinzipiiert die reale Welt, zu der sowohl die natürliche als auch die geistige (die subjektive wie die intersubjektive) Welt gehören. Als von der idealen Welt prinzipiiert ist dem objektiven Idealismus alles Seiende werthaft, wenn auch in verschiedenem Grad, der sich nach der Entsprechung der relevanten Entitäten mit der idealen Welt richtet.

Wichtig ist in diesem Zusammenhang, daß das Verhältnis von Natur und Geist in einem fundamentalen Sinn zweideutig ist. Einerseits ist, wenn man unter Natur die ganze empirisch erfahrbare Realität versteht, auch der Geist Teil der Natur; jedenfalls ist er durch die Natur vermittelt. Andererseits ist der Geist eben nicht bloß ein Teil der Realität neben einem anderen – da er das Außereinander der Natur im Erkennen aufhebt, diese idealisiert, kann er zugleich als Rückkehr aus der Natur zur Idee gedeutet werden. Wenn die logische Welt die Thesis ist, dann ist die Natur die Antithesis; und als reale Struktur, die zugleich der Einsicht in das ideale Prinzip der Natur fähig ist, ist der Geist die Synthese. Die Synthese ist freilich stets auch Negation der Antithese. und in sofern ist der Geist zur gleichen Zeit Teil der Natur und deren Negation.

Offenbar ist diese antinomische Bestimmung des Geistes unabdingbar, wenn wir verstehen wollen, wieso es zu der ökologischen Krise kommen konnte. Wäre der Geist *nur* Teil der Natur, dann wäre sein außerordentliches Zerstörungspotential gegenüber der Natur nicht erklärlich; wäre er eine *vollständig* selbständige Substanz, dann wäre die Naturzerstörung nicht potentiell selbstmörderisch. Die Negation der Natur durch den Geist findet auf zwei verschiedenen Ebenen statt, die streng zu unterscheiden sind. Einerseits negiert der Geist die Natur, indem er sie erkennt, ihr Außereinander im denkenden Begreifen aufhebt, die idealen Strukturen erfaßt, die sie durchwalten. Freilich impliziert dieses Begreifen, als Akt nur des Geistes, keine reale Zerstörung; es läßt die Natur, wie sie ist, und durchleuchtet sie nur. Andererseits kann der Mensch als der Organismus, in dem der Geist Fleisch geworden ist, die Natur real vernichten; eben diese Fähigkeit erreicht in der ökologischen Krise, deren Zeugin unsere Generation ist, ihre weltgeschichtliche Klimax. Es liegt auf der Hand, daß der Geist die Natur nur dadurch zerstören kann, daß er Fleisch geworden ist; ansonsten könnte er gar nicht in die Natur intervenieren. Nur insofern er selbst partiell Natur ist, kann sich der Mensch gegen die Natur wenden, wenn auch das Ausmaß seiner Auflehnung gegen die Natur von seiner Geistigkeit abhängt.

Aber nicht nur läßt sich sagen, daß der Mensch, insofern er zur Hälfte Naturwesen ist, Natur zerstören *kann;* insofern er organisches Naturwesen ist, *muß* er dies tun. Im zweiten Hauptsatz der Thermodynamik liegt begründet, daß der Organismus die eigene höhere Ordnung nur um den Preis der Vermehrung der Unordnung in seiner Umwelt erhalten kann. Eine Ontologie, die sich an diesem harten und unerbittlichen Gesetz der Realität vorbeilügt, wird nie überzeugen können; und auch und gerade von einem objektiven Idealismus ist zu erwarten, daß er das Gesetz vom Fressen und Gefressenwerden zur Kenntnis nimmt, das die organische Welt in so furchtbarer Weise beherrscht. Versucht man den Ort des Lebendigen im Ganzen des Seins zu bestimmen, so erkennt man folgende Spannung – gerade wenn man den Sinn der Natur in der Rückkehr zur Idealität erblickt, wie sie im Geiste statthat. Auf der einen Seite geht im Organismus das Licht der Subjektivität auf; in der Selbsterhaltung, später in der Empfindung des Organismus wird eine Form von Reflexivität verwirklicht, die den Geist vorbereitet. Andererseits bedeutet die Bildung subjektiver Zentren eben auch die Durchbrechung der Kontinuität des anorganischen Seins; die Höherentwicklung impliziert die Entgegensetzung des einen subjektiven Zentrums zunächst gegen seine anorganische Umwelt, dann gegen ein anderes subjektives Zentrum. Während sich die ganze nur anorganische Materie assimiliert – aber immerhin im Kampf um den Lebensraum andere Pflanzen verdrängt und vernichtet – bedarf das heterotrophe Tier organischer Nahrung; und erst hier tritt eigentlich ein, was man Naturzerstörung nennt. Denn die chemische Umwandlung von anorganischen Stoffen würde man nicht Zerstörung nennen; mit diesem Ausdruck meint man vielmehr die Tötung des Lebendigen, die Vernichtung der organischen Form. Immerhin ist die Tötung eines Organismus, das sein Leiden, wenn es denn empfindet, wenigstens nicht auszudrücken vermag, noch nicht eigentlich empörend; Herbivoren können kaum schwermütig stimmen. Das Auftreten von Karnivoren, das Töten von Tieren, zumal Vertebraten, durch andere Tiere ist es, was dem Sein immer wieder einen Anschein von sinnloser Grausamkeit gibt – jedenfalls in der Betrachtung jener Geistwesen, die allein die Frage nach dem Sein zu stellen vermögen. Freilich besteht schwerlich ein Zweifel daran, daß das Erscheinen von Karnivoren die Entwicklung des Geistes in der Natur begünstigt hat. So wie die tierische Heterotrophie Lokomotion und Sinneswahrnehmung überhaupt erst nötig gemacht hat, so ist deren Vervollkommnung und die erste Formung, von so etwas wie Intelligenz durch die Jagd des Tieres auf das Tier beschleunigt worden.

Die faszinierenden kybernetischen Relationen zwischen den Populationen von Beutetieren und Jägern, die in Gleichungen von bewundernswerter Symmetrie beschrieben werden können, sind hier nicht näher zu thematisieren. Von Wichtigkeit ist die Tatsache, daß die Jäger auf die Beutetiere angewiesen sind: Sie leben von ihrer ständig erneuten Negation, und das setzt ihr stets wiederholtes Dasein voraus. Nimmt die Population der Beutetiere ab, dann schrumpft auch die der Jäger, die sich nicht mehr ernähren können, was den Beutetieren wieder Gelegenheit zur Zunahme gibt. Die dialektische Natur dieses Typs von Relation läßt es als Glücksfall erscheinen, daß eine vollständige Negation der Beutetiere nicht möglich ist: Sie wäre nur scheinbar ein Triumph der Jäger, in Wahrheit ihr Tod. An diesem kurzfristigen und kurzsichtigen Triumph werden die Jäger durch ihre Geistlosigkeit gehindert, die eine systematische Jagd unmöglich macht; und eben diese Geistlosigkeit erweist sich als ein Segen.

Daß der Mensch das ökologische Gleichgewicht in so tiefgreifender Weise stören konnte, hängt daran, daß er das intelligenteste aller Tiere ist. Beides, Geistigkeit und Organizität, ist in ihm vereint; nur beide zusammen können zur ökologischen Krise führen. Aber *muß* diese Verbindung dieses Resultat zeitigen? Ich habe anderswo zu zeigen versucht, daß in den fünf Naturbegriffen, die in der menschlichen Geschichte unterschieden werden können, eine Logik waltet, die auf eine immer stärkere Entgegensetzung von Geist und Natur hinausläuft und ihren Höhepunkt in der Cartesischen Metaphysik mit ihrer Entgegensetzung von res extensa und res cogitans erreicht[20]. Eben diese Entwicklung läßt sich in der Tat als Fortsetzung jenes Prozesses deuten, der mit der Entstehung des ersten Organismus begann – das subjektive Zentrum vertieft sich immer mehr in sich selbst, bis es schließlich das autonome, der Natur und der Gemeinschaft entfremdete Ich der neuzeitlichen Subjektivität wird. Insofern kann man die menschliche Kulturgeschichte durchaus als Fortsetzung der Naturgeschichte deuten – in der globalen Naturzerstörung durch die Industriegesellschaft wird nur ein Prinzip auf die Spitze getrieben, das im organischen Sein schon präsent ist und vermutlich im Sein selbst angelegt ist. In der ökologischen Krise – und dem, was wir aus ihr machen – muß das Sein gewissermaßen Farbe bekennen, den Grundwiderspruch offenbaren, der ihm eignet.

Aber worin genau besteht dieser Widerspruch, und läßt er sich auflösen? Wie schon gesagt, läßt sich die ganze Naturentwicklung durchaus als Fortschritt hin zum Geiste deuten, und wenn wir uns selbst und die metaphysische Reflexion, die wir betreiben, noch ernst nehmen wollen, können wir auch gar nicht umhin, die Entwicklung hin zum Geiste positiv zu bewerten. Gleichzeitig basiert diese Entwicklung auf zunehmende Entgegensetzung subjektiver Zentren zum umgebenden Sein, und diese Entgegensetzung müssen wir heute, wo sie auf eine Katastrophe hinauszulaufen droht, zu überwinden, zumindest zu beschränken suchen. Aber ist der Geist, sosehr er auf die Beschränkung dieser Entgegensetzung angewiesen ist, um zu überleben, nicht wesensmäßig Negation der Natur?

Ich habe schon gesagt, daß die Negation der Natur durch den Menschen doppelt ist: einerseits insofern er Organismus, andererseits insofern er Geistwesen ist. Wäre er nur Geistwesen, könnte er der Natur nicht schaden; wäre er nur Organismus, könnte er ihr nicht in dem Maße schaden, in dem er es tut. Anthropologisch adäquat kann der Mensch nur erfaßt werden, wenn er zugleich als Organismus und Geistwesen gedeutet wird; und offenbar hat diese Doppelheit seines Wesens einen tieferen Grund in der Verfaßtheit der fundamentalen Kategorien. Denn so wie im System der apriorischen Kategorien eine Kategorie wie Sein, insofern sie ihrer Form nach Begriff ist, die Kategorie »Begriff« präsupponiert, diese aber die einfachere Kategorie »Sein« als Element ihrer Bedeutung voraussetzt, so kann auch nur das organische Sein dem Geist in der Welt eine ontische Grundlage geben; den *Sinn* seines Seins erhält aber das Leben nur aus dem Geist, zu dem es sich entwickelt. Die Doppelheit von Form und Inhalt, die für das Logische so kennzeichnend ist, spaltet sich im Menschen in Geist und Leben. Das metaphysische Rätsel des Menschen besteht gerade darin, daß in ihm das wechselseitige Angewiesensein von Idealität und Realität in der empirischen Welt sichtbar wird; und die ökologische Krise ist letztlich Ausdruck der Verschärfung dieser Dualität zum absoluten Gegensatz.

In der modernen Industriegesellschaft scheint die ewige Spannung zwischen Vitalem und Geistigem im Menschen in radikaler Weise verkehrt zu sein. Denn offenbar ist die geistige Erfassung der Naturgesetze in der neuzeitlichen Wissenschaft etwas, das man ceteris paribus positiv einschätzen muß, werden doch allein dadurch die Naturgesetze »für sich«. Aber die Pointe der modernen Industriegesellschaft besteht gerade darin, daß sie die ungeheure geistige Leistung wissenschaftlicher Naturerkenntnis zur Befriedigung abgelegenster Bedürfnisse instrumentalisiert, die der Mensch als domestizierter Organismus haben mag. Die letztliche Geistlosigkeit, die man bei manchen hochintelligenten Einzelwissenschaftlern antrifft, resultiert eben daraus, daß die Erkenntnis der Natur nicht auf ein ideales Ganzes bezogen ist, sondern der Befriedigung äußerer Bedürfnisse dient. Freilich ist dafür gesorgt, daß die Überbetonung des Nützlichkeitswertes in der Wertehierarchie den modernen Menschen keineswegs glücklicher macht; denn durch die Dazwischenschaltung immer neuer Mittel zur Befriedigung elementarer Bedürfnisse können die vitalen Werte nur verkümmern[21]. Ab einem gewissen Punkt wird der Wille des Lebens, seine Umgebung zu beherrschen, kontraproduktiv; indem es zu seinen Zwecken die mechanischsten Mittel einsetzt, beraubt es sich seiner ursprünglichen Vitalität und damit des einzigen möglichen Sinnes seiner Tätigkeit. Es regrediert ins Anorganische.

Aus dem Gesagten folgt, daß zur geistigen Bewältigung der ökologischen Krise keineswegs eine Verabschiedung der traditionellen metaphysischen Hochschätzung des Geistes oder gar der Vernunft erforderlich ist. Man tut der Industriegesellschaft viel zu viel Ehre an, wenn man sie für vernünftig hält und meint, Kritik an ihr müsse auf den Irrationalismus rekurrieren. Die Lebensphilosophie wird uns nicht aus der ökologischen Krise herausführen, da ja diese nur die letzte Konsequenz der Entwicklung des Lebens ist. Nur eine Philosophie, die das Leben als die Grundlage des Geistes und den Geist als die Wahrheit des Lebens denkt, hat Aussichten, die ökologische Krise metaphysisch adäquat zu interpretieren. Um die Entwicklung der Moderne angemessen zu bewerten, ist es ferner entscheidend, scharf zwischen Geist und neuzeitlicher Subjektivität zu unterscheiden. An der Auszeichnung des Geistes, des idealisierenden und begreifenden Prinzips, ist aus begründungstheoretischen Gründen nicht zu rütteln. Aber die neuzeitliche Subjektivität, dieses Prinzips intensivster Vereinzelung, das sich aus dem Sein des Absoluten, der Natur und des intersubjektiven Geistes herausreflektiert hat und sich über seine innere Leere und furchtbare Einsamkeit durch den infiniten Regreß immer neuer Bedürfnisse hinwegtäuscht, kann nicht das Ziel des Universums sein. Eine umfassende Analyse und Kritik der Funktionsgesetze, die sie treiben und die ihr Verhalten in dualen zwischenmenschlichen Beziehungen, im Wirtschaften, in der Politik, in der Kunst, in der Religion und eben auch im Naturverhältnis bestimmen, ist ein dringendes Desiderat der Gegenwartsphilosophie. Und dies nicht nur aus zeitkritischem Interesse[22]; allein eine solche Untersuchung könnte konkret nachweisen, wie grotesk der Anspruch der neuzeitlichen Subjektivität ist, das Sein aus sich zu generieren: sie, die in ihrer Seinsvergessenheit nur eine innere Entwicklungstendenz des Seins selbst – diejenige zur Bildung subjektiver Zentren, in denen es allein für sich werden kann – zu ihrem Höhepunkt führt.

Allerdings: Gerade weil es das Sein ist, das sich in der neuzeitlichen Subjektivität ausspricht, gerade weil sie nicht eine Struktur eigenen Rechtes ist, die von außen in die Welt gefallen ist, kann sie auch nicht völlig funktionslos sein; gerade der Seinsphilosoph kann sie nicht nur verurteilen, sondern muß in ihr etwas Affirmatives anerkennen, zumindest vermuten. Die Anwendung dialektischer Kategorien auf das Verhältnis von Natur und Geist läßt in der Tat die Hoffnung keimen, daß deren Entgegensetzung, die in der modernen Industriegesellschaft gipfelt, nur transitorisch ist. Transitorisch wird sie zwar in jedem Fall sein – auch wenn sich der Mensch zerstört, wird die Natur, in welch verstümmelter Form auch immer, überleben. Aber dies wäre nur ein Rückfall auf einen früheren naturgeschichtlichen Zustand, der einmal wieder zur gegenwärtigen Situation führen müßte, während sich die Hoffnung auf eine *Versöhnung* von Natur und Geist richtet. Will man diese Versöhnung in ein System der Philosophie einordnen, dann ließe sich sagen, daß der triadische Systementwurf des reifen Hegel, der aus logischer Idee, Natur und Geist besteht, mit Bezug auf die ökologische Krise durch einen tetradischen ersetzt werden muß, wie er sich beim frühen Hegel findet. Denn im triadischen Systementwurf ist der Geist Negation der Natur, Rückkehr aus ihr zur Idee. In dem tetradischen Entwurf ist hingegen die Antithesis, entsprechend ihrem negativen Wesen, in sich gedoppelt. In diesem

Sinne müßte man sagen, daß der Geist, solange er noch der Natur entgegengesetzt ist, mit dieser zusammen die Antithese zur These der logischen Idee bildet. Erst die Versöhnung von Natur und Geist kann als Synthese bezeichnet werden; erst sie überwindet die Entgegensetzung des Seins in Reales und Ideales, die für die empirische Welt so kennzeichnend ist. Eine Versöhnung von Natur und Geist kann übrigens nicht nur im Geiste stattfinden – in dieser Annahme liegt wohl der größte Irrtum Hegels (nicht nur des Vulgärhegelianismus). In der intersubjektiven Welt der Kultur, in der die einzelnen Subjekte nur über ihre leibliche Verwirklichung füreinander dasein können, ist eine Einheit von Natur und Geist schon gegeben; und es kommt in der Geschichte der menschlichen Kultur wesentlich darauf an, eine Integration der menschlichen Gemeinschaftsformen in die umfassende Natur zu erreichen. Um eine Synthese wird es sich bei einer solchen Integration nur handeln, wenn die Freiheit der Moderne respektiert wird – freilich eine Freiheit, die in der aus Einsicht entspringenden Bindung an die Gesetze des Kosmos ihre Vollendung findet.

Ob Homo sapiens sapiens diese Versöhnung mit der Natur beschieden ist, wissen wir nicht. Für die Metaphysik ist die Beantwortung dieser Frage auch irrelevant. Denn der Metaphysik geht es in der Tat um das Allgemeine und um das Zeitliche nur, sofern in der Zeit allgemeine Entwicklungsgesetze wirken. Wir haben gesehen, daß sich in der Zeit die logische Dualität von Inhalt und Form der Kategorien in Gestalt des Gegensatzes von Leben und Geist auslegt, der in der ökologischen Krise nur seine höchste Zuspitzung erhält. Aufgrund der ontologischen Fundierung der ökologischen Krise hat die Annahme viel für sich, daß, sollte es in unserem Kosmos andere endliche Vernunftwesen geben, sie alle einmal durch die ökologische Krise hindurchgeschritten sind oder hindurchschreiten werden. Jede Kultur wird über kurz oder lang eine der neuzeitlichen Subjektivität analoge Struktur hervorbringen, damit aber auch ein verwandtes Programm der Naturbeherrschung mit der Gefahr der Selbstzerstörung. Ob diese Gefahr in dieser oder jener Kultur endlicher Vernunftwesen Realität wird oder nicht, ist, wie gesagt, kein metaphysisches Problem. Sicher ist es aber eine ethische Aufgabe – und zwar nicht nur eine, sondern *die* vorrangige –, auf diesem Planeten alles zu tun, damit eine Versöhnung des Menschen mit der Natur zustande kommt. Denn zumindest was diesen Planeten betrifft, hat das Sein sich uns anvertraut. Nicht nur für kommende Generationen haben wir eine Verantwortung; auch die bisherige Seinsgeschichte hängt in ihrer metaphysischen Rechtfertigung an uns. Scheitern wir, sind die drei Milliarden Jahre bisherigen Lebens auf diesem Planeten in einem bestimmten Sinne vergeblich; gelingt uns die Synthese, wird ex post auch die Naturgeschichte legitimiert. Das Ausmaß der Verantwortung mag uns schrecken;

es mag uns aber auch die Kraft geben, die wir benötigen, um den Aufgaben der nächsten Jahrzehnte gerecht zu werden, in denen es sich entscheiden wird, was das Schicksal des Seins ist.

Biographie

Vittorio Hösle, geboren 1960 in Mailand, promovierte 1982, habilitierte 1986, war 1988 Associate Professor with tenure an der New School for Social Research in New York und ist seit 1993 ordentlicher Professor für Philosophie in Essen. Hauptwerke: Wahrheit und Geschichte, 1984; Hegels System, 2 Bände, 1987; Die Krise der Gegenwart und die Verantwortung der Philosophie, 1990; Praktische Philosophie in der modernen Welt, 1992.

Anmerkungen

1. Vgl. Demokrit, in: *Die Fragmente der Vorsokratiker,* Griechisch und Deutsch von H. Diels, Siebente Auflage hrsg. von W. Kranz, 3 Bde., Berlin 1954, 68 B 34.
2. Vgl . zu dieser Art des Zugangs M. Seheler, Die Stellung des Menschen im Kosmos, Bonn 1988.
3. Man müßte die im folgenden skizzierte Position weitaus eher mit dem subjektiven Idealismus eines Fichte verbinden, wenn es nicht gerade Hegels Analysen der modernen Welt wären, an die sie anknüpft. Hegels objektiv-idealistische Naturphilosophie hat der Vulgärhegelianismus stets ignoriert.
4. Ich beziehe mich im folgenden besonders auf sein letztes Buch: Aufstand für die Natur. Von der Umwelt zur Mitwelt, München/Wien 1990.
5. Die drei Positionen scheinen mir im Sinne einer dialektischen Entwicklungslogik aufeinander zu folgen. Mir selbst ist der scharfe Gegensatz zwischen I und III erst durch die geistige Begegnung mit dem späten Heidegger klar geworden; seine Größe zu sehen *hat* mich mein Kollege und Freund Professor Dr. Reiner Schürmann gelehrt.
6. Ich darf mir gestatten, auf mein Werk »Hegels System«. 2Bde. Hamburg 1988 zu verweisen, das Hegel in einer vom Vulgärhegelianismus stark abweichenden Weise rekonstruiert.
7. Eine Ausnahme innerhalb der Ritterschule ist Robert Spaemann.
8. Vgl etwa sein Buch: Fortschrittsreaktionen. Über konservative und destruktive Modernität, Graz/Wien/Köln 1987.
9. Siehe etwa seine Aufsatzsammlung: Apologie des Zufälligen, Stuttgart 1986.
10. Person und Eigentum. Zu Hegels »Grundlinien der Philosophie des Rechts« §§ 34-81, jetzt in: *Materialien zu Hegels Rechtsphilosophie,* hrsg. von M. Riedel, 2 Bde., Frankfurt 1975, II 152-175.
11. Die Zahl der Epigonen von Heideggers Spätphilosophie ist Legion; in Italien ist etwa E. Severino zu nennen.

12. Vgl. dazu meinen Aufsatz: Heideggers Philosophie der Technik, erscheint in *Wiener Jahrbuch für Philosophie 23* (1991).
13. Siehe etwa R. Groh/D. Groh, Weltbild und Naturaneignung. Zur Kulturgeschichte der Natur, Frankfurt 1991.
14. Platons Lehre von der Wahrheit. Mit einem Brief über den »Humanismus«, Bern/München 1947.
15. Die Zeit des Weltbildes (1938), in: *Holzwege,* Frankfurt 1977, 75-113. Zu erinnern ist hier natürlich auch an Husserls Krisis-Schrift.
16. Vgl. A. Schopenhauer, Parerga und Paralipomena: kleine philosophische Schriften, II 1, Kap. 12, § 156, in: *Zürcher Ausgabe, Werke in zehn Bänden,* Zürich 1977, Bd. IX, S. 325: »Wenn man, so weit es annäherungsweise möglich ist, die Summe von Noth, Schmerz und Leiden jeder Art sich vorstellt, welche die Sonne in ihrem Laufe bescheint; so wird man einräumen, daß es viel besser wäre, wenn sie auf der Erde so wenig, wie auf dem Monde, hätte das Phänomen des Lebens hervorrufen können, sondern, wie auf diesem, so auch auf jener die Oberfläche sich noch im krystallinischen Zustande befände.«
17. Siehe zu der historischen Entwicklung der kosmischen Einfühlung M. Scheler, Wesen und Formen der Sympathie, Bern/München 1974, 87 ff.
18. Über die Unmöglichkeit, das erkenntnistheoretische Grundproblem evolutionistisch zu lösen, vgl. meinen Aufsatz: Tragweite und Grenzen der evolutionären Erkenntnistheorie, in: *Zeitschrift für allgemeine Wissenschaftstheorie 19* (1988), 348-377.
19. Die Krise der Gegenwart und die Verantwortung der Philosophie, Transzendentalpragmatik, Letztbegründung, Ethik, München 1990. Die wichtigsten Beiträge zu einer objektiv-idealistischen Naturphilosophie stammen von D. Wandschneider; vgl. sein Buch: Raum, Zeit, Relativität, Frankfurt 1982.
20. Philosophie der ökologischen Krise, München 1990, 48 ff. Dieses Buch ist, ebenso wie die vorangegangenen Überlegungen, stark von Hans Jonas beeinflußt; vgl. insbesondere: Organismus und Freiheit. Ansätze zu einer philosophischen Biologie, Göttingen 1973.
21. Vgl. dazu M. Scheler, Das Ressentiment im Aufbau der Moralen, Frankfurt 1978, 92 ff.
22. Von besonderer Wichtigkeit ist, daß viele der heutigen Kritiken an der Industriegesellschaft einem noch tieferen Grad des Subjektivismus entspringen, als er bisher die Geschichte bestimmt hat; diese Kritiken lösen nicht, sie verschärfen die Krise, die die neuzeitliche Subjektivität über die Welt gebracht hat.

Dieser Aufsatz erschien erstmals in: Prima Philosophia 4 (1991), 519-541; er wurde wiederabgedruckt in: Praktische Philosophie in der modernen Welt, München 1992, 1995.

Ingvar Johansson

Perception as the Bridge between Nature and Life-World

Paper read at the XIth Internordic Philosophical Symposium, 11-13 August 1995, Odense University, Denmark; slightly revised.[1]

Abstract
The main claim in "Perception as the Bridge Between Nature and Life-World" is that philosophy once again has to discuss the old problem of direct realism. According to modern psychology of perception we are never in our perceptions in direct contact with the external world, but in our everyday lives we take direct veridical perception for granted most of the time. Our culture contains an epistemological contradiction. Therefore, phenomenological philosophers should allow themselves to drop the method of epoché, and analytic philosophers should not confine themselves to language analysis. In the paper, some peculiar consequences of direct realism are highlighted. Modern direct realists have to accept that veridical perception (a) is x-ray perception (i.e. we perceive through *material things), (b) is backward perception (i.e. we perceive* backwards *in time), and (c) that such perception contains a connection at a distance; they also have to accept (d) that our ego has no determinate spatial and temporal limits. The main alternative to direct realism seems to be some kind of monadology. It is claimed, however, that a monadology is even worse off than direct realism is. Therefore, the philosophical problems of direct realism have to be discussed.*

Something is rotten in the state of our knowledge. Science imposes a gulf between nature and the life-world which is invisible to both scientists and philosophers.

(By 'nature' I mean the world as it would be if man passed out of existence; by 'life-world' I mean the perceptual world in which we live our everyday lives. The world in which we meet other people, talk with them, work with them, quarrel with them, but also the world in which we come across and work on things. Nature, I here take for granted, exists independently of man, whereas, of course, our life-world does not.)

The Cartesian-Lockean heritage

In our philosophically non-reflective lives, we all of us take it for granted that we often perceive a man-independent nature. In our life-world (and, I think, in the life-world of most – probably all – cultures) nature is part of the life-world. Modern perceptual psychology, however, has since long implicitly taught that we do not directly perceive nature. One might think that one of the aims of perceptual psychology is to explain the mechanisms we use to perceive the world, but perceptual psychology puts forward theories which tell us that in our perceptions we cannot be in contact with nature. Of course, nature is regarded as one kind of *cause* of our perceptions, but such causes are regarded as wholly external to our perceptual acts. Our life-world subscribes to direct realism, our science subscribes to indirect (representative) realism. This is not acceptable; especially not since science nowadays is part of the life-world, too. Our life-world is incoherent. Something philosophical has to be done.

When modern philosophy emerged, both Descartes and Locke sketched the outlines of what was, some centuries later, to become the specialized sciences of perceptual psychology and sensory psychophysics. According to their story, ordinary veridical perception consists of a causal chain starting in the thing to be perceived, then passing through space to our body, into our body, and into our sensory organs. By different mechanisms the causal process is assumed to proceed through the body and in the head, in order to end somewhere in the brain. Here, at last, the perception itself is said to occur. Hence a perceptual act in which a thing is perceived is necessarily distinct from this thing itself, both spatially and temporally. The thing and the corresponding perception must be spatially distinct since the thing and the brain are in different places, and they must be temporally distinct since the causal process takes time. Furthermore, things and perceptions are categorially different. Things are material but perceptions are mental. The Cartesian-Lockean philosophy of perception implies that nature is wholly outside our life-world. Locke wrote as follows:

> This is certain: that whatever alterations are made in the body, if they reach not the mind; whatever impressions are made on the outward parts, if they are not taken notice of within, there is no perception. Fire may burn our bodies with no other effect than it does a billet, unless the motion be continued to the brain, and there the senses of heat, or *idea* of pain, be produced in the mind; wherein consists *actual perception*.[2]

Descartes made the same point in the following way:

> We must know, therefore, that although the mind of man informs the whole body, it yet has its principal seat in the brain, and it is there that it not only understands and imagines, but also perceives; and this by means of the nerves which are extended like filaments from the brain to all the other members, with which they are so connected that we can hardly touch any part of the human body without causing the extremities of some of the nerves spread over it to be moved; and this motion passes to the other extremities of those nerves which are collected in the brain round the seat of the soul, as I have just explained quite fully enough in the fourth chapter of the Dioptrics. But the movements which are thus excited in the brain by the nerves, affect in diverse ways the soul or mind, which is intimately connected with the brain, according to the diversity of the motions themselves. And the diverse affections of our mind, or thoughts that immediately arise from these motions, are called perceptions of the senses, or, in common language, sensations.[3]

Locke remained on the abstract level of the considerations presented in these quotations, but Descartes tried to fill in the concrete details of the causal process. He put forward many hypotheses about different kinds of particles moving around in our body. In particular, he thought that there are some extremely small material particles, misleadingly called *animal spirits*, which are able to connect the sensory organs and the brain. There is no philosophical reason for learning about this detailed picture today. It was presented mainly in *L'homme*, which was published after his death. However, in figure 1, three drawings from that book are reproduced.[4]

Both Descartes and Locke were ontological dualists, although, epistemologically, Descartes was a rationalist and Locke an empiricist. Let us look at the relationships between their ontologies and their epistemologies. For an empiricist, an ontological dualism between mind and matter creates an insurmountable epistemological problem. Bertrand Russell, for one, has made this point forcefully:

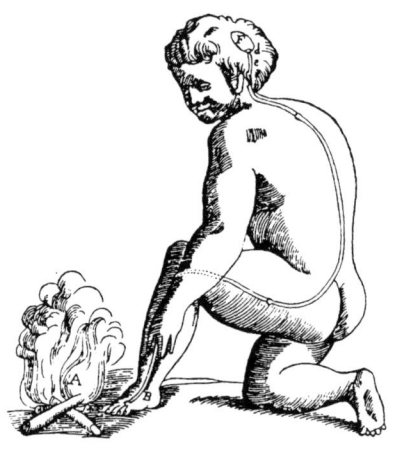

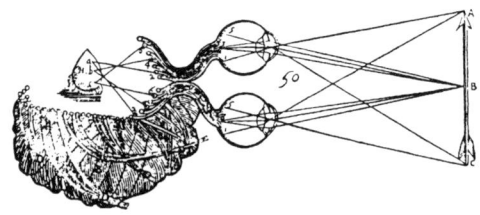

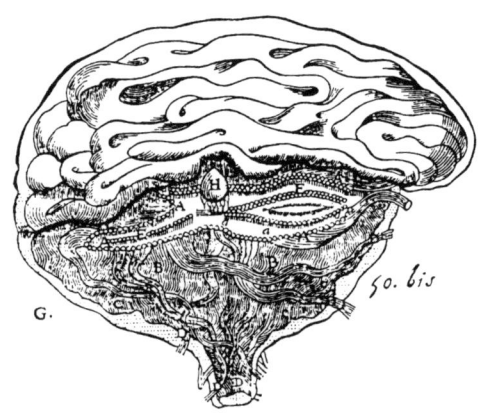

Figure 1.

> In all this, Locke assumes it known that certain mental occurrences, which he calls sensations, have causes outside themselves, and that these causes, at least to some extent and in certain respects, resemble the sensations which are their effects. But how, consistently with the principles of empiricism, is this to be known? We experience the sensations, but not their causes; our experience will be exactly the same if our sensations arise spontaneously. The belief that sensations have causes, and still more the belief that they resemble their causes, is one which, if maintained, must be maintained on grounds wholly independent of experience. The view that 'knowledge is the perception of the agreement or disagreement of two ideas' is the one that Locke is entitled to, and his escape from the paradoxes that it entails is effected by means of an inconsistency so gross that only his resolute adherence to common sense could have made him blind to it.
>
> This difficulty has troubled empiricism down to the present day.[5]

Most post-Lockean British empiricists, from Berkeley to Russell, have freed themselves from Locke's inconsistency by becoming ontological idealists or phenomenalists. Although rationalists do not have exactly the same epistemological problem, they have one which is structurally similar. How does reason, which resides in mind, come to know anything about material *particulars*? Descartes was of the opinion that in order to silence all doubts about the existence of the external world, a proof for the existence of God was needed. Most of the great rationalist continental thinkers who followed Descartes, became, like Leibniz, idealists. Kant, of course, retained the thing in itself but made it unknowable. In my opinion, no materialist thinker has so far really solved the Cartesian-Lockean problem of perception. A metaphysical realist should be able to connect nature and the life-world.

Modern physics and perceptual psychology has discovered a lot about all the material processes which are necessary for veridical perception, and have shown that Descartes' detailed hypotheses were false. Broadly speaking, collisions between material particles have been replaced by electromagnetic interaction and chemical reactions, and animal spirits have been replaced by synapses and neurons, but nonetheless the abstract picture is the same. It implies an ontological gulf where nature and life-world are kept apart. Perceptual psychologists take the existence of a man-independent nature for granted, but, according to their theories, no part of nature can be a real part of a perceptual act.

It is possible to distinguish between three different paradigms or perspectives "that inform contemporary investigations of perception".[6] One, "the inference and empiricist perspective", is closely connected with Locke, although its major figure is Hermann von Helmholtz. According to this perspective, perception consists of two parts, sensation and interpretation; and interpretation is regarded as built up only out of earlier sensations. Association of ideas is the main explanatory principle. A distinction between sensation and interpretation is also to be found in "the Gestalt perspective", but here interpretation is seen as stemming from innate ideas and from mind's own creative ability. Descartes, Kant, and Gestalt psychologists are among those who should be placed in this paradigm. However, differences notwithstanding, both the empiricist and the Gestalt perspective imply the dualism between nature and life-world which I have described.

The third theoretical perspective, which I would like to call the Gibsonian perspective,[7] denies that veridical perception can be split up into two parts, sensation and interpretation. The founding father, J. J. Gibson,[8] distinguishes between sensory receptors which respond to stimulus *energy* and perceptual systems which respond to stimulus *information*. The perceptual (visual, auditive, etc.) systems are assumed to be active, to interact with each other, and to be able to respond *without any process of interpretation* to stimulus information. The concept of stimulus information is one of Gibson's theoretical creations. According to Gibson, if one takes into consideration all light, reflected as well as non-reflected, it is possible to demonstrate that this *ambient light* contains structures and invariants which contain information about the environment. These structures and invariants can remain the same even when frequencies and intensities of the light change. The properties which sensory psychophysics has studied, e.g. frequencies and and intensities of electromagnetic radiation, is given a very subordinate role. The receptors in the eyes cannot discover such invariants, but, Gibson claims, the visual perceptual system can. He also assumes that our perceptions often give us correct information about nature. Sometimes, as in the following quotation, he even seems to be a direct realist in the sense that I use this term.

> It seems to me that these hypotheses make reasonable the common sense position that has been called by philosophers direct or naive realism. I should like to think that there is sophisticated support for the naive belief in the world of objects and events, and for the simple-minded conviction that our senses give knowledge of it.[9]

In spite of this quotation, and in spite of all the philosophical advantages which I think Gibson's perspective has compared with the other ones, he is not a real direct realist. Stimulus information is assumed to travel by means of electromagnetic radiation from the things perceived to the perceiving persons. The uptake of stimulus information is made at the surface of the body. Even in Gibson's theory, a thing perceived seems to be regarded as being wholly external to the perceptual act in which it is perceived. Gibson has never discussed the problems which I shall try to highlight below under the headings *connection at a distance*, *x-ray perception*, *backward perception*, and *the changeful limits of our ego*. Gibson might be called an epistemological realist but not an ontological realist. He says that veridical perception contains no process of interpretation and that it give us direct knowledge of the world, but he does not say that a veridical perceptual act *contains* parts of that which is perceived.

If we abstract from the differences between Descartes, Locke, and competing perspectives within modern perceptual psychology, we find a common core which can be illustrated as in figure 2 (where there are two persons who perceive the same tree). The point of the picture is that the Cartesian-Lockean heritage is monadological in its ontological import. Every mind is closed within itself. It is numerically distinct both from all other minds and from all external things and states of affairs which are said to be perceived in veridical perception. In contradistinction to Leibniz's monadology, however, the monadology of perceptual psychology has a materialistic basis. Perceptual acts are assumed to have material causes, and different minds are assumed to be connected with different material bodies. Bodies can directly interact with each other, but the minds cannot. When two

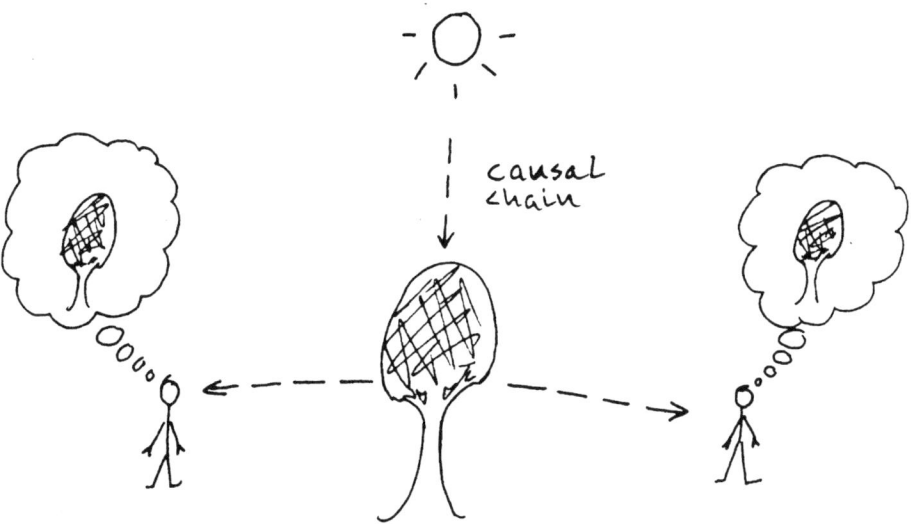

Figure 2.

Figure 3.

people look into each other's eyes, the situation can be pictured as in figure 3. According to perceptual psychology, if you look into your beloved one's eyes, you will really not see her eyes. You will only see eyes in your own mind which are partially caused by her eyes. If she whispers sweet words, you will only hear words which exist in your own mind. A sad story, I would say. Ontological narcissism, as it may be called, is the necessary consequence of such a theory.

Phenomenology and Analytic philosophy

If we look at 20th century philosophy, there is not much awareness of the problem I have sketched. There are mainly two reasons for this neglect: the focus on logic and language within analytic philosophy and the 'bracketing' of the sciences within the phenomenological movement. Since we owe the concept of life-world to Husserl and Scheler, I shall first comment on the phenomenological movement.

The central concept of phenomenology is that of *intentionality*. Perceptions and thoughts are the main examples of intentional acts. In both perceptions and thoughts we are *directed* at something; sometimes at something existing, sometimes at something non-existing. The aim of phenomenology is to study phenomena as they are given in our intentional acts. In order do to this accurately, according to (the middle late) Husserl, we have to perform the *epoché*, i.e. we have to suspend judgements. In particular, we have to bracket, or put within parentheses, all scientific explanations of how the phenomena to be studied are caused. Such explanations, it is claimed, refer to entities which are external to the phenomena in question. Also, we should bracket the question whether anything transcends intentionality. In this way the whole Cartesian-Lockean problem is simply put within parentheses. It was not to be dealt with, neither epistemologically nor ontologically, by phenomenologists.

Later on Husserl himself introduced the methods of transcendental and eidetic reductions, and other phenomenologists made other changes. But there is one thing all these changes within the phenomenological tradition have in common, the Cartesian-Lockean problem is pushed aside. According to the phenomenologists, when two people in the life-world perceive the same tree, they do perceive the same tree, and when two people look into each other's eyes, they do see each other's eyes. In the life-world we are direct realists, and most phenomenologists seem to rest content with knowing this. The method of epoché (and similar procedures) gives us the nature of the life-world but not the real man-independent nature which natural scientists think they are studying, it gives us the intersubjectivity of the life-world but not real intersubjectivity rooted in man-independent nature. Not even so-called realist phenomenologists (e.g. Roman Ingarden and John Wild) have taken the implications of natural science seriously. This is very clear in a recent book in this tradition with the telling title *Back to 'Things in Themselves'*.[10] Here, the traditional epoché of phenomenology is very explicitly thrown away. The author argues for the existence of objective knowledge of a mind-independent world, but he does not discuss the Cartesian-Lockean problem of perception in spite of the fact that he writes that "Phenomenology proper is so far from being opposed to causal explanations of things that it even calls for them."[11]

The Cartesian-Lockean view emphasizes that there is a causal chain directed *from the perceived thing to the perceiving person*, whereas 'the lifeworld view' emphasizes that there is intentionality directed *from the perceiving person to the perceived thing*. If both kinds of directedness are represented by an arrow, the arrows will point in diametrically opposed directions (see figure 4). It can be noted that many theories of perception in antiquity really assumed that in vision there is a causal process which has the same direction as visual intentionality. Something was assumed to emanate from the eye and go *from the eye to the thing perceived*. John Burnet, in his famous *Early Greek Philosophy*, says that "what is characteristic of Greek theories of vision as a whole, /is/ the attempt to combine the view of vision as a radiation proceeding from the eye with that which attributes it to an image reflected in the eye."[12] He also writes:

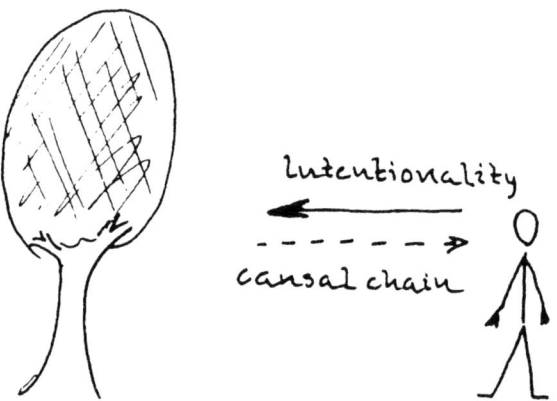

Figure 4.

/Empedokles'/ theory of vision is more complicated; and, as Plato makes his Timaios adopt most of it, it is of great importance in the history of philosophy. The eye was conceived, as by Alkmaion, to be composed of fire and water. Just as in a lantern the flame is protected from the wind by horn, so the fire in the iris is protected from the water which surrounds it in the pupil by membranes with very fine pores, so that, while the fire can pass out, the water cannot get in. Sight is produced by the fire inside the eye going forth to meet the object.

Empedokles was aware, too, that "effluences," as he called them, came from things to the eyes as well; for he defined colours as "effluences from forms (or 'things') fitting into the pores and perceived." It is not quite clear how these two accounts of vision were reconciled, or how far we are entitled to credit Empedokles with the theory of Plato's *Timaeus*. The statements quoted seem to imply something very like it.[13]

Phenomenology, in particular the technique of the epoché, has in my opinion taught us a lot about the content of various perceptions. However, if we want a whole world-view we cannot in principle suspend our judgements about presumed causal explanations and try to be free from ontological commitments. The method of epoché has done its job and we have to face the conflict between the explanations of perceptual psychology and the findings of phenomenological philosophy. Something has to change somewhere. But let us first take a quick look at analytic philosophy.

Analytic philosophy has contained two main sub-traditions. One with Gottlob Frege and Bertrand Russell as the great ones among the founding fathers, and the other with G. E. Moore in a similar role. In the first one, philosophy came to be identified with conceptual analysis, logic and the construction of artificial languages; in the second sub-tradition, philosophy was in some way or other to be confined within the limits of ordinary language. However, as is often the case, the founding fathers were somewhat atypical; at least in the beginning. Russell was a real metaphysician who (now and then) advocated phenomenalism, and in the paper which triggered off Moore's career, *The Refutation of Idealism*,[14] Moore defended direct realism without any appeals to common sense or to ordinary language. Later on, of course, he changed strategy and tried to make common sense the final arbiter in both epistemology and ontology. Founding fathers apart, the important thing now is that in both these sub-traditions natural science, realistically conceived, was put aside and philosophy was restricted to language. Each in their own way, like the phenomenological movement, put realist science within parenthesis.

In the Russellian line of analytic philosophy, science was highly esteemed, but it was claimed that philosophers *as philosophers* could not say anything about the world. Scientists were accorded a monopoly on claims about the world; philosophers could only indirectly be of help in the attempt to get knowledge about the external world. Philosophers could analyse the concepts of science but no more. This is the so-called under-labourer conception of philosophy. Logical positivism, which belonged to this sub-tradition, turned most scientific theories into instrumentalist theories by means of their principle of verifiability. Ontological problems were claimed to be literally meaningless. This means that it is impossible to discuss what I have called the Cartesian-Lockean heritage.

In the ordinary language tradition science was given no prominence at all. Moore's classic *A Defence of Common Sense*[15] could just as well have been called *A Defence of the Life-World*. Common sense is for Moore more secure than science. Later on, Gilbert Ryle and the so-called Oxford Philosophy, explicitly claimed that the central aim of philosophy is to analyse ordinary language; or, to use Ryle's phrase, "determine the logical geography of concepts" and "rectify the logical geography of the knowledge which we already possess".[16] In Ryle's *The Concept of Mind* this move amounts to almost exactly the same thing as the epoché of the phenomenological movement. Before he mounts his attack on the Cartesian ghost in the machine he says that: "It will be argued here that the central principles of the doctrine are unsound and conflict with the whole body of what we know about minds when we are not speculating about them."[17]

It was also within Oxford philosophy that the life-world conception of *agency* first entered analytic philosophy. I think there is a simple reason why ordinary language philosophy is so close to the phenomenological philosophy of the life-world. Without perception there is no language, and ordinary language is permeated by ordinary perception. In everyday life, we *say* we simply see a tree or see another person because that is the way the world is *perceptually presented* to us. At Royaumaunt in France 1958, Oxford philosophers met phenomenological philosophers at a conference. Ryle read a paper called *Phenomenology versus 'The Concept of Mind'*.[18] In the discussion which followed both Herman van Bréda and Maurice Merleau-Ponty stressed that there are strong similarities between Ryle's views and those of the phenomenological tradition. Van Bréda said:

> It seems to me – and I will conclude with this minor point – that many phenomenologists practice in Europe, after Husserl, the same genre of analysis which occurs at Oxford; but they do not have the same temptation – pardon my use of this word – to hypostatize language [*langage*], to hypostatize expression [*langue*], to hypostatize the concept and the word; in this instance the Oxford analysts show themselves to be excellent Platonists, which Husserl is not.[19]

Merleau-Ponty made in the discussion it clear that he had worked with Ryle's book,[20] and he started his contribution as follows:

> I have also had the impression, while listening to Mr. Ryle, that what he was saying was not so strange to us, and that the distance, if there is a distance, is one that he puts between us rather than one I find there.[21]

So much for phenomenology and analytic philosophy in relation to science and the Cartesian-Lockean problem. Similar things can be said also about the philosophy of later Wittgenstein and German hermeneutics. In my opinion, these traditions have taught us a lot about ordinary language, scientific language, perception and intentionality in general, but they are all wrong in denying the Cartesian-Lockean problem admission to philosophy.

Connection at a distance

Phenomenology has taught us that reductive materialism is obviously false. We all intermittently have intentional acts (veridical and illusory perceptions, images, acts of imagination, dreams, thoughts, etc.). This is impossible to deny. It is a truth as secure as any scientific truth; and intentionality cannot possibly be reduced to the kind of categories which make up natural facts in general or neurophysiological facts in particular. Ordinary materialist properties (like having shape, mass and electromagnetic properties) and relations (like being larger, being at a distance from, and being caused by) do not have the kind of directedness which constitutes intentionality.[22] Not even a velocity has the same kind of directedness as thinking and perceiving have, even though a velocity "points" in space.[23] I agree completely with John Searle when, in his book *Intentionality,* he writes:

> My own approach to mental states and events has been totally realistic in the sense that I think there really are such things as intrinsic mental phenomena which cannot be reduced to something else or eliminated by some kind of re-definition. There really are pains, tickles and itches, beliefs, fears, hopes, desires, perceptual experiences, experiences of acting, thoughts, feelings, and all the rest. Now you might think that such a claim was so obviously true as to be hardly worth making, but the amazing thing is that it is routinely denied, though usually in a disguised form, by many, perhaps most, of the advanced thinkers who write on these topics. I have seen it claimed that mental states can be entirely defined in terms of their causal relations, or that pains were nothing but machine table states of certain kinds of computer systems, or that correct attributions of Intentionality were simply a matter of predictive success to be gained by taking a certain kind of "intentional stance" toward systems. I don't think that any of these views are even close to the truth…"[24]

Intentionality cannot be denied. Let us now investigate the peculiarities of that intentional phenomenon we ordinarily call veridical perception, and let us see whether veridical perception can be interpreted in a way which solves at least some of the problems which perceptual psychology poses for it. The first thing to be noted is that veridical perception contains what might be called *connection at a distance*. In the perception of a tree (see figure 2), the perceiving person is by intentionality connected with the tree despite the spatial distance between them. In veridical perception there is, so to speak, a 'hop' in space. A real material unit like a stone (i.e. *not* an aggregate like a number of stones spread out on the ground) is usually thought of as being compact in space, i.e. all its parts are contiguous in space. Veridical perception, however, is different. When a person perceives a thing, the person is at a particular place in space and the thing at another. The visual act connects the person and the thing without 'filling out' the space between them.

In physics, *action at a distance* has ever since Newton been looked upon with suspicion. The gravitational forces of Newtonian mechanics looked mysterious even to Newton himself. How can the sun momentarily affect the earth which is eight light minutes away? How is this distance bridged? Causality means contiguity between cause and effect, but the concept of action at a distance denies this contiguity. Action at a distance is an occult relation. Like telepathy and telekinetics it connects cause and effect by a 'hop' in space.

Independently of whether or not *action* at a distance is possible, the actual existence of *connection* at a distance by means of intentionality is undeniable. It reoccurs in every everyday perception. Nor has anyone really denied it. But most philosophers have been content to say that it must be a mental phenomena, as though this classification would make it more easy to comprehend.

In our life-world there are colours, shapes, and a lot of other properties which are taken to be given facts. Whatever their ontological status is, they do exist. Similarly with connection at a distance. It is a fact that entities which are spatially apart can be directly connected. Whether these entities and the connection itself should be regarded as material, as spiritual, or as something else, may be open for discussion, but not that this kind of connection exists.

X-ray perception

In what follows I shall assume that life-world veridical perception often really is veridical; I shall assume that direct realism is true. And by direct realism I do not mean that form which reduces intentionality to material states and dispositions and which ought to have another name.[25] By direct realism I mean the view that in acts of real intentionality we can be in direct contact with material things and states of affairs.

In veridical perception we reach out towards persons, things, and states of affairs in the world, and sometimes we become connected with them. How, then, one might ask, is this peculiar connection at a distance related to the material things which occupy the intervening space?

According to all our knowledge, be it science or common sense, usually we see through the air. Sometimes, of course, we see through glass or water. The general conclusion is that in visual veridical perception we perceive *through material things*. Connection at a distance is here *not* connection across empty space; it is connection across a materially filled space. Superman is said to have x-ray vision. He can see *through* material buildings. My point is that, apart from perception in outer space, all visual veridical perception can be called x-ray vision.

Michael Polanyi has drawn attention to facts about perceiving which amount to a similar conclusion with regard to the tactual sense, too.[26] Often, tactually, we perceive *through* material things which do not belong to our body. When we write with a pen we are not aware of the hand touching the pen. Instead, we are aware of the pen's touching of the paper. Similarly, when we use a hammer we feel the hammer against the nail, or even the nail against the wood, but not the hand against the hammer. When we are skiing we do not feel our feet against the ski but the ski against the ground.

If we only could be in direct contact with that part of nature which is at the the limits of our body, then we should only see the air just in front of our eyes, and we should only feel what the hands and feets actually meet. This, however, is simply not the case. Often we do, to summarzie the last two sections, perceive *through* material things *to* natural facts which are *at a distance* from us.

Backward perception

Phenomenology tells us that if in veridical perception we can perceive nature, then we do it by means of connection at a distance and x-ray perception. Let us now repeat what today's science tells us. It says that there is some kind of energy flow from a perceived thing to the body of the perceiving person, and it also says that it takes some time for the energy to move from the thing to the person in question. Therefore, we have to accept that intentionality which is connection at a *spatial* distance is also connection at a *temporal* distance. When we perceive a thing, we do not perceive it as it is now. We perceive it the the way it was structured when the relevant energy (according to Gibson: electromagnetic radiation with stimulus information) left the thing. This view, by the way, is not strictly confined to science. There are life-world situations which display the phenomena. Thunder comes after the lightning, and when one sees a man hammering at a great distance the blows are heard after they have been seen, and *this difference is perceived*.

The difficulty with intentionality through time, in comparison with instantaneous intentionality, is that it implies that one is in direct contact with states of affairs which no longer exist. Connection at a spatial distance can be rather difficult to accept, but, as first presented, it is nevertheless a relation between a perceiving person and a perceived state of affairs which exist simultaneously. Temporal connection at a distance, on the other hand, connects a presently perceiving person with an earlier existing state of affairs. The farther away the perceived fact is, the more obvious is this temporal relation. Perception of distant stars is the paradigm example. We can see stars which no longer exists. If this really is veridical perception, then veridical perception is *backward perception*.

I have maintained that *most* 20th century philosophers have, in different ways, avoided the problem of direct realism. One of the exceptions to the rule is Roderick Chisholm. He has written the following:

> The belief that people perceive only appearances or that they cannot perceive physical things often results from what seem to be philosophical paradoxes. For example, when we learn about the velocity of light and about the distances of the stars we see at night, we may begin to wonder whether we do see the stars we think we see. And when we are told that stars sometimes disrupt and become extinct and that possibly some of those we see tonight ceased to exist hundreds of years ago, we may feel that there is some paradox involved in supposing that we can perceive anything at all. But the paradox arises only because we tend to assume, until we are taught otherwise, that any event or state of affairs we perceive must exist or occur simultaneously with our perception of it. We tend to assume, more generally, that S can perceive *a* at *t* only if *a* exists at *t*. If we combine this assumption with what we know about the finite velocity of sound and light, perhaps we can derive the conclusion that no one perceives any of the things he thinks he perceives. But to assume that S can perceive *a* at *t* only if *a* exists at *t* is no more reasonable than to assume that S can receive or reflect light from *a* at *t* only if *a* exists at *t*. The perception of a star that is now extinct should be no more paradoxical than the action of such a star on a photographic plate or its reflection in the water.[27]

To my mind, Chisholm does not take 'the problem of star perception' seriously enough. I agree with him that "the paradox arises only because we tend to assume, until we are taught otherwise, that any event or state of affairs we perceive must exist or occur simultaneously with our perception of it". But there is more to it than Chisholm recognizes. His presumed solution, i.e. the similarity he finds between perception and causality, does not exist. That, today, we can receive light from a non-existing star is of course no mystery. Such light has an existence which is independent of the star which emitted it a long time ago. There is a *causal chain* through time, but each part in such a chain exists only at one moment, and there is no direct connection between two parts which are not contiguous in time. In veridical perception it is different. Chisholm has no clear grasp of the concept of connection at a distance. If direct realism is true in relation to things around us, then we perceive backwards in time, but it is then an extremely short time interval, almost infinitesimal, which we bridge. However, if direct realism is true even for star perception, then we can perceive backwards over a huge time interval. Mostly, we do in one and the same perception perceive things at different distances from us. This means that veridical perceptions of the world are *extended backwards in time*. This is what we have to teach ourselves if we want to be direct realists, but Chisholm doesn't even hint at this. As far as I know, there is only one philosopher who has stated this feature of perception clearly, and that is Samuel Alexander at the beginning of this century, but, for some reason, he mentioned it only in a footnote.[28]

In the former section I claimed that *connection at a distance*, which is a feature of veridical perception, is something other than *action at a distance*, which (if it is at all possible, which I think it isn't) is a kind of causality among material entities. Similarly, *backward perception* is a feature of veridical perception which must not be conflated with *backward causation*, which (if it is at all possible, which I think it isn't) is a kind of causality among material entities. In the next section we shall see that the existence of these features means that the limits of our ego are undetermined and very changeable.

The changeful limits of our ego

What I have said about veridical perception has repercussions for our conception of the human ego. The history of philosophy contains several different ontologies of the ego which I find false in every important respect. I have already mentioned one such ontology, reductive materialism. Another easily refuted metaphysics is the one which takes intentionality on the one hand, and materialist categories on the other, to be merely different ways of apprehending the same phenomena. Such a Spinozist multiple aspect theory is reflexively inconsistent. The phrase 'different ways of apprehending' presupposes the category of intentionality. An act of apprehension is an intentional act, which means that a Spinozist view amounts to saying that intentionality and materialist categories relate to the same substance apprehended in different intentional acts. The last use of 'intentional act' cannot be replaced by any phrase contaning concepts which only refer to materialist or other non-intentional categories, which means that 'the intentional aspect' as a whole cannot possibly be equivalent with 'the materialist aspect'.

The falsity of ontologies which, like those of Descartes, Locke, Leibniz and Berkeley, regard the ego as a *spiritual* substance, is not as total as that of reductive materialism. Such substance ontologies of the ego do not deny the existence of irreducibly mental phenomena, but they lack a clear conception of intentionality. They have not noted a certain feature of intentionality, *the non-substantiality of the ego*, which Heidegger and Sartre[29] brought to our attention.

Heidegger characterises man by saying, among other things, that man's situation in the world is one of "Geworfenheit" (= thrownness). Man is in a sense throwed, flung, or cast out into the world. Sartre describes the essence of man as a Nothingness. Both descriptions, at bottom, focus attention on the fact that the directedness of intentionality is in many, perhaps most, intentional acts not apparent at all in the acts themselves. When we are fascinated by something we are observing, we are just 'thrown out' in the object; we do not perceive ourselves perceiving. We are aware only of the perceived object. The same goes for perceptions accompanying concentrated actions. All there is is the action. We are lost in it. Following Sartre, I shall "call such a consciousness: consciousness in the first degree, or *unreflected* consciousness".[30]

The directedness of intentionality has two poles. One may speak of a 'to-pole' (an intentional object or correlate) and a 'from-pole'. If, now, in a reflective intentional act (i.e. consciousness in the second degree), we try to make the from-pole of an earlier act (i.e. the presumed ego) into the to-pole of this later reflective act, what do we find? When we make an earlier intentional act itself into an intentional correlate, i.e. the to-pole of the present intentional act, we find between the 'from-pole' and the 'to-pole' of the unreflected consciousness nothing similar to a relation between things. In the latter case – think for instance of a perception of the relation of being larger than – we perceive two things and a relation between them. In an *unreflected* intentional act directed towards nature we perceive things and states of affairs but *no* relation between ourselves and the intentional correlates in question. Therefore, it is adequate to say that the to-pole is something, whereas the from-pole of intentionality is empty. The ego which is assumed to exist in the from-pole seems to be thrown out into the to-pole or to be a kind of nothingness, or, better, emptiness.

It should be noted that when a reflective (second degree) intentional act is directed at the from-pole of an unreflected (first degree) act and discovers the corresponding emptiness, the reflective act is not directed at its own from-pole. This from-pole has the same emptiness, but in order to see it a third order act which has the second order act as its intentional correlate is needed.

That the from-poles of intentional acts are empty does not mean that they do not exist. Their existence may be compared to (but not identified with) that of the void (in non-relational conceptions of space). Where there are no things (or fields) in space there is void, but void is not nothing. It is empty space. The from-pole of intentionality is empty but nonetheless it is something. It belongs to reality.

The emptiness or nothingness of the ego is, it is important to note, only an emptiness on the level of intentionality itself. As stressed by another phenomenologist, Maurice Merleau-Ponty, intentionality so to speak radiates from our body.[31] When in reflective acts we are looking for the from-pole of intentionality, we will always find a material body. Moreover, *our own* material body. In this sense we find something, but not what we are looking for. We look for our soul but we find our body. We find a substratum for intentionality. Perceptions are perspectival and they refer back to our body. Only an Aristotelian account of the soul can comprehend this feature of intentionality. Intentional acts presuppose for their existence something which is not part of themselves, namely a body with a nervous system and a brain. The ego, therefore, is neither only a Nothingness nor only a "Geworfenheit". It is a complex unity with both a body and intentionality; the body is a substratum upon which intentional acts are emergent properties.

Looking upon Heidegger and Sartre from this Aristotelian point of view, Heidegger puts too much emphasis on the to-pole and Sartre puts too much stress on the emptiness of the from-pole of the ego. For Heidegger the ego seems to be merely "Geworfenheit", merely the indwelling in the perceived objects and facts; and for Sartre the ego seems to be nothing. The ego is not a pure "Geworfenheit", nor is it merely Nothingness, but neither is it a spiritual or material substance. It is intentionality fused with a body.

Since having perceptions (and having the capability of having perceptions) is part of the essence of human egos, egos cannot have the kind of spatial limits which material things have. Material things are enclosed in a space volume, whereas the ego in veridical perceptions reach out from the body into the world at a distance. Intentionality is not the only kind of phenomena which deviates from the things-with-properties or substance-accidence scheme. Relations like 'being larger than' and 'being more circular than' are not confined to a compact space volume either. Instances of such relations exist in the scattered particulars they relate. The point I want to make, however, is not that intentional acts are some kind of relations. In my view, on the contrary, intentionality is a category distinct from both external, internal and grounded relations.[32] Reality contains several categories which, from the perspective of a substance-accidence scheme, have peculiar spatial limits. Therefore, one should not look for the spatial limits of the ego the same way one looks for the spatial limits of a material thing and its (monadic) properties.

Some things are easy to think, some things are hard. The spatial limits of material objects are easy to think, the spatial limits of the ego is hard to think. Material objects have rather well defined spatial limits even if the limit, like that of a shrinking balloon, is rapidly changing. But intentionality behaves in a different way. It is not limited by other material objects nor by other intentional acts. In veridical perception the ego is fused with natural facts, and the spatial limits of the ego are the spatial limits of its intentional acts. Wherever an intentional act turns the non-perceiving of material things into perceiving, the spatial limit arises. The ego is *not* spatially confined to its body in spite of the fact that its intentional acts are existentially dependent upon the body. Intentionality makes the ego spatially undetermined. Normally, the limits of our ego are changing. At one moment we are looking at states of affairs close to us, and at the next moment we are looking at more distant states of affairs.

The common sense distinction between oneself and external things is easily turned into false philosophical ontologies of the ego, where an inner-outer distinction is wrongly made identical with a distinction between subjective (= mind-dependent) and objective (mind-independent) phenomena. In relation to material things, the distinction between being inner and being outer is clear. What is within the spatial limit of the thing is inner, and that which is outside the limit is outer. But since intentionality does not have the same kind of spatial limits, we are not allowed to think the inner-outer distinction of the whole ego in the same way as we can think the distinction in relation to its body.

Usually, we perceive pains as located within our body. The same is true of our heart beats, of tired muscles, of nervous stomachs, and of other similar phenomena. In cases like these, the intentional correlate is both mind-dependent and inside our body. Subjectivity and inwardness here go together. We perceive ordinary things, plants and animals as located outside our body. Here, objectivity and outwardness go together; the intentional correlates are both mind-independent and outside our body. However, when we perceive the *colours* of the things in question, these intentional correlates are both mind-dependent and outside our body. We have subjectivity and outwardness together. The same is true in visual illusions and hallucinations as well as in tactual illusions like the "phantom pains" of amputated legs. If all mind-dependent intentional correlates are said to be inner, in contradistinction to mind-independent correlates which always are outer, then 'inner' looses its original contrast with 'outside the body', and, consequently, has to take on a completely new meaning. A meaning which has to turn all intentional correlates into inner entities, and we are back into the ontologies of idealism or dualism. In such ontologies nature can never be perceived.

In some intentional acts (like dreams and imaginations) the intentional correlate (the dream and imagination, respectively) is wholly mind-dependent, whereas in other acts (like veridical perception) some parts of the intentional correlate (for instance a material thing) are mind-independent and some parts (for instance colours) are mind-dependent. In the latter cases there is a fusion of mind-dependent and mind-independent parts. *Our egos are not spatially confined within the limits of our bodies*, this is the ontological truth to remember.

The ontology of the ego now sketched contradicts ordinary psychological (and Humean) projection conceptions in which secondary qualities, like colours and other life-world qualities, are projected onto nature. When, with a projector, we project a picture on a screen, there is a picture inside the projector which by means of a light beam is copied on the screen. However, most life-world qualities do not first exist inside our head in order, later, by means of a 'perceptual beam', to be copied out in the world. Their primary existence is outside our body. The projection metaphor is adequate only in those cases of writing and drawing when we know in advance what to write and what to draw. Here, first there are thoughts and then there are corresponding outward-oriented perceptions.

Just as the feature of connection at a distance implies that our egos are not spatially confined within the limits of our bodies, so the feature of backward perception implies that *our present egos are not temporally confined within the limits of the present*. If we are in direct contact with past states of affairs, part of the ego must be extended into the past. The time limits of our egos are, just like the spatial limits, undetermined and changeful. However curious this may seem, it should be noted that, according to the claims put forward here, the ego is never in veridical perception extended into the future. Also, I want to repeat, the closer to the perceiving body a perceived state of affairs is, the closer it is to the present. Our body only exists actually in the present, although it can preserve its identity through time. The body is never extended in time outside the present, only some acts of intentionality are.

Life-world in contact with nature or monadology

If we want to claim that, in our life-world, we do really perceive parts of nature, then we have to accept that veridical perception is x-ray perception, backward perception and connection at a distance; we also have to accept that our ego has no determinate spatial and temporal limits. Peculiar features. Perhaps they are too odd to believe in. But, we have to ask, on what grounds are we to take the decision to accept them or reject them? Since most philosophers nowadays are fallibilists in epistemology, the problem is not that I cannot *prove* that in (so-called) veridical perception we are in contact with nature. The only thing a fallibilist can do is to estimate the reasonableness of this view in comparison with other possible alternatives. Of course, one should choose the most credible view; or, as in this case, the least incredible alternative. In order to reject veridical perception, we have to find an ontological alternative which is cheaper. What, then, are the main alternatives to real veridical perception?

For many thinkers reductive materialism gives us the truth about perception, but, as is clear from my earlier remarks on this view, I regard reductive materialism as the most incredible of all views. It simply denies the obvious fact of connection at distance. Therefore, to my mind, the main alternative is the claim that connection at a distance is possible only in a completely mental sphere. In idealist conceptions and in indirect realism there is no need to postulate either x-ray perception or backward perception. If all intentional acts are wholly mental, then it is tautologically true that x-ray perception (i.e. perception through material things) is impossible. Backward perception, on the other hand, is not ruled out in principle, but there seems to be no reason at all to claim that there is a temporal distance between the perceiving person and that which is perceived. Note, though, that connection at a distance is not explained away. It is merely maintained that connection at a distance is wholly mental. There is no denial of my claim that the existence of connection at a distance is an indisputable fact.

If we dismiss idealism, be it old-fashioned or linguistic, then 'the mental alternative', taken together with perceptual psychology, implies a monadology. We are back in some kind of Cartesian-Lockean ontology. Every person is confined within his own mental world. The only connection which exists between people and between people and things are causal relations in the material part of reality. If we are not to abandon completely the belief that our life-worlds have something in common, we are forced in this ontology, as was Leibniz in his, to postulate a predetermined harmony among all the numerically different mental spheres. Fundamentally, we each live in our own mental world, but the worlds have great similarities with one another. Ontologically, we are as beings with a consciousness, in contradistinction to clumps of pure matter, completely and helplessly isolated from one another. My life-world is only mine and your life-world is only yours; even when our bodies, which are part of nature, are as close to each other as they can be. If life-world and nature is kept apart, the life-world breaks apart, too.

As far as I can see, our fallibilist ontological choice today consists, to put it sharply, in either accepting a monadology or accepting a direct realism wich contains the peculiarities of connection at distance, x-ray perception, backward perception and undetermined limits of the ego. In my opinion, the monadological alternative is more incredible than direct realism with its implications.

What is most difficult to accept in the kind of naive realism, or life-world realism, which I am advocating, is of course that part which is not directly in keeping with genuine naive realism, namely the view that one perceives across or through time, not at one particular moment. But, I want to stress once again, 'through time' is always connected with 'through space'. The farther we get in time, the farther we have to get in space. Normally, when in one and the same instant we are looking at several things whose spatial distance to us varies, we perceive them as simultaneous. According to the view I have argued for, this must be wrong. Space cannot in veridical perception open itself towards more distant states of affairs without time's also opening itself – and vice versa. It is an illusion that ordinary veridical perceptions are momentary in time. If this is accepted, then it is not too difficult to accustom oneself to the view that one can perceive backwards through time.

The perceptual bridge and other bridges

The problem of perception is merely one of a number of ontological problems which need to be solved before we get a stable philosophical connection between life-world and man-independent nature. Apart from the problem of perception, there are also the problem of agency (or of mental causation) and the connected problem of how to reconcile (to speak with Kant) causality of freedom with causality of nature. In our life-world we take it for granted both that our will can affect our body and that our actions are not wholly predetermined by natural laws, be they deterministic or statistical; indeterminism is something other than freedom.

I shall not discuss the problems of agency and determinism here, merely mention that they, like the problem of perception, can be viewed from a new perspective now that fallibilism reigns supreme in epistemology. Fallibilism means that neither ontologists nor scientists can speak with the voice of the one who has recourse to absolute truth. Philosophers can contest science and scientists can contest philosophy. A philosopher who contests science, need not and should not, regard himself as a 'master-scientist' standing above science; and a scientist who contests philosophy, need not and should not, take recourse to scientific views. This means, among a lot of other things, that the reductive views of the natural scientists should not have too much authority in ontology. Science cannot in and of itself show that the life-world experience of agency is false, and that, therefore, the concept of freedom should be wholly replaced by that of causality of nature.

The existence of agency implies that the future cannot be wholly predetermined. Something must be open. This means that veridical perception *through time into the future* is impossible. Forward perception conflicts with agency, but backward perception does not. And I have only argued for backward perception.

Conclusion

I do think that we are philosophically entitled to say that we, in our life-world, can be in contact with nature and with each other. However, since I regard my ontological views as fallible, I shall end by letting Nature herself speak. I can hear her saying: "To be perceived, or not to be perceived: that is the question." She is looking at a skull. A philosopher's skull. She wants it alive again.

Biography

Ingvar Johansson is associate professor at the Department for philosophy and philosophy of science, Umeå University, Sweden. He has been working both within philosophy of science (main work: *A Critique of Karl Popper's Methodology,* Scandinavian University Books 1975) and in ontology (main work: *Ontological Investigations,* Routledge 1989). He is member of the board for the Nordic Institute for Philosophy.

Notes

1. This paper develops thoughts that I have earlier argued for in my *Ontological Investigations*, Routledge: London 1989, chapter 13.7. Apart from the participants in the discussion at Odense, I want to thank Kevin Mulligan, Stefan Hansson, and Torbjörn Jakobsson for helpful comments.
2. Locke, *An Essay Concerning Human Understanding,* vol. one, book II, chapter IX, section 3.

3. Descartes, *Principles of Philosophy*, part IV, principle CLXXXIX.
4. They are, in turn, figures 7, 29, and 38 from *L'homme*.
5. Russell, *History of Western Philosophy*, Allen & Unwin: London 1974, p 591.
6. Irvin Rock, *Perception*, Scientific American Books: New York 1984, p 5. What follows is in close accordance with Rock's views as presented on pp 8-13.
7. Rock, ibid. p 12, calls it "the stimulus perspective".
8. See *The Senses Considered as Perceptual Systems*, Houghton Mifflin: Boston 1966.
9. *Reasons for Realism. Selected Essays of James J. Gibson*, eds. E. Reed & R. Jones, Lawrence Erlbaum Ass.: London 1982.
10. Josef Seifert, *Back to 'Things in Themselves'*, Routledge & Kegan Paul: London 1987.
11. Ibid. p 28.
12. Burnet, *Early Greek Philosophy*, London 1920, p 194.
13. Ibid. p 248-49.
14. Reprinted in Moore, *Philosophical Studies*, London 1922.
15. Reprinted in Moore, *Philosophical Papers*, London 1959.
16. Ryle *The Concept of Mind*, Hutchinson: London 1975, pp 8 & 7.
17. Ibid., p 11.
18. See Ryle, *Collected Papers,* vol. 1, chapter 11, Thoemmes: Bristol 1990.
19. Merleau-Ponty, *Texts and Dialogues*, (eds. Silverman & Barry, Jr.) Humanities Press: London 1992, p 61.
20. Ibid. p 67.
21. Ibid. p 65.
22. I have given a detailed argumentation of this irreducibility thesis in my *Ontological Investigations*, Routledge: London 1989, chapter 13.5.
23. For detailed arguments for this view see my paper 'Intentionality and tendency: How to make Aristotle up to date', in K. Mulligan (ed.) *Language, Truth and Ontology*, Dordrecht: Amsterdam 1992.
24. Searle, *Intentionality*, Cambridge University Press: Cambridge, 1983, p 262.
25. I am thinking of philosophers like D. M. Armstrong, *A Materialist Theory of the Mind*, Routledge: London 1968, and G. Pitcher, *A Theory of Perception*, Princeton UP: New Jersey 1971.
26. *Personal Knowledge*, Harper: New York 1962, chapter 4:5.
27. Chisholm, *Perceiving: A Philosophical Study*, Cornell UP: New York 1957, p 153.
28. See 'The method of metaphysics; and the categories', *Mind N.S. 21*:1-20, p 3 note 2 (1912). He says that any experience means "compresence within the world of the experiencer and the experienced", and the footnote reads "Perhaps I should say at once that compresence does not mean simultaneity in time. I am compresent with a past event which I apprehend. And indeed the events I perceive always are past, by however small an interval. Compresent means simply belonging to the same universe."
29. I am thinking of their famous books *Being and Time* and *Being and Nothingness,* respectively. Sartre´s position, however, is more lucid in his *The Transcendence of the EGO,* Noonday Press: New York 1957.
30. *The Transcendence of the EGO*, p 41.
31. *Phenomenology of Perception*, Routledge & Kegan Paul: London 1962.
32. See *Ontological Investigations,* chapter 13.5.

Simo Knuuttila

Plenitude, Reason and Value: Old and New in the Metaphysics of Nature

Abstract
The questions of the origin of the universe dealth with in modern physical cosmologies are analysed from the point of view of their argumentative patterns. Contemporary models of ultimate explanations are then compared with similar ways of thinking in the history of philosophy. It is shown how critical evaluation of contemporary physical metahysics gains form an acquaintance with the classical discussions of the nature of modalities, explanation, and understanding.

There are scientists who think that a mathematical unified theory of all forces and elementary particles and of the structure of space and time is feasible. Some of them believe that they almost have such an all-embracing theory from which the physical and cosmological properties of the world can be deduced by the application of reason alone. The questions of the origin of the universe and the cosmological conditions of life dealt with in this kind of literature have become popular themes even in the media. (See, e.g., Barrow 1990, Davies 1992.)

The desire for scientific completeness accompanies a desire for a unified picture of the world, and these are traditionally considered virtuous scientific longings. I assume that most scientists do not believe in any great final fulfilment of these desires, at least not in the near future, and there are lots of philosophers who have found the whole idea of a final completion of science as badly confused, though it has often figured in the modern conception of scientific progress since the days of Paracelsus and Bacon. In any event, it is remarkable that this view is as popular as it is and that it is particularly applied to those interpretations of quantum physics and cosmology which show similarities to classical metaphysical theories. This scientific or semi-scientific interest in ultimate explanations has for its part stimulated philosophical investigations of the nature of metaphysical questions and arguments and the ways in which they possibly make sense.

In the first part of this paper, I shall discuss some features of the modern metaphysics of the universe and nature from the point of view of its argumentative patterns. In the second part I shall compare certain aspects of the modern models of ultimate explanations with similar ways of thinking in the history of philosophy.

1. Modes of Explanation in the Metaphysics of Nature

Most physicists believe that the universe is expanding and that its clusters of galaxies are flying away from each other at an increasing speed, as is taken to be revealed by the systematic redshifting of the light from distant sources. In the Big Bang theory, all separations are assumed to extrapolate back to zero at an apparent beginning about fifteen billion years ago. It is also assumed that the initial conditions of the expansion were fixed during a very short time after the beginning and that the situation then was largely at variance with the observed laws of nature. The theories pertaining to the initial stage of cosmic evolution are pretty much on the speculative side, but they are described in popular works on modern cosmology as if they were its main achievements.

The living systems of Earth are based upon the chemical properties of carbon and their combination with hydrogen, nitrogen, phosphorus, and oxygen. According to current cosmological theories, these elements are the results of nuclear reactions in the interior of stars which have been blown out into space when the stars have exploded. These biological elements are then incorporated into molecules, planets, living organism, and people. The conditions necessary for the evolution of stars and life were fixed before the expansion which is subjected to the known laws of nature, and these initial presuppositions had to be very much those they are. If some basic constituents of nature were not within one per cent of their present values, then the required elements of life would not exist in the universe.

Is there any explanation for the fact that of the seemingly countless possible initial conditions those that actually obtained were the ones that allowed for life? One might think that there is nothing to be explained, since there had to be some conditions and the actual ones were not less likely than any others. But the point of the question is usually taken to be slightly different.

It is first assumed that life and consciousness are something special and it is asked why it was precisely the universe in which there are conscious beings that was produced. (For the discussions of the fine-tuning of the universe, see Barrow and Tipler 1986.)

Some physicists, philosophers, and theologians have argued as follows. If the fine-tuning of the Big Bang just mentioned is a mere coincidence, the probability of this accident is very low. As the coincidence explanation is that unlikely, it is more reasonable to think that the Big Bang was fine-tuned, because God or some purposeful intellect chose to produce life. Even though God's existence was not very probable, it is more probable than the extreme improbability of the accidental fine-tuning of the Big Bang. Therefore the designer theory provides a better explanation.(See, e.g., Swinburne 1990, Davies 1992, Craig in Craig and Smith 1993.)

Other writers have suggested that there are many universes which are not causally related to each other and which have emerged from similar Big Bangs. If there were enough of them, it would not be strange that in some of them conditions were right for life. In arguing for this approach, Derek Parfit (1992) asks whether we have any reason to believe in the many worlds hypothesis. He thinks that we have since the existence of many worlds would explain the appearance of fine-tuning without reference to a divine agent. This makes it less puzzling. The arguments in the discussion of the relative simplicity of explanations are not very different from those formulated in the 17th and 18th century debates about natural theology. I shall not comment on this theme. It has been also remarked that the question itself is unclear in many ways. As for the specialness of life, Peirce has already mentioned that there is no natural way to quantify the intrinsic improbability of the different requirements for life. Furthermore, we can imagine that the initial conditions could have been different from what they are, but we don't know whether the alternatives are real possibilities. (For some further epistemic problems dealt with in works on the so-called Anthropic Principle, see Barrow and Tipler 1986, Bertola and Curi 1989.)

The traditional Big Bang theory suggests that the universe began at the beginning subsequent to a singularity at which the space-time and the laws of nature were broken down and from which anything could come out. In the chaotic inflationary modifications of this picture, it is assumed that minute local regions can inflate independently of all the others by different amounts determined by their local conditions which may vary in a random fashion. The idea of arbitrarily many worlds is also included in different vacuum fluctuation theories.

Some general conceptual presuppositions of these theories can be formulated as follows. There are numerous possible universes which can be actual in different combinations, and it is also possible that there is no universe at all. We could call the possibilities which cover all alternative conjugations of causally independent possible worlds as universal possibilities. One extreme of the universal possibilities is that all worlds exist and another it that nothing ever exists. Between these boundaries, there are countless combinations of particular possible worlds. The traditional Big Bang theory takes the Big Bang singularity as a brute fact. Quentin Smith (1993) has argued that it is reasonable to believe that the Big Bang singularity occurs uncaused and that its future cannot even in principle be predicted. The critics have found it strange to think that the actual universe began to exist from nothing and without any cause. Their views can be classified in four groups: (1) the universe is probably infinitely old, (2) the universe began to exist and its beginning was caused by God, (3) the universe is because it is of a certain kind, (4) evidence in unsufficient to enable us to decide the questions of this kind.

Smith's view does not deviate from the starting point of traditional metaphysics that there cannot be any causal explanation of existence as such, but in the traditional theories this was considered the reason why there must must be something which is necessarily existent. (See, e.g., Leibniz's treatise 'On the Ultimate Origination of Things' in Leibniz: *Philosophical Writings*, ed. G.H.R. Parkinson 1973, 136-7.) If we should decide between the pictures of the universe as a temporally finite brute fact and as an infinitely old brute fact, I think that most people would choose the second alternative. It is less at variance with generally accepted basic assumptions and hence less puzzling – one is not obliged to think that something begins from nothing. If the universe is in some way infinitely old, it is possible to ask why it is so. What would be the decision between the pictures of an infinitely old contingent universe and an infinitely old necessary universe or a universe caused by a necessary being? If it is possible that nothing exists, there is no necessary being. The theists should either think that it is impossible that nothing is or that God is not a necessary being.

Some thinkers have accepted the inflationary scenario due to the fine-tuning arguments. The obtaining of the global possibility which includes our world and many other worlds is easier to explain than the universal alternative which includes only our world, if both are random and without an ultimate explanation. As far as this line of thought is the main motivation for many worlds theories, they can be regarded as naturalistic metaphysical theories. They offer reasons to believe that one universal possibility obtains rather than another, but they do not attempt to explain why there is something rather than nothing.

The theories of the uncaused beginning and the world ensembles theories are not the only alternatives to metaphysical theism (2). In the paper quoted above Derek Parfit describes one further contemporary approach (3) as follows. In traditional metaphysics as well as in the discussions motivated by recent cosmological research it is often thought that reality has some special features, such as being maximal, being the best possible, having the most elegant mathematical structure or providing the optimal conditions for life. If the universal possibility actually realized has such a special feature, it seems hard to believe that it only happens to have it. We could assume that some possibility obtains because it is the best or the simplest or the least arbitrary or because it makes reality maximal or its fundamental laws are mathematically the most beautiful. "If some possibility obtains because it has some feature, that feature selects what reality is like. Let us call it the Selector. A feature is a plausible Selector if we can reasonably believe that, were reality to have that feature, that would not merely happen to be true." Although there are universal possibilities which are special in the sense of having a plausible selector, in the largest range of the global possibilities there is an arbitrary set of messily complicated worlds without any selector. If ours is one such world, it has no explanation of any kind. It is a brute fact.

If reality were randomly selected and there were no explanation of why it is as it is, one could ask why that should be true. It is not logically necessary that it is so and has no explanation, because there are other explanatory possibilities. It would therefore make sense to ask why the actual universe is a brute fact, if it is a brute fact. But all explanatory possibilities raise this same further question, if they are not self-explanatory. In order to show that this does not frustrate the quest for the existence of anything, Parfit suggests that we should think as follows. Our world may seem to have a selecting feature, and we might reasonably suspect that the world exists because it has this feature. That hypothesis might lead us to confirm that our world does have this feature. Asking why in this primary sense may lead us to see truths about the whole world or, if ours is not the only world, about the whole universe. Even if all explanations must end with a brute fact, the brute fact need not enter at the lowest level.

This way of looking at ultimate explanations is largely based on the form of argument included in John Leslie's axiarchic theory of why the universe exists (1989). On Leslie's view, the universe exists because it is good that it does so. There is a best way for reality to be, which directly explains why reality is that way. It is supposed that there are evaluative truths which are 'creatively effective'. That the universe exists as a result of 'ethical requirement' makes it look designed, even if it has not been. Abstracting from the special content of this argument, its formal structure, in Parfit's terminology, is as follows. One universal possibility has a plausible selecting feature. This is the possibility that obtains, and it is reasonable to think that it obtains because it has this feature.

This line of thought is an application of the principle of sufficient reason. What is methodologically interesting in it is the attempt to formulate some kind of abductive logic of an ultimate explanation that is neither causal nor teleological in any traditional sense. It is possible that when our knowledge of the universe increases, some basically new types of explanation become part of our intellectual culture. Relative to our present knowledge, it is wise not to have very strong opinions about whether the universe has any metaphysically special features, though it is not irrational to feel that way and to think that it exists just for that reason. But perhaps it is not less irrational to feel that the world has no such features and to think that it has no explanation. (See Smith 1993.) If there were good reasons in the future to believe that the world exists because it is of certain kind, it is not clear whether people would change their way of living for this reason. To be a human being is something very different from being a particle or a universe even when the ultimate answer to the question of why they are would be the same. It is somewhat disappointing that all contemporary selector candidates are taken from traditional metaphysical discussions. Perhaps one should not be very optimistic regarding the future developments of this line of thought.

2. Defining Possibilities

The notion of possible worlds used above is metaphysical and not the standard conception of possible worlds used in the so-called possible worlds semantics. Metaphysically possible worlds are causally independent universes. The above classification of them deviates from the tenets of ancient philosophy in many ways. For one thing, it is assumed that nothingness is one alternative. There is a long tradition which has found this view totally unintelligible. Accepting the null possibility destroys the (Scotist or Leibnizian) proof of God's existence where the possibility of a necessary being implies its actual existence. It is also assumed above that the maximal universal possibility is a special case which would need explanation. Those ancient thinkers who thought, as the atomists did, that the conception of the plurality of worlds makes sense, took it for granted that they are all actual. The same view was also put forward by some Renaissance thinkers, including Bruno. One can find related ideas in some many-worlds interpretations of quantum cosmology (see Gale 1990.) Let us have a look at at the history of this notion.

The idea that all genuine possibilities or types of possibilities will be realized has not been unusual in the history of philosophy. In his famous book *The Great Chain of Being* (1936) Arthur A. Lovejoy studied the history of three basic ideas of Western thought. One of them he called the Principle of Plenitude, the view that no genuine possibility remains unrealized. Lovejoy gives several examples of the Principle of Plenitude from Plato to Schelling, but the general approach of the book is not without problems. Contrary to what Lovejoy thought, the Principle of Plenitude is not a unit idea which different authors at different times have made use of or included in their philosophical systems as an unchanging element. As shown by Jaakko Hintikka (1981), it is rather a special view of the balance sheet between possibility and actuality which individual authors have applied to quite different conceptions of possibilities. Correspondingly, the principle has had different meanings for them.

It is commonly thought that John Duns Scotus made a remarkable contribution to the emergence of the modern idea of what could be called the theory of modality as referential multiplicity, i.e. the theory that the meaning of modal notions is basically spelled out with the help of the model of synchronic alternative states of affairs. The notion of logical necessity refers to what obtains in all alternatives, the notion of possibility refers to what obtains at least in one alternative, and that which is logically impossible does not obtain in any conceivable state of affairs. This basic model can be applied to more restricted real modalities by modifying the alternatives and it can also be given a diachronic interpretation.

The principle of plenitude plays no role in this analysis of the meaning of modal notions, but in ancient philosophy it was included in the standard philosophical interpretations of the modal terms. Several different modal paradigms were used and distinguished in ancient philosophy, but none included the view of synchronic alternatives just mentioned. In ancient modal theories, modal terms were taken to refer to the one and only historical world of ours, and it was commonly thought that all generic types of possibilities had to prove their mettle through actualization. All ancient schools of philosophy accepted the view of the necessity of the present formulated in Chapter 9 of Aristotle's *De interpretatione*, and it was correspondingly assumed that what always is, is by necessity. Although some elements of the theory of the diachronic model of modalities occur in different authors and unrealized individual possibilities were touched on in this connection, the idea of synchronic alternatives was not applied in ancient modal philosophy. (For the history of modal conceptions in ancient and medieval philosophy, see Knuuttila 1993.)

The new theory came to be discussed in early medieval thought, originally with a theological motivation. Some twelfth century authors called it the Christian view of possibility, as distinct from the received philosophical conception of possibility. It seems, however, that the significance of the new modal semantics was not fully recognized before John Duns Scotus, William Ockham and Jean Buridan who developed it in a way which shows striking similarities to contemporary possible worlds semantics. Late medieval modal logic and semantics was well-known to Leibniz who has been mistakenly regarded as the creator of this interpretation of modal terms.

The emergence of possible worlds semantics in late medieval thought changed philosophical discussion of many traditional questions. Theories assuming that all possibilities will be realized had now to explain which kinds of possibilities were meant and why this view was taken to be true of possibilities of that kind. Perhaps the most significant metaphysical consequence of the new modal thinking was that the actual universe was taken to be one possible world, some alternatives to which were regarded as physically possible and some as conceptually possible. The question of how the borderline between these different types of necessities and possibilities should be drawn was found interesting and difficult, not least because the new distinction implied a radical re-evaluation of the traditional concept of nature: its laws and structures were no longer considered logically necessary.

Some analogical problems are treated in recent cosmological and physical theories. These theories have altered our picture of the universe and they have influenced our general modes of thinking to some extent. The changes are not as deep as in late medieval times, however. Although the modal terms are much used in the discussions of quantum indeterminacy, chaotic processes, initial conditions and other related themes, they are mainly employed in a whay which is in accordance with the rules codified in the possible worlds semantics. The creation of this modal semantics was a more radical innovation than what has taken place in modern science. It demanded profound reorganization of the basic level of understanding. It is of some interest to notice, however, that the distinction between physical and logical possibilities is often dealt with in contemporary physical and cosmological literature and that some new problems are encountered in this connection. Contrary to what has been sometimes maintained, the ideas of statistical laws and probabilistic potencies or propensities have a long tradition in the history of philosophy. (Knuuttila 1993.) The interesting new problems are connected with certain other aspects of the theories.

One motive for keeping to the distinction between physical and logical possibilities is the felt importance of some kind of demarcation between science and fiction. But if the empirical results are imbedded in theories according to which the initial conditions and even the laws of nature can be different in different existing universes, it becomes difficult to fix the limits of what should be regarded as physically possible. Let us look at Quentin Smith's arguments (1993) for the view that Big Bang singularity is the first uncaused physical state. Smith accepts the traditional view of natural possibility as something which is consistent with the known laws and some initial conditions of nature. The singularity is said to be a real physical state in which all known natural laws break down. If it is real, it must be possible, but apparently it is not physically or naturally possible in the traditional sense. There are similar problems in the many worlds theories with respect to initial conditions. It is thought that there are possible states of affairs which generate the domain of physical possibilities. They do not belong to physical possibilities, but they are actual in the same reality in which physical possibilities are actualized. A satisfactory theory of physical possibilities would be very helpful here.

3. The Metaphysics of Understanding

There are important and well-known differences between the metaphysics of Plato and Aristotle, but both of them postulate an eternal and invariant formal level of being which makes particular things what they are and which can make the human soul a conscious copy of the formal basic structure of reality. This double function of the formal level as the shaper of being and intellect made Plato's and Aristotle's epistemology extremely realistic and gave the philosophy the high distinction of making the soul directly acquainted with the ultimate basis of reality. Plato and Aristotle proceeded to the formal structure of being from the question of why the universe is as it is: why it seemingly includes a great variety of invariant modes of being, why it has just those modes of being it has, and why the human mind tends to see it as an ordered whole. They thought that when the intellect comes to know the formal structure of reality, it becomes a conscious instance of the universal code of everything. It has then an inside view into the ultimate foundations of being and sees the visible world as its imitation or explication.

It is typical of this approach that the perfection of the intellect takes place through a certain participation in the intelligibility of the universe and not through an interpretation of it. The same view is later repeated in slightly different terms in Stoic and Neoplatonic philosophy. As the intelligible structure (ideas, forms, Logos) was considered eternal and necessary, there was no reason to ask whether it could be different, and as far as this structure was connected with a possibility of its visible imitation or instantiation and it was thought that no generic possibility remained unrealized, the existence of the visible universe was not found a puzzling question at all. I think that it is this unified view of being and understanding which even now makes ancient metaphysical thought, often in a more Spinozist form, attractive to many people. It offers a romantic non-Kantian answer to the question of what comprehension of things is.

Nobel prize-winning particle physicist Steven Weinberg writes: "There is one clue in today's elementary particle physics that we are not only at the deepest level we can get right now, but we are at a level which is in fact in absolute terms quite deep, perhaps close to the final source." Weinberg concludes that the fact that the rules which have been discovered become increasingly coherent and universal is probably not an accident, but "there is a simplicity, a beauty, that we are finding in the rules that govern matter that mirrors something that is built into the logical structure of the universe at a very deep level." What does it mean to find a theory of the structure of reality that is deep in absolute terms? Apparently it is a theory which does not pose further questions and to which other partial explanations are reduced. As for the beauty and simplicity of such a supertheory, Albert Einstein stated that "a theory which in its fundamental equations explicitly contains a constant would have to be somehow constructed from bits and pieces which are logically independent of each other; but I am confident that this world is not such that so ugly a construction is needed for its theoretical comprehension." Einstein's view of the ultimate truth did not include logically independent parts: "I cannot imagine a unified and reasonable theory which explicitly contains a number which the whim of the Creator might just as well have chosen differently, whereby a qualitatively different lawfulness of the world would have resulted." (For these quotations, see Barrow 1990.)

If the main structure of the universe were algorithmically compressible in the way some scientists believe, it would certainly be a significant feature of reality. It would not be a metaphysical selector, however, because it is assumed to be the only consistent theory of reality. When it is thought that all prima facie contingent constants can be eliminated from the theory of everything, the universe would be necessarily as it is and wholly understandable through the unified theory. Those who have found this view attractive are motivated by ideas which are not very different from those on which Plato and Aristotle based their general views of the aim of natural philosophy and which made them to feel at home in the universe.

Modern theories of everything should also unite their adherents to the ultimate structure of being and make them its conscious instances. A realist interpretation of an ultimate mathematical code provides the same form for the universe and for informed minds. This way of thinking exceeds the alleged dichotomy between explanation and understanding as two different modes of cognitive orientation. It has been said that explanation pertains to nature which remains strange and external to us and understanding concerns the experience of being which is internal and familiar to us. But comprehending the ultimate mathematical structure of reality would be understanding oneself as the fully informed consciousness of this structure.

The number of the philosophers who regard this as a real option is not very large. The others have to be satisfied with much more mundane ideas about comprehension and understanding, except the metaphysical theists. They are inclined to interpret many of the possibly felt special features of the universe as hallmarks of its divine designer. This line of thought has, of course, a long history. As distinct from the classical cosmological view, cosmological theists usually assume that there are countless possible universes. The actual order of things is taken to include certain remarkable aspects which make it unreasonable to think that its existence is a mere coincidence. It speaks about its designer.

The traditional criticism of the Thomist teleological argument has been that seeing natural processes as teleologically planned says more about the conceptual models of the interpreter than about reality. Similarly if God is supposed to be very intelligent, algorithmic compressibility of reality is not something God needs, but it is useful for human understanding. That simple is beautiful is also something which corresponds to human needs. This kind of criticism is relevant with respect to most forms of non-theist selector metaphysics as well. Perhaps the main attraction of the designer model is not very different from the attraction of ancient metaphysics. In the same way designer metaphysics offers an ultimate explanation of finite being and at the same time an answer to the questions of why it is understood and what it is to understand it – in this case it is said to mean to participate in an already existing infinite thinking of the first thinker. In both theories, intelligibility itself is taken as simply given.

As for the more mundane approaches, such diverse thinkers as Kant, Heidegger, and Wittgenstein have all thought that we are bound to accept the human form of knowledge and consciousness simply as a given fact, because we cannot, as it were, go outside them to tell what they really are. I think that there is something wrong in this line of thought. (Cf. Kusch

1989, Hintikka 1986) When it is said, for example, that semantics is ineffable, because one cannot go outside language to say what it is, it could be answered that language can be regarded as a calculus which can be reinterpreted, changed and replaced step by step. One could see semantic relations as inexhaustible rather than unaccessible. Similarly we can improve our view of what comprehending things is and deepen our understanding of how understanding makes things understandable without any a priori limits. If understanding is regarded as relative to historically contingent modes of signifying and synthesizing, analyzing our conceptual tools and their history may reveal important things about the construction of puzzle of reality, even if it does not solve it.

Biography

Simo Knuuttila is Research Professor at the Academy of Finland. His works include *Modalities in Medieval Philosophy* (1993) and several articles on the history of ancient and medieval philosophy. He has edited, a.o., the books *Reforging the Great Chain of Being* (1981), (together with Jaakko Hintikka) *Logic of Being* (1986), and *Modern Modalities* (1988). He is managing editor of the New Synthese Historical Library.

Bibliography

Barrow, J., *Theories of Everything. The Quest for Ultimate Explanation*, Oxford: Clarendon Press 1990.
Barrow, J. and Tipler, F. (eds.), *The Anthropic Cosmological Principle*, Oxford: Oxford, University Press 1986.
Bertola, F. and Curi. U. (eds.), *The Anthropic Principle*, Cambridge: Cambridge University Press 1989.
Craig, W. and Smith, Q., *Theism, Atheism, and Big Bang Cosmology*, Oxford: Clarendon Press 1993.
Davies, P., *The Mind of God. Science and the Search for Ultimate Meaning*, London: Penguin Books 1992.
Gale, G., 'Cosmological Fecundity: Theories of Multiple Universes' in J. Leslie (ed.) 1990.
Hintikka, J., 'Gaps in the Great Chain of Being' in S. Knuuttila (ed.), *Reforging the Great Chain of Being*, Dordrecht: Reidel 1981.
Hintikka, M. B. and J., *Investigating Wittgenstein*, Oxford: Blackwell 1986.
Knuuttila, S., *Modalities in Medieval Philosophy*, London: Routledge 1993.
Kusch, M. *Language as Calculus vs. Language as Universal Medium. A Study in Husserl, Heidegger and Gadamer*, Dordrecht: Kluwer Academic Publishers 1989.

Leibniz, *Philosophical Writings*, ed. G. H. R. Parkinson, trans. by M. Morris and G. H. R. Parkinson, Totowa, N. J.: Rowman and Littlefield 1973.

Leslie, J., *Universes*, London: Routledge 1989.

Leslie, J. (ed.), *Physical Cosmology and Philosophy*, London: Macmillan 1990.

Lovejoy, A., *The Great Chain of Beig. A Study of an Idea*, Cambridge, Mass.: Harvard University Press 1936.

Parfit, D., 'The Puzzle of Reality', *Times Literary Supplement*, July 3, 1992.

Swinburne, R., 'Argument from the Fine-Tuning of the Universe' in Leslie (ed.) 1990.

II

Britt D. Andresen, Helle Balsby, Cathrine Egeland, Mette Richter, Henriette Vognsgaard and Ulla Wiborg Johansen

Identity and Ethics[1]*

Abstract
With a point of departure in the thesis that woman is located in a world already defined, structured and interpreted by men, this essay discusses different aspects of the relationship between female identity and socialization.

Traditionally, theoretical philosophy has been separated from practical philosophy. Furthermore, the philosophical subject has been regarded as an ahistorical and genderless entity. Even though philosophers have regarded the philosophical subject as ahistorical and genderless, they nevertheless claim that women are incapable of philosophizing[2]. The history of philosophy is primarily thought by men and written and told to men. These men have thought that their thinking transcended their sex and claimed that women cannot philosophize because of their sex. Yet the theme of sex/gender has not received an adequate treatment from professional philosophers. The traditional way of conceiving women is that women cannot deal with abstract matters because they are too attached to nature. Only males are defined as creatures of reason.

With this inheritance the female student of philosophy begins her study. She can either choose to identify with the way tradition has defined her sex, i.e. as nature, passive, unfree or she can choose to identify herself with the way tradition has defined males, i.e. as rational, active and free. The majority of female students tend to identify themselves with the definition of the male sex, i.a. because this definition has positive connotations. This implies that female students read what male philosophers have said about the male sex as if it was said to cover the female sex as well (cf. footnote 1).

However, what if these two definitions are untenable? What if the two sexes are not to be defined as two complementary opposites. I.e. where man is defined first and given the positive predicate of freedom. This definition is given in Rousseau in his "Émile", where woman is defined and given the negative predicate of unfreedom and is situated in the home in order to be able to facilitate the male's life in freedom. This way of constructing the relationship between the two sexes constitues the bourgeios ideal of education. What if these definitions of man and woman are wrong? How can we then continue to identify ourselves with the positively loaded male subject that we read about when we study philosophy? And how will a new way of thinking change the concept of rationality?

Identity and socialization

In this essay we will discuss the relationship between identity and ethics based on the following thesis: Our identities as women and men are connected with contradictory processes of socialization[3]. This implies that we end up implementing theories and practices (maintained or) prescribed by a patriarchal power structure which in many ways are opposed to what we want as feminist philosophers or just good and decent people[4].

When we here talk about identity, we are not thinking of an identity independent of a *physical* and *socio-cultural position* in a particular society with certain economic and social structures as well as certain structures and relations between the sexes. Thus we will define identity as the result of an individual and collective historical and relational process of socialization. I.e. our identitites are firstly connected to our own and to common "memories" (understood as embedded knowledge, deriving i.a. from our physical, bodily and spatial imbeddedness in the world). Secondly, the people we have been and still are surrounded by (parents, siblings, friends, authorities etc.).

We think that it is very fruitful to connect identity with ethics because when we *describe* ourselves, i.e. when we try to find out who we are, we can't avoid also *prescribing*, i.e. who and what we *ought* to be, and especially what others have thought and still think we ought to be. This "ought to" is expressed in different processes of socialization: explicit processes of socialization are e.g. family, political institutions and education systems; implicit ones are e.g. commercials and language. The borderline between explicit (where we are directly told what we ought to do) and implicit processes of socialization is not always clear. These processes do not always correspond to one another, but oppose and even negate each other. What we have been told we "ought to do" via the different processes of socialization that we have been through is ambiguous. Different images of women are represented as vague and diffuse end-results of different processes of socialization. Different processes of socialization present different images of women, representing different ideals, interests and values. More or less conscious values influence the way we sort the items of information. When we as a feminist philosophers want to study the concept of gender identity[5] we must pay attention to these processes of socialization. It is necessary to examine them.

> We live in a capitalist and patriarchal society. The capitalist aspect becomes more and more clear – even the university is seen as a firm with customers (other firms) and products (students). In this essay, however, we intend to concentrate on the patriarchal aspect. We are aware, though, that capitalism is closely related to the present version of patriarchy which, as Maggie Humm has observed, is largely *"...a system of male authority which oppresses women through its social, political and economic institutions."*[6]
>
> In our focussing on the historical oppression of the female sex, we do not intend to victimize women; we have simply become aware of how the historical oppression is still underlying the way we structure life in modern society. We would like to give some examples of oppression. In Denmark women did not enter the university until 1875 – why? Women did not get the vote until 1915 – why? These facts are not just of historical interest. We continue to live with them and the ineqalitiy they have created among men and women.
>
> It makes a difference to have *"...the historical memory of oppression or exclusion, as women, rather than being the empirical referent for a dominant group, like men."*[7]

Human historical memory is for the most part a male memory. Men have interpreted the world for thousands of years, while the female voice has been silenced. World history has been written from a male perspective, male experiences have been favoured both concerning what history has been about and the basis for selecting what is relevant to include in a history book. But women compared to men are situated physically and socioculturally in other positions in society.

This difference has been, and still is, manifested in departments of philosophy – both in theoretical and practical matters – as *institutionalized disqualifications* of women. As students of philosophy we are also part of a process of socialization derived from institutionalized philosophy. The images of women are either negative or completely missing from the process. Nevertheles these are a part of our socialization as female students of philosophy. As an example mention may be made of the fact that students of philosophy are taught what men have said to other men about men's capacities. In other words, philosophical discourse has been essentially a male discourse. These images imply that we are introduced to interests and values which result in an institutionalized way of sorting information. As feminist philosophers this leaves us in a problematic situation, because we have realized that from time to time we filter information which is both interesting and relevant just because this information traditionally has been seen as irrelevant. It is in this way we implement theories and practices which go against or negate what we wish as feminists philosophers.

Identities, language and values

We are all born into a world already defined, structured and valued. A world where men have interpreted women for at least 2500 years; this has resulted in in a negative way of conceiving femininity. The question is whether this definition of women would have been the same if women had had the same opportunity as men to develop language, i.e. to define and to name. Another question is *why* this traditional definition of women is of any interest in 1995. As we have all been told, women have already obtained the same rights as men!

We think that the traditional definition of the female sex is still of interest i.a. because it is embedded in the language which we use to understand world and reality and used for ordering and categorizing the phenomena of the world. The language in which the individual woman interprets herself and others, is the one in which the definition and derogation of the female sex is embedded.

This accentuation of the historicity of language and of human beings is the one of the approaches that can be used to criticise traditional metaphysics. That human nature is ahistorical has been called into question. It has been asked whether or not the cultural context, the historical period and natural language have had an influence on the development of human consciouness and identity. The majority of thinkers in the 20th century have discussed human historicity as a central idea, e.g. Heidegger, Foucault and Wittgenstein. Many feminists carry on these philosophers' ideas and thoughts but feminism introduces a new perspective to philosophy. It comes as no surprise that this specific perspective concerns the question of sex. Woman has always been defined in terms of her sex; only man is seen as having the possibility to transcend sex. Woman is seen as unable to transcend the sphere of partiality and reach universality, a possibility which is open for man only.

We are told that philosophy is about universal matters; if so, why construct the discourse by excluding women's reflections? Have male philosophers dealt with what is universal? Or do philosophers thought on the contrary reveal that the philosopher was a male? Both women and men are able to say something shared by both the sexes – some male philosophers have also done so. Our point is that not until women enter the history of philosophy it is made explicit what applies to human beings and what applies to men alone in the philosophers' arguments.

Many feminists criticise a concept of language where it is seen as representing reality in a one-to-one correspondence. This concept of language is too narrow and is valid only in some simple cases, e.g. the word *table* representents the physical table or the word *cup* represents the physical cup. Is the relationship just as simple with the word *man*? *Man* means both human being and a male human being. Why is this so? Is this a coincidence?

According to Dale Spender this is not the case. When using the word *man* to cover both a human being and a male human being it is assumed that the male sex contains the female sex. This assumption is by feminists called the *male-as-norm-syndrome*. That the word *man* is used to cover human beings in general and the male human being is no coincidence. The following is inspired by Dale Spender's *Man Made Language*.

In *Man Made Language* Dale Spender notes that in 1553 Thomas Wilson insisted that is was more natural to place the man before the woman, as in husband and wife, brother and sister and son and daughter[8]. The reason for claiming this was the assumption that the man comes first in natural order and that the male superiority ought also to be visible in language. Since Wilson's audience was exclusively a male audience nobody protested against this assumption (women were not allowed to enter the institutes of higher education).

In 1646 Joshua Poole stated that *the male gender was the worthier gender*[9]. In 1746 John Kirkby formulated his "Eighty Grammatical Rules". He wrote; *"Rule number Twenty One stated that the male gender was more comprehensive than the female"*[10]. This rule was now handed down to generation after generation of male grammarians. Thus it becomes grammatically correct to say "he" when a person's gender is not known. Today we use "he" and "man" unconsciously to cover the human norm, but Dale Spender's point is that those grammarians who introduced it were not so unconscious. If there had been any female grammarians who had had the possibility to develop and influence the patterns of language, the precedence of the male category would not exist[11].

If men control the development of language and if language has been working in men's favour, because as Dale Spender points out; *"men have not only provided themselves with more – and more positive – words, but they (have also) ensured that they had more opportunities to use them"*[12], how then does this influence the socialization and identity of women? How can she avoid, in her being active in a patriarcal society, reproducing what she wants to fight? In a patriarchy woman learns to see herself from a male point of view, she learns to compare herself to the male standard and she learns to devaluate what has to do with being a woman, i.a. because she via language lives with male definitions of herself.

We will now give some examples of this from our academic world. Words that originally were applied to men and are now used for both sexes can be illustrated by the two words "bachelor" and "master". "Bachelor" means both a person who has a three-year degree at a university *and* an unmarried man. The word is loaded positively. An unmarried woman is called a "spinster". "Spinster" originally meant at woman who spins, but has gra-dually come to mean*; "a woman who remains unmarried beyond the usual age for marrying"*[13]. The word is highly negatively loaded. Woman is seen and assigned value in relation to man. "Master" both means a man who rules others and has control, authority or power over others, head of household an a superior, but the word "master" is a university degree, too. The female word for "master" is "mistress", but "mistress" does not have the same connotations as "master", meaning instead a kept woman, a lover. This example shows that the two words both meaning "authority over others" have their meaning extended in such a way that "master" expresses the highest authority and "mistress" expresses a relational existence.

Language is not a static value-neutral medium. Language is continuously developing. It reflects world and reality interpretations developed in historical specific societies. This does not mean that women cannot understand a given language but that they should be highly sensitive to those interpretations which are inherent in language.

Dale Spender, refering to Muriel Schulz, talks about a *"systematic, semantic derogation of women"*, meaning that *"words become negative when they shift into the female sphere"*[14]. When a word (or a social position) becomes associated with women it is no longer suited for men[15]. In Dale Spender's words; *"All words – regardless of their origin – which are associated with females acquire negative connotations, because this is a fundamental semantic rule in a society which constructs male supremacy. When the same word shifts from being positive to be negative once it has moved from refering to a male to refering to a female, then the logic lies not in the word (and what it represents) but in the sex. The way meaning is created in our society depends upon dividing the world into positive-masculine and negative-feminine"*[16].

Human beings have access to a given language, which humanizes us. At the same time, we are socialized to see the world in a certain way. One of the principles of feminist thought is to note that society has been constructed with a one-sided favourising of the male sex. Power has been ascribed to men, reaching from economic power to the control of language. Feminists interested in the relation between language and society work on tracing the social bias between the sexes present in the language, showing that the values and world interpretations of one sex are predominat. Interpretations of the world are seen from a male perspective; they can be traced in everday language. Male perspective means that the point of departure is taken in the male subject, the male being seen as the norm and the female, as the derivation from the male norm[17]. One of the things that feminists criticise tradition for is its androcentrism, that tradition is centred round the male (subject). E.g. in the Bible:

"The man said; 'This one at last is bone from my bones, flesh from my flesh! She shall be called <u>wo</u>man for from man she was taken' ". (Genesis 2, 23).

"<u>Wo</u>man" derives from "man", "<u>s</u>he" derives from "he", "<u>fe</u>male" derives from "male", in Hebrew "i<u>s</u>ja" (Issah) (woman) derives from "isj" (is) (man) and in Latin "virago" (woman) derives from "vir" (man).

Speaking of human beings in general, we often imagine them having male bodies. "Homo erectus" is masculine. Homo means both a human being in general and a male human being, but a woman is seldom imagined when speaking of "homo erectus" – and also the grammatical inflection is of course masculine. In Hebrew "Adam" means human being in general, but at the same time it is the name of the first male human being according to the Bible[18].

We have now seen how language is a part socialization. Also, how it influnces female and male identities.

Another part of socialization is modern media.

Identity and Ethics *161*

Identity and mass media

In our modern information society[19], we consider ourselves as being enlightened. The more information we get, the more enlightened we become (we believe). This is a vulgar version of the western concept of progress. The mass media are an essential source of information – especially television, films, pictures and images.

We are bombarded with pictures and images. Some of them we barely notice, while others make a certain impression and stay in our minds for a long time. We regard the first mentioned as a threat because we do perceive them, but not sufficiently to be able to sort them out critically. Therefore they "sneak in" and influence our interpretation of the world.

When items of information are not "digested" properly, messages which influence our lives (our understanding of what it means to be a woman or a man and our personal identity) in a way we do not notice right away easily creep upon us. As an example of this we could mention the traditional sex roles, which still play a central role in today's commercials. At first sight commercials seem harmless, normally being understood as an appeal to buy this or that. But what we want to focus on is what other implicit messages we receive and how they correspond to the gendered bourgeois ideal of education.

Women as well as men are still presented in accordance with the traditional sex roles.

In order to maintain our competitive society it is no longer sufficient to sell products. Every product embodies a certain lifestyle. We do not just buy yoghurt; we buy health, well-being and beauty. The target group is female consumers, because it is still (according to commercials) the woman who takes care of the well-being of the family.

The capitalist slogans are: "You are what you have" and "You become what you buy". For instance, you become beautiful if you buy exactly this or that shampoo. All this we know ad nauseam. But there is more to it. In spite of so-called equality, it is still mainly women who do the laundry, change nappies, clean the house, cook the healthy food and, last but not least, take care of their looks. The woman and her looks are regarded as being vital for her in order to become "really happy". At the same time, woman is objectified and her identity manipulated because it is in the interst of the market to keep the consumer in the faith (and hope) that happiness is someting you can buy at the nearest chemist's.

Many women will agree with this interpretation and their may agree with the fact that it is a delusion. But why, then, do we actually buy these products which promise eternal youth, beauty and wealth when we know very well that the products do not work that way? Do we want to be tricked? Do women want to be identified as the beautiful, slim and devoted housewives who use the "right" products? Is this really what women are interested in ?

Is it not – i.a. – the commercials' representation of a happy and slim woman with a career and family that make some women starve themselves and therefore end up physically and mentally damaged? The story goes: As long as you don't get too fat, old and wrinkled, life will turn out perfect. Especially if a man is willing to give his contribution to a happy family you can take care of.

This is, we think, what women in western culture confirm by their implied acceptance of the commercials' way of representing women. At the same time there are some ethical consequences which are far-reaching; Mum makes the dinner and attends to the house while dad is out taking care of the rest of the world. Our descendants are indirectly raised to think that the happy life implies this pattern of sex-roles and they are taught that what really matters in life is the material objects you can buy.[20]

Now the question is whether we want such a development, or whether we want something more and something different for the generations to come. As feminist philosophers we think that such problems must be considered if we are to be able to transcend the ancient male/female dichotomy which has influenced most of the western history of philosophy.

We have now reached the end of this paper and together with the philosopher Rosi Braidotti we will ask the two questions : "What can motivate a women's choice of/for philosophy? How can one go on doing philosophy?"

How do we as feminist philosophers proceed in a patriarchal tradition – a tradition which may be exhausting its possibilities? In the history of philosophy the patriarchal tradition has been selecting and sorting information. Until now (and still) we have been (and still are) philosophizing on the premises of the patriarchate and therefore it has been problematic to put forward new and radical premises for thinking. We think that philosophy is in an urgent need of new thinking. Partly because the most influential theories of the tradition[21] have failed to see that sexual difference is a philosophical issue. In order to make sure that philosophy is a continuous process it is necessary to think in a new radical way and to think in a constructive way. If we continue solely to philosophize according to the premises of the tradition, we risk exhausting our possibilities. We think we are bound to adopt a critical attitude towards the tradition in order to stay sensitive to vital and important issues. For instance; How do we as women define and identify ourselves in a patriarchal culture?

The American philosopher Susanne K. Langer published "Philosophy in a New Key" in 1942. This title indicates the need of *a new key* in philosophy in order to be able to think in an innovative and radical way. Langer used the musical term *new key* to show the possibility of switching from one key to another to vary the tune and thereby create possibilities for variations. In Langer's opinion, philosophy has played in one and the same key for centuries. Langer's indication of the need of a new key was not meant as a systematic rejection of som venerable ancestors but rather meant as an attempt to show that philosophy needs new thinking in order not to become uninteresting.

For biographical information, see note 1.

Notes

1* We are six women working together in a feminist philosophical study group, at Odense University.

There are many reasons why this study group came into being. First of all, we wondered why we were not introduced to female philosophers in the classes we attended on the history of philosophy. Did female or feminist philosophers never exist? We soon realized that they did and therefore we wanted to find out why they were not included in our curriculum.

Furthermore, our study group has also been a place where we are free to experiment with the fact of being women *and* philosophers in a patriarchal philosophical tradition.

Our study group is also a place where we aim at *thinking with* and not against each other. This presupposes that we individually *and* as a group accept each other's strengths and weaknesses and use these in a constructive way.

Working together also means that we accept the strength of thinking together instead of expecting to be credited for our own individual contribution. By the way, it is probably by sharing one's thoughts that it will show whether these thoughts are potentially fruitful or not. In the light of the overall glorification of individualism it might be difficult to realize and to accept that we stand together, are a group, are interdependent and have mutual responsibilityand and that we then are stronger and have a greater possibility to reach a higher level of creativity. The development of creativity is favoured by working collectively. However, our experiences also show that it has been very difficult to set aside individualism.

Our point of departure was a desire to think and write together – we wanted to discuss theses, arguments and examples and to read and rewrite each other's papers. The most important thing for us as feminist philosophers is to focus on the group work as a process *and* a method in order to be able to continue philosophizing.

Finally, in our attempts at working in a group and via the process we have been through we have become aware of the strengths and respect we gain *as* a group.

2. As far as we are concerned, Kant never changed his opinion about women expressed in the pre-critical (vorkritische) text "Beobachtungen über das Gefühl des Schönen und Erhabenen" (Bruno Cassirer, Berlin, 1922). Let us give you two examples from this text: *"Denn es ist hier nicht genug sich vorzustellen, dass man Menschen vor sich habe, man muss zugleich nicht aus der Acht lassen, das diese Menschen nicht vor einerlei Art sind."* (p. 270). This has very strange implications for the relationship between women and ethics. Kant founded morality in principles and man's duty is then to act out of esteem for these principles. But according to Kant women are not capable of principles or overall rules: *"Man wird ihr [the woman's] gesamtes moralisches Gefühl und nicht ihr Gedächtnis, zu erweitern suchen und zwar nicht durch allgemeine Regeln, sondern durch einiges Urteil über das Betragen, welches sie um sich sehen."* (p.272). And another place in "Beobachtungen" Kant says: *"Ich glaube schwerlich, dass das schöne Geschlecht der Grundsätze fähig sei..."* (p. 273). A disqualification of woman because of her sex.
3. For an elaboration of this thesis, see Jørgen Døør and Cathrine Egeland: "Dialectical and feminist philosophy – an understanding and critique of everyday life in modern capitalism." Paper presented at the conference "Culture and everyday life in differentiated societies", Aalborg University, 1995.
4. We use both "feminist philosophers" and "good and decent people" as criteria, because we do not operate with an absolute distinction between theory and practice. Our theory has consequences for our way of living.
5. We are aware of the problems attached to the sex/gender distinction. The distinction was originally introduced to stress the difference between culturally constructed femininity and what were considered to be biological facts (materiality). The distinction seemed necessary because male philosophers failed to recognize the importance of cultural influences in shaping socalled female and male characteristics. However, the sex (referring to biology)/gender (referring to culture) distinction maintains the dualism between the natural/essential on one side and culturally constructed identities on the other. The distinction keeps an important question in focus though: How is it possible to refer to natural and essential female and male identities – and can we completly avoid operating with some kind of naturalness?
6. Maggie Humm: "The Dictionary of Feminist Theory", Second Edition, Prentice Hall/Harvester Wheatsheaf, 1995, p. 200.
7. Rosi Braidotti: "Embodiment, Sexual Difference and the Nomadic Subject" *Hypatia* vol.8, no.1 (Winter) 1993, p. 8.
8. Dale Spender, "Man Made Language" Pandora Press, 1994.
9. ibid. p. 147.
10. ibid. p. 148.
11. ibid. p. 150.
12. ibid. p. x.
13. Webster Word Histories.
14. Dale Spender, Man Made Language, p. 16.
15. ibid. p. 17.
16. ibid. p. 18. Connected to this we would like to stress that it is not sufficent to make words political correct when society as a whole is extremly political uncorrect i.e. oppressive.
17. Examples of 'male-as-norm' from the history of philosophy: *"In appearance too a boy is like a women, and the women is as it were an infertile male (...).*, Aristoteles,

"De Generatione Animalium I", 728 a. 17. Clarendon Press, Oxford, 1992, p. 49. *"Dicit enim Philosophus, in libro de Generat. Animal., quod femina est mas occasionatus. Sed nihil occasionatum et deficiens debuit esse in prima rerum institutione. Ergo in illa prima rerum institutione mulier producenda non fuit."* (Philosopher says, in the book "De Generatione Animalium, that the women is an accidentally caused man. (Occasionare – zufällig verursachen. cf. Thomas Lexicon von Ludwig Schutz, Stuttgart, 1958.) But nothing coincidental and defective was created at the first creation. Therefore in this first creation women was not made. (our translation))

Thomas Aquinas "Summa Theologiae", first part, 92nd question, 1. article 1. Marietti, 1952, p. 450.
18. Biblisch-historisches Handwörterbuch, Vandenhoech & Reprecht in Göttingen, 1962.
19. Society is split into two spheres the public and the private. Importance has only been ascribed to the public sphere not noticing its dependence on the private. Essential to the private sphere is nurturing, caring and providing safety. Essential to the public is competition and aggression. The dependence of the public sphere on the private is seen in the work done in the homes in order to make the workforce able to keep on producing. Whit out the possibility of recreation at home one would not be productive as modern society demands. In this way these so-called "female ways of being" (essential to the private sphere) provide the basis of our modern society. Therefore it is astonishing that they have been ridiculed and underestimated.
20. Consumerism might of course also be criticized from an environmental point of view.
21. Here we define the tradition exclusively as the tradition we are taught and examined in at Odense University.

Henrik Bruun

Nature as a Symbol of Identity
– Planning a Case Study in the Finnish Archipelago Sea

Abstract
To what extent is nature a part of human identity? This question is discussed in relation to the people living in the archipelago of southwestern Finland. Charles Taylor's interpretation of identity as a framework for evaluation, is taken as a starting point. To what extent is the archipelago environment a part of this framework among people living there? Potential answers are presented, drawing on some of the literature in the field. Emphasis is put on the way in which archipelago people are represented, or represent themselves, in different contexts. The conclusion is that the whole question is rather complex, since there are many ways in which nature can be a part of human identity.

1. Introduction

The present text has been developed in close connection to Richard Langlais' human ecological work *Reformulating Security*.[1] Langlais investigates how the Inuits of north-eastern Canada understand security. His interviews reveal a close relation between security concerns and the question of identity. They also confirmed the importance of the biophysical environment for Inuit identity. A fundamental meaning of security was thus perceived to be the possibility of continuing to have a certain kind of relation to the land – an interpretation that challenges that of the traditional, state centered, and militarily oriented security policy.

Langlais' work contains a lot of material that could be developed further. Here I want to discuss the question of identity. What is identity and what place does nature, or environment, have in it? These two questions have to be answered in different ways. The first is a theoretical concern, and I will try to explain my way of understanding "identity" with the help of a well known philosopher, Charles Taylor. The second question must be answered empirically. I will present a case study that will be carried through during the next few years. The discussion will be focused on some of the problems and the expected results of such a study.

2. What is meant by "identity"?

"Identity" has been an important concept in the environmental discourse since the first texts of Arne Næss on deep ecology. According to Næss people could get a more profound relation to the environment by identifying themselves with the field of ecological relations they are a part of. In this way they would get a broader self-conception; they would no longer see themselves as isolated egos, but rather as points in an integrated field. Næss claims that this kind of ontological connectedness would have ethical implications in the sense that we, in deciding what to do, would consider the needs of the whole of the field, instead of *only* ourselves and the people who are directly affected by our actions.

> The greater our comprehension of our togetherness with other beings, the greater the identification, and the greater care we will take. The road is also opened thereby for the delight in the well-being of others and sorrow when harm befalls them. We seek what is best for ourselves, but through the extension of the self, our 'own' best is also that of others. The own/not-own distinction survives only in grammar, not in feeling.[2]

Næss' thoughts on identification have inspired a wealth of literature on the subject.[3] There seems to be a general feeling, among theses authors, that the question of identity has something to do with ethics. It is, however, seldom explained in what way identity and ethics are connected. One reason for this is that the meaning of identity is taken as obvious; something on which one does not need to elaborate.

My view is that we in fact never define ourselves as atomic egos. Our self-conception is always formed in a process of communication in which we define ourselves by identifying with certain communities or certain types of people. "I am a student," "I am a woman," "I am a Finn," "I am a human being," "I am a living being" – all of these ways of explaining who you are implicate a sense of being connected to the other units of the mentioned category. This is why movements like regionalism, nationalism, and feminism, to mention some examples, can be so strong. I also suspect that our ways of identifying ourselves quite often contain a sense of integration with nature. Regionalist and nationalist movements often use the local nature as a symbol of the togetherness. And if these symbols are to work in the regional or national rhetorics, people must feel that they are significant. Even the feminist movement has used a special relation to nature as one of the symbols of femininity.

I do not think that the "identifying with" – approach is the best one when trying to understand identity and its connection to ethics. One reason is that there are so many ways in which you can identify with something. In the previously mentioned study by Langlais, it is shown how important "the land" is for the identity of the Inuit people living on Ellesmere Island. To be Inuit is about being able to survive in the arctic environment. "The land," which does not signify only the land but also the sea, is the central element and could be said to be a symbol for the ecology of the area. The Inuit identity is built on the feeling of being a part of the ecological system, to be able to maintain their nisch in it. In practice it is a question of having time to be out "on the land," to know how to hunt, to be able to take care of oneself in the rough environment, to understand what the clouds say about tomorrows weather, to eat meat, to be familiar with the movement patterns of the caribou, to know how many animals you can kill without endangering the regeneration of the population, to learn the geography of the vast land areas, to know how to build a tent, and so on. It is this complex of relations and interactions that is the foundation of the Inuit identity.[4]

> Inuit respondents themselves considered that without the complex of attributes that hinge upon the relation to the land, their identity and way of life as Inuit is threatened, which leads to the conclusion that the loss of this identity and way of life would mean that "post-Inuit" people would be without any particular, distinguishing reasons for living anywhere, and the continuing to live in Ellesmere would be without any particular meaning at all.[5]

The feeling of being a part of the ecology of an area is founded on a worldview that understands reality as an ecology. With this worldview as an axiom there is no need to speak about a sense of identity with, for example, the animals. To shoot a caribou is not the same as shooting a part of yourself, while the destruction of the caribou population as a whole would be equal to the destruction of a part of yourself as an Inuit. Not because the caribou population is a part of the Inuit in any mystical extended sense, but simply because the caribou hunt is so important for these people.

> All of the Inuit respondents mentioned the importance of being able to hunt animals for their idea of what it was to be Inuit.[6]

This was one example of "identifying with" nature. Now, it is obvious that one could identify with the same environment in other ways, for example in ways that would exclude caribou hunting. "Identifying with" is thus too general. It is the mode of identification that is interesting, and that has implications for our actions. It is now time to turn to the Canadian philosopher, Charles Taylor, and his book *Sources of the Self*.

3. Identity as a Framework

My intention is not to present the contents of Taylor's book, but rather to use some of his concepts as tools for my discussion on identity.

Do identity and ethics have anything to do with each other, as Næss and others seem to believe? Does the answer to the question "who am I?" have any ethical relevance? In the first instance we might be inclined to say "no". But Taylor asks us to look at the problem from another angle. How would I react if someone accused me of wasting my life, of leading a worthless (meaningless) life? With what right could someone accuse me of something like that? According to Taylor, accusations like this must proceed from some frame of reference. There must be some kind of measure for what is a meaningful life and what is not. The accusation of a wasted life, thus, proceeds from an idea of what a meaningful life would be. And with this starting point the accusation is not only an insult, but also a condemnation with ethical dimensions.[7] One could think of an Inuit father on Ellesmere Island who accuses his son of being a bad Inuit, when the latter, maybe influenced by television and other media, wants to move to the south. The expression "bad Inuit" would then be a moral judgment which is motivated by the incapability, or the lack of will, of the son to maintain the Inuit relation to the land. Taylor calls this type of judgments *strong evaluations*.

According to Taylor our moral reactions consist of two components: moral intuition and statements on human nature. An understanding of moral statements demands an ability to feel disgust for what they forbid and a longing for what they request. Without the intuitive feeling that there is something negative in pain we would not be able to understand an ethics that forbids us to cause pain in others. The moral intuition is something, at least partly, learned.[8] Different times and different cultures can form variable moral intuitions. In certain cultures for example honour is perceived as the ultimate sign of the meaningfulness of life, in others self-control is considered more important and in still others everyday life (work, reproduction, and family) or even the act of creating.[9] What is seen as a meaningful life dependes on what you think human life is all about. In the last instance, therefore, the strong evaluations fall back on an ontology of the human being, that is, on *statements on the nature of human beings*.[10]

Much of Taylor's book can be read as a criticism of what he calls an "action centered ethics".

> "Morality," of course, can be said and often is defined purely in terms of respect for others, the category of the moral is thought to encompass just our obligations to other people. But if we adopt this definition, then we have to allow that there are other questions beyond the moral which are of central concern to us, and which bring strong evaluation into play. There are questions about how I am going to live my life which touch on the issue of what kind of life is worth living, or what kind of life would fulfill the promise implicit in my particular talents, or the demands incumbent on someone with my endowment, or of what constitutes a rich, meaningful life – as against one concerned with secondary matters or trivia. These are issues of strong evaluation, because people who ask these questions have no doubt that one can fail to lead a full life. To understand our moral world we have to see not only what ideas and pictures underlie our sense of respect for others but also those which underpin our notions of a full life.[11]

Strong evaluations can, according to Taylor, only be made against the background of a framework, that is, a set of qualitative distinctions. "To think, feel, judge within such a framework is to function with the sense that some action, or mode of life, or mode of feeling is incomparably higher than the others."[12]

The set of qualitative distinctions is our framework of evaluation. It is strongly attached to our feeling of identity. Or rather, personal identity *is* the framework of our evaluations.[13] It is an answer to the question "Who am I?", or in other words, "What is of vital importance for me?". We have seen that the Inuit identity is more than just a perspective of life. It is, with Taylor's words, "the frame within which they can determine where they stand on questions of what is good, or worthwhile, or admirable, or of value."[14] Taylor continues with words that can be compared with the Langlais-quotation in section 2.

> ...they are saying that were they to lose this commitment or identification, they would be at sea, as it were; they wouldn't know anymore, for an important range of questions, what the significance of things was for them.[15]

4. Essentialism versus constructivism

> ... an identity is something that one ought to be true to, can fail to uphold ...
> Our identity is what allows us to define what is important for us and what is not.[16]

My conclusion from the discussion above is that we, if we want to understand the ethical relevance of nature for a certain human being (or group or culture), must know what position nature has in his horizon, that is, in what he defines to be a meaningful life. In simple terms: if nature has no important place in what you consider to be a "full life" then it has no ethical relevance for you. Or: if a "full life" would be unthinkable without certain interactions with nature then there is a relevance. What this relevance is depends on what kind of relations we are talking about.

I will do my empirical research on the people living in the archipelago of south-western Finland, an area that is called the Archipelago Sea. The people in this area are mainly Swedish speaking and, when they want to bring attention to where they live, they call themselves "skärgårdsbor" ("skärgårdsbo" in singular form: "one who lives in the archipelago." I will translate the singular form of skärgårdsbo with "archipelagoite" and the plural form with "the archipelago people")[17]. My question is: What is the position of the archipelago as a natural environment in the identity of an archipelagoite? What does it mean to be an archipelagoite? What kind of life does this word indicate, implicate or maybe even *impose*?

The discourse of identity is broad and diverse. Although space does not allow any extended discussion on different ways of interpreting "identity" there are some important things that this discourse teaches us, some traps that we should avoid. One way of categorizing different conceptions of identity is to distinguish between essentialistic and constructivistic interpretations. The first is typical for the nationalistically inspired research on "the soul of the people." The idea is that one really expects to find a common core, "something that characterizes all of us, and that distinguishes us from all other people." The constructivist interpretation does not necessarily deny such a homogenity, but claims that it is constructed rather than found. Historians, linguists, cultural researchers etc., thus, did not *find* a national identity but *constructed* it by trying to find it.[18]

The essentialist and the constructivist interpretations of identity are fruitful as long as they do not demand monopoly on the concept. Identity is not *only* a question of essence. If we, with Taylor, understand identity to be a process of relating oneself to a vision of what a meaningful life would be, it is clear that this vision must be represented in some way – through myths, traditions, religious and philosophical writing, poems, art, and, of course, historical research. These representations are not only human constructions, but often, if not always, carry ideological contents. If identity is about defining what is meaningful, and if it further is a mechanism for forming alliances between people with the same vision, it cannot avoid being caught in the web of power relations in society. Identity, by its nature, cannot be pure in the sense that essentialists often seem to assume that it is. The purity is contaminated by ideology and power.

But, on the other hand, identity is neither a "pure construction", if we with that expression would signify something without any foundation in the subject (individual or group). Identities are of emotional nature. If we cannot feel that a certain way of life "X" is meaningful, then this way of living does not work as the measure against which we evaluate ourselves. Since identities are constructed through processes of communication, we can of course change our way of interpreting "X". This change in interpretation would be complete when we *feel* that we want to, and should, live in the X way. Identity is never only ideology and manifestation of power relations. It is always also a question of communication, interpretation and emotion.

When asking questions about the meaning of nature for the archipelagoite we should thus remember the following:

– We should not assume that all the archipelago people share the same vision of a meaningful life just because they happen to live in the same area, even if this area is of a very special character. We have to avoid blue-eyed essentialism. There are other facts influencing identity (like profession, gender, age, and so on). On the other hand, the fact that profession, gender, age etc. affect identity does not necessarily exclude the importance of the biophysical environment. In stead of discovering one meaning of the archipelago as an environment forming identities, we might discover several meanings.

– We should not believe all that is said about the archipelago people.

There is a lot of rhetorics going on, with different actors definig the situation in the archipelago according to his interests. The identity of the archipelago people is very often used as a legitimation of certain kinds of politics, both by the archipelago people themselves and by other actors. We have to get under this rhetorical surface.

– We should be aware of the fact that we by "discovering" meanings also construct them, and, thus, that we also are an actor in the field of human interaction in and around the archipelago.

5. The Archipelago

In Finland there are several archipelago-areas, both in the sea and in the lakes. The largest is the one between Hankoo in the east and the main land of Åland in the west, that is, *the Archipelago Sea*. Geomorphologically the region is very diverse, with some areas dominated by land and others by the sea. The circumstances can be quite different depending on the size of the islands and the extent to which the sea dominates their climate and ecology. Along the coast we have several relatively large islands which ecologically are similar to the coastal areas of the main land, and which economically and infrastructurally are fully integrated with the main land. This has been called *the inner archipelago*. Further out the islands get smaller, often forming clusters. Here the distribution between land and sea is more or less equal (*the middle archipelago*). The island ecologies of the middle archipelago have a special archipelago character, partly because of the influence of the sea, but also as a consequence of the ecological history of the islands. The continual process of land elevation makes the archipelago a dynamic landscape, always changing. New islands rise from the sea (*the outer archipelago*), older ones get colonized by plants and animals. A process of succession takes place.

Economically and infrastructurally the middle archipelago used to be quite isolated from the main land. Even if there never was total self sufficiency, most of the time the economy has had a local character. The subsistence strategies have varied with seal and sea bird hunting, collection of eggs and feathers, agriculture and fishing as important elements through most of history. Despite a high degree of infrastructural isolation before the time of the steamship – and later the car, the telephone and electricity – the interaction with the cities of the main lands surrounding the archipelago (that is, with Turku, Stockholm, Reval and Helsinki) has been of great importance for a long time. Today most of the large islands of the middle archipelago are connected with the main land through roads (on the islands) and bridges and ferries (between the islands). The smaller islands are still isolated. Economically the area is quite integrated with the main land economy, although the local informal economies still have some importance. Most families pursue a plural subsistence strategy, with wage work and agriculture as important ingredients. In the 1960s and 1970s there was a depopulation crisis in the region, caused by the centralization of the main land economy which, together with improved transportation, undermined the local economies. In the 1980s the archipelago society was revitalized, partly as a result of the Finnish regional policies (the public service sector was the most important factor for new employment during this time) and partly as a consequence of the new possibilities opened up by fish cultivation in the sea. In this way the archipelago societies have been able to avoid becoming pure service establishments for the main land tourism in the summers – the destiny of much of the Stockholm archipelago. Today around 7 000 people live in the middle archipelagos of the Archipelago Sea.[19]

I have spent some space to give a short description of the middle archipelago. The reason is that most of the people we would call archipelago people live in this area. The Finnish archipelago law (instituted in 1981: a law setting the goals for development in the archipelago areas of Finland) defines "archipelago" as being an area that lacks permanent road connections (bridges or tunnels) to the main land. This relative lack of communicative integration is considered to give the islands their special archipelago character, that is, a certain degree of isolation. From the perspective of the dominating paradigm of development isolation is a problem. The law states that a municipality can be called an archipelago municipality (and thus have a special status when money is distributed or when projects are implemented) if its archipelago character can be considered "an essential *hindrance* for the development of the municipality" (my italics).

As already mentioned, "archipelago people" refers to those who live in the archipelago, that is, to those who have this environment as their home. The decision of who to call an archipelagoite is always somewhat arbitrary. It cannot be made on ethnical grounds, since there is no such ethnic group that would differ from people on the main lands of Finland or Åland. Neither is there a linguistic homogeneity – most of the archipelago people in the Archipelago Sea have Swedish as their mother tounge, but in some areas the Finnish speaking people dominate. There is not even a common history bound to a specific geographical area. Land elevation and historical development have constantly been changing both the area that could be called "archipelago" and the settlement patterns in this area. Still "archipelagoite" is a common concept, and it is used in much the same way as the names of ethnical groups.[20]

It is a fact that there are people calling themselves archipelago people, obviously finding the archipelago as a source for, or symbol of, their identity. From a human ecological point of view this is interesting. The modern, industrialized world is not exactly full of people explicitly determining their identity on geomorphological or ecological grounds. But what does it mean to be an archipelagoite? In what sense does the archipelago influence identity? Or, in other words: What is it with the archipelago that makes it a suitable symbol of identity for some people?

These questions must be answered empirically, mainly through interviews. But we might be able to get some hints of what results to expect by investigating what has been said about the archipelagoite in the literature about the archipelago.

6. The Historical Archipelagoite

We have to distinguish between the description of the historical archipelagoite, on the one hand, and the modern on the other. The previous is a rather mythological figure, almost always described in a positive manner. Thus, for example, the tendency to be suspicious towards strangers or the importance attached to exclusive ownership of land has been interpreted as a kind of adaptation to the archipelago circumstances.

The historical archipelagoite is considered to have been firmly integrated with his environment.

> The subsistence of the archipelago people used to be based on a complicated system of production forms mirroring the dynamics of the natural year. The further out in the archipelago one came, the greater the integration between work and the rythms of nature. One kind of work succeded the other. It was difficult to distinguish any main occupation.[21]

This intensive interaction with nature can today be seen not only in the vast amount of geographical names in the archipelago reflecting "the traditional production forms, the means of transport, and the knowledge of the sea, weather and wind,"[22] but also in the linguistic differentiation between different kinds of islands and ices – to mention two examples. Thus depending on structure, form, size and situation, landstructures in the sea have been called skär, häll, sank, båda, klack, gadd, sten, klint, klack, knuv, knall, syl, kobbe, klobb, klubb, kläpp, ör, haru, grund, grynna, rev, land, holme or ö (island).[23] In winter, ice was both a blessing and a problem. On the one hand, it made transportation easier, on the other hand, it could be very dangerous. Knowledge of the character of different ice formations was crucial. Thus, depending on the date of its forming and its structure ices have been called isskum, blåis, blankis, skrovelis, kärnis, klingis, klinghal is, rändis, isrätjen is, tallriksis, sättis, sörjeis, snöis, pipis and råd.[24]

The historical archipelagoite is seldom described as an exploiter of nature, although historical records show that the picture of a "harmony between man and nature" in the archipelago societies can be questioned.[25] He is rather described as a *steward* of nature.

> One should be aware of that nature can be taxed and cultivated, but it cannot endure pure utilization and exploitation.
> This the archipelago people have respected since old times.[26]

Or, as Ole Torvalds expresses it in his poem "Skärgårdstider:"

> We do not exactly do
> everything in the best and wisest of ways
> but rough owners
> we have not been
> rather tolerable stewards.[27]

Although biologists stress the ecological richness of an ecotone like the Archipelago Sea, and some sociologists point out that the archipelago society actually used to be quite well off compared to the general standard of living on the main land, there is a very persisting picture of the hardships of the traditional archipelago life. The historical archipelagoite, as he is often described, realized the lutheranian ideal of the simple, hard working man – conservative because of necessity, loyal to his fellows, hospitable towards strangers as long as he had control over the situation. Solidarity and equality are often mentioned as characteristics of the traditional archipelago society, although these also have their limitations if we pay attention to historical facts. But there is another side to this life in harmony and virtue. The relative isolation of the archipelago society has given it a sense of independence, although it in fact was quite dependent on for example the tax and trade regulations of the main lands. This independence, which metaphorically has been described as "the freedom of the islands," was expressed in different ways, positively as a richness in initiatives or negatively as an opposition to central government. In the beginning of this century, when alcohol was prohibited in Finland, many archipelago people made their living as smugglers.

The traditional archipelagoite is most often a male, although recently there have been several attempts to draw people's attention to the archipelago women in history. The importance given to male activities might be a reason to why it is often the archipelago as a production landcape that is emphasized as a source for the identity of the archipelagoite. It is the hunting, fishing and cultivating man we learn to know. Thus, we seem to know less about how the archipelago was experienced as a home, as a place in which the emotional side of life has its course. The emotional bond is, rather, assumed, normally in quite an unspecified manner, as a consequence of the the productive dependence on nature.

> ... the genuine archipelago society is a social form of adaptation that has been developed and shaped in an almost perfect interplay with nature. During the long development and under continous influence of the hard pressure of the maritime environment, man in the archipelago has been forced to adapt to the physical, biological and psycological conditions put up by nature. The result was early an archipelago society that relied on an almost pure biological ground; man became a consuming and producing element in the ecosystem of the archipelago, in principal governed by the same forces as the other elements of the system. We dare to call this genuine archipelago society a happy, almost complete society.[28]

7. Archipelago People Today

The picture of the historical, genuine archipelagoite and his archipelago society is important not *despite* of its mythical character, but precisely *because of* it. Today's archipelago people are often considered to be heirs of the described features, both by themselves and by others. A female physiotherapist from Kimito, one of the larger islands that is considered to be a part of the inner archipelago, goes beyond the male image of the historical archipelagoite when identifying with the historical archipelago women:

> Actually I feel as a continuation of a series of enterprising archipelago women ... How could the archipelago women have made it in previous times without their independent initiative. The men where out on the sea for long periods while the women took care of the fields and the animals.[29]

This feeling of being a heir of a special relationship to nature and life is what is most often claimed to be what characterizes the archipelagoite of today.

> He who was born and has grown up in the archipelago will probably never more feel good if he moves to the main land. There he won't feel free, nature is totally different – I myself, at least, always feel caught, although I don't live in any city.[30]

> Maybe one doesn't exaggerate when one says that there is something in the genetic type of certain people that responds to the character of the archipelago in a similar way that a key fits a certain lock. Far from all people likes it in the archipelago, may be they find it to be too unpredictable, too rough, too insecure, but the group of people that belong to the archipelago is almost in a supernatural way spelled by it, for ever and indissolubly.[31]

The bond to nature, as expressed in the subsistence pattern and life style of the archipelagoite, is often considered to be a fact with epistemological and political consequences. The archipelagoite considers himself, or is even considered by others, to be the one who should be in charge of the development of the archipelago – not only because this is his home, but also because he has a deeper knowledge of the nature of the archipelago and the needs of the archipelago society. In the old days, it was the archipelago people themselves who...

> decided how the resources of land and sea were to be used in a way that was appropriate and lenient towards nature. I am sure that the archipelago people of today are just as capable as their ancestors to formulate rules for the practical use in accordance with the demands of our time. These demands are in many ways different than before, but they are hardly more difficult to handle than the problems that the first inhabitants of the islands had to face ... But it is the people of the archipelago that itself has to be allowed to decide how the fishing, pasture, cultivation of plants, hunting, forestry and free time activities should be regulated within the combined units of production and nature conservation that the geographical circumstances have created.[32]

> To live on a small archipelago island with a relatively clean air, clean water, somewhat of an income and the people you wish to see around you. That should be close to the ideal.

> Of course life is far away from always like this, the worst "dirt in the eye" are our bureaucrats and politicians (who can be found tens of kilometers in on the main land) and who so often "run over" us, hardly at all respect our special way of living and surviving, in many ways decide about our doing and being without being familiar with the circumstances.[33]

The special way of understanding the archipelago and life there is often interpreted in ethical terms as a special set of values. Thus, one author claims that the logic of the tourist industry ("to get the visitors to spend as much money as possible") to be incompatible with the "basic values of the archipelagoite concerning fellow humans and tradition."[34] Another author, Marlen Öhberg, suggests that it is the way of organizing work in the archipelago that gives rise to different values. According to her the modern economy of the cities makes people value wage work as a source of self-esteem. To be an independent, modern woman means to have a job, instead of staying at home. But in the archipelago with its still important informal economy wage work cannot, and should not, be given the same value.

> The reason to why the values of big society or in this case all the values of the feminist movement cannot be transferred to the archipelago society, is among other things that the working day in the archipelago society is not split up in work and leasure in such a strict way, that the households are small and must manage to do most things themselves.[35]

In the old days independence came as a function of isolation. Today it seems to be considered an important value, maybe one of the most important. In relation to the land, independence means being in control, in other words, owning it. Private ownership seems to be interpreted as a security against the undertakings of the central government.[36] But it is also reported to be a hindrance against collective projects among the archipelago people.

> The nature of people here is that they don't want to join any enterprises – everyone wants to have his own and make his own decisions. Everyone is a little bit like this. It is also often the case that the archipelago people don't want to borrow money from the bank. They are afraid of having loans. It has always been like this, people want to do it on their own.[37]

8. The Achipelago as a Symbol of Identity

Can anything be said about the position of nature in the identity of the archipelagoite? Could he be said to have an identity based on ecological awareness in the modern sense? This is a question that is very difficult to answer. On the one hand the archipelago people have been very fast in picking up the concepts of the environmental discourse. They have also been working together with main land environmental groups against different exploitative projects, for example the planned large scale waterways through untouched areas in the archipelago. On the other hand, the archipelago people have also been involved in conflicts with the environmentalists concerning some of the productive usages of nature, for example forestry on the islands, sea bird hunting and the cultivation of fish in the sea. Several archipelago people were also reported to have been sceptical against the implementation of a national park in the archipelago. It is however difficult to draw any conclusions from these incidents since the problem might have been the fact that "outsiders" – in the national park project it was even the central government – or even worse, "white collar people," "put their noses further and further/into what we do and what we don't/ what we can do and what we can't/with forest and bird hunting/ and the right to build and everything else that is ours".[38]

There is, however, another source of information on the extent to which ecological concerns direct, or rather, do not direct the life of the archipelago people. This source is the group of people who have moved to the archipelago explicitly because of a desire to live what, with a modern vocabulary, could be called "an ecological life."

> I am a woman who wants to live in the archipelago, originally I come from a big city. I want to live close to the sea – to have open views around me, land, forests, few people and a lot of silence.
> A small cottage (or a big one!), some land, a bridge, a boat, and a cow-house. An oldfashioned dream, but so incredibly real for me.
> But this doesn't correspond to the expectations of the archipelago people I have met AT ALL – not the least! There seemed rather to be room (or ONLY room) for an efficient private entrepreneur or wage worker who would prefer to live in a terrace-house, have road-metalling and street-lighting! (It was because of the asphalt and the lighting I once wanted to move away from the city!)[39]

This new group of archipelago people who want to "dig in our land, sow our seeds and see the crops grow" tell us of a totally different "genuine (inborn) archipelagoite" than the one that is traditionally described. They report of suspiciousness against things that are unfamiliar, of a lack of self-esteem that leads to an unreserved admiration of the ways of the big society, which in its turn takes its expression in feelings of inferiority and unnecessary rudeness against people from the cities. Marlene Öhberg is probably right in her hypothesis that one reason to the hostility might be the different situations of the two groups – the inborn archipelagoite, on the one hand, who never chose to live in the archipelago, "it just happened," and the, often academically educated, outsider who has chosen to lead an "alternative life."[40] The archipelago, thus, can be interpreted both as "a place where you happen to live," and as a chosen "alternative" to something else. We have here two different cognitive landscapes, the archipelago as a home and a place for subsistence, and the archipelago as a place for moral fulfilment. Within these two ways of understanding the archipelago different things seem to be considered important. In both cases the archipelago as an environment is significant, but for the one group its importance derives from its character of a home and a production landscape, while for the other the character of an ecologically rich and, thus, morally significant landscape gets more attention. Both groups seem to value the small scale of the archipelago society, although in different ways. The genuine archipelagoite often emphasizes the possibility to be one's own master, while the new archipelagoite might appreciate the enduring face-to-face contacts that have become so rare in the cities. The inborn archipelago people might see the small scale societiy as a protection towards outside forces, while the ones who move there to live alternatively are fascinated by its transparence and the possibility it gives you to make a difference (to influence what happens with your community). As one of the new archipelago people expresses it:

> To take responsibility for something more than yourself, implies that the human being develops and matures, that she can create herself a space for life that leads towards togetherness and happiness.[41]

Now, I do not know how significant this group of "alternative" people is out there in the Archipelago Sea. Probably they are not that many. There are other reasons to move out to the archipelago, for example if you marry someone living there. But however small this group is, its experiences are enlightening when we try to understand what the archipelago means for the people living there. In this case we see that there seems to be at least two ways of being deeply integrated with the biophysical dimensions of the archipelago; one that is more natural (in the sense that the archipelago is and has always been one's home) and practical, and another which is more of a reflexive and moral nature. Actually the fact that there are different paths of integration is more interesting than the answers to "who thinks what?". It is possible that quite a few "genuine archipelago people" today understand and support the interpretation of the archipelago as an alternative and morally significant landscape. This might either lead to conflicts within themselves or between them and those who keep to the traditional interpretation. If the city-cultures admiration of wage work could be spread to the archipelago in the 1960s and 1970s, then today's urban longing for the purity and beauty of unspoilt (which does not necessarily mean *untouched*) nature and for the authencity of small scale society should be spread even more efficiently.

> For the archipelago people it has its significance to interpret the world from an archipelago perspective. The worldview that described the cities as obvious centers of the world and everything called archipelago or rural area as that which is "outside" or "beside" is out-of-date and invalid. The earth can be described as a gigantic archipelago; the universe can be experienced as an eternal sea filled by islets and reefs. Everyone has to contribute with his own vision in order to formulate the new worldview we need today.[42]

9. The Meaning of Places in Modern Identities

As can be seen in some of the quotations above, the reason given for the deep integration with environment of the historical archipelagoite was his interaction with it through his involvement in primary production (hunting, agriculture, fishing and so on). Today the archipelago society is very different. Wage work within the service sector plays a major role in getting money for the expensive equipment that is needed to live in the modern archipelago. People own cars, glass fibre boats, televisions, micro owens, satellite antennas and mobile telephones just like anyone on the main land. They send their children to schools where they learn the same things as every child in all of Finland. Even from the outer islands (at least the ones with ferry connections) you can reach a big shopping center within a few hours. What is left of the special character of archipelago life?

Nils Storå hits the core of the question when discussing the loss of the knowledge of different forms of ice in the archipelago. The traditional knowledge is lost as the elements of nature, like the ice, lose their importance for every day life of the archipelagoite.

> The knowledge of ice belongs to the patterns of maritime adaptation that have lost their previous importance, which probably means that many archipelago people experience the ice as a rather alien element. One can wonder if the loss of this and other maritime patterns of adaptation decreases the possibilities of the archipelago people to identify their environment of life and thus has consequences for a factor like the well-being of people, difficult as it is to define. Against this background it seems important to investigate how the archipelago people themselves understand the archipelago as their environment of life, and how this conception changes.[44]

It is possible, maybe also probable, that the archipelago as an environment, still has an important meaning for people. Although much has changed, the life in the archipelago still has its unique character; the relative isolation, the small-scale societies, the dependence on plural subsistence strategies and, of course, the archipelago as an biophysical environment. And although less and less people have primary production, with all that this means for the sense of interacting with nature, as their main occupation, fishing, hunting and cultivating still have some importance, although now as "free time activities".

The discussion has led us back to the broader issue of how identities are constructed. Many authors have suggested that the role of *place* for identity has changed as a consequence of modern mobility and mediation of information. According to Anthony Giddens modernity is characterized by its reflexivity, that is, the tendency to constantly examine and reform social practices "in the light of incoming information about those very practices."[45] At an individual level this reflexivity is reflected in the process of defining one's self-identity. Modern identity formation is characterized by a relatively high level of reflexivity.[46] Identity is no longer *only* a question of external relations – like, for example socioeconomic position – but should be developed within a sphere of authencity and emotionally based relations, or, as Giddens calls them, pure relations.[47] The implication of modern reflexivity seems to be a change in the role of places for identity formation. In pre-modern societies places were central for personal identity 1) as a location where you spend most of your life and with which you interact continuously, and 2) as a location in which you are anchored through all those external social relations defining who you are. In modern societies transport systems move people around the world and media move the world into people's living rooms. Modern human beings thus interact with many places every day. At the same time the relative dissolution of the importance of external social relations changes the sense in which we are anchored in places. Emotionally based relations are not automatic in the same way as external relations are, but must be worked on. There is always a risk that the relation will come to an end. This means that place appears as a frame and location for our emotional development rather than as a determining structure. When we ask ourselves who we are, and thus, whom we want to be and where we have come in relation to this, we interpret our past as a emotional development through important places. Places, of course, are not purely physical locations, but also social and natural contexts. The reflexivity of modern identity forming means that we have to reflect on the meaning of places, and that the meaning of one place is never final. When reflecting in this way we write a geography of ourselves, and this geography is in a constant flux.

How will all this affect the study presented in this paper? One important thing seems to be that the meaning of the archipelago for people living there must be understood in terms of lifestyle rather than geographical location. The essence of the archipelago as part of personal identities is not its character of being a physical source for those identities, but rather its value as a symbol of a certain way of living. Giddens defines lifestyle as "a more or less integrated set of practices which an individual embraces, not only because such practices fulfil utilitarian needs, but because they give material form to a particular narrative of self-identity."[48] So even if many of the old practices (bird hunting, fishing, cultivation, moving in the sea or on the ice, and so on) have lost their meaning as necessities for subsistence in the archipelago, they still might form a set of practices integrated and specific enough to be gathered in the word "arcipleagoite." The symbolic value of "archipelago" for identity forming would thus be its reference to a certain desired way of living, that is, to an ideal set of practices and the social and natural contexts within which these should be realized.

Biography

Henrik Bruun (1966) is a doctoral student at the Human Ecology Section, University of Göteborg. His field of research encompasses interpretations of nature, security issues, and life in coastal and archipelago areas. His educational background includes a Masters in philosophy at the University of Helsinki.

Notes

1. Richard Langlais, "Reformulating Security; A Case Study from Arctic Canada," *Humanekologiska skrifter 13*, Göteborg 1995.
2. Arne Næss, *Ecology, Community and Lifestyle*, ed. David Rothenberg (Cambridge; Cambridge University Press, 1989): 175.
3. See Warwick Fox, *Toward a Transpersonal Ecology; Developing New Foundations for Environmentalism* (Boston&London: Shambala, 1990) for references.
4. See especially chapter 2, "Ellesmere as relational field," in Langlais, "Reformulating Security."
5. Langlais, "Reformulating Security," 285.
6. Langlais, "Reformulating Security," 279.
7. Charles Taylor, *Sources of the Self* (Cambridge; Cambridge University Press, 1992): 4.
8. Taylor, *Sources of the Self*, 8.
9. Taylor, *Sources of the Self*, 44.
10. Taylor, *Sources of the Self*, 5.
11. Taylor, *Sources of the Self*, 14.
12. Taylor, *Sources of the Self*, 19.
13. The point that identity must be understood in relation to what one wants to be should be valuable for deep ecologists who normally discuss identity in terms of "identifying with" for example a specific landscape. The extended Self should not be understood as an elimination of the boundary between the person and his environment, but rather as a definition of good life in terms of co-existence rather than domination. Identity is founded on ontological statements, just as the deep ecologists claim, but these statements concern human beings in general and not any specific one. The kind of life I want to realize in interaction with nature is absed on my view of man's position in nature, rather than on the process of personal identification with nature. Or, put in another way, personal identification must be based on more general statements on the nature of human being.
14. Taylor, *Sources of the Self*, 27. Taylor is of course not speaking of the Inuit here, but of people in general defining themselves according to nationality, religion, ideology, and so on.
15. Ibid. I want to point out that the presentation here is descriptive rather than normative. The fact that people's identities are of normative character does not implicate that anything can be legitimized by showing that it is part of someone's identity. "What can we say about something being important for a full life, according to *our* sense of identity, but that is not recognized by people who have another sense of identity than ours?" This very important question, posed by Langlais in a private letter, is left open in this paper.
16. Taylor, *Sources of the Self*, 30.
17. "archipelagoite" might feel a bit artficial as a concept. I have chosen it with reference to the fact that people living on islands can be called islanders. On the other hand, I did not want to use this latter concept, since living in an archipelago is not necessarily the same as living on an island. I also considered using the Swedish term (skärgårdsbo), just like the Inuits are called Inuits (which in their language means "the people"), but decided not to do that since it gives a false impression of ethnicity and homogenity.

18. A discussion on constructions of national identities can be found in Benedict Anderson, *Den föreställda gemenskapen; reflektioner kring nationalismens ursprung och spridning* (Göteborg; Daidalos, 1993). The problems of finding regional identities are dealt with in for example Sven B. Ek, "Regional identitet; ett besvärligt kapitel," *Den regionala särarten*, ed. Barbro Blomberg & Sven Olof Lindqvist (Lund: Studentlitteratur, 1994).
19. Gunda Åbonde-Wickström, "Befolkning, bosättning, bebyggelse i skärgården," *Kontakt och konflikt i skärgården*, Nordenskiöldsamfundets tidskrift 49 supplementum (Helsingfors, 1989): 143.
20. See for example Nils-Hinrik Aschan, "Skärgården och rekreationslivet," *Skärgård i omvandling; Miljö och människa i Finlands skärgård* (Borgå; Rabén & Sjögren, 1975): 201.
21. Nils Storå, "Den gamla skärgårdskulturen och dess framtid," *Skärgård i omvandling*.
22. Bo Lönnqvist, "Skärgård och identitet," *Skärgård* 2/1993, 4.
23. Håkan Kulves & Göran Harberg, *Skärgård; sammanbrott eller utveckling?* (Borgå: Albert Bonniers förlag, 1971): 19-26; Leif Lindgren & Torsten Stjernberg, "Benämningar på olika land," *Skärgårdshavets nationalpark*, red. Lindgren&Stjernberg (Borgå: WSOY, 1986): 14-16.
24. Nils Storå, "Skärgården som livsmiljö; anpassning, variation och förändring," *Kontakt och konflikt i skärgården*, 47. These names have, however, been collected from all of the Finnish archipelagos – not only from the Archipelago Sea.
25. See for example the following articles in *Kontakt och konflikt i skärgården*: Stig Jaatinen, "Stabilitet och instabilitet i skärgården," 17; Nils Storå, "Skärgården som livsmiljö," 41, and Göran Bergman, "Kan skärgårdens landskap, fauna och flora bibehållas när människan använder skärgården på andra sätt än förr," 98-99.
26. Anders Danielsson, "En skärgårdsbo ser på skärgårdens framtid," *Skärgård i omvandling*, 239.
27. Ole Torvalds, "Skärgårdstider," *Kontakt och konflikt*, 152.
28. Kulves & Harberg, *Skärgård; sammanbrott eller*, 9.
29. Ingrid Sandman, "Gunnevi Vesterlund: 'Skärgårdsföretagaren liknar en martall,'" *Skärgård* 1/1991, 8-9.
30. An archipelagoite (from the Ekenäs archipelago) quoted in Birger Ohlson, "Finlands skärgård som en del av jordens arkipelager," *Skärgård i omvandling*, 11.
31. Kulves & Harberg, *Skärgård; sammanbrott eller*, 19.
32. Danielsson, "En skärgårdsbo," 240.
33. Gun Jansson, "Deltagarkommentar," *Skärgårdsliv på kvinnovis*, Nordisk Ministerråd, NORD 1987:47, 24.
34. Torsten Stjernberg, "Skärgårdens folk och närsamhället; människan i skärgården," *Kontakt och konflikt*, 141-142.
35. Marlene Öhberg, "Kan man vara avvikande i skärgården," *Skärgårdsliv på kvinnovis*, 56-57.
36. Christoffer Taxell, "Samhällsutvecklingen och skärgården," *Kontakt och konflikt*, 55-56.
37. Archipelagoite quoted in "Vår syn på möjligheterna att få arbete," *Skärgård i omvandling*, 174.
38. Torvalds, "Skärgårdstider," 152.
39. Eeva-Stiina Snellman, "Deltagarkommentar," *Skärgårdsliv på kvinnovis*, 15.
40. Öhberg, "Kan man vara," 55-60.

41. Öhberg, "Kan man vara," 55.
42. Mariella Lindén, "De tre kvinnorna – mytens användbarhet," *Skärgård* 1/1991.
43. Ea Blomqvist, "Skärgården som natur- och kulturmiljö," *Kontakt och konflikt*, 10.
44. Storå, "Skärgården som," 48.
45. Anthony Giddens, *The Consequences of Modernity* (Cambridge; Polity Press, 1995): 38.
46. Anthony Giddens, *Modernity and Self-Identity; Self and Society in the Late Modern Age* (Cambridge; Polity Press, 1994): 75-76.
47. Giddens, *Modernity and*, 88-98.
48. Giddens, *Modernity and*, 81.

Bibliography

Anderson, Benedict. *Den föreställda gemenskapen; reflektioner kring nationalismens ursprung och spridning.* Göteborg: Daidalos, 1993.
Archipelagoite quoted in "Vår syn på möjligheterna att få arbete," *Skärgård i omvandling; Miljö och människa i Finlands skärgård.* Borgå: Rabén & Sjögren, 1975.
Aschan, Nils-Hinrik. "Skärgården och rekreationslivet." *Skärgård i omvandling; Miljö och människa i Finlands skärgård.* Borgå: Rabén & Sjögren, 1975.
Bergman, Göran. "Kan skärgårdens landskap, fauna och flora bibehållas när människan använder skärgården på andra sätt än förr." *Kontakt och konflikt i skärgården.* Nordenskiöldsamfundets tidskrift 49 supplementum. Helsingfors, 1989.
Blomqvist, Ea. "Skärgården som natur- och kulturmiljö." *Kontakt och konflikt i skärgården.* Nordenskiöldsamfundets tidskrift 49 supplementum. Helsingfors, 1989.
Danielsson, Anders. "En skärgårdsbo ser på skärgårdens framtid." *Skärgård i omvandling; Miljö och människa i Finlands skärgård.* Borgå: Rabén & Sjögren, 1975.
Ek, Sven B. "Regional identitet; ett besvärligt kapitel." *Den regionala särarten*, ed. Barbro Blomberg and Sven Olof Lindqvist. Lund: Studentlitteratur, 1994.
Fox, Warwick. *Toward a Transpersonal Ecology; Developing New Foundations for Environmentalism.* Boston & London: Shambala, 1990.
Giddens, Anthony. *The Consequences of Modernity.* Cambridge: Polity Press, 1995.
Giddens, Anthony. *Modernity and Self-Identity; Self and Society in the Late Modern Age.* Cambridge: Polity Press, 1994.
Jaatinen, Stig. "Stabilitet och instabilitet i skärgården." *Kontakt och konflikt i skärgården.* Nordenskiöldsamfundets tidskrift 49 supplementum. Helsingfors, 1989.
Jansson, Gun. "Deltagarkommentar." *Skärgårdsliv på kvinnovis*, Nordisk Ministerråd, NORD no. 47 (1987).
Kulves, Håkan and Göran Harberg. *Skärgård; sammanbrott eller utveckling?* Borgå: Albert Bonniers förlag, 1971.
Langlais, Richard. *Reformulating Security; A Case Study from Arctic Canada.* Humanekologiska skrifter 13. Göteborg: Human Ecology Section, Göteborg University, 1995.
Langlais, Richard. Private letter, 17.8.1995.
Lindén, Mariella. "De tre kvinnorna – mytens användbarhet." *Skärgård* 1 (1991).
Lindgren, Leif and Torsten Stjernberg. "Benämningar på olika land." *Skärgårdshavets nationalpark.* Eds. Lindgren and Stjernberg. Borgå: WSOY, 1986.

Lönnqvist, Bo. "Skärgård och identitet." *Skärgård* 2 (1993).

Næss, Arne. *Ecology, Community and Lifestyle*. Ed. David Rothenberg. Cambridge; Cambridge University Press, 1989.

Ohlson, Birger. "Finlands skärgård som en del av jordens arkipelager." *Skärgård i omvandling; Miljö och människa i Finlands skärgård.* Borgå: Rabén & Sjögren, 1975.

Sandman, Ingrid. "Gunnevi Vesterlund: 'Skärgårdsföretagaren liknar en martall'." *Skärgård* 1 (1991).

Snellman, Eeva-Stiina. "Deltagarkommentar."*Skärgårdsliv på kvinnovis*, Nordisk Ministerråd, NORD no. 47 (1987).

Stjernberg, Torsten. "Skärgårdens folk och närsamhället; människan i skärgården." *Kontakt och konflikt i skärgården.* Nordenskiöldsamfundets tidskrift 49 supplementum. Helsingfors, 1989.

Storå, Nils. "Den gamla skärgårdskulturen och dess framtid." *Skärgård i omvandling; Miljö och människa i Finlands skärgård.* Borgå: Rabén & Sjögren, 1975.

Taxell, Christoffer. "Samhällsutvecklingen och skärgården." *Kontakt och konflikt i skärgården.* Nordenskiöldsamfundets tidskrift 49 supplementum. Helsingfors, 1989.

Taylor, Charles.*Sources of the Self.* Cambridge; Cambridge University Press, 1992.

Torvalds, Ole. "Skärgårdstider." *Kontakt och konflikt i skärgården.* Nordenskiöldsamfundets tidskrift 49 supplementum. Helsingfors, 1989.

Åbonde-Wickström, Gunda. "Befolkning, bosättning, bebyggelse i skärgården." *Kontakt och konflikt i skärgården.* Nordenskiöldsamfundets tidskrift 49 supplementum. Helsingfors, 1989.

Öhberg, Marlene. "Kan man vara avvikande i skärgården," *Skärgårdsliv på kvinnovis*, Nordisk Ministerråd, NORD no. 47 (1987).

Dan Egonsson
Man's Place in Nature

Abstract
In this paper I will defend a kind of human-centred perspective regarding how to deal with ethical questions where the interests of humans and animals and respect for nature are involved. This perspective, I believe, is not speciesistic in the sense of arbitrarily picking out the interests of one particular species as counting for more than the interests of all other species. Nor does it claim that the natural environment is valued only for human use and enjoyment. Instead it is an attempt to rationally justify a view according to which humans have a special although not a unique place in relation to the rest of creation.

I believe that human beings are morally special but also that there is room for direct duties to other creatures and objects in nature. My position might therefore be described as some kind of compromise between traditional anthropocentrism and radical anti-speciesism or environmentalism. I will argue that, given a subjectivistic theory which holds that values orginate exclusively in relation to valuing subjects, and given that human beings have a special value compared to other species and objects in nature in the eyes of other human beings, then we have a point of departure for a defence of human dignity, suggesting that man has some kind of superior moral standing in creation.

In this paper I will consider a fundamental ethical question, namely, whether or not human beings have a special moral standing in creation. Recently the idea that such a standing exists has been vigorously attacked from different directions. For instance, Richard Ryder and many others have called one version or manifestation of this idea "speciesism", i.e. the idea that the interests of the members of a particular species, just by virtue of being interests of that particular species, count for more than the interests of members of other species. *If* speciesism is morally objectionable, then the way we have treated nature and other species is a moral tragedy. Others, for instance Paul W. Taylor, have attacked the idea that humans have a special standing from an even broader perspective and have argued that anthropocentrism or a human-centred environmental ethics – according to which the natural world is valued only as object for our use and enjoyment – should be replaced by a life-centred or biocentric one – according to which our duties towards nature do not stem from the duties we owe to humans.

I want to argue for a kind of human-centred perspective on how to deal with ethical questions where the interests of humans, animals and respect for nature are involved, which, I believe, is not speciesistic in the sense of arbitrarily giving priority to the interests of a particular species. Neither does it claim that the natural environment is valued only for human use and enjoyment. Instead it is an attempt to rationally justify a view in which we humans have a special although not a unique place in relation to the rest of creation.

I believe that human beings are morally special but that there is also a place for direct duties to other creatures and objects in nature. My position might therefore be described as some kind of compromise between traditional anthropocentrism and radical anti-speciesism or environmentalism. The present paper, however, is merely an outline of a position to be developed.

1.

One crucial distinction which we have already touched upon is that between having a direct and indirect value or moral importance. According to Taylor, anthropocentrism claims that nature has a value which is derived from other values and that only human beings are directly valuable.

However, this talk of a direct value of human beings has to be analysed. What does it mean to say that some being or property has a direct value?

At least two different things can be meant by it. Either that the property in question is important in itself and not because of the fact that the property is typically found together with some other property, or that the property is important in itself and not merely as an instrument or necessary condition for the actualization of other values.

Many philosophers have thought that being human is *indirectly* important in the first sense. For instance Kant believed that human beings occupy a special place in creation by virtue of the fact that they have an intrinsic worth or dignity. One important formulation of the categorical imperative in *Groundwork of the Metaphysics of Morals* reads: "Act in such a way that you always treat humanity, whether in your own person or in the person of any other, never simply as a means, but always at the same time as an end" (1964: 97). In this we humans are different from all other living objects on earth. Only human beings can be the object of direct duties, and "as far as animals are concerned, we have no direct duties. Animals are not self-conscious and are there merely as a means to an end. That end is man" (*Lectures on Ethics*: 239).

However, in view of the distinction made above, this is not an expression of the idea that being human is directly valuable. In spite of Kant's language, being human has importance only in so far as it is combined with being a rational agent, who is capable of making his own autonomous decisions.

The reason why rationality and autonomy are important for Kant has of course to do with his view of morality: the moral law is the law of reason, and, in James Rachels's words, "rational beings are the embodiment of the moral law itself" (1993: 129). Furthermore, the moral law is autonomous in so far as its validity does not depend on desires and feelings, whereas rational beings are autonomous in the sense that their actions might be motivated independently of the pursuit of happiness. Morality, and humanity in so far as it is capable of morality, alone has dignity.

I interpret this as an expression of the idea that being human is morally important in the sense that this property is typically combined with being a rational being capable of autonomous choice and therefore morality. And this is a plain example of indirect importance in the first sense above.

What might seem somewhat strange is that Kant does not, as far as I know, explicitly consider the question of whether those human beings who lack this capacity – for instance infants and imbeciles – also lack dignity, which would be the natural conclusion. On the other hand, he is eager to emphasize that dignity is not to be conferred only on human beings, but on all rational beings, whether or not they are human.

In order to endow the property of being human with this kind of indirect value one needs not be a Kantian. Many philosophers think that in order to be able to want something you have to have a concept of the object of your want. If the attitude of desiring is a propositional attitude, or involves such an attitude, a necessary condition of having such an attitude seems to be understanding the proposition one desires to be true. A necessary condition of this understanding in turn seems to be having the concepts figuring in it (cf. Michael Tooley 1983: 104).

If this reasoning is correct, you cannot desire to continue living unless you have a concept of your future life, and in order to have such a concept you have to be self-conscious, at least to a certain degree. Thus, if you believe it morally important (which many non-Kantian philosophers indeed do) not to thwart a desire to go on living, you will also think that the capacity for self-consciousness is a morally significant property.

This will not, however, be an intrinsic significance, since an individual may have this capacity without caring whether or not he will exist in the future; that is, self-consciousness according to this reasoning is relevant only as a prerequisite of a desire to go on living (or of a desire not to go on living). Therefore, being human is morally important in virtue of the fact that humans *commonly* display self-consciousness.

Actually this is an example of a combination of the first and second distinction between direct and indirect values. Being human is typically associated with being self-conscious – being human is therefore indirectly important in the first sense. Being self-conscious, on the other hand, is indirectly important in the second sense, since this property is valuable in virtue of what it makes possible, for instance valuing one's own life.

In short, we have considered two distinctions which can be hidden in talking of the direct importance of a property. First, properties which have an *intrinsic* importance, in contrast with being *associated* with other properties (which can be directly or indirectly important). Second, properties which are *intrinsically* important, in contrast with being *instrumentally* important.

I want to argue that being human might be intrinsically important particularly in the first sense and that that is partly what gives this property a special moral standing. However, once again, this kind of importance is not exclusively bestowed on that property, but might be conferred on other objects as well – in culture and nature.

2.

One important problem in the theory of value concerns whether something can be valuable only in relation to a valuing subject or if something can be valuable – given that there exists something valuable – whether or not a subject has any attitudes towards it. ("Attitude" might be understood in a wide sense. Thus Steve Sapontzis calls the former position "an affective value theory" which "holds that values originate with feelings, such as pleasure and pain, fulfilment and frustration, joy and sorrow, excitement and depression, and so forth", 1993: 271. By "attitude" I mean particularly something related to preferring.)

This is the classical question of subjectivism *versus* objectivism. One problem which the subjectivists have to solve is how to account for the fact that we normally seem to have moral attitudes towards objects because we think these objects valuable (positively or negatively) in some way or another, whereas the truth according to subjectivism has to be described the other way round: objects are valuable in virtue of subjects having attitudes towards them. And, briefly, one problem with objectivism has to do with explaining what kind of fact it is that something is valuable, if it is not ultimately a fact about our own or another's attitudes. Furthermore, how do you as an objectivist explain the fact that a value judgement is intrinsically motivating in a way that a factual judgement is not?

My ambition is not to show that the problems with objectivism are more difficult to solve than the problems with subjectivism (although I believe that is the case) but rather to show that you may believe that being human is in itself morally important whether you are an objectivist or subjectivist about values. If you believe that being human is intrinsically important you can, if you are a subjectivist, mean by this that the property is intrinsically important *for humans*, i.e. human beings place a special value on being human in itself, a value that is not dependent upon what is associated with belonging to that species.

I will proceed from the assumption that subjectivism is true. The reason is that I want to show that there is a sense to be given to the idea of a human dignity even from a subjectivistic perspective, although subjectivists mostly deny this very idea. Furthermore, subjectivists often deny as well that we should give intrinsic weight to the fact that for instance an entire species may disappear, or to the fact that a valley's ecosystem is destroyed, although I believe that doing so makes sense from a subjectivistic point of view.

3.

Many philosophers have questioned one of the more important assumptions that I proceed from, namely, that being human *is* intrinsically important for humans. They have questioned what Roger Wertheimer describes in the following way:

"Let us call the kind of moral status most people ascribe to human beings *human (moral) status*. The term refers to a kind of independent and superior consideration to be accorded an entity, not to the kind of entity to be accorded the consideration, so it is not a definitional truth that human beings have human status. But most people believe that being human has *moral cachet:* viz., a human being has human status in virtue of being a human being (and thus each human being has human status). Call this the *Standard Belief.* That most people accept it is an empirical fact" (1974: 107-8).

But is it an empirical fact? One remarkable thing is that there is empirical evidence which seems to contradict this proposal of a Standard Belief. For instance, in Sweden there was an investigation carried out in 1986-7, led by Anders Jeffner, which attracted a great deal of attention. The investigation concerned, among other things, whether or not people think that there is a moral difference between human and non-human beings. (I will not here consider the scientific reliability of the investigation.)

When asked whether one ought to show more respect to a human being than to other living beings, 43% answered "no", 37% "yes" and the rest did not know how to answer the question. This was of course surprising, but a follow-up investigation seems to confirm that two Swedes out of three believe that humans and non-humans are equally valuable, which is an even stronger conclusion!

However, I am very sceptical of these results. One reason is that when asked why they regard humans and animals as equally valuable, 93% in the investigation answered that they believe that everything which is alive is equally valuable. I certainly do not know of a single person who in practical life behaves as if there is no value difference between different kinds of living organisms. That attitude would not only prescribe a radical change in our treatment of animals and nature but would also prescribe reverence for micro-organisms such as viruses. In choosing whether to save from a burning house our neighbour's ten-year-old daughter or an invisible micro-organism (for instance an AIDS virus) in a test tube, you would, if you had the belief in question, consider the choice to be morally indifferent – you could just as well save the micro-organism. (If you prefer not to call the virus a living organism, a comparison can be made instead between a human being and, for instance, a potted geranium.) I am absolutely sure that the majority of Swedes would reject such a conclusion.

Likewise, in my view it is hard to reconcile the fact that only about 30% believe that a human being ought to be shown more respect than other kinds of living beings with the fact that a majority of us in everyday life do not act as if this is what we actually believe. For instance, most of us eat meat without protesting, and I find it difficult to believe that someone who is serious in his denial of a difference in worth between humans and animals really would continue to do that (unless *ex hypothesi* the thought was that humans and animals were equally *worthless*). It is true that we have formed habits which might be very difficult to extinguish, but the point is that it seems troublesome to claim that humans and animals are of equal value against the background of these habits.

These examples are enough to show that we have reason to question the *seriousness* of the attitude expressed in Jeffner's investigation. We have to distinguish between what we *say* about the values we embrace and what values we *actually* embrace. And I think this is true in whatever sense we understand an evaluation – there has to be some connection between our valuations and actions or at least action tendencies.

However, this is not to say that Jeffner's investigation lacks importance. On the contrary, I believe it might point to an interesting change in our attitudes to other animals and to nature – people nowadays are *more* liable to reject an anthropocentric ethic, which might be interpreted as a tendency to a more radical change in the future. There are more vegetarians in the Western countries nowadays than, say, 25 years ago and I guess that in the future there will be even more. I welcome this development for various reasons, but we must beware of not overinterpreting the attitudes expressed in the investigation. And as long as the anthropocentric point of view dominates it will have subjectivistic importance.

4.

If there exists a Standard Belief, then we are prepared to make priorities among different kinds of beings merely on the basis that some of them biologically speaking are humans.

But the kind of importance we attach to species membership which is manifested in the Standard Belief, if I am right in my assumptions, will both be possible to grade and to confer on non-human species. To be morally special is something relative, and even if it should turn out that we humans, as far as the subjective and intrinsic value is concerned, are morally special compared to the rest of creation, that will not mean that all other species are on an equal moral footing.

Take as an example a bird-watcher and nature-lover. I assume that this person not only wants it to be the case that birds and other animals with a certain physical appearance exist in nature. She has (normally) also wants concerning the genetic structure of these animals. For instance, if a bird-watcher wants it to be the case that a certain kind of rare bird does not become extinct, I suppose she would not be content to know that it might be possible to breed birds of another species the physical appearance of which would be identical with the rare bird's. This shows that in this case species membership is something important in itself – a bird-watcher does (normally) not only want to look at birds with a certain kind of physical look, she wants them to be of a certain species as well. Furthermore, some non-human species are more valuable in her eyes than some others.

An intriguing question is whether or not something ought to be added here, namely, that in this example it is species membership as a result of an evolutionary process that is important in itself. When Ronald Dworkin discusses the phenomenology of nature's sacredness he says:

"Geneticists have created plants that we find instrumentally valuable: they produce food and may save lives. But we do not think that these artificially produced species are intrinsically valuable in the way that naturally produced species are" (1993: 78-9).

This may give rise to the following question. Suppose a species becomes extinct but that geneticists in the future may create an animal with exactly the same structure as that of the extinct species, would the created animal be as valuable (for instance in a normal bird-watcher's eyes) as the original one? (Here I assume that we have a species concept that would allow us to say that the original and the created animal were of the same species. This could be put in question, of course, i.e. whether or not some kind of historical continuity also is necessary for the identity of a species.)

We will have to guess, and my guess is that many people would think that something valuable *is* lost in the created animal, and if that is true then we have to admit that species membership of a certain being may be important in itself, as long as we talk of an individual which is not created by genetic manipulation. At least, to be a result of such a process will make one's value as a member of a certain species *less* than it would have been if the genetic set-up was instead the result of a "natural" process.

However, one might object that in our example from the bird-watcher we have a case where non-human species membership is indirectly rather than directly valued – she wants there to exist birds of a certain species in order to be able to watch them. But I believe it possible to point to examples where this is not the end of the matter. Lovers of nature may not only want a certain species to exist for the sake of the pleasure of watching (or listening to) it, they may also want it to exist independently of *any* pleasure that it could produce in humans, directly or indirectly.

At least this sounds very realistic in my own ears. If I should hear of a very rare and shy owl never directly observed by any human, I might spontaneously want it to be preserved. And that would not be because of the possibility of observing the owl in the future. On the contrary, it would be better if the owl also in the future remains the mysterious kind of animal it has been in the past. And the same kind of thought experiment will work for other kinds of animals – deep-sea fish, beetles and so on. And since I do not think I am unique in this respect, that means we have examples where intrinsic value is conferred subjectively also on non-human species of animals.

In these examples we have considered intrinsic value conferred on certain objects on the basis of genetic structure. This is not the only possible basis for such values. For instance, we may also consider a wild river or a mountain as intrinsically valuable. That is, we may consider its existence valuable whether or not it may be used for some further purposes, and also whether or not someone is aware of its existence.

Summing up, the property of being human might well remain something special and important also when we take this importance to be an effect of our capacity to confer intrinsic value on objects. However, it does not seem to be a *unique* value which only humans have – what is special about us humans is rather that we probably have this value to a greater extent than do the animals.

5.

The only thing that seems unique as far as this value is concerned is that humans probably are the only beings able to *confer* it on objects.

The reason why this is so has of course to do with mental capacity. Consider the Standard Belief, which I said was a value conferred on the property of being human by humans. One big difference between humans and non-humans in this regard seems to be that only humans may have a concept of what it is to belong to a certain species; only humans have a concept of what it is to be a member of a certain species over and above having a certain appearance, a certain smell, displaying certain behaviour-patterns, and so on.

Assigning intrinsic value to an object does not only require having a concept of the object, but also being able to value the object in a certain way. Consider once again the Standard Belief. For a subjectivist, the important element in this attitude is particularly a preference concerning the well-being of members of the species *Homo sapiens*. Assigning intrinsic value to an object means wanting that object to exist and prosper independently of what that may mean to me (as the person who values). Therefore, we may borrow a term from R. M. Hare (originally from Dworkin) and call this an "external preference". Hare takes this class of preferences "as consisting of those preferences which are for things other than experiences of the preferrer" (1989: 177).

And now I have to speculate, but I doubt that this kind of preference is particularly frequent among non-humans. It is hard to believe that a dog wants its master to prosper independently of whether or not the dog itself has any experiences of this. Again the problem seems partly to be conceptual – perhaps the dog lacks a concept of what it means for its master to have a life independently of the life they have in common. But even if it has got the appropriate concepts, it does not seem very realistic to believe it would put them together in a valuation like the one described. On the other hand, this kind of valuation is common among human beings – a mother may very well want her children to prosper also after she has died.

This reasoning can easily be transferred to objects like wild rivers and mountains, and so on. Even if an animal had a concept of what it takes for a river to be a wild river and even if it had a concept of what it would be for the wild river to exist independently of the animal's experiences, it seems unrealistic to imagine that the animal has a valuation to the effect that the wild river should continue to flow independently of what effects this might have on the animal's experiences.

Therefore, I believe that the kind of valuation which according to a subjectivist is the basis of intrinsic values might be found exclusively, or at least with very few exceptions, among human beings. This means that man in some fundamental sense is the source of the intrinsic value that might be conferred also on natural objects and which in turn may be a basis for direct duties towards them; that is, duties that have as their primary object the protection of these objects independently of the consequences for human experiences.

6.

Now let me try to formulate some kind of conclusion. I believe there is a sense in which beings and objects in creation, and particularly human beings, can be said to have intrinsic value, even in a theory according to which values originate exclusively in subjective attitudes, such as preferences, emotions, and so.

This may seem to be a fairly modest conclusion, but actually I think that many philosophers have neglected this sense of what it takes to be intrinsically valuable. Consider, for instance, the following passage from Peter Singer's book *Practical Ethics* (second edition):

"The drowning of the ancient forests, the possible loss of an entire species, the destruction of several complex ecosystems, the blockage of the wild river itself, and the loss of those gorges are factors to be taken into account only in so far as they adversely affect sentient creatures. Is a more radical break with the traditional position possible? Can some or all of these aspects of the flooding of the valley be shown to have intrinsic value, so that they must be taken into account independently of their effects on human beings or non-human animals?" (1993: 276). Eventually Singer rejects the idea of an intrinsic value to be ascribed to the valley.

I believe that Singer in his treatment of intrinsic value conflates the two distinctions which I have discussed above. He says: "Something is of intrinsic value if it is good or desirable *in itself*; the contrast is with 'instrumental value', that is, value as a means to some other end or purpose" (1993: 274). Even though Singer talks of what is desir*able* in itself and not what is desir*ed* in itself, I believe that the contrast here concerns the general distinction between value as an end and value as a means. (Let us call this distinction 1.) However, in the first passage this is not a natural reading of intrinsic value. A more natural interpretation is that he wants to contrast an object having value independently of the object's effects on sentient beings and an object having value exclusively *in virtue of* the effects of the object on sentient beings (distinction 2), that is, a distinction that recalls our distinction between objective and subjective value (though as I understand subjectivism an object can be valuable for a subject even when it does not have any direct experiential effects on the subject; but let us ignore this difference).

Therefore, proceeding from distinction 1 we may argue that the abovementioned aspects of the valley have intrinsic value, but nevertheless deny that they have intrinsic value considering distinction 2. And in view of his subjectivistic point of departure Singer may well agree with this.*

Biography

Dan Egonsson was born in 1956. He is a Doctor of Philosophy and presently working as Postdoctoral Fellow at Lund University. He has previously published *Interests, Utilitarianism and Moral Standing* (1990).

Bibliography

Dworkin, Ronald (1993). *Life's Dominion*, London: HarperCollins.

Hare, R. M. (1989). "Universalizability and the summing of desires: Reply to Ingmar Persson", *Theoria*, Vol. LV, Part 3, pp. 171-7.

Jeffner, Anders (1988). *Människovärde och människovärdering*, Uppsala Universitet, Tros- och livsåskådningsvetenskap, Rapport.

Kant, Immanuel (1963). "Duties to Animals and Spirits", in *Lectures on Ethics*, trans. Louis Infield, New York: Harper & Row, pp. 239-41.

Kant, Immanuel (1964). *Groundwork of the Metaphysic of Morals*, trans. and analysed by H. J. Paton, New York: Harper & Row.

Rachels, James (1993). *The Elements of Moral Philosophy*, New York: McGraw-Hill.

Sapontzis, Steve (1993). "Aping Persons – Pro and Con", in P. Cavalieri & P. Singer (eds.): *The Great Ape Project*, London: Fourth Estate, pp. 269-77.

Singer, Peter (1993). *Practical Ethics*, sec. ed., Cambridge U. P.

Taylor, Paul W. (1986). *Respect for Nature*, Princeton U. P.

Tooley, Michael (1983). *Abortion and Infanticide*, Oxford: Clarendon Press.

Wertheimer, Roger (1974). "Philosophy on Humanity", in R. L. Perkins (ed.): *Abortion: Pro and Con*, Cambridge & Massachusetts: Schenkman, pp. 107-28.

* I wish to thank Ed Damron and Toni Rønnow-Rasmussen for valuable comments.

Martin Ishøy
Kants *Critique of Judgement*, the Inherent Ethics

Abstract
*The teleological judgement (*Urteilskraft*) gives reason to assume an aim (*Zweck*) in nature. The foundation of this aim is the noumenon/supersensible substrate. This is also the foundation of the moral reason. There is a twofold point in the present short-communication. First the teleological judgement of some phenomena in the natural world can give guidance for an environmental ethical behaviour. The second point is that the best motivation for a moral attitude towards the environment emerges from an encounter with the sublime in nature, because such an encounter results in* Achtung, *which constitutes the moral feeling. A sublime natural phenomena could be called "a natural alien".*

Kants *Critique of Judgement*, the inherent ethics

It is the aim of the *Kritik der Urteilskraft* (= Critique of Judgement) to bridge the gab between (scientific) knowledge and moral. Based on freedom, moral decisions cannot in any way be caused by physical nature. The object of empirical knowledge (*Naturbegriff*) is held in a representation (*Anschauung*) without any access to the thing in itself. The object of science is an *Erscheinung*. The object of the idea of freedom (*Freiheitsbegriff*) is conceived in itself, but no representation is achievable, and therefore there is a boundless gab between these two departments (*Natur/Freiheit*).

Nevertheless it *must* be possible for them to concure, or else it would be impossible to realize, or to bring into existence, the objects of the idea of freedom.

Kant makes it clear that there is a bridge, and that this is the reflective judgement, the central topic of the *Kritik der Urteilskraft*. Unlike the other two departments, the judgement doesn't have a *Begriff*, it is not conceptual subsumptive. Bridging the gab between scientific and moral knowledge, reflective judgement must apply some means that, unlike natural concepts, enable the person to conceive freedom, while still making sensible nature intellegible.

The way the judgement reveals the unity of pure and practical reason, is by drawing attention to the phenomenon *Zweckmässigkeit*, which is a feature in art and nature, that cannot be understood by pure reason. It cannot be subsumed under an universalizing concept (a "universal"). It can only be understood granted freedom as co-constituent condition. By means of the idea of freedom, a human being is able to constitute an aim. Though, in a judgement about *Zweckmässigkeit* one doesn't know the aim as an aim. No human being is the aiming agent. Only, one has to conceive the object as constituted by an aim. So the object is regarded as "aimlike", *Zweckmässig*. *Zweckmässigkeit* is the principle of reflective judgement. It could also be translated into "purposive", but I think that translation would suggest too much of psychology.

Kant divides the *Kritik der Urteilskraft* in two parts, the *Critique of aesthetic judgement* and the *Critique of teleological judgement*. In the *Critique of aesthetic judgement* the aimlikeness, *Zweckmässigkeit*, is aesthetic. This means that it is subjective in the sense that it refers to the capacities or faculties in the judging subject. The conception of the object is aimlike regarding a free interplay of the faculties of cognition, which is not governed by a law, but by freedom. The object is aimlike for this interplay, and the result of this interplay is *Wohlgefallen*, the special feeling of pleasure and displeasure (maybe one could say "feeling of perfection and negation of perfection"). This feeling, which has the same universal validity as an idea (*Begriff*) is important for the final part of this short-communication.

In the *critique of teleological judgement* the aimlikeness is "logical", which means that it refers to the object, but not being an object of pure reason, it cannot be subsumed under any *begriff*. Therefore Kant says that in its teleological activity, the judgement in judging the object is purely reflective. In the aesthetic judgement, the feeling of *Wohlgefallen* was equivalent to an idea. In the teleological judgement there is no such feeling. There is no special feeling, but the object of teleological judgment indicates a practical reason in organic nature. Only, we cannot know the content of this reason scientifically. We cannot know ostensively – or we cannot come up with any proof about – the situation, this "reason in nature" is aiming at. All we can do is to judge the particular phenomenon as aimlike for an apparent aim. In one way it is possible, of cause, to know the "aim" of, for example, an oak tree. The aim is the growth and bloom of the tree. Though, this aim behind the aimlikeness in nature, we can only know as a final state, which we can conceive empirically "*für uns*", but not in it self.

From the above follows, that on the basis of aimlikeness both the aesthetic and the teleological judgement reveals the supersensible substrate, or noumenon, in the empirical world. The reflective judgement recognizes freedom at stake in the sensitive world.

The supersensible substrate is the unconditioned condition, not only for pure and empirical knowledge, but also for acts of freedom (meaning: it is the condition for an aim, and therefore also for aimlikeness). In its revelation of the noumenon (supersensible substrate), the aimlikeness calls to mind (or compels) the moral law.

Now, it is my point, that since the noumenon is the origin of both the moral law and the aimlikeness in the natural world, Kants view is not anthropocentric (antropocentrism being the view that humanness is the decisive criterium for moral relevance). Kants apparent anthropocentrism is qualified by being determined by what is the foundation of both nature and humanity.

In its purity, the moral law is strictly formal. The essential principle is that no act can be allowed which violates freedom (or violates freedom except for the sake of freedom). Not every human act can be contained in the moral law: only those acts which is guided by or aimed at freedom. This is the reason for Kants exclusion of heteronomy in the foundation of moral reason. No satisfaction of any natural inclination can decide the right moral behaviour.

Since aimlikeness is the sign of freedom in nature, not any act having its reason outside human beings, is an act out of heteronomy. Contrary to this: since the ethical norm is "concordance with freedom", and aimlikeness is the sign of an aim, which is only possible on the basis of freedom, the logical aimlikeness can be regarded as the basis of an ethical norm. When acting with consequenses for nature, it is a violation not to take into consideration the aims of nature indicated by the aimlikeness. When the dynamics of nature is acknowledged as aimlike, not respecting them as aims in themselves (though not fully intelligible) is a violation of the moral law.

To give a brief example, one could point to our untempered use of fossil fuel and the resulting escalating greenhouse-effect. The greenhouse-effect is not – or only to a very limited degree – caused by moral regards, *and* it is a symptom of disrespect for the features in nature which gives reason to the assumption of aimlikeness.

We talk about natural boundaries for certain kinds of trees, spruce e.g. These boundaries are not fixed once and for all. They can move during millenia. But when the greenhouse-effect causes the southern boundary of the russian taiga, or forrest, to move northwards at a speed at least ten times faster than ever, and when this implies that vast areas are impoverished in a most unnatural way, then it is a clear expression of lack of respect for the dynamics of nature.

So far, the ethical importance of judgement has emerged from the *teleological* judgement. This is so because the respect for nature is due to a feature in nature; the aimlikeness.

When it comes to the question of the driving force behind an ethics towards nature, I think that the *aesthetic judgement of the sublime* provides a motivation for an ethical attitude towards the non-human environment. In my view both the sublime and the beauty, which is also subject for aesthetic judgement, provide not only motivation for the attitude, but also reason to respect natural occurrences. But that (latter) topic will not be treaten here.

The driving force, or *Treibfeder*, behind morality is *Achtung*, the feeling of respect towards the moral law. The moral law humiliates the natural inclinations towards particularistic satisfaction. As a parallel to the teleological aimlikeness' indication of an aim in nature outside humans, the aesthetic judgement provides a feeling of an aim in nature. This feeling brings either pleasure or displeasure, as mentioned above, due to either a harmonious or a disharmonious interplay of the faculties of cognition. Referring to a harmonious interplay the feeling of beauty results in pleasure or perfection. However, the present focus concerns the feeling of the sublime, which is the feeling of *Unlust*, displeasure or negation of perfection. It refers to disharmony. This feeling springs from an experience that exceeds our capacity to conceive. The experience of the sublime resist both subsumption and the free interplay of the faculties of cognition. Instead of reminding us emotionally of an aim, it seems to us to violate every aim of ours. An exampel of the sublime could be a thunderstorm or a rock of a very strange shape. It is exciting. It doesn't bring the mind into a harmonious state of free interplay. On the contrary, it seems to violate any calmness and harmony. But exactly for this reason, I think, it follows that one must assume an aim in the sublime, but an aim opposed to any aim of ours. Or more precisely; it indicates an aim that transcends our capacity of conception. The pleasure of the free interplay in the mind is caused by the aimlikeness' assumption of an aim, but it is an aim, which is not constituted by us. In the same way, the violation seems to be caused by a strange or alien aim, which is not ours.

The feeling of the sublime is acquainted with *Achtung*, the feeling of respect for the moral law. Both violates our natural preferences. Referring to this violation, Kant writes that the sublime is the best representation, *Vorstellung*, of the moral law[1]. This violation humbles our natural preferences, and brings about that our will is determined by the supersensible substrat or noumenon.

My idea is that the encounter with the sublime, alien, anti-human phenomena, the otherness, in nature humbles us, and opens our eyes for the ethical importance of the freedom in the non-human natural world.

In the search for reasons for respect of nature, I think that for the motivation to preserve nature, it is important to focus on the "alien" aspects of nature. The feeling of encountering the sublime triggers the attitude of respect exactly as does *Achtung*. It is close at hand to title the feeling of the sublime in nature: "*Achtung* for the moral law manifest in nature".

The main idea of the above is, that despite Kants humanism, his text, *Kritik der Urteilskraft*, clearly indicates an environmental ethics, which doesn't exclude non-human nature from immediat moral relevance. Contrary to a widespread assumption, I therefore think, that "anthropocentrism" is a false term when applied to Kant. A better alternative would be "noumenocentrism", referring to the unity of pure and practical reason, and thus to the foundation of the human and non-human world.

I have not been referring to art, which obviously is a central aspect in the *Kritik der Urteilskraft*. Post scriptum, I would like to mention, that according to several interpretations of art today, the central point in the judgement of art is not – as for Kant – the beauty, but exactly the sublime. This is true, even if we do not have a romantic view of art. I think that for instance, the point in Bertold Brechts *Verfremdungstheater* is very close to my interpretation of sublimity. Therefore, true art can have the same impact on our mind as (kantic) sublime nature. There is no contradiction in the truth of art and environmentalism.

Biography

Martin Ishøy (born 1962) is Cand. Theol. and Ph.D. in environmental ethics. He carried out his Ph.D.-programme at the Centre for Social Science Research on the Environment (CeSaM), and Department of Systematic Theology, Aarhus University. Denmark.

Notes

1. *Kritik der Urteilskraft* p. 120.

Bibliography

Immanuel Kant; *Kritik der Urteilskraft*, Herausgegeben von Karl Vorländer, Hamburg: Meiner, 1990. Pagenumbers refer to the third *Originalausgabe*, 1799.

Immanuel Kant; *Grundlegung zur Metaphysik der Sitten*, Herausgegeben von Karl Vorländer, Hamburg, 1965 (1785).

Kevin Jardine; "Truslen fra Taigaen", *Global Økologi*, Juni, 1995 (based on *The Carbon Bomb: Climate Change and the Fate of the Northern Boreal Forests*, Greenpeace International, Amsterdam).

Jonas Nilsson

Rationality, Substantive Belief, and the Metaphysical[1]

Abstract
In this paper I discuss the relation between substantive beliefs and standards of rationality in science. I present Dudley Shapere's account of the connection between them, and his theory about how both standards and substantive beliefs can be rationally discussed and changed. His theory of the rationality of prospective reasoning is then used as a basis for a discussion of how other philosophers of science have treated a certain class of substantive beliefs, which have been referred to as "metaphysical". Philosophers like Kuhn and Lakatos have treated metaphysical beliefs – along with standards of rationality – as belonging to a separate level of science, and as being exempt from direct rational criticism. I suggest that these views about the status of metaphysical beliefs in science are due to an overly narrow understanding of the resources for rational argumentation in science, and that Shapere's theory provides a better understanding of the function and rational status of metaphysical beliefs. In a concluding section, I discuss briefly how Shapere's ideas might be brought to bear on the question of the rationality of philosophical enquiry.

Introduction

How are rationality and substantive beliefs related to each other? Do they depend upon each other, so that, e.g., what we believe about the world influences what we take to be rational? Or are they rather independent of one another, so that they can be studied in isolation from each other? Can the form and the content of reasoning be kept strictly apart?

In this paper I will present the views of Dudley Shapere, a philosopher of science who denies that such a separation can be made. Instead he claims that the content, or the substantive beliefs, and the standards of rationality in science are intimately connected. Substantive beliefs influence what counts as rational, and standards of rationality change with such beliefs.

After presenting Shapere's account of scientific rationality, which constitutes the main part of the paper, I will discuss how other and earlier philosophers of science have treated a certain sort of substantive beliefs, which have been referred to as "metaphysical". Beginning with the views of the positivists and Popper, I shall go on to Thomas Kuhn and Imre Lakatos and their thoughts about the role of the metaphysical in science, and its connection with rationality.

These views on the relations between metaphysics and rationality will then be contrasted with Shapere's. The purpose of doing this is to bring out both the importance and the function of metaphysical assumptions for rational enquiry, as described by Shapere.

Finally, I will discuss how these ideas from the philosophy of science might be relevant also for rationality in philosophical enquiries.

Dudley Shapere on Rationality and Substantive belief in Science

According to Dudley Shapere, to investigate scientific rationality is to study the kind of reasoning that takes place in science, to examine what counts as *reasons* in scientific practice. About such reasoning, he makes some claims: 1) Such reasoning is complex, and cannot be adequately understood if rationality is reduced to some single or a few rules or sets of criteria. 2) There is a rationale in the reasoning which takes place in the so called "context of discovery", which means that accounts which focus exclusively on the justification (or rejection) of theories lead to distorted views of scientific rationality. 3) What counts as reasons in science is to a large extent dependent on the content – the substantive beliefs – of science, and therefore formalistic approaches to scientific rationality are misguided. 4) Everything in science is open to change, not only substantive beliefs but also beliefs about what counts as a reason for or against something.

Shapere has what he calls a "domains approach" to science. A domain is a body of associated items of information, which becomes an object of scientific study if it satisfies certain conditions:

(1) The association is based on some relationship between the items.
(2) There is something problematic about the body so related.
(3) That problem is an important one.
(4) Science is 'ready' to deal with the problem.[2]

One purpose behind his introduction of the concept of a domain is to bring out the fact that there are scientific problems of different sorts, of which the problem for theories to account for facts or observations is only one kind. This type of problem he labels "problems of *theoretical inadequacies*", and explicates them as problems for theories to account for their domains. There are also "domain problems", which have to do with clarifying and delimiting the domain, and "theoretical problems" concerned with how to give deeper accounts (in the form of new theories) of specific domains.

As has already been said, a domain is a body of items of information, having certain characteristics which suggest that there are deeper connections among the items. It is these deeper connections a theory is supposed to account for, explaining the relations between and the characteristics of the items of the domain. The concept of a domain, says Shapere, is supposed to replace – or rather displace – the traditional distinction between observation and theory, which he believes has been an obstacle to the understanding of science. A domain can include older "theories and theory-determined entities"[3], as well as what is usually referred to as "observations". The periodic table of chemical elements, e.g., was an important part of a scientific domain for which a theoretical account was sought, and that table included such information as quantitative determinations of the specific masses of the different elements, an ordering of elements in respect of that property, and knowledge about other properties about those elements.[4]

Another important concept for Shapere is "background information". That is information which has come to be accepted (for reasons I shall later specify), and which is not itself part of the domain under study although it is taken to be relevant to it. It is on the basis of such prior background information that a domain is taken to actually *be* a domain, i.e., something that consists of items among which there really *are* relevant relations.

Domains are not static, but change. Investigation of a domain, or changes in background information, may lead to inclusion or exclusion of certain items, to the splitting up of what was thought to be one domain into two smaller ones, or to the unification of domains which were once considered to be separate.

Such domains are what scientific theories are supposed to account for, according to Shapere. The theory is supposed to explain – perhaps in terms of newly introduced entities at some more fundamental level – the characteristics of the items of the domain and the relations between them. An example is how a theory of the internal structure of atoms explains, e.g., the periodicity and discreteness of the differences of specific masses among the elements in the periodic table, why different elements with similar chemical properties are similar in that way (due to the distribution of electrons into different "shells"), or why certain substances have identical chemical properties but different masses (they are explained as isotopes).

Shapere says that there are six questions concerning domains, their problems, and the solutions of such problems, which must be answered in order to give a satisfactory account of scientific reasoning. Three of the questions concern the type of reasoning which governs scientists 1) in regarding a certain set of items of information to be related so as to form a domain, 2) in refining and modifying the description of those items, and 3) in deciding that something in a domain is problematic and should be investigated. I shall not say much about these questions.

The other questions are the following:

> 4. What considerations lead to the generation of specific lines of research, and what are the reasons (or types of reasons) for considering some lines of research to be more promising than others in the attempt to resolve problems about the domain?
> 5. What are the reasons for expecting (sometimes to the extent of demanding) that answers of certain sorts, having certain characteristics, be sought for those problems?
> [–]
> 6. What are the reasons (or types of reasons) for accepting a certain solution of a scientific problem regarding a domain as adequate?[5]

As I have already mentioned, Shapere claims that there are scientific problems of different kinds: domain problems, theoretical problems, and problems of theoretical inadequacies. Generally, philosophers of science have concentrated almost exclusively on the latter kind – which concern question 6. – dealing with problems for theories of accounting for observations (falsifications, anomalies, how evidence verifies or makes theories probable). Now Shapere says that in relation to such inadequacies, one should make a further distinction between theories that are *incorrect* (and are to be rejected), and such that are merely *incomplete* in regard to its domain (in which case they may still be fundamentally correct but in need of supplementation). About this, he claims, judgments can often be made on the basis of background information. And he holds, generally, that the reasoning which takes place in the face of theoretical inadequacies contains considerations of many different kinds, which cannot be reduced to rules of a purely formal nature.

In relation to problems of theoretical inadequacies, the question arises as to which part of the system it is that is responsible for the inadequacy. Shapere claims that there are often *reasons* for attributing the error to one, or a limited number of parts of the system. He writes:

> Rather than emphasizing the *logical* viability of alternative ways of resolving problems, what we need to study closely is the rough rationale that often exists in science for the circumstances in which and the order in which we subject the ingredient accepted ideas to suspicion and, correlatively, the order in which we seriously consider new alternatives.[6]

First, Shapere holds that it is important that the beliefs (and standards) that are used in a problematic situation have a history, in which they have, up til then, been more or less successful, and in which more or less strong reasons to doubt the correctness of specific elements may have assembled. On the basis of judgments about the success or lack of it of particular elements in previous enquiry, it may be possible to argue that some part or parts of the system are more likely to be incorrect than others.

Another way of reasoning in the face of theoretical inadequacies is connected to the role of conceptual devices such as simplifications. Shapere says that in science one can give reasons for considering something to be, e.g., a simplification rather than a realistic treatment. This is something that is established in the light of accepted information concerning the subject matter. (Background knowledge from classical electricity and classical mechanics, e.g., entailed that in an atom *both* the nucleus and the electrons revolve around a common center of force, and therefore one of Bohr's early theories of the atom had to be a simplification since it described the nucleus as not moving.) Shapere even proposes a *principle of non-rejection of theories* in relation to this:

> when a discrepancy is found between the predictions of a theory and the results of observation or experiment, do not reject the theory as fundamentally incorrect before examining areas of the theory in which simplifications have been made which might be responsible for the discrepancy.[7]

These are two ways of reasoning in cases of theoretical inadequacies. Two things should be noticed about them: the first is that Shapere regards appeals to the histories of enquiries as legitimate and important sources for scientific reasoning. The second is the way in which prior information available at the time provides resources for reasoning about how to overcome problems.

This will turn out to be important for Shapere's view about the nature of "metaphysical" beliefs in science.

Questions 4. and 5., on the other hand, concern reasoning in the so called "context of discovery", the prospective reasoning which leads scientists to approach a problem in one, or some, particular ways among the logically possible ones, and to try to find an explanatory theory of a particular kind (why, e.g., did scientists aim at constructing a compositional theory of the elements in the periodic table, rather than any other of the logically possible alternatives?).

Shapere's thesis is that such reasoning – and scientific reasoning generally – cannot be divorced from the content – the substantive beliefs – of science. Actually, he says about science that "its rational procedures depend wholly on the content of belief rather than on purely 'formal' considerations, and they develop as that content develops."[8]

I shall focus on the connection, described by Shapere, between substantive beliefs and rationality.

"Rationality", as I will use it here, is a complex concept, with different parts. A concept of rationality is something that is embodied in practices of enquiry, and which decides (in some sense of 'decides') what counts as a reason for or against something. So when Shapere is trying to give an account of scientific reasoning, I would say that he is articulating a concept of scientific rationality.

So, according to Shapere, the standards of rationality of science cannot be separated from substantive beliefs about the world (or some aspect of it), and thus cannot be reduced to anything that is purely formal.

Among the things that are included in the concepts of rationality of science, are answers to the following questions: How is it determined that something is problematic (and is thus to be studied and accounted for)? What theoretical solutions are possible given the information making up a problematic domain? What methods are appropriate in solving a problem? What counts as evidence for or against beliefs (or, more narrowly, what counts as an observation?)? What counts as an explanation of a domain, i.e., as a solution to a theoretical problem? What are the goals of investigations?

Scientific reasoning cannot be understood without taking account of all of these aspects of rationality, and, Shapere claims, in any given field at any given stage in science, answers to the questions above are given largely in terms of the current *content* of science. They are *not* answered only in terms of, e.g., formal relations between "theory" and "observations".

That something is a domain and that there is a problem concerning this domain, is established in the light of prior information (beliefs) of two kinds: first there is the information making up the domain, consisting of, e.g., the description and classification of the items. Second, there is background information, i.e., beliefs which have come to be accepted but which are not themselves part of the domain.

These kinds of prior information establish similarities and dissimilarities between items, that some of these are significant while others are superficial, and thus suggest that deeper accounts can be given of certain relations of similarity. Examples from the history of science of items (or sets of items) that have been more deeply related in this way, are the phenomena of static and galvanic electricity (for which a deeper, unifying explanation was given by Faraday), or the phenomena of electricity and magnetism (explained by Maxwell).

Here, Shapere claims, the reasoning which leads scientists to claim that something is a problem that needs to be investigated, is based on the content of substantive beliefs, not on, e.g., formal or abstract requirements of increase in empirical content, or the like.

As we have seen, Shapere maintains that there is a rationale in reasoning in the so called "context of discovery" in science, i.e., in the reasoning which leads scientists to solutions of their problems. So, given that a problem has been identified, what does the reasoning which leads to a solution – a solution of some particular kind – look like?

His idea is that the characteristics of the domain, supplemented by background information, specifies not only that there is a problem, but that there is a problem of a *particular kind*, i.e., a problem for which a particular sort of theory is to be expected as a solution. As an example of such reasoning, leading from the characteristics of a domain to the expectation of a certain sort of explanatory theory for it and the generation of lines of research to find such a theory, Shapere mentions the case of the periodic table of chemical elements and the attempts to find a deeper theory for it.

He claims that in that case a particular pattern can be discerned in the reasoning which led the scientists involved to expect and to try to find a compositional theory of the chemical elements, a pattern which can be brought out as a "principle of compositional reasoning":

> To the extent that a domain D satisfies the following conditions or some subset thereof, it is reasonable to expect (or demand) that a compositional theory be sought for D:
> (Ci) D is ordered;

(Cii) the order is periodic;
(Ciii) the order is discrete [...], the items having values which are [...] integral multiples of a fundamental value;
(Civ) the order and periodicity are extensive, detailed, and precise;
(Cv) compositional explanatory theories are expected for other domains;
(Cvi) compositional theories have been successful or promising in other domains;
(Cvii) there is reason to suppose that the domain under consideration is related to such other domains so as to form part of a larger domain.[9]

Certain things should be noted about such a principle. First of all, it is a principle of reasoning in the "context of discovery". Second, it refers to specific, "theoretical" characteristics of the items of information making up the domain ("ordered", "periodic", "discrete", etc.) and to background information (theories of other domains, etc.) – not to "observations" or "basic statements" in a traditional empiricist manner, nor to conventionalist notions of, e.g., "simplicity". Third, it does not constitute any kind of algorithm, and does not dictate unequivocal answers in all cases. Shapere says that in connection to such principles, rationality becomes a matter of degree:

> the pursuit of a certain line of research in the expectation of finding a compositional theory for a given domain is more rational, the more of points (Ci) to (Cvii) are satisfied, and the more each of them is satisfied.[10]

But although such principles do not provide us with a *logic* of discovery, i.e. often they do not give us decisive answers, they do place severe restraints on scientific reasoning and have important functions in guiding research. Science would not be the rational enterprise that it has come to be without such principles, Shapere claims, and therefore they should be seen as legitimate parts of the concepts of rationality of science.

Shapere discusses another such principle, which is of special interest. It is the "principle of evolutionary reasoning", and he extracts it from his examination of a case in physics: the problems of making spectral classifications of stars, and of giving a theory which could explain such a classification. Such an explanation was given in terms of a theory of stellar evolution. Shapere says that the reasoning in that case is captured by the following "principle of evolutionary reasoning":

(Ei) If a domain is ordered, and if that ordering is one which can be viewed as the increase or decrease of the factor(s) on the basis of which the ordering is made, then it is reasonable to suspect that the ordering may be the result of an evolutionary process, and it is reasonable to undertake research to find such an answer (which we have called an evolutionary theory).

(Eii) The reasonableness of such expectation is increased if there is a way (for example, by application or adaptation of some background information such as a theory from another domain, whether unrelated or [preferably] related) of viewing that sequential ordering as a temporal one, and still more if a way is provided of viewing that ordering as having a temporal direction.[11]

Condition (Eii) refers to background information. In the actual case, this background information consisted of available information about how the colours of hot bodies change during cooling, which suggested a way of fulfilling (Eii).

Later on, this principle was applied also to the domain of the chemical elements of the periodic table, for which a theory of the evolution of the various elements was eventually given. In that case, the theory of stellar evolution functioned as background information which was adapted to the domain so that it made it possible to view the sequence of elements as stages in an evolutionary process.

What makes this principle particularly interesting is that it was a *new* principle which was introduced at a rather late stage in science, while it had not been applied before. Shapere suggests that the acceptance of the principle of evolutionary reasoning in the physical sciences should to a large extent be seen in the light of the success of Darwin's theory of biological evolution. This opened up new possibilities for scientific explanation and reasoning, by providing a model of explanation which could be adapted to other fields. However, that those modes of explanation and reasoning were reasonable also in physics could not be established simply by virtue of their success in biology, but had to be indicated in a stronger and more specific way by other background information which could be seen to be more directly relevant to particular physical domains; information about colour changes of cooling bodies for spectral stellar classification, and theories of stellar evolution for the explanation of the table of chemical elements. Thus, what counts as reasons in science remains linked to the content of science.

Actually, it is a crucial point in Shapere's account that there are no sharp distinctions between the content of science and the standards of rationality (principles or criteria) employed within it. They are not wholly distinct levels, but *interact* with each other. Content (beliefs about the world) shapes standards of rationality, by generating principles of reasoning, theoretical goals, rankings of the importance of problems, beliefs about what is relevant to what, what is to count as evidence, etc:

> I have argued that it is the content of scientific belief that shapes our 'standards' or 'criteria' of what counts as reasons or as reasonable in science, and that such 'standards', far from standing above and independent of science, are as much a part of the activity of science, of the processes of discovering and coming to understand, as are the substantive beliefs themselves; indeed, in many ways they are indistinguishable from the latter. The activity of science is not well described in terms of two distinct *kinds* of statement, substantive and criterial; what occurs is better conceived in terms of statements playing different roles in different circumstances.[12]

The standards of rationality guide the further development of the content of science, which, in turn, leads to changes in the standards of rationality, and so on. So, according to Shapere, the standards (or principles or criteria) of rationality in science are open to revision and rejection just like substantive beliefs are.

I would like to distinguish three different ways in which substantive beliefs influence standards of rationality:

a) Specific beliefs, which have been successful, become normative principles. This normative function they receive by being used to specify, e.g., what adequate explanations look like, and what the goals of enquiries are. Examples of such norms based on successful beliefs, given by Shapere, are "'Try to explain all phenomena in terms of matter in motion'", and "'So construct explanations of elementary particles that they take the form of renormalizable locally gauge-invariant field theories.'"[13] Another example might be the belief that the world is deterministic, and the corresponding standard of explanation which requires that theories should be deterministic.

b) Substantive beliefs can be used to criticize existing standards of rationality. An example of this might be the success of statistical theories in physics, which has led to a rejection of the deterministic standard of explanation. But such critique in the light of substantive beliefs may be directed even against standards that do not refer to specific beliefs, as is evidently the case with, e.g., the rules of logic (where the distributive laws may, or may not, be put in question by interpretations of quantum mechanics).

c) Finally, the content of substantive beliefs has to be added if the normative principles are to do their work. Shapere claims that such principles tell us very little about what is reasonable if they are divorced from such beliefs. The concepts of "success" and "freedom from specific doubt", e.g., which are central in Shapere's account of scientific rationality, receive their determination only in relation to content. What does success, under different circumstances, amount to? What are, under specific circumstances, reasons for doubting something (e.g. doubting that a theory is realistic rather than a simplification)?

Furthermore, the standards of rationality resemble substantive beliefs in that they are justified in a similar way; not by being shown to be necessary and unalterable, but by the (contingent) fact that they have been successful and are free from specific doubt. Shapere claims that all of our beliefs, including beliefs about what is rational, are contingent in this way, and that they are all, in principle, open to the possibility of doubt and revision or rejection.

I shall now deal with some more general aspects of the standards of rationality in modern science, as described by Shapere.

An important part is a method of investigation which Shapere calls the "*piecemeal*" or "*domains approach*". This means that particular areas are isolated and treated as separate objects of study, and that explanatory theories are sought for such isolated "domains", rather than for the whole of nature.

Related to this is an aspect which is, according to Shapere, common to both everyday and scientific understandings of rationality: that if something is to count as a reason, it must be *relevant* to the subject matter under discussion. He argues that

> since the characteristics and boundaries of that subject matter and the relevance thereto of proposed considerations can themselves be subject to debate, it follows that whether a given consideration counts as a 'reason' depends crucially on how definitively the subject matter can be formulated and how clearly the relevance of proposed considerations can be established.[14]

The clearer the delineation of subject matter and the information that is relevant to it, the tighter the reasoning. Therefore, Shapere claims that the development of science and scientific rationality partly consists "in a gradual discovery, sharpening, and organization of relevance relations".[15]

The domains approach has important consequences for another part of modern scientific concepts of rationality; that the beliefs used in science should be *successful* and *free from specific doubt*. The notion of the "success" of theories, e.g., becomes tied to their ability to account for the domains for which they are responsible:

> With the full adoption in science of the piecemeal (domains) approach to the search for knowledge, the 'success' of a theory has come to be judged, in large part, in terms of how completely and precisely it accounts for the items of its domain.[16]

This approach, or this part of the concepts of rationality, has been adopted in science because it has proven to be successful. And its adoption has had consequences for other aspects of rationality – e.g. for what it *is* to be successful.

But at the same time, another aspect has been included (or perhaps maintained) in the concepts of rationality of science, viz. the goal of *unification*. Scientists have been able to transfer knowledge about some domains to others, and to give unifying accounts of different domains. So, due to the successes of using this method, unification has come to function as a goal in science.

The last aspect of scientific rationality as described by Shapere, which I shall discuss, is what he calls "internalization". It is a principle which he expresses like this: "Aim at the internalization of scientific reasoning".[17]

In Shapere's account, this concept of "internalization" is very important. Actually, it can be said to relate other aspects of rationality – such as relevance, success, freedom from doubt – to each other and to other concepts or claims which figure in his account of science, e.g., domains, background information, the denial of sharp distinctions between content and standards, or the claim that everything in science is open to change.

Then what does he mean by "internalization"? It is a process, he says, in which science tries to make its reasoning self-sufficient, or autonomous, so that it does not have to rely on any considerations external to itself (material drawn from, e.g., common sense, religion or philosophy). Shapere writes that

> science aims at becoming, as far as possible, autonomous, self-sufficient, in its organization, description, and treatment of its subject-matter – at becoming able to delineate its domains of investigation and the background information relevant thereto, to formulate its problems, to lay out methods of approaching those problems, to determine a range of possible solutions, and to establish criteria of what counts as an acceptable solution, *all in terms solely of the domain under consideration and the other successful and doubt-free beliefs*

which have been found to be relevant to that domain; that is, to make its reasoning in all respects wholly self-sufficient.[18]

In other places, he says that the aim is to be able to proceed on the basis of only the information making up domains, and such background information which is claimed to be relevant to those domains (included in that background information are the standards of rationality employed in science; methods, goals, standards of explanation, principles of reasoning, and so on). What is important about this, is that according to Shapere such information (beliefs and standards) must meet certain requirements to qualify as legitimate background information. As he writes in the passage quoted above, they must be successful and free from specific doubt.[19]

This accords with Shapere's general view of scientific development as a process in which scientists use the best beliefs available to acquire more and better beliefs. The point of the internalization is that the beliefs (and standards) that are accepted and used as a basis for further research should be such that there are good reasons – as judged by standards current at specific times and in specific fields – for accepting and using them. The goal of this process is that *all* elements of science should be scrutinized like this, including the standards of rationality (as well as what has been called "metaphysical" assumptions about ultimate aspects of nature).

Thus, the principle of internalization is connected to Shapere's denial of the thesis that standards of rationality form a separate level within science and are immune to revision in the light of substantive beliefs. He writes:

> Such interpretations of science are fundamentally misguided. For a central aim of science is – has become – wherever possible to *remove* such distinct 'levels', if they exist, in favor of an integrated approach, 'internalizing' the separate levels to achieve an *interaction* of ideas (methods, standards, *etc.*) in which all of them are subject to revision or rejection in the light of what we learn about nature.[20]

What the requirements for being counted as internal to science are, may change in the course of enquiry – requirements may be dropped or added. And the meaning of such requirements – what success is, or what reasons for doubt are – depends on the content of scientific belief, and thus their meaning may change when the beliefs do. Also, the process of internalization is not a necessary feature of science (according to Shapere, *nothing* is): it has not always been part of it, and it is possible that it may cease to be so in the future. Its status is not different in this respect from that of other elements of science. Of course, scientists are not able to rely only on things that meet such requirements, but the normative principle to aim at internalization has still come to be adopted. Shapere writes that

> with the increasing successes achieved through seeking and respecting such constraints, continued respect of them wherever possible has become a normative guiding principle of science; and it has become a goal of science to try to achieve a state where its reasoning can be fully autonomous and integrated.[21]

Shapere's account of scientific rationality has important consequences for the role of metaphysical beliefs in science. In order to bring out Shapere's view of such beliefs, I shall contrast it with the accounts given by some other philosophers of science.

The metaphysical in Science: Kuhn and Lakatos

Positivists wanted to claim that what they considered as metaphysical statements – in distinction from empirical or scientific ones – were meaningless. This attempt, which was never successfully carried through, was based on theories of meaning as dependent on verification or confirmation (or reducability to a physicalistic language).

Popper argued against such theories of meaning, and against attempts at demarcation between scientific and non-scientific statements based on them.

Against the positivists, he argued that metaphysical statements are not meaningless, and that the demarcation criteria of the positivists were mistaken and would exclude large parts of science while, contrary to their intentions, many metaphysical statements could be construed so that they met the criteria.[22]

Popper himself concentrated primarily on the question of how to demarcate science from other fields. According to him, a statement or theory is scientific if it is falsifiable, i.e. if it entails some basic statements and can thus be empirically tested. Statements which are not falsifiable, he labelled "metaphysical". That does not mean that they are meaningless, however. They can also, according to Popper, be critically discussed, in spite of the fact that they are irrefutable. Actually, Popper displays an ambiguous attitude towards metaphysics. A metaphysical theory may be developed into a testable theory, and thus become scientific. He also says that metaphysical ideas may have important heuristic functions within science. But he stresses that one should always strive to make theories or statements testable, and eliminate metaphysical elements in science.

In later philosophies of science, the metaphysical was often taken in the Popperian sense of irrefutable. An important difference from Popper and the positivists was that these philosophers regarded the metaphysical (the unverifiable or irrefutable) as something inescapably internal to science, and as necessary for scientific work. Two such philosophers are Thomas Kuhn and Imre Lakatos.[23]

According to Kuhn, the history of science consists of successions of different *paradigms*, guiding scientists at particular times and in particular areas. They have two important characteristics: a) they do not consist only of theories or propositions, and they cannot be fully articulated; b) the components of the paradigms are not refutable (or verifiable), and are thus metaphysical in the Popperian sense. The irrefutable, metaphysical paradigm governs the activity of the scientists working within it, prescribing what counts as a fact, an observation, a problem, an explanation, etc. The components of the paradigm are not arrived at through research – but are instead a necessary condition for research to be possible at all. In the "Postscript – 1969" to the second edition of his book *The Structure of Scientific Revolutions,* Kuhn discerns the following kinds of components of paradigms: 1) "symbolic generalizations"; 2) "metaphysical parts of paradigms", or "beliefs in particular models"; 3) "values"; 4) "exemplars".[24] It is particularly the second kind of component which is of interest here.

At certain points in history, such paradigms are rejected or abandoned as wholes, and are replaced by entirely new ones.

In Lakatos' philosophy of science, the fundamental unit of appraisal is what he calls "scientific research programmes", within which series of theories are developed. Such research programmes have a "hard core", and a "negative heuristic" which says that the hard core is to be treated as irrefutable. This means that no accepted basic statements are allowed to contradict anything in the hard core. Instead such falsifications are to be blamed on auxiliary theories, which make up a so called "protective belt". A "positive heuristic" specifies how this protective belt is to be developed and how falsifications are to be dealt with. Thus, the hard core, being irrefutable, is metaphysical in Popper's sense. So the hard core remains unaltered through the lifetime of a programme. The programme, as a whole, is rejected when another research programme, with a different hard core, emerges and is more successful than the earlier one.

What I have referred to as metaphysical in science as described by Kuhn and Lakatos, is so also in a more traditional sense, since these parts of science refer to what is taken to be the fundamental or underlying principles on the area in question. A paradigm, according to Kuhn, includes a metaphysical world picture. These elements of science specify the basic characteristics of (at least) a part of reality, which is what metaphysics has often been understood to be concerned with.

Something is characteristic about these treatments of the metaphysical in science. It is seen as something which is in itself irrefutable or unverifiable, but which is necessary for scientific research, and for the testing of theories or statements at some "lower" level. Metaphysical assumptions function so as to make critique, reasoning or testing possible at lower, empirical levels, but are themselves seen as exempt from such questioning. What is tested or questioned is rather the paradigm or programme as a whole. In Lakatos' case, this critical testing is done in relation to the empirical content of theories and their relative empirical success. That is, the metaphysical is seen as constituting some sort of *separate level* within science.

I believe that this is mistaken, and that this way of looking at the metaphysical is the result of mistaken or too narrow ideas about scientific rationality. I think that Shapere preserves the insights of Kuhn and Lakatos concerning the importance of the metaphysical, while avoiding this mistake.

Shapere on Kuhn, Lakatos and the Metaphysical

Shapere agrees with Kuhn and Lakatos that the kind of substantive beliefs they refer to as metaphysical are important to science. He also agrees with Kuhn that there is a relation between such beliefs and standards of rationality.

What he disagrees with is the status and function they assign to the metaphysical. In both Kuhn and Lakatos, a part of science is treated as fundamental for scientific activity, and is taken to form a separate level which is treated by scientists as exempt from direct critique (paradims or hard cores). Of course, neither Kuhn nor Lakatos claims that these parts of science are incapable of being undermined and rejected. On the contrary, a paradigm may have anomalies which eventually lead to its rejection (Kuhn), and a research programme may be superseded by a rival programme (Lakatos). But they both see the paradigm or hard core as a unitary whole, which is in its entirety kept unchanged during the lifetime of a paradigm or programme, after which it is rejected *as a whole*, and replaced by an entirely new one.

My impression is that their views about metaphysics stem from mistaken views about rationality. Lakatos, e.g., allows only one kind of consideration in cases of conflicts between theory and observation (one that is based on increase in empirical content), and does not allow a rationale in the reasoning about which part of the system to attribute the error to, nor in the reasoning involved in the construction of a solution of the problem. Instead he says that some parts of the system are treated as irrefutable, by "methodological decision", and that the other parts of it may be changed in any way as long as that change constitutes a "progressive problem shift".

According to Shapere, the possibilities of rational reasoning in such contexts are much greater (since concepts of rationality are *complex*), and therefore it is unnecessary to take the view about the metaphysical that Lakatos does (as well as Kuhn). He says:

> There are a great variety of such general types of considerations: the knowledge-seeking enterprise is not, nor has it ever been, governed by some *single* sort of consideration like verifiability, falsifiability, or observability. It is [...] the business of the philosophy of science to delineate this complex network of general types of considerations and their interplay.[25]

About Lakatos and scientific research programmes, Shapere writes that

> I am arguing that such programmes are more fruitfully viewed in terms of the problems and background information which produce them than in terms of some overarching approach which is accepted rather arbitrarily – as the views of Imre Lakatos ultimately imply.[26]

On Shapere's account, a body of background beliefs which have come to be accepted, does function in descriptions of subject matters, in observation situations, in formulations of problems and methods, etc., and some such beliefs may shape scientific activity to a large extent. But he claims that they do not form any inseparable unity. Different beliefs are brought to bear in different situations, and although some of them do so in very many situations, there is according to Shapere

> no one belief or set of beliefs ('high-level background theory' or 'paradigm') which functions in one single way to 'determine' ('shape', or whatever) every scientific activity in every situation in a 'tradition'.[27]

Furthermore, he holds that all elements of science – including "metaphysical" beliefs, and standards of rationality – are in principle open to doubt and revision or rejection, and the reasoning which leads to such doubt arising can be directed towards *specific* such beliefs (or standards) rather than applying indiscriminately to the whole cluster of beliefs that are supposed to make up hard cores or paradigms.

A corollary to this is Shapere's claim that scientific change is piecemeal and gradual rather than revolutionary. Substantive beliefs, including metaphysical ones, as well as standards, are reconsidered in the light of new information, and parts that there are specific reasons to doubt are revised or replaced, and in this process both fundamental assumptions about the world and standards of rationality may come to be drastically changed. These changes are gradual, however, and Shapere further claims that even radically different stages in the history of science are connected by "chains of reasoning". This means that science proceeds from one position to another in a process in which the steps are taken in the light of the best reasons available at that time.

The concept of "internalization" is relevant to the question of the metaphysical. According to Kuhn and Lakatos, a whole set of metaphysical assumptions are accepted together, used in guiding research, and eventually, in retrospect, evaluated, as a whole, in respect of the success in puzzle-solving or the empirical growth they generate. To aim at the internalization of scientific reasoning, on the other hand – as Shapere claims that scientists have come to do – amounts instead to trying to accept and use only such beliefs or standards that meet certain requirements; that in the previous history of enquiry they have been successful and free from specific doubt, and that they are considered to be relevant to the subject matter in question. So Shapere writes as follows:

> In contrast to their role in Kuhn, and presumably also Feyerabend, even the highest-level (in the sense, now, of most widely-adopted and pervasively functioning) background beliefs are, in *mature* science, subject to ever-stricter constraining conditions[.][28]

If Shapere is correct in claiming that the principle of internalization is a part of scientific concepts of rationality, then scientists should strive *not* to make any beliefs (or standards) immune to critique, and instead let all kinds of beliefs interact with each other, using the best established beliefs available to criticize and improve existing metaphysical beliefs (and standards of rationality). I.e., scientific beliefs should not be allowed to be "metaphysical" in the Popperian sense of "irrefutable" or "exempt from critique".

So science should try not to rely on beliefs that do not meet such requirements (something which scientists, however, often are unable to do). But Shapere still claims that scientific work requires assumptions which are metaphysical in another sense, viz. that of making claims about fundamental aspects of reality, claims which are "widely-adopted and pervasively functioning" in research.[29]

A reason for the importance of such beliefs, is that they give rise to normative principles which function as standards of rationality. A belief that reality ultimately consists only of matter moving about in a void, provides scientists with a goal for their enquiries and with a standard of adequate explanations of phenomena. A belief to the effect that the world is deterministic, gives rise to a standard of explanation according to which theories of a statistical type are inadequate as fundamental (or realistic) explanations.[30] So such beliefs come to function as reasons, determining at least partly the goals to be attained in science, what counts as possible or reasonable solutions of problems, what counts as simplification and what as realistic, etc. And, according to Shapere, the resources such "metaphysical" beliefs provide scientific reasoning with are necessary if science is to be a rational enterprise.

They should be treated with caution, however, and whenever possible scientists should try to use only such beliefs that have proven themselves successful and free from specific doubt. And metaphysical beliefs that are used without meeting such requirements should be subjected to the same criticism as other beliefs, and if possible be legitimated, revised or perhaps rejected.

Rationality and Metaphysics in Philosophy

In this concluding section I would like to make some remarks about what might be the consequences of applying Shapere's ideas about rationality and the metaphysical to *philosophical* enquiries. I shall be speaking very generally, and what I say will have the character of guesses and suggestions.

Shapere claims that the rationality of scientific reasoning depends on the complexity and specificity of the standards of rationality in science, and the strong claims they entail about what counts as a reason. In order to become a rational enterprise, and to make progress in rationality, science has had to make claims about what rationality in enquiry is, which go far beyond what can be shown to be common to any and every enquiry. Such standards are introduced, justified and developed within the histories of those scientific enquiries within which they are used, and it is only in that developing context of beliefs and standards that they *can* be rationally discussed.

The same holds for metaphysical beliefs (in Shapere's sense of very "widely-adopted and pervasively functioning"[31] beliefs). Science needs such beliefs, just as it needs those "strong" standards of rationality with which they are often connected. But such beliefs are to be judged by the best standards of rational belief internal to science itself, and whether they are acceptable or not depends on the functions they have in enquiries, and how well they fulfill these functions.

This is what Shapere expresses by saying that all aspects of science – substantive beliefs as well as standards – are "contingent", in the sense that they have to be *learnt* in the course of enquiry, and that they cannot be discovered and justified in abstraction from the concrete development of science itself (by philosophers, e.g.).[32]

Now, I would like to make the bold conjecture that the same is the case with all (or at least many) forms of enquiry, including typically philosophical ones. They too need complex, strong standards of rationality if reasoning is to be effective, standards which include specifications of the goals to be attained, criteria of what are acceptable solutions of problems, what kind of knowledge from other areas that can legitimately be appealed to, and so on.

I also believe that metaphysical beliefs play important roles in many philosophical enquiries, and that they are used in deciding what is problematic about a subject matter, that they exclude certain logical possibilities and thus set limits to what can count as reasonable, and that they determine theoretical goals.

In philosophy of language, e.g., I would say that metaphysical beliefs about language speakers (that they are in some sense finite) and linguistic competence (that speakers can, potentially, produce an infinite number of meaningful utterances) function importantly to determine that there is a problem, what the problem (or problems) are, and what is to be demanded of an adequate theory of language – not to talk about beliefs about entities of meaning, etc. In moral philosophy, different standpoints have different metaphysical beliefs about, e.g., determinism and free will, the relation between reason and passion or desire, the possible sources of motivation for human agents, personal identity, or theological questions. In epistemology, metaphysical beliefs may be about Platonic ideas or Aristotelian forms, or about the non-existence of objects of knowledge that are independent of cognitive acts.

So, rational enquiry presupposes both metaphysical beliefs and strong standards of rationality. But how is the employment of particular such standards and beliefs to be justified? Shapere claims that the beliefs and standards of science are legitimated or criticized within the history of science itself, in the light of the best beliefs and standards available at any given time – *not* in a more traditionally philosophical manner by showing them to be necessarily true (of the world or of all possible experience), or essential for enquiry or rationality as such (by analyzing the "meaning" of "rationality" or "scientific", e.g.). So Shapere would say that the resources for rationally criticizing or justifying scientific standards of rationality and metaphysical beliefs are only available within the ongoing enquiries of science itself, and such criticism or justification is based on how these elements function in these investigations (are they successful or not? Are they perhaps inconsistent with other elements which have proven equally or more successful? Can one achieve the same, or equally good, results without using them?).

My opinion is that this is appropriate for philosophical enquiries, too. If a certain form of moral philosophy, e.g., has built into it metaphysical beliefs about human agency, or a standards of rationality according to which moral theories should have particular characteristics – then how should such beliefs and standards be evaluated? In analogy with Shapere's account of science, I propose that they should be tried out in the course of enquiry (do they work well or do they lead to problems? Can the same success be achieved by using other beliefs? Could problems be solved if a particular belief or standard were rejected or replaced?). And they should be continually evaluated and revised in the light of the best existing standards and beliefs acknowledged by those working within that enquiry.

This can be rephrased by saying that the resources required for rational enquiry – both metaphysical beliefs and strong standards of rationality – are only available within *traditions* of enquiry. For the rational evaluation of, e.g., specific metaphysical beliefs, depends on forms of reasoning which require other metaphysical beliefs, as well as complex standards of rationality. This also means that the *histories* of enquiries become central for rational evaluation, since an important part of the evaluation of particular beliefs refers to how they have fared in the previous history of the enquiry.

This is not a plea for traditions of a "Kuhnian" kind, where adherents would accept, uncritically, a core or paradigm which is left as an undisputed, untouched foundation for enquiry. The present approach, departing from an analogy with Shapere's account of science, does mean that rationality requires using and building upon *some* set of metaphysical beliefs and strong standards of rationality. But any particular member may be critically discussed and possibly rejected or modified. If Shapere's concept of "internalization" can be applied to forms of enquiry other than modern scientific ones, like philosophy, one aim in philosophical enquiries would be to try to make the metaphysical assumptions that are at work in investigations explicit, to evaluate them in the light of other existing standards and beliefs, and to try to rely only on such metaphysical beliefs that there are good reasons for accepting. In this process of development, many (or perhaps even all) of the initial beliefs and standards of a tradition may come to be replaced.

The aim of the process of internalization is to attain a state where, internal to a tradition, there are good reasons for deciding what is acceptable or unacceptable, what is relevant or irrelevant, and what counts as good reasons. But the less a tradition has managed to achieve of such self-sufficiency, the less effective its reasoning will be. It will be more difficult to reach agreement about what is problematic about subject matters, about what kinds of considerations that are relevant in enquiries, about what adequate solutions of problems should look like, and so on. In such situations, it will be unclear how to choose between different and incompatible metaphysical beliefs, standards of rationality or theories. This will inescapably be the case in early phases of enquiry into some subject matter. Shapere mentions, as an example, the situation in Greek natural philosophy,

> where the possibility of agreement about such questions as the origin of the world (or worlds), the divisibility or indivisibility of matter, the nature and pervasiveness of change, and the interpretation of specific natural phenomena seemed so remote that reaction against the very undertaking of such inquiries finally set in. [–] The very formulations of the issues, where clear, tended to vary from one thinker to another, and the appropriate tools for their resolution was itself a matter of disagreement.[33]

He adds that such problems "are by no means absent even from the most modern period. For the ideal of complete autonomy of scientific investigation has not, even yet, been realized."[34] But through the historical development of science, scientific reasoning has become more and more constrained, Shapere claims, and therefore more rational.

I would like to claim that the same inability to rule out possibilities, to distinguish the relevant from the irrelevant, and to choose between incompatible formulations of and theories about subject matters, can arise for quite another reason: because of the adoption of a conception of rational enquiry which *denies* that rational reasoning depends on resources made available within specific traditions, and that rational justification (of both metaphysical beliefs and standards of rationality) has a historical character. This is a conception of rationality which demands that substantive beliefs or norms should be judged by *universal* standards of rationality, and that these standards must be such that they can be shown to be valid for any rational, or reasonable, person. I believe that this is the case with most areas of philosophy, and that it is the adoption of such conceptions of rationality which explains the – perennially noted and criticized – inability to reach agreement on fundamental matters, and "make progress", in philosophy.

Readers familiar with the work of Alasdair MacIntyre might protest now that I am conflating Shapere's account of scientific reasoning with MacIntyre's theory of tradition-constituted rationality. But I would argue that, despite what I take to be differences of emphasis rather than of substance between them, Shapere's description of scientific reasoning and development conforms splendidly to MacIntyre's general account of the development and rationale of traditions of enquiry. And at this point of my suggestion, MacIntyre becomes crucially important.

For what would happen if it were allowed that philosophical rationality requires the use of, e.g., metaphysical assumptions and standards of rationality, which cannot be sufficiently argued for (or against) in advance of enquiry, but rather have to be evaluated for the way they – later – turn out to function in those enquiries themselves?[35] If different traditions would form around different sets of metaphysical beliefs and standards of rationality, would not the result be some form of relativism, where we would have no means of resolving disagreements between traditions?

It is questions such as these MacIntyre has tried to answer in his later work.[36] There, he shows how a tradition can be shown to fail, in its own terms, as a rational enterprise, and how different traditions can be compared to each other. An account of MacIntyre's theory is beyond the scope of this paper, but what MacIntyre shows that is of importance to my suggestion here, is that accepting a conception of rationality as tradition-constituted and hence accepting the possibility of a plurality of research traditions, does not lead to relativism, but rather opens up a way to rationally evaluate and eventually rule out fundamental possibilities which cannot be rationally chosen or rejected in advance of the outcomes of the enquiries they function within.

The possibility of rationally comparing rival traditions of enquiry can be said to compensate for the element of arbitrariness that marks the choice of initial sets of beliefs and standards from which traditions depart. This arbitrariness is further circumscribed by the possibility, described by Shapere, of reasoning about and replacing or modifying both metaphysical beliefs and standards of rationality in the light of what is learnt in enquiry *within* a tradition.[37]

I have suggested that metaphysics – in the sense of "widely-adopted and pervasively functioning" beliefs about aspects of reality – is needed and used in both scientific and philosophical enquiries. But what about metaphysics as a separate area or discipline? According to the views of Shapere and MacIntyre presented here, the prospects for that are rather limited. What the nature of time, or space, is, or what the categories figuring in a true theory about nature are, is something that is to be discovered and argued for within science itself. Similarly, I think that beliefs about human nature cannot be properly judged in abstraction from the roles such beliefs play in enquiries in e.g. psychology, sociology or moral philosophy.

This is not to say, however, that metaphysicians are not needed. On the contrary, I believe that in many investigations there are metaphysical assumptions at work – sometimes unrecognizedly – which need to be brought out and discussed. Rather, I am suggesting only that metaphysics cannot lay claim to being separate from nor privileged in relation to other forms of enquiry.

Biography

Jonas Nilsson is a postgraduate student in theoretical philosophy at Umeå University in Sweden. He is currently writing a dissertation with the title *Rationality in Enquiry: Changing and Conflicting Standards of Rationality*. Jonas Nilsson was born in 1969.

Notes

1. This paper was presented at Nature and Lifeworld. XIth Internordic Philosophical Symposium, Odense Denmark, 11-13 August, 1995.
2. Shapere, "Scientific Theories and their Domains", p. 279.
3. Shapere, "Scientific Theories and Their Domains", p. 283.
4. See Shapere, "Scientific Theories and Their Domains".
5. Shapere, "Scientific Theories and Their Domains", p. 278.
6. Shapere, "The Character of Scientific Change", p. 223.
7. Shapere, "Scientific Theories and Their Domains", pp. 305-6. In the Bohr case, this simplification was discovered to be the source of a disagreement between the theory and observations of certain spectral lines from stars. The adjustment of the theory on this point removed the disagreement, and led to predictions of previously unobserved spectral lines, which were subsequently found.
8. Shapere, "Observation and the Scientific Enterprise", p. 39.

9. Shapere, "Scientific Theories and their Domains", pp. 289-90.
10. Shapere, "Scientific Theories and Their Domains", pp. 290.
11. Shapere, "Scientific Theories and Their Domains", p. 298. The word within square brackets is inserted by Shapere.
12. Shapere, "The Character of Scientific Change", p. 226.
13. Shapere, "Observation and the Scientific Enterprise", p. 37.
14. Shapere, "Observation and the Scientific Enterprise", p. 29.
15. Shapere, "Observation and the Scientific Enterprise", p. 30.
16. Shapere, "Observation and the Scientific Enterprise", p. 31.
17. Shapere, "Observation and the Scientific Enterprise", p. 37.
18. Shapere, "Introduction", in *Reason and the Search for Knowledge*, p. XXIII.
19. This means, as I have already pointed out, that references to the histories of enquiries are central to scientific reasoning according to Shapere. In this his thinking strongly resembles that of Alasdair MacIntyre.
20. Shapere, "Introduction", in *Reason and the Search for Knowledge*, p. XXIV.
21. Shapere, "Introduction", in *Reason and the Search for Knowledge*, p. XXXII.
22. See Popper, e.g. in "On the Status of Science and of Metaphysics", "The Demarcation Between Science and Metaphysics", or *Realism and the Aim of Science* pp. 159-216.
23. See Kuhn's *The Structure of Scientific Revolutions*, and Lakatos' "Falsification and the Methodology of Scientific Research Programmes".
24. Kuhn, *The Structure of Scientific Revolutions*, pp. 182-7.
25. Shapere, "The Character of Scientific Change", p. 218.
26. Shapere, "On the Relations Between Compositional and Evolutionary Theories", p. 196, note 3.
27. Shapere, "Introduction", in *Reason and the Search for Knowledge*, p. XXXI.
28. Shapere, "Introduction", in *Reason and the Search for Knowledge*, p. XXXI.
29. Shapere does not discuss this explicitly, but that this is his position is evident from his statements of some scientific normative principles which correspond to such substantive, metaphysical, beliefs. Since he argues both that such principles have a place in science, and that at least many of those principles are based on successful substantive beliefs, then he should be taken to accept the employment of such beliefs in science.
30. It should be noted that both of these beliefs, and the principles corresponding to them, have been seriously questioned, and, in the first case at least, rejected.
31. Shapere, "Introduction", in *Reason and the Search for Knowledge*, p. XXXI.
32. See Shapere, "Introduction", in *Reason and the Search for Knowledge*, pp. XXVII-XXX, XLIV-XLV.
33. Shapere, "Introduction", in *Reason and the Search for Knowledge*, p. XXVII.
34. Shapere, "Introduction", in *Reason and the Search for Knowledge*, p. XXVII.
35. This is a misleading way of stating it, suggesting perhaps that philosophical enquiries would have to start "from scratch" (whatever that might mean). It is instead the case that in every philosophical area, there already exists a great variety of more or less developed standpoints, from which traditions could develop further.
36. See his *Whose Justice? Which Rationality?*, and *Three Rival Versions of Moral Enquiry*.
37. I do not mean to say that we should let a thousand flowers bloom. In terms of the botanical metaphor, the point is rather that if we want to breed beautiful or interesting flowers, we should not restrict ourselves to studying only seeds, but rather plant seeds of different kinds and wait to see what they grow into, until we make our decisions.

(Another possible analogy, in the other direction, concerns the prospects of cross-breeding. But I will not go into that here.)

Bibliography

Kuhn, T. S., *The Structure of Scientific Revolutions*, 2nd rev. ed., University of Chicago Press, 1970 (1st ed. 1962).
Lakatos, I., "Falsification and the Methodology of Scientific Research Programmes", in Lakatos and Musgrave, A. (eds), *Criticism and the Growth of Knowledge*, Cambridge University Press, 1970.
MacIntyre, A. *Three Rival Versions of Moral Enquiry. Encyclopaedia, Genealogy, and Tradition*, Duckworth, London, 1990.
MacIntyre, A., *Whose Justice? Which Rationality?*, Duckworth, London, 1988.
Popper, K., "On the Status of Science and of Metaphysics", in his *Conjectures and Refutations*, 5th rev. ed., Routledge, London, 1989 (1st ed. 1963).
Popper, K., "The Demarcation Between Science and Metaphysics", in his *Conjectures and Refutations*.
Popper, K., *Realism and the Aim of Science*, Rowman and Littlefield, Totowa, New Jersey, 1983.
Shapere, D., "Observation and the Scientific Enterprise", in Achinstein, P. and Hannaway, O. (eds.), *Observation, Experiment, and Hypothesis in Modern Physical Science*, MIT Press, Cambridge Mass., 1985.
Shapere, D., "On the Relations Between Compositional and Evolutionary Theories", in Ayala, F. J., and Dobzhansky, T. (eds.), *Studies in the Philosophy of Biology*, University of California Press, Berkeley and Los Angeles, 1974.
Shapere, D., *Reason and the Search for Knowledge*, Reidel, Dordrecht, 1984.
Shapere, D., "Scientific Theories and Their Domains", in Shapere, *Reason and the Search for Knowledge*.
Shapere, D., "The Character of Scientific Change", in Shapere, *Reason and the Search for Knowledge*.

Per Nilsson
Critical Theory and Nature

Abstract
Early critical theory, as it was developed by Horkheimer, Adorno and Marcuse, seemed to be a promising approach for developing a philosophy of ecological concern. However, the problems this theory faced and the utopian solution to those problems met a substantial critique from within the critical theory camp itself by above all Jürgen Habermas. Habermas' version of critical theory have, on the other hand, been exposed to a lot of critique from thinkers with ecological concern. They claim that his distinction between speaking and non-speaking nature and the two different forms of rationality (communicative and instrumental) they are subjected to makes an philosophy of ecological concern impossible. In this paper I will examine the critique delivered primarily from Joel Whitebook and Gunnar Skirbekk. I will argue that their critique misses the target and that a philosophy of ecological concern very well might be developed from Habermas' version of critical theory. It will be a more anthropocentric but less utopian philosophy than his predecessors theory.

Introduction

One might think that the schemes and concepts developed within Critical theory, especially the theme of the domination of nature, would be promising for developing a philosophy of ecological concern. Carolyn Merchant states in the introduction to the volume *Ecology: Key Concepts in Critical Theory* that domination has been one of our century's most fruitful concepts for understanding human-human and human-nature relationships. One can say that this concept, developed by Horkheimer and Adorno in the book *Dialectic of Enlightenment,* was useful for describing the problems they associated with the modern world or modernity, that is, the period from the Renaissance and Reformation to the era of state capitalism in the twentieth century. They called it the concept of Enlightenment and it epitomised the ideology of the modern world. Horkheimer and Adorno think that modernity has strong potential for totalitarian politics, an incapability of controlling technology and strong tendencies for dehumanisation in the social world and destruction of the environment.

In forming the concept of domination they draw on Bacon's old credo that knowledge is power. They think that this form of knowledge and the science to which it gives rise is symptomatic for the scientific age after Bacon. The most prominent token of this knowledge is technology.

> The concordance between the mind of man and the nature of things that he had in mind is patriarchal: the human mind, which overcomes superstition, is to hold sway over a disenchanted nature. Knowledge, which is power, knows no obstacles ... Technology is the essence of this knowledge.[1]

The concept of domination, as a critical concept, directly appealed to spokesmen for an ecocentric view of the world (that is a view in favour of valuing nature in all its aspects for its own sake.) Those spokesmen have claimed that an application of instrumental reason to all spheres of life will lead to less freedom for man. This critical examination of the relationship between man and nature in terms of domination was seen as the most radical innovation of early critical theory. However, Horkheimer and Adorno were not concerned with an ecological philosophy, it was rather a philosophy of human emancipation they tried to develop. As a by-product, one might say, the concept of domination also seemed useful for ecological philosophy.

As Horkheimer and Adorno saw it the human alienation from nature began in the ancient world with the sense of a self distinct from the external world. This sense led to a denial of the internal nature in human beings.[2] In order to create a self separated from nature this alienation is necessary, and in order to achieve this, nature has to be disenchanted.

Horkheimer and Adorno used critical theory to expose the underlying instrumental reasoning that they saw behind both scientific thought and capitalist society. They regarded the rationalisation process of the Enlightenment as a negative dialectic that will lead to a domination of both the outer nature of the external world and inner nature of man himself. Man seeks emancipation from nature through domination of it. But the rather paradoxical fact is that man also is a natural creature and the domination of external nature leads to a domination of internal nature, in other words, the domination projected on outer nature projects itself on man.[3]

> The very spirit that dominates nature repeatedly vindicates the superiority of nature in competition... The subjective spirit which cancels the animation of nature can master a despiritualized nature only by imitating its rigidity and despiritualizing itself in turn.[4]

The result of this domination, or power, is that nature becomes reduced to abstract material. Accordingly, nature is objectified and its sole purpose is to be dominated and used. What the rationalisation processes of the Enlightenment have done is to demystify nature in a Weberian sense. Horkheimer and Adorno mean that if we accept natural science, and especially physics, as the only way to apprehend nature we will look at a material demystified object without any meaning more than its use.

If the goal is human emancipation and happiness, instrumental rationality should not govern the relationship between man and society or between man and nature. Robyn Eckersley puts it like this: "Human happiness would not come about simply by improving our techniques of social administration, by treating society and nature as subject to blind, immutable laws that could be manipulated by a technocratic elite."[5] The same can be said if the goal is to avoid the destruction of the environment, at least if we are to accept the thesis of a monistic theory of rationality in the way it was formed by early critical theory. The solution to the historical impasse in our time, would accordingly be a reconciliation with nature.[6] This solution is the utopian ideal of early critical theory, an ideal clearly stated by Marcuse and more secretly nurtured by Horkheimer and Adorno.

As I will try to show below, this problem is eliminated in the dualistic theory of Jürgen Habermas. The problem of that theory is that it also seems to make a reconciliation with nature impossible. However, I will argue that this fact does not make a philosophy of ecological concern impossible. On the contrary, such a philosophy might very well be developed from the theory of Habermas, although it will be more anthropocentric than the theory of his predecessors but also less utopian.

Habermas' theory of nature

Habermas' own theory is an advance according to the points of critique against early critical theory. He argues that it is not just a sober examination of historical forces that results in the pessimism of the early Frankfurt school. It is rather a result from incorrect and tacit theoretical presuppositions assumed at the outset. He also develops a transcendental argument to provide the epistemological and normative ground for critical theory. He offers a superior theoretical grounding for critical theory, but his transcendentalism excludes with necessity every attempt at a reconciliation with nature. Theoretical rigor is reached at the cost of the utopian ideal of early critical theory.

The fundamental mistake of his predecessors is, according to Habermas, the monistic character of early critical theory. Instead he introduces a dualistic framework. The logic of instrumental rationality governs the domination of external nature and the logic of communicative rationality governs that of internal nature. The main difference between those two forms of rationality is that while the former aims at reification, the latter makes reification a possible but pathological outcome.

Habermas' theory is also a more important reason than the utopian goal of the early Frankfurt school as to why critical theory has failed to become a foundation of an ecological philosophy. Habermas sees the ecological movement more as an indicator of the motivation and legitimation problem of the advanced capitalistic societies than as the bearer of emancipatory ideas. He has analysed the appearances of new social movements and ecological problems as grassroot resistance against colonisation tendencies within the life-world (the feminist movement is an exception which he sees as emancipatory). He regards those movements, as well as the antinuclear movement etc., as essentially defensive in character. Their attempts to develop contra institutions and liberated areas from within the life-world is seen as unrealistic.

> The intervention of large-scale industry into ecological balances, the growing scarcity of non-renewable natural resources, as well as demographic developments present industrially developed societies with major problems; but these challenges are abstract at first and call for technical and economic solutions, which must in turn be globally planned and implemented by administrative means.[7]

However, Habermas' general dissociation from the green movement is more radical than this. It originates from his break with the negative dialectic, as well as with what he regarded as the utopian goal of reconciliation with nature that was the trademark of early critical theory. Such a goal is, according to Habermas, neither necessary nor desirable for human emancipation. Instead he regards the rationalisation process of the Enlightenment as something positive, contrary to his predecessors.

In his early theory, stemming from *Knowledge and Human Interest*, Habermas launched the idea of different kinds of cognitive interests, that is the technical, practical and emancipatorial cognitive human interests. Those interests are related to three different forms of action and three different types of science; empirical-analytic, historical-hermeneutic and critical-social science based on self reflection. The technical human interest is the interest of dominating nature. This interest stems from the fact that man has to work in order to survive and it develops into a technological mastering and a scientific explanation of nature. The practical human interest is the interest in communication stemming from the fact that man is a social and verbal being and it develops into historical-hermeneutic disciplines. The emancipatorial interest at last is guided towards self reflective liberation from distorted and reified forms of consciousness.

There seems to be a limit between communicative subjects and non-communicative objects. In order to be emancipated one has to be a communicative subject, in other cases one is an object that falls under the technical human interest and so an object of possible instrumental control. The only way for science and technology to know nature is, according to Habermas, in instrumental terms since that is the only way it can efficiently secure our survival as a species. There seems to be no way for nature to be emancipated in Habermas theory.

> ...Only if men could communicate without compulsion and each could recognise himself in the other, could mankind possibly recognise nature as another subject: not, as idealism would have it, as its Other, but as a subject of which mankind itself is the Other.
> Be that as it may, the achievements of technology, which are indispensable as such, could surely not be substituted for by an awakened nature.[8]

I will examine some of the claims in Habermas' theory in order to a) explicate what might be a problem for ecological thought in his notion of nature[9] and b) examine if the 'science of life,' that is biology, can be at hand in questioning the theory. In doing this I will start by elaborating the problem as I see it within his theory of nature as only conceivable from the outlook of the technical human interest.[10]

Habermas' theoretical progress and his doctrine about nature both arise from the same source, that is, his transcendentalism, or quasitranscendentalism as he prefers to call it. By means of reflection on the evolution of man this categorical framework takes shape. This means that the categories instrumental and communicative are the framework within which the basic modes of human knowledge and action develops.

The transcendentalism of Habermas reminds us of that of Kant, but where they differ the most is in the fact that Kant's transcendental subject is singular while Habermas' is plural. The unity of Habermas' plural transcendental subject can be made clear through considering the conditions of the emergence of the human species. At some point in time, in accordance with the laws that govern the evolution of the pre-human nature (or in Habermas words nature-in-itself) something unique occurred, the emergence of man. Since man lacks specialised instinctual endowments, and since he, as a child, is in need of care longer than other species, language and communication originated as both a possibility as well as a necessity for the species.

> The human interest in autonomy and responsibility is not mere fancy, for it can be apprehended a priori. What raises us out of nature is the only thing whose nature we can know: language. Through its structure, autonomy and responsibility are posited for us. Our first sentence expresses unequivocally the intention of universal and unconstrained consensus.[11]

Habermas states that Hegel is right against Kant when he says that it is impossible to locate a transcendental subject outside of history, a subject who stands over the object he constitutes. The genesis of the transcendental subject occurs in the very realm that comprises its object domain, i.e., the realm of history. At the same time Habermas finds himself on the same side as Marx concerning Marx' critique of Hegel. Habermas and Marx see the grounding of man's mind in nature. The problem this arises originates in the fact that the knowing subject, which constitutes nature as an object of knowledge, is itself a product of nature. Habermas attacks this risk of circularity by making a distinction between objective nature, subjective nature and nature-in-itself. Further nature-in-itself can be divided in evolutionary pre-human nature and something similar to Kant's thing-in-itself. Joel Whitebook formulates this notion in the following way:

> Thus, pre-human nature produces the human species in the course of natural evolution and that created species possesses a subjective nature which constitutes objective nature as an object of possible experience and knowledge. The particular makeup of the species is such, according to Habermas, that objective nature is constituted as an object of possible technical control. Furthermore, knowledge of objective nature is, in a Kantian fashion, knowledge of a system of appearances, and something like a Ding-an-sich must be posited as lying behind our apprehension of objective nature. Unlike the Kantian Ding-

an-sich, however, Habermas' is not a quasi object affecting our receptive apparatus. Rather, it is simply a theoretical posit which must be made to indicate the externality, contingency and facticity of nature which conspire to confound any arbitrary interpretations we seek to impose on it.[12]

Thomas McCarthy poses the question if not the materialistic claim, that if pre-human nature produces subjective nature which in turn produces objective nature as an object of possible control, does it not throw Habermas back into a pre-critical ontology that goes against his transcendental approach? The problem however is that the pre human nature or nature-in-itself is a postulate that we must presuppose. In Habermas' words: "Nature-in-itself is therefore an abstraction, which is a requisite for thought."[13] I cannot see how this throws Habermas back into a pre-critical ontology, unless his epistemology implies an ontology. I would say that it is important to distinguish Habermas' work in *Knowledge and Human Interest* from works in ontology. The main point is what we can know, not what there is, and so this pre-human nature, or nature-in-itself is just what he claims it to be, a postulate.

As we have seen, a dialectic of, or philosophy about, nature (in the sense of early critical theory) becomes impossible in the theory of Habermas. This is due to the fact that the knowledge we validly can claim about nature within the framework of transcendental philosophy is the type of knowledge we apprehend from natural science, that is, nature is constituted as an object of possible technical control. Natural science should here be understood as constitutionally instrumental and, at least potentially, technological.

Habermas thinks that there is something unsurpassable in modern natural science. Modern science and technology represent man's most refined and sophisticated means in order to carry through the interest in instrumental control. If Habermas' argument is right, that is, technology and science are something that has to be seen as a project for the whole of mankind, that is, science and technology are not unique for the occident world, then there is no way that we can develop a qualitatively new science of nature, and a new technology that corresponds to this new science[14]. This becomes, as we have seen impossible. Whitebook applies a strategy to challenge Habermas on this claim. He tries to challenge him from a position within the philosophy of science.

According to Whitebook biology might very well be an example of an anomaly for Habermas' philosophy of science. An examination of biology seems, according to him, to be the most fruitful way to criticise Habermas on those issues. This approach would examine a discipline that will remain immanent to science. By this approach one avoids the risk of contradicting the present standards of intersubjective rationality.

The Norwegian philosopher Gunnar Skirbekk also makes three remarks concerning Habermas' notion of nature in connection to the technical interest. The first remark he raises is also connected to how we should regard biology, that is, under which cognitive interest can it be placed. Habermas does talk about nature as constituted by the technical interest encountered as moving objects and this sounds, according to Skirbekk, as though he has physics in mind. However I would not say that this is correct. I presume that Habermas is convinced that the technical interest is sufficient to account for biology. Whitebook posits the same question: if the entire realm of human cognition can be subdivided in the terms of the three cognitive interests where should we place biology? According to Habermas' scheme, and since nature does not communicate, we have to place biology under the technical interest with its instrumental rationality. This is then, according to Whitebook, the way we have to approach non-human life, as objects of possible control.

> Our only possible cognitive relation to other living beings in this scheme is one transcendentally oriented to technical domination. Moreover, it must be assumed that, in order to preserve his scheme of cognitive interests, Habermas would have to subscribe to the reductionist program for biology – a position which is problematic on both empirical and theoretical grounds.[15]

While, according to Whitebook's interpretation, everything on the sub-human level, life included, should be approached from the point of view of the technical interest, that is, from the area of instrumental rationality. The human capability of communication is the only thing which remains within an otherwise totally mechanistic universe. I would say that this way of argumentation is wrong. As long as it is scientific knowledge we seek, we must approach animals (as well as the bodies of humans) from the technical human interest. Whitebook seems to be overly polemical in his argumentation. Even if this interest apprehends nature as an object of possible control it does not entail any application of its result. It is also quite possible for us to hold other attitudes toward nature than a scientific one. I have earlier stated that we can hold aesthetic, moral and ethical standpoints to nature and I am convinced that there a numerous of other attitudes that are quite possible for us to hold. A key word here is objectification. It seems to me as if Habermas uses the concept of objectification in a limited sense. The natural sciences objectifies nature in accordance with the technical interest. Outside the natural sciences, however, we have a different relationship to that what is objectified. An example is medicine and the human body. While medicine objectifies the human body in accordance to the technical interest, I for one do not think that we in our daily life look up on the human body as a physical thing which should be dominated. This kind of objectification is restricted to science and technology and not to our practise in daily life.

Another problem (a more interesting one) for Habermas in relation to biology is the ontological hiatus between speaking and non-speaking nature. He seems to cross over this hiatus in a some what illicit way. We should, according to him, understand the apparent teleological behaviour in animals by reasoning 'privately'(a term used by Whitebook) from the view of human intentionality. Whitebook writes that: "while the idea of private reasoning may make sense in the context of Aristotelian metaphysics, where a continuity of beings is presupposed, in Habermas' case, where no such continuity is assumed, it strikes me as peculiar."[16] We have seen that this hiatus is a result of Habermas' approach to combining materialism with transcendentalism and it cannot be crossed until an adequate account of how pre-human nature actually produces human nature has been given. This account should not, according to Whitebook, be given by a reference to 'private reasoning'.

> ... does this type of reasoning not pre-suppose that there is some continuity between non-speaking and speaking nature – some "Community of Life" – by virtue of which "private" reasoning can legitimally take place? And once we can reason privately in a backward direction, what is to prevent us from reasoning in a forward direction and conceiving of pre-human nature as incipient spirit? This notion of incipient spirit might, in turn, form a basis for an ecological ethics from a naturalistic perspective.[17]

However what does Habermas say? The reference is made to a discussion on ethology, that is, the study of animal behavior. Is it possible to analyse behavior without reference to intentions and meanings? According to Habermas, this is impossible.

> For an anticipation of intentional relationships has slipped into the theoretical approach unnoticed. Behavior itself is defined as intelligible behavior; it only appears to be "objective." Behavior is always interpreted from the perspective of a situation we interpolate from our own [human] experience.[18]

One can say that Habermas' argument is that our understanding of animal behavior is derived from human behavior and then applied privately onto animals. The question is if there is another way? If we take as an example a dog which wags its tail and tries to lick us in the face, this behavior is interpreted as if the dog is happy, that is the dog is in the intentional state of happiness. Without going into the problem of knowing about other minds, I must confess that to me it seems to be a big enough problem to know what goes on in the head of other people, not to mention what goes on in my own. The problem becomes even bigger, I would assume, when it comes to know what goes on in the head of the dog which represents another specie. Is an incipient spirit the answer and if it is how can we reach the necessary knowledge about it? I cannot see a solution to this problem, and Whitebook's suggestion of an incipient spirit does not convince me of being an answer.

Skirbekk's second remark also concerns the problem of how to sharply differentiate nature from what is not nature. He does not, however, suggest an incipient spirit, but refers to the realm of communication. Animals do communicate and we can to some extent decode their communication. We have a possibility to some degree to understand nature in the sense of animal life. We should also remind ourselves how we communicate with babies, mentally retarded or senile persons. This would be an attempt to cross the ontological hiatus between human and pre-human nature by referring to nature as communicative. What Skirbekk elaborates is an ethical gradualism between man and nature. Since some animals do communicate on the semantic level – for instance chimpanzees and maybe dolphins – it is difficult to use a principle of communication and language capability to differentiate between human beings and nature. However, animals might communicate within their own species to some degree but they seem to lack the capability of pragmatic, reflective and discursive use of language. This seems to be a capability which is restricted to humans, and so we cannot involve ourselves directly in discourses which depends on this capability with animals. Skirbekk's solution is an advocatory principle, that is, some humans should speak in the interest of animals in practical discourse just as some people speak on behalf of unborn fetuses, mentally retarded or senile persons and so on. However, I would say that this would lead us back to the problem of private reasoning in one way. Those who speak on the behalf of animals would do so out of their own – human – experience and so we are back at the ontological hiatus. Such a principle could be used anyway but it would still be from an anthropocentric point of view. There is nothing to stop us, as humans, from applying this principle or any other ethical principle when it comes to our discussion of nature. What is important is that we as communicative, competent and responsible beings, agree on how to view nature and the ecological problems which face her and us today.

The third remark from Skirbekk concerns what we usually refer to as 'soft' contra 'hard' technology. This remark can be stated in this way: if we regard all rational actions concerning nature as structured by the technical cognitive interest, we end up with a too hard behaviour even when we approach the non-animal nature. Skirbekk uses an example in order to intuitively illustrate this point: "... a sailboat moves along in harmony with winds and waves in a way which a cabin cruiser does not. To be sure both follow the laws of physical nature. In this sense there is nothing un-natural in either case."[19] It is not a question of evaluating the two vessels, that is, to propose that the sailboat is preferable to the cabincruiser, it is rather a reminder of the notion of nature, or the view of the technological control of nature. If we approach the question from the physical aspect there is no difference between the two vessels but, according to Skirbekk, from a biological, geographical or meteorological point of view there is a difference. The sailboat works its way with winds and waves while the cabincruiser fights its way through them.

> If step by step we open our example to the entire ecological environment – with plants, birds and fish – the difference between the silent non-polluting, and non extractive sailboat and the polluting and extractive cruiser becomes even more striking. In short, the crudeness of the Habermasian notion of technical interest and control tends to blur an ecologically important difference between biologically hard and soft technologies.[20]

This argument seems interesting but I can not see how this perspective is ruled out by the technical interest. If we look at the sailboat it can without problem be placed under the technical interest, as can biology, meteorology and geography from this perspective. Is it not the technical interest itself that can tell us why the sailboat works? The question of application of 'hard' contra 'soft' technology is something that should be elaborated in a free discussion among communicatively competent discussants. I can not see why this could not take place within Habermas' theory.

While writing this paper my thoughts has revolved around the question: what makes Habermas' notion of nature unsympathetic to people with ecological interest? It is not as though his theory implies some misuse of nature and its inhabitants. One reason is surely the strong anthropocentricism it entails, that it places humans high above nature. However, I am convinced that we can reach far in developing a philosophy of ecological concern within the realm of Habermas' philosophy. The benefit of the theory is that it seems to be possible to develop such a philosophy without referring to some utopian solution. If we elaborate two positions a) preserving nature in order to obtain a sustainable future for mankind and b) preserving nature in the interest of nature itself, I think that those two positions could function together when it comes to come to grips with the acute problems mankind is facing today. If on the other hand, we would like to argue for position b), then I can understand the worries over Habermas' theory. I think that such a philosophy would have to start in ontology and move to ethics and back again.

Biography

Per Nilsson (1963) is a Ph.D. student at the department of Philosophy and the philosophy of science at Umeå University in Sweden. He is currently writing a dissertation with the working title Ecology and Rationality.

Notes

1. Max Horkheimer and Theodor W. Adorno, *Dialectic of Enlightenment,* (New York: The Continuum Publishing Company, 1994), p. 4.
2. One might say that the domination of man which is the result of the domination of nature come about when the instrumental rationality is applied in society, that is, when it is used to govern the relationship between human beings and the society.
3. This is what we can call a monistic theory of rationality. If instrumental rationality is seen as the dominating rationality in our time, and if it is applied to all spheres of life this is the outcome.
4. Horkheimer and Adorno, *Dialectic of Enlightenment,* p. 57.
5. Robyn Eckersley, "The Failed Promise of Critical Theory," in *Ecology: Key Concepts in Critical Theory,* ed. Carolyn Merchant (New Jersey: Humanities Press, 1994), p. 66.
6. In the theory of Herbert Marcuse this reconciliation is expressed in terms of liberation of nature, see Herbert Marcuse, *One Dimensional Man,* (Boston: Beacon Press, 1964).
7. Jürgen Habermas, *Theory of communicative Action*, transl. Thomas McCarthy (Cambridge: Polity Press, 1987), vol. 2, p. 394.
8. Jürgen Habermas, "Technology and Science as "Ideology," in *Toward a Rational Society,* transl. Jeremy J. Shapiro (London: Heinemann Educational Books Ltd, 1971), p. 88.
9. See Joel Whitebook, "The Problem of Nature in Habermas," in *Telos* 40 (1979); p. 41-69, Gunnar Skirbekk, "The Pragmatic Notion of Nature," in, *Rationality and Modernity,* (Oslo: Scandinavian University Press, 1993), p. 169-190; Thomas McCarthy, *The Critical Theory of Jürgen Habermas,* (Cambridge, Mass: MIT Press, 1978), p.

110-125; Stephen D. Parson, "Explaining Technology and Society: The Problem of Nature in Habermas," in Philosophy of the Social Sciences, Vol. 22 (1992), 218-230.
10. I am not sure of this theme. As I see it the argument of Habermas is in epistemology and his critics claims that he makes an ontological claim in this argument. The only way I can see the problem arise is if the epistemological claim of Habermas implies an ontological claim.
11. Jürgen Habermas, *Knowledge and Human Interest*, second ed. transl. by Jeremy J. Shapiro (London: Heineman Educational Books Ltd, 1978), p. 314.
12. Whitebook "The Problem of Nature in Habermas," p. 49.
13. Habermas, *Knowledge and Human Interest*, p. 34.
14. For an opposite view, sufficiently critisised by Habermas in "Technology and Science as 'Ideology'," see Herbert Marcuse, *One Dimensional Man.*
15. Whitebook,"The Problem of Nature in Habermas," p. 59.
16. Whitebook,"The Problem of Nature in Habermas," p. 60.
17. Whitebook,"The Problem of Nature in Habermas," p. 61.
18. Jürgen Habermas, *On the Logic of the Social Sciences*, transl. by S. W. Nicholsen and J. A. Stark (Cambridge Mass: MIT Press, 1988), p. 72.
19. Gunnar Skirbekk, "A Pragmatic Notion of Nature," in *Rationality and Modernity,* (Oslo: Scandinavian University Press, 1993), p. 177-178.
20. Skirbekk, "A pragmatic Notion of Nature," p. 178.

Bibliography

Eckersley, Robyn. "The Failed Promise of Critical Theory." In *Ecology: Key Concepts in Critical Theory.* Ed. Carolyn Merchant. New Jersey: Humanities Press, 1994.

Habermas, Jürgen.*Theory of Communicative Action.* Transl. T. McCarthy. Oxford: Basil Blackwell Ltd, 1991.

Habermas, Jürgen. *Knowledge and Human Interest.* Transl. Jeremy J. Shapiro. Second ed. London: Heineman Educational Books Ltd, 1978.

Habermas, Jürgen. *On the Logic of the Social Sciences.* Transl. S. W. Nicholsen and J. A. Stark. Cambridge Mass: MIT Press, 1988.

Habermas, Jürgen. "Technology and Science as 'Ideology.'" In *Toward a Rational Society.* Transl Jeremy J. Shapiro. London: Heinemann Educational Books Ltd, 1971.

Horkheimer, Max and Theodor W. Adorno. *Dialectic of Enlightenment,* New York: The Continuum Publishing Company, 1994.

Marcuse, Herbert. *One Dimensional Man.* Boston: Beacon Press, 1964.

McCarthy, Thomas. *The Critical Theory of Jürgen Habermas.* Cambridge, Mass: MIT Press, 1978.

Merchant, Carolyn, ed. *Ecology: Key Concepts in Critical Theory.* New Jersey: Humanities Press, 1994.

Di Norcia, Vincent. "From Critical Theory to Critical Ecology." In *Telos* 22. (Winter, 1974-75).

Parsons, D. Stephen. "Explaining Technology And Society: The Problem of Nature in Habermas." In *Philosophy of the Social Sciences.* Vol. 22 No. 2. (1992).

Skirbekk, Gunnar. *Ecophilosophical manuscripts.* Bergen: Ariadne forlag, 1992.

Skirbekk, Gunnar. *Manuscripts on rationality*. Bergen: Ariadne forlag, 1992.
Skirbekk, Gunnar. *Rationality and Modernity.* Oslo:Scandinavian University Press, 1993.
Whitebook, Joel. "The Problem of Nature in Habermas." In *Telos* 40. (1979).

Sami Pihlström

The Pragmatist Critique of Metaphysics and the Nature of Man[1]

Abstract
Traditionally, pragmatists have attacked metaphysics – not in the logical positivists' way but in their own particular way. In our time, the most devastating neopragmatist critique of metaphysics has been presented by Richard Rorty. He wants to lead us to a "post-Philosophical culture" by giving up the old-fashioned metaphysical and epistemological tradition of "systematic" philosophy. He thinks that he is following the classical American pragmatists (e.g., William James) in this effort.

Rorty's conception of philosophical problems is shown to be flawed on the basis of pragmatism itself. The key idea is that pragmatism presupposes philosophical (even metaphysical) reflection and, in particular, a philosophical conception of humanity. In my view, we need a normative and non-reductively naturalist picture of human nature. In James's philosophical anthropology, for example, such human characteristics as activity and courage are combined with a metaphysical view of man's place in nature. Hence, Rorty's thesis that the classical Kantian questions (in particular, the question "What is man?") can just be given up is very un*pragmatistic and disastrous – also from the point of view of the fundamental problems that we, as human beings, are confronting today (e.g., the ecological crisis).*

1. Introduction

In recent years, some "neopragmatists" have radically attempted to undermine many of the traditional problems of philosophy. For example, in philosophy of science, Arthur Fine has defended an anti-metaphysical view labeled NOA ("the natural ontological attitude"), according to which we should simply accept the ontological commitments of science without trying to interpret or problematize them philosophically.[2] Stephen Stich, in turn, has argued for a strong form of pragmatism, according to which we should not even care whether our beliefs are true or false.[3] Furthermore, many defenders of "minimalist" theories of truth have claimed that there is, in fact, no special philosophical problem related to the notion of truth: the Tarskian formula "'p' is true iff p" tells us everything that needs to be told about truth.[4] Sharing this attitude, Richard Rorty, who explicitly considers himself a pragmatist, has advocated a version of pragmatism suggesting the end of philosophy as a systematic enterprise.

Of course, (meta)philosophical critique of metaphysics has a long history. If I had to present a full treatment of this topic, I would have to begin with Kant and discuss Nietzsche and the logical positivists, among others, at length. But now the very idea of there being any kind of "philosophy" in any traditional sense (usually assumed by "traditional" critics of metaphysics) is called into question by Rortyan neopragmatists. In particular, the very idea of there being any philosophical issue of humanity is questioned.

I do not hope to persuade the reader to entirely reject these fashionable neopragmatist lines of thought. After centuries of seemingly endless philosophical speculation about various issues, some of them are quite refreshening. But I do think that they are deeply problematic – *philosophically* problematic – and, in the end, untenable. In this paper, I shall examine the rejection of metaphysical reflection in Rorty's pragmatism in particular, thus paying attention to the question of the status of metaphysics (especially the metaphysics of man, i.e., the problem of human nature) rather than on questions related to truth, knowledge, rationality, and so forth. My inquiry can be understood as a metaphilosophical or perhaps meta-metaphysical one. Obviously, however, something about the notion of truth, for example, must be said in such an inquiry. I am going to argue that Rorty and his fellow pragmatists are seriously mistaken, on the basis of pragmatism itself. Endorsing (neo)pragmatism as a general philosophical position which emphasizes (1) the practice-ladenness of all human projects, including philosophical ones, and (2) the uselessness of any sharp dichotomy between "theory" and "practice", I also defend (3) the human pragmatic need to engage in metaphysical reflection on human nature. Moreover, I contend that the problem of human nature is, for the pragmatist, one of the deepest problems in philosophy. Thus, I shall try to make a positive point by first treating Rorty's form of pragmatism as a negative example. I shall not try to save traditional metaphysics as such, but I hope I will be able to make sense of the idea that the pragmatist can attempt to reformulate and redefine metaphysical issues by her pragmatic means (i.e., to transform them, not eliminate them). This is what James, in my view, wanted to do.

Before turning to my rather general metaphilosophical thesis, we must take a look at Rorty's famous repudiation of the Western tradition of philosophy. His attack turns on his claim that traditional philosophical problems are mere confusions – a claim closely connected with his physicalism. I shall begin by sketching what I take to be his overall argument, focusing on his deconstruction of traditional philosophy of mind, since this theme carries us most naturally to the issue of human nature.

2. Overcoming Metaphysics

As is well known, Rorty argues in his *Philosophy and the Mirror of Nature* (1980) and in many other works that the mind-body problem, originated in its modern form by Descartes and Locke, is a mere confusion, a contingent product of the history of philosophy. The distinction between "the physical" and "the mental" should not be ontologized (pp. 29-32). The mistaken idea that there is, within a human being, a "mind" or "consciousness" whose relation to the material reality is in some way problematic is labeled the idea of "our glassy essence" by Rorty.[5] We should, he suggests, manage without such "mirror" metaphors. (See especially *ibid.*, ch. 2; cf. Rorty 1989, ch. 2.) Rorty is, clearly, a materialist (in the 1960s and 1970s he advocated "eliminative materialism"), but he reminds us that the materialist need not accept any metaphysical "identity theory" of the mind (Rorty 1980, pp. 114-119). This is, of course, quite trivial, if the materialism favored is eliminative: there just *is* no mind to identify with brain activity.

In his article 'Non-reductive Physicalism', Rorty (1991, p. 114) defines "physicalism" as the view that "every event can be described in microstructural terms, a description which mentions only elementary particles, and can be explained by reference to other events so described". This definition undoubtedly sounds (ontologically) reductionistic. Rorty goes on to say that even the event of Mozart's composing a melody can, in principle, be described in this physicalistic way (*ibid.*). However, this doctrine can be combined with the claim that a relation of "reduction" can take place "merely between linguistic items, not among ontological categories" (*ibid.*, p. 115). A linguistic reduction can never show that "X's are *nothing but* Y's", since an "X is what it is and no other thing" (*ibid.*). But since there simply is no "ontological category" of "mind", we should, I think, understand Rorty as saying that there is no question of reduction because there is nothing to reduce (in any ontological sense). "Elimination, hence no reduction" would seem to be Rorty's formula. He writes:

> So to be a physicalist is, on this non-reductionist account, perfectly compatible with saying that we shall probably continue to talk about mental entities – beliefs, desires, and the like – forever. Such talk is not metaphorical, does not need to be bracketed, does not need to be made more precise or scientific, does not need philosophical clarification. (*Ibid.*)

This point is related to Rorty's acceptance of Davidson's view that metaphors do not have meanings[6] and especially to Davidson's idea that "reasons can be causes", that is, that "mental" and "physical" events can be seen "as the same events under two descriptions" (*ibid.*, p. 114). Davidson's philosophy is presupposed by Rorty most clearly in the question concerning the relation between language and the world. Rorty's central Davidsonian thesis is the denial of genuine semantic relations between sentences and non-sentences: "things in the world do not make sentences (nor, *a fortiori*, beliefs) true" (*ibid.*, p. 116). He argues for an "anti-representationalist" view of language-world relations. Linguistic items do not represent non-linguistic items, and thus the traditional problem of realism vs. anti-realism is not a genuine problem at all (*ibid.*, Introduction).[7]

Rorty extends these ideas into a general naturalist account of the relation between a human being and the environing world. This happens by taking three steps. First, one should follow Peirce in regarding beliefs "as tools for handling reality" rather than "as representations of reality". Second, one should follow Quine in "blurring the distinction between necessary and contingent truths". The third step is the genuinely Davidsonian one: that of dispensing with relations of "making true" and realizing that there are only causal relations between the human subject and its environment. (*Ibid.*, pp. 118-120.) On these grounds, Rorty finds no special philosophical interest in the question of "how things look from the inside" of the human subject:

> The fact that human beings can be aware of certain of their psychological states is not, on this view, any more mysterious than that they can be trained to report on the presence of adrenalin in their bloodstreams, or on their body temperature, or on a lack of blood flow in their extremities. Ability to report is not a matter of "presence to consciousness" but simply of teaching the use of words. The use of sentences like "I believe that p" is taught in the same way as that of

sentences like "I have a fever". So there is no special reason to cut off "mental" states from "physical states" as having a metaphysically intimate relation to an entity called "consciousness". To take this view is, at one stroke, to eliminate most of the problematic of post-Kantian philosophy. (*Ibid.*, p. 121.)

To understand Rorty's eliminationist attitude more clearly, we may briefly take a look at his statements on the issues of realism and truth. In his system, as in any physicalistic system, there is (as there presumably must be) a place for a world in a realist sense. Rorty says that he does not end up with anti-realism or idealism, though he rejects both realist theories of reference and the correspondence theory of truth (and *all* other "theories" of truth as well). Though the Rortyan pragmatist drops the idea of a sentence being true or false because of some relation of "making true" obtaining or failing to obtain, in the correspondence sense, between the sentence and the way the world is, he thinks that there is a world "out there" which we did not make up. But the world does not tell us any truths: "The world is out there, but descriptions of the world are not." It is we, humans, who formulate linguistic expressions which may be true or false. (Rorty 1989, pp. 4-7.) The world just is there. It has no real function in semantics or epistemology. In Rorty's earlier phrase, it can be said to be "well lost" (see his 1982, ch. 1).

In particular, the Cartesian conception of the mind as a "mirror of nature" leads to the problem of skepticism and to epistemological considerations in order to refute skepticism. Skepticism is inevitable, if knowledge is regarded as accurate representation of reality. According to Rorty (1980, ch. 4), epistemology is as historically contingent and "optional" as philosophy of mind is. This conclusion is based on Sellars's, Quine's, and Davidson's arguments against the "myth of the given", the analytic/synthetic distinction, and the scheme/content dualism (respectively). In rejecting the idea that knowledge is accurate representation of reality, Rorty also wants to put aside the philosophical problem of reference. As an invention of philosophers, the notion of reference is an artificial and unnecessary construct: the commonsense notion of "talking about" is enough for our purposes. We need not ask whether there are things connected with the use of linguistic terms by a relation called "reference". (*Ibid.*, pp. 287-292; Rorty 1982, ch. 7.) Similarly, the correspondence theory of truth is empty or trivial. There is no philosophically interesting theory of truth to be formulated. (Rorty 1980, pp. 281-282; 1982, p. xvi; 1989, pp. 8-9.) The role of philosophy concerned with metaphysical and epistemological questions is, in our secularized culture, as peripheral as that of theology. Its classical problems have ceased to be relevant. To be an anti-representationalist is to stop thinking about the traditional notions of truth, reference, and knowledge.

Rather than trying to secure a foundation for knowledge, we should, Rorty contends, pragmatically and "therapeutically" inquire into the interaction between human beings. In a naturalistic spirit, Rorty advocates "epistemological behaviorism", according to which philosophy cannot say anything about truth and knowledge that could not be said by common sense, history, biology, etc. (Rorty 1980, pp. 175-176.) "Philosophical problems" of knowledge cannot be "solved"; they must be "dissolved" (*ibid.*, pp. 219-220, 229-230). In short, by abandoning such old problems, Rorty seems to be led to the conclusion that there is nothing philosophically mysterious in human beings. In a sense, we *simply* are parts of matter, although this does not prevent us from being complex cultural entities. The pragmatistic attitude that Rorty favors is "relaxed". There is no need to pursue dead-end philosophical puzzles concerning man's being (epistemically, referentially or conceptually) related to reality.

Even though Rorty accepts the existence of a world "out there", we can, in his view, only compare two descriptions of a thing with each other, never a description with a thing in itself. Different vocabularies or ways of describing things serve different purposes, and there is no such thing as the world's or Nature's "own" vocabulary, as there is no such thing as a purpose which would be "closer to reality" than other purposes. (Rorty 1982, pp. 153-154; 1989, p. 20; 1991, pp. 91-92.) Thus, while trying to avoid anti-realism, Rorty rejects "metaphysical realism".[8] As pragmatists, we should not attempt (like a "mirror of nature") to accurately represent a reality structured in its own way entirely independently of us and our purposes. Rather, we live in a world of actual human projects, in a *praxis*, in which truth as correspondence is simply irrelevant:

> In the end, the pragmatists tell us, what matters is our loyalty to other human beings clinging together against the dark, not our hope of getting things right. James, in arguing against realists and idealists that "the trail of the human serpent is over all," was reminding us that our glory is in our participation in fallible and transitory human projects, not in our obedience to permanent nonhuman constraints. (Rorty 1982, p. 166.)

By trivializing the notion of truth, Rorty tries, on my interpretation, to *trivialize realism*. Traditionally, the problem of realism has been considered deep and important, because it is the most general way of reflecting on the relation between man and the world. But Rorty, as an eliminative materialist, does not find anything interesting in this relation. The underlying idea is his *trivializing of the problem of humanity*.[9] Being human is, we seem to be told, philosophically unexciting. As Rorty puts it at the end of one of his recent papers,

> ... lots of different developments in our century – Freudian accounts of inner moral conflicts, ethnographic descriptions of alternative forms of social life, experimentalism in literature and the arts – have made it steadily easier for us to substitute Deweyan questions such as, Which communities' purposes shall I share? and What sort of person would I prefer to be? for the Kantian questions, What Should I Do? What May I Hope? What is Man? (Rorty 1995a, p. 15.)

Still, we are supposed to respect others' humanity and participate in "human projects", without even asking what kind of beings we, as men, are. What is going on here?

From the description of the contingency and dead-ends of Western philosophy Rorty moves on to his own radical view on the possibilities of future philosophizing: "Pragmatists are saying that the best hope for philosophy is not to practice Philosophy." (Rorty 1982, p. xv.) He thinks that we should abandon "Philosophy" and be satisfied with "philosophy", i.e., some sort of free (more or less "Deweyan") cultural discussion and criticism. In a "post-Philosophical" culture, philosophy would simply have become such "edifying" discussion. (See *ibid.*, pp. xxxvii – xliv and chs. 2 and 12; cf. Rorty 1980, ch. 8.) Philosophy as reflection on traditional philosophical problems would then have come to an end.[10] It would not have disappeared as an academic subject or as a project of constructing large visions, but problems like the nature of being, the nature of man, the relation between the subject and the object, language and thinking, etc., would not interest post-philosophers. (Rorty 1982, pp. 31-32; cf. 1980, pp. 393-394; 1991, pp. 99, 187.) Metaphilosophically speaking, we should understand the historically contingent nature of philosophy and reject the dream of philosophy as the "mother of sciences". Simultaneously, we should drop the question of what philosophy "really" is. (Rorty 1982, pp. 222-225.)

In discussing the possibility of "post-Philosophy", Rorty praises not only Dewey but also Wittgenstein: "What gives Wittgenstein's work its power is, I think, the vision of a point where 'we can cease doing philosophy when we want to.'" (*Ibid.*, pp. 35-36.)[11] The undeniable fact that we have reached the threshold of a "post-Philosophical" culture through confusing traditional concepts and problems is also expressed by an allusion to Wittgenstein: "Philosophers like Davidson and Derrida have, I think, given us good reasons to think that the *physis – nomos, in se – ad nos*, and objective – subjective distinctions were steps on a ladder that we can now safely throw away." (Rorty 1991, p. 193.) *Via* a Wittgensteinian or quasi-Wittgensteinian conception of our various forms of life as the basis of our language-games, Rorty's view of philosophy culminates, in the end, with politics and social engagement. Philosophy must be a part of the "conversation of mankind" (see Rorty 1980, p. 389 ff.). The Rortyan pragmatist is above all interested in the conversationel community we live in. The ways in which the members of the community use their language, their capacities of finding edifying and inspiring vocabularies and metaphors, are more important than truth, knowledge, or rationality. These latter notions have significance only within a community, language-game, culture, or *ethnos*.[12]

I shall try to show that Rorty's eliminationist account of man is in deep tension with (Jamesian) pragmatism and that, as a result, what he calls "pragmatism" is, in its insistence on avoiding metaphysics, disastrously unpragmatistic. At least it is unpragmatistic from the point of view of my favorite form of pragmatism.

3. Preserving Metaphysics

What is, then, wrong with Rorty's view? One plausible answer lies at the very center of his position, in his related doctrines of physicalism and anti-representationalism. On the most general level, Rorty's account of the relation between language and the world leads to an unacceptable conception of human communication, including philosophy. These are conceived as mere "discussion" or "conversation" (cf. Rorty 1980, ch. 8) with no hope of ever achieving any real contact with the world, extra-linguistic reality. If our words and sentences never refer to anything, how can we discuss anything? What we can do is just speak – or go on writing, in Derrida's sense.[13] This is, to my mind, an unacceptable picture of what kind of beings we language-using humans are.

On the other hand, *if* Rorty somehow allows some kind of referentiality or representationality in language – something to account for the fact that it is possible for us to talk about different things rightly or wrongly, to make true or false statements about reality – he seems to face another problem. We have seen that he accepts all the following: (1) there is a real natural world independently of human language(s); (2) in language, we can "talk about" things, if not refer to anything in the philosophical sense of "refer"; (3) there are only causal relations between language(s) and the world. How does this position *pragmatically* differ from the highly reductive views of those naturalists or physicalists who advocate "causal theories" of reference? Either Rorty completely fails to make sense of human language-use by eliminating all connections between linguistic expressions and what they are supposed to be *about*, or else he ends up with a "causalistic" reduction of these word-world relations, employing a more or less philosophical concept of reference, which he says he does not find intelligible at all.[14]

Putnam has attacked Rorty's views as fiercely as he has attacked metaphysical realism. In his view, what both Rorty and such naturalizers of epistemology as Quine (among others) fail to notice is that "there is no eliminating the normative".[15] Putnam argues that Rorty (at least in *Philosophy and the Mirror of Nature*) is a cultural relativist, and that cultural relativism is, surprisingly, "one of the most influential – perhaps the most influential – forms of naturalized epistemology extant, although not usually recognized as such" (Putnam 1983, p. 235). As related to the issues of relativism and normativity, the debate between Rorty and Putnam has focused on the notion of truth. Putnam (1994, p. 331) declares that both Quine and Rorty agree on what he himself finds shocking, that is, "that 'truth' is an empty notion". Putnam has constantly argued for a "substantial" concept of truth, one in which 'true' refers to a genuine and, most importantly, *normative* property that a sentence, statement, or belief may have or lack. "Redundancy", "disquotational", or "minimalist" conceptions of truth fail to make sense of the normativity of our linguistic practice – of the fact that the notion of truth serves our need to recognize that we sometimes get things right, sometimes wrong. If Quine (1990) is right in claiming that "immanent truth" (truth within a language) is all we have or need, then Rorty is right and, moreover, Derrida is right in saying that "il n'y a pas de hors-texte" (Putnam 1994, p. 341). For Putnam this is unacceptable.

Rorty (1992, p. 418), in turn, has reacted by noticing that, in demanding that truth should be conceived as a "normative property", Putnam has "come to that place of philosophy where, as Wittgenstein says, 'one just wants to utter an inarticulate sound.'" The key to his disagreement with Putnam lies, of course, in his naturalism (or "Darwinism", as he now also calls it). He claims that Darwinism is "a useful vocabulary" for formulating the general pragmatistic position on which he and Putnam agree (Rorty 1993, p. 447); consequently, he gives a pragmatic argument for thoroughgoing naturalism:

> We should see what happens if (in Jean-Paul Sartre's words) "we attempt to draw the full conclusions from a consistently atheist position," a position in which such phrases as 'the nature of human life' no longer distract us from the absence of a God's-eye view. The first

> step in conducting this experiment should be to set aside the shards of the subject-object, scheme-content, and reality-appearance distinctions, and to think of our relation to the rest of the universe in purely causal, as opposed to representationalist, terms... I think that my differences with Putnam come down, in the end, to his unhappiness with such a purely causal picture. (*Ibid.*, p. 449; cf. also pp. 460-461.)

What is at issue is, precisely, the availability of a "purely causal", fully naturalistic picture of man (rather than just theories of truth). The strength of a Putnamean reply to Rorty will also, in part, depend on whether a viable version of naturalism can be constructed in a way acceptable to him.

Rorty's naturalism, again, turns on anti-representationalism (*ibid.*, pp. 448-449) and on an ultra-pragmatist project of avoiding "fruitless, irresolvable, disagreements on dead-end issues" (i.e., traditional metaphysical and epistemological issues) by transforming such issues into "cultural politics" (*ibid.*, p. 457). In my view, this hardly escapes – despite Rorty's claims to the contrary (e.g., *ibid.*, pp. 446-447) – his old "end of philosophy" line of thought. He still thinks that naturalism can "dissolve", or eliminate, all fruitless philosophical puzzles. In his most recent work, Putnam has once again responded to Rorty's responses by pointing out that while his own views have become "increasingly realist", "Rorty has moved from his physicalism to an extreme linguistic idealism which teeters on the edge of solipsism" (Putnam 1994, p. 306). He points out (*ibid.*) that Rorty's (1993) response (to his [i.e., Putnam's] contention that the human mind cannot be fully "naturalized", i.e., that it cannot be thoroughly described in non-intentional and non-normative language), with its insistence on the idea that the irreducibility of one "vocabulary" to another does not imply anything ontological, is "an odd move indeed for some one who claims the very vocabulary/reality distinction has to be given up". As we saw, this was also Rorty's point in his 'Non-Reductive Physicalism'. Rorty appears to be led to a self-refuting paradox by appealing to a distinction between reality and the vocabularies in terms of which reality is described.

This short excursion to the Rorty vs. Putnam debate was intended to show that neopragmatists are not at all undiverged in their opinions concerning the realism issue. Yet, Putnam and Rorty agree in rejecting precisely the sharp metaphysical distinction between "reality" and our "vocabularies". They both reject metaphysical realism, and here I follow their pragmatism. Many of Rorty's ideas *are* acceptable – and, conversely, many of his critics fail because of their commitments to metaphysical realism. I find Rorty's skepticism regarding the possibility of describing the world in terms of the world's "own" vocabulary completely justified. Moreover, I endorse his overall view on the history of philosophy: philosophical problems, emerged in the course of the past 2500 years, are *of course* contingent products of history – as contingent as we ourselves are, once we have given up idealistic or religious convictions of a divine purpose functioning in and through history. We need not, and should not, postulate any aprioristic, ahistorical, essentialist set of philosophical problems. There are no necessary and sufficient conditions for a problem to be a philosophical one. Problems change, as we do; metaphysical reflections and outlooks are historically relative. We are not, for example, philosophically interested in angels, with whom the medievals were concerned. Finally, I also feel some sympathy to Rorty's naturalistic program in general, even though I do not think that his particular formulation of it is successful.

However, as against Rorty's account of the nature of philosophical problems, one may simply claim that the historical contingency of a certain problem does not imply its unreality. The pen on my table exists only contingently, as any given thing presumably does. The existence of whatever there is in the world is contingent at least in the pragmatist sense that whatever we actually identify as an entity or a thing of some kind could be identified differently.[16] Our classifications of things could be quite different from what they in fact are. Nevertheless, even though I could (if I had chosen a rather peculiar conceptual scheme) regard my pen and my table as a single entity, the pen, as I (contingently) identify it, is a real pen. It exists as a pen. I can, of course, throw a bad pen away and get myself a better one; similarly, I can take a pragmatic attitude to philosophical problems. Rorty is, however, quite overhasty in his claim that we should reject all traditional problems of philosophy. He emphasizes the "solidarity" of historically contingent communities and accepts only "conversational" standards and criteria of truth and rationality internal to such communities;[17] on the other hand, he is prepared to step outside *his own* (philosophical, metaphysical, epistemological) community to tell us that we should bury systematic philosophy. It is not easy to see how he could react to the following simple counter-argument raised by the defender of traditional, systematic philosophy: "*We philosophers* do not accept your 'post-Philosophy'". Indeed, as Susan Haack (1993) has argued – in order to show that Rorty thoroughly misunderstands Peirce[18] – the dichotomy between "Philosophy" and "philosophy" is untenable. There are, according to Haack (p. 413 ff.), at least three dimensions of this false dichotomy in Rorty's work: first, the dualism of Philosophy taking science as an idol and Rortyan philosophy "as a genre of literature or literary criticism"; secondly, the dualism of truth as "mirroring" (i.e., the truth of the representationalist) and as "not the sort of thing one should expect to have a philosophically interesting theory about";

thirdly, the dualism of "transcendental principles" and "conventions of conversation".[19]

We can say, then, that Rorty's criticism of traditional philosophy is inconclusive, because he ignores the possibility of constructing an analogical argument – with a contrary conclusion – based on the notion of community, *ethnos*, practice, or form of life. This amounts to defeating Rorty by using his own weapons. *Our* form of life is such that we cannot give up the systematic problems of philosophy, including some difficult metaphysical and epistemological questions.[20] As pragmatists, we can regard this as a feature of our *philosophical practice*, or, if we want to use Wittgensteinian terminology, *our philosophical form of life*. Rorty merely prefers a certain unphilosophical form of life to philosophical ones. Or, to put it in a yet other manner, he does not pay due attention to the fact that our *life-world* may be philosophically loaded – in a way which makes that very life-world itself problematic. (Consider, for example, the life-world of a philosopher who participates in a philosophical symposium on the concept of life-world.) This way of attacking Rorty might appear to stretch the notions of life-world and form of life beyond their useful application. One might argue that these notions, by definition, denote something "everyday", "ordinary", or non-philosophical. But I would like to suggest that, *for a philosopher*, there is no genuine separation between philosophy and life. Philosophy is not such a clean and tidy academic subject.

On the other hand, the Rortyan pragmatist will not find it easy to stop philosophizing. Sometimes Rorty only seems to give up philosophy. Indeed, Putnam accuses him of certain *philosophical* prejudices: Rorty (in the company of many other contemporary philosophers) is unable to accept the "pre-philosophical" picture that our thoughts and statements can be about the world, that our language can represent the world, and so forth. His anti-representationalism is, on Putnam's account, a *wrong* way of formulating the "impossibility" that we confront in rejecting metaphysical realism (cf. Conant 1994, pp. xxiv-xxxiii). The *unintelligibility* of metaphysical realism is not a matter of some sort of inability of ours or of our failure to be able to do something:

> I agree with Rorty that we have no access to "unconceptualized reality." ...But it doesn't follow that language and thought do not describe something outside themselves, even if that something can only be described by describing it (that is by employing language and thought); and, as Rorty ought to have seen, the belief that they do plays an essential role *within* language and thought themselves and, more importantly, within our lives. (Putnam 1994, p. 297; cf. 1995, ch. 2.)

The viability of a more or less realist notion of representation can thus be argued for pragmatically, by appealing to its role "within our lives". Rorty is, according to Putnam, simply wrong in claiming that it plays no such role. Putnam goes on to say that the unintelligibility of the idea that we could compare our language and thought with reality "as it is in itself" entails the corresponding unintelligibility of the idea that this comparison is "impossible". Thus, Rorty's rejection of metaphysical realism "partakes of the same unintelligibility". Putnam, on the contrary, rejects both sides of the coin (i.e., both Rortyan anti-representationalism and metaphysical realism) and wishes to "recover our ordinary notion of representation". (Putnam 1994, pp. 299-300.)[21]

I do not think that Putnam's "ordinary notion of representation" is philosophically innocent; on the contrary, it seems to me that, unfortunately, Putnam himself (almost) slides into mere Rortyan "talking about" in his latest writings on language and reality.[22] What is relevant here is, however, that Putnam confronts Rorty's position by tracing it back to its general philosophical presuppositions. We should also recognize that naturalism, including Rorty's particular brand of "non-reductive physicalism", is inevitably a philosophical position. Most importantly, it is a philosophical (though "Darwinian") conception of man. In any event, then, Rorty should be able to support his views by means of philosophical arguments – if he wants to justify them at all. Let us, therefore, once again raise the issue of ontological realism. Despite some of his clearly anti-realistic remarks, Rorty turns out to be an ontological realist, as was already observed. The spatio-temporal (physical) world exists quite independently of human mental states or capabilities.[23] However, the relation between realism and pragmatism is not unproblematic. In agreement with other pragmatists, Rorty emphasizes the familiar contextuality of ontology, that is, the fact that "all objects are always already contextualized" (Rorty 1991, p. 97) and that, once the opposition between the context and the contextualized thing is dropped, "there is no way to divide things up into those which are what they are independent of context and those which are context-dependent" (*ibid.*, p. 98).

Arguably, Rorty's strong physicalist realism is incompatible with the idea (typical of pragmatism) that we should not try to reach and represent uncontextualized reality "as it is in itself" (see Holówka 1990). Rorty seems to presuppose that the world, abstracted from our classifications and contextualizations, just is physical. In any event, it is very problematic for him that he must use ontological language in order to state his "pragmatism". How can a "post-Philosopher" start from ontological statements, such as the recognition of the existence of an external world? Furthermore, how can language used by an "anti-representationalist" refer to anything, even to the world, which Rorty nevertheless thinks exists independently of us? What kind of language does he use in saying all that he says? In short, how can he claim that he has stepped beyond the problem of realism? His ontological statements not only include, as such, a challenge to engage in the dispute over the issue of realism, but his own (realist and pragmatist) ontological claims are not easily reconcilable. The claim that traditional metaphysics is avoided is, then, false.[24]

We might even attempt a tentative formulation of a short armchair argument against the project of undermining the problem of realism. If Rorty thinks that this problem (or some other problem of traditional, systematic philosophy) is a "pseudo-problem", he in a sense claims that, *as a philosophical problem*, it is unreal. It is not a real problem, in his view. (Perhaps it has been more or less "real" in a distant philosophical community of the past, but it no longer is, or at least it no longer should be. Post-Philosophers have finally recognized its unreality.) If we are ontological realists even in a modest sense, i.e., if we accept, as Rorty does, that there is some kind of a reality external to and independent of our mental states, we may also accept that there are some man-made cultural artifacts, emerged in the course of history and causally dependent on the lives of some famous philosophers as well as on books written by them, that we call philosophical problems – whatever is the right (reductive or non-reductive) ontological analysis of them.[25] In making the claim that the problem of realism is unreal, Rorty seems to be making a claim about reality. Thus, he is an anti-realist with regard to philosophical problems, especially with regard to the issue of realism. This anti-realism, as a reaction to a special case of the general issue of realism, of course reintroduces the very same issue, which he thinks he has abandoned.

However, Rorty considers himself an edifying philosopher or an "ironist" (see especially his 1989) who can use language without committing himself to any *views* about reality. The most critical passage of *Philosophy and the Mirror of Nature* is, I think, the following one:

> ...edifying philosophers have to decry the very notion of having a view, while avoiding having a view about having views. This is an awkward, but not impossible, position. ...We might (when we say something) just be *saying something* – participating in a conversation rather than contributing to an inquiry. Perhaps saying things is not always saying how things are. Perhaps saying *that* is itself not a case of saying how things are. (Rorty 1980, p. 371.)

Now, it is impossible to follow Rorty to this absurdity.[26] His view on the nature of philosophical conversation, which he even applies to himself, puts a full stop to all conversation. He can go on conversating only by ceasing to conversate. If the language that we use does not refer to anything – if our use of it is not an attempt of any kind to state anything about the way things (in however pragmatic sense) are – it is difficult to understand what it even is to use language. "Conversation", in which one just "says something" and does not express any views about anything, is not conversation at all in the sense of a (minimally rational) human dialogue, in which one can get things right or wrong. The (moderate) pragmatist should, I would argue, insist on this latter kind of rationally conducted conversation in which participants make genuine commitments to genuine views.

The "conversation" that the extreme Rortyan pragmatist participates in by writing about "pragmatism" and "post-Philosophy" is, on the basis of her own criteria, mere pseudo-conversation: she tries to (meta)philosophize about the relations between philosophical discourse and something external to this discourse (other discourses, science, the world, the supposed relation between language and the world, etc.) – even though there should be nothing interesting in these relations from her point of view. If the relation between language and the world, for instance, is of no philosophical interest but is just one more causal relation, why should we even be interested in philosophical (or "post-Philosophical", as it were) discussion of the relation between that relation, on the one hand, and traditional philosophy of language, on the other? Why should we even be interested in ourselves as philosophizing human beings? Or is there some metaphilosophical level on which traditional issues become relevant, after all?[27]

4. The Human Metaphysical Need: Why Philosophical Anthropology is Ineliminable

I have critically considered the Rortyan suggestion that metaphysical and epistemological issues should be overcome by taking a radically pragmatic turn. I have argued that the issue of realism is fundamental for the pragmatist, too, and that Rorty is unable to escape it. No end of philosophy (or metaphysics) is in sight for us, even if a Wittgensteinian "peace of thought" may sometimes be our goal for a moment.[28] After having discussed Rorty's views on naturalism, physicalism, and realism, we are now able to defend the pragmatist's need of metaphysics in general and "philosophical anthropology" in particular.

While there cannot (for us philosophers) be an end of philosophy or even an end of metaphysics, one can speak about the various "ends" of metaphysics. In a recent defense of metaphysics against postmodernism and related challenges, Robert Kane (1993, p. 415) identifies two: (1) "Objective Explanation", that is, "the goal of understanding, in Aristotle's terms, the principles or reasons, the *archai kai aitiai* of things, which will account objectively and comprehensively for what is, and why"; and (2) "Objective Worth", the pursuit of which is the pursuit of understanding "what is *objectively valuable and worth striving for*". Postmodernist critics are skeptical about both of these ends (*ibid.*, p. 417 ff.). However, Kane argues, their criticism only succeeds in disputing the view that objective explanation and objective worth could be known with absolute certainty. "The metaphysical quest" must be admitted to be "radically contingent" – we should be anti-foundationalists, as Rorty and other pragmatists typically think – but Kane points out that the two central ends of metaphysics are still "legitimate objects of aspiration". (*Ibid.*, p. 421.) The choice between a metaphysical and a (Rortyan) post-metaphysical culture is, he argues, a "real pragmatic choice": it concerns the way we want to live our lives and what we want to strive for. (*Ibid.*, p. 427.) Thus, what Kane provides us with (even though I consider some of his statements *too* friendly to metaphysics to be acceptable by a pragmatist) is a *pragmatic argument for traditional philosophy*. Since the traditional ends of metaphysics are not unattainable or incoherent, they are, in his view, also worth striving for: belief in "objective Truth and Goodness", on which these ends are based, and the striving for them "vivify human efforts and give meaning to life" (*ibid.*).

William James, even though he was not a lover of traditional metaphysics, could well have written these words. Pragmatically, metaphysics, which "inquires into the cause, the substance, the meaning and the outcome of all things" (James 1911, p. 22), is indispensable because of its human relevance. It can make human life significant, and such significance is a good reason for philosophizing. We can appeal to the pragmatic goal (i.e., "end") of philosophy in arguing that it has not come and probably never will come to an end (as long as there are intelligent beings in the universe). At least *we* cannot end it: we will have to go on reflecting on the deepest questions people have asked and will continue to ask about our place in the universe. For us, it still seems impossible to find the human condition unexciting and uninteresting.

Thus, if my reading of James is even close to a correct one, he was not a Rortyan pragmatist. For him, as for Kane, philosophical problems, even metaphysical ones, were real and meaningful; he was tolerant with respect to metaphysical questions and wanted to find out the genuine, pragmatic meaning of them (cf. e.g. Meyers 1971). He also wanted to present a philosophically relevant theory of truth. An "end of philosophy" would not have been a positive achievement for him; philosophy as mere Rortyan "edification" or "conversation" would not have been philosophy at all for him, either (cf. Seigfried 1990, pp. 294, 417). I wonder whether those who read James as a "post-Philosopher" are familiar enough with his posthumous 'Philosophy and Its Critics' (1911, ch. 1), a beautiful piece defending philosophy against its enemies (e.g., Comtean scientistic positivism).

Any purely "first order" philosophical (metaphysical) problem, say, the problem of realism, can of course be put aside, at least for a while.[29] To introduce some more technical terminology, this is equivalent to saying that the problem of realism need not, at a certain moment, be a part of one's philosophizing in the sense of the Kantian *Schulbegriff* of philosophy. Yet, for a philosopher in the sense of the *Weltbegriff* of philosophy, there seems to be no way of dispensing with the genuineness of the issue.[30] *Pace* Rorty, we must reaffirm the human (pragmatic) value of philosophical wonder. Philosophizing is a *natural* element of a distinctively human form of life. Thus, we get a naturalistically acceptable but definitely non-reductive defense of philosophy and metaphysics.

Rorty's particular version of naturalism – his "non-reductive physicalism" – is unacceptable, because, as noticed above, in the end Rorty accepts no relations between a physical human organism and its environment except strictly causal ones. Unless there are irreducible semantic and referential relations involved in our normative practices of coping with the world – unless human beings can (naturally) think about the world, refer to it, and discuss its features with each other, as well as (in Putnam's terms) sometimes get something right and something wrong – there just is no human form of life as we know it. But the rejection of Rorty's view does not necessarily lead to the rejection of naturalism. The fact that *we are* humans and lead a human form of life is itself, in a broad sense, a natural (though normative) fact of our existence, based on empirical biological, psychological, and social conditions. Why do philosophers feel the need to reduce this fact to something else? Reduction does not remove the mystery of human natural life, but only hides it.

The recognition of our human situation as essentially tied to normativity requires neither any strong metaphysical theory of normative issues nor any metaphysical theory of humanity purporting to give us the timeless essence of man. It is most important to formulate *our anti-reductionist* naturalism as an *anti-foundationalist* and *anti-essentialist* naturalism, too. Our language-games and forms of life "naturally" change. This was also Wittgenstein's (1953, 1969) view: the language-games that we play are not fixed once and for all, but they are in a constant dynamical process of change, entangled with the change of our life. There are no metaphysical or epistemological guarantees, on a sane naturalist and pragmatist account of man-in-the-world. Nonetheless, we have no choice but to be in contact with the world, act in the world, go on living normative human life as parts of the world.

I have already expressed my conviction that there is no simple way in which the pragmatist could follow Rorty in abandoning traditional philosophy. Now I wish to make this same point more specifically with regard to James's attitude to the metaphysical project of understanding the nature of humanity. We have to take a brief look at James's philosophy of religion, because it is in this context that his views on man are best developed.

Despite his supernaturalism, James argues for his "melioristic" religion by relying on a premise which could be taken to be a naturalistic one – again, naturalistic very broadly speaking, in a non-reductive sense. In the last chapter of *Pragmatism*, for example, he remarks that "it would contradict *the very spirit of life* to say that our minds must be indifferent and neutral in questions like that of the world's salvation" (James 1907, p. 137; my emphasis).[31] For James, a certain conception of human nature is, thus, the ultimate premise. If the creator of the world offered us a universe which is "not certain to be saved", a world whose perfection is "conditional" and whose safety is "unwarranted", i.e., a world whose characters would be involved in "a real adventure, with real danger", aiming at a salvation of the world through co-operative efforts, James (*ibid.*, pp. 139-140) contends that a human being who is "normally constituted" and loyal to "our old nurse Nature" could not refuse to accept the offer (even though it would not be an offer safe enough for optimistic absolute idealists who crave for absolute security). Again, the remark that our "need of an eternal moral order is one of the deepest needs of our breast" (*ibid.*, p. 55) can be considered a naturalistic one, relying on a non-reductive and pragmatic view of human nature. According to James, to people who are not interested in such long-term metaphysical issues as the ultimate fate of the world, one can only say, "you do injustice to *human nature*" (*ibid.*; my emphasis). The fact (which is, according to James, a fact of human existence) that some deep metaphysical and religious issues make a difference to our lives – in the sense that there is a pragmatically meaningful question about their truth or falsity – cannot be escaped. This is, moreover, a normative fact of our nature. James seems to think that we not only do, but also ought to, engage in metaphysical reflection on ultimate issues.

We can surely question James's specific "theory" of the human nature, for example by arguing (quite plausibly, perhaps) that men are much more passive and effortless creatures than James thought. James may be in the grip of his actively melioristic picture of man and the world. Still, it should be clear that some "theory" of man is needed in support of his religious position. In fact, *The Varieties of Religious Experience* (1902) was subtitled 'A Study in Human Nature'.[32]

Without accepting James's religious views, one can say that he bases his argumentation (in this case with regard to religion, but in other contexts, too) on an account of what it is to be a human being. The Kantian question, "What is man?", is thus in the heart of his pragmatism – and, in my view, of pragmatism in general. It is man with reference to whom reality is structured, even though we can, from our human standpoints, think and say that the world would exist even if we ourselves did not exist. The conceptual schemes and practical points of view through which alone things can be meaningfully said to exist (or fail to exist) are nevertheless man-made. To avoid excessive anthropomorphism, we can, and should, observe (from our human points of view) that we are not literally at the center of the universe. Still, the nature of humanity is, inevitably, the ultimate issue in philosophy – for us. Even the questions "What (if anything) is God?", "What is the world?", and "Why is there something rather than nothing?" are secondary. We might say that, in James's case, a conception of human nature functions as a (non-reductively) naturalistic premise of his substantial religious views (which are admittedly supernaturalistic).

Furthermore, the problem of the nature of man is pragmatically vital for us precisely because of our contingent, historically evolving human condition. What the contemporary ecological crisis, for example, means for us is dependent on what kind of beings we think we ourselves, as men, are. Facing the threat of a global destruction of human and non-human nature, we need to know (or at least seriously ask) whether we are, in a reductionist sense, "merely" natural beings, material parts of nature, or whether some of our abilities are "higher" than nature (and if so, in what sense). We also have to try to determine what one should mean by "nature" in posing these questions.

I cannot engage in any detailed examination of the problem of man here. My view *is* naturalistic, but it differs from Rorty's naturalism. The moderate, non-reductive naturalism that the pragmatist should (in my view) favor accommodates the irreducibly normative character of human culture and form of life, even though it regards man, including all his cultural capacities, as a product of nature. It should also accommodate such pragmatic characteristics of man as his capacity to act purposively, possibly his Jamesian courage, etc. More metaphilosophically, the pragmatic-normative conception of man needed should account for man's metaphysical need – the fact of human nature that man cannot avoid inquiring into the ultimate, deepest questions of what the world is like and what he himself is like. It should, thus, also account for itself. This circularity is not vicious but virtuous (and inevitable). Moreover, I am not supposing that philosophical anthropology should be elevated to the status of "first philosophy" in any Aristotelean, Cartesian, or Kantian sense. The moderate pragmatist who finds the problem of man inescapable can agree with Rorty (1991, p. 193) on the fact that "there is no 'objective truth' about what the human self is *really* like". She can, and should, give up metaphysical realism, also with respect to human nature. My pragmatist account of the ineliminability of philosophical anthropology is, then, entirely compatible with the view that there is no autonomous "first philosophy" (as Quine, Rorty, *et al.* have urged for a long time). Philosophy is, in our days, inextricably intertwined with sciences, arts, politics, and social life. But to say that there are close links between such areas of culture is not to say that there is no philosophy any longer or that all our old problems have been dissolved.

According to James, the human worth of a philosophy is the decisive criterion of its viability. In his little book on pragmatism, John P. Murphy describes this idea as follows:

> ...it is a basic principle of James's philosophy ... that the conditions of acceptability of a philosophy are just as important (perhaps even more important) as its truth conditions. James's point is that, in the last analysis, it is always our nature – human nature – not the nature of reality in general, which must decide what we are to think about the nature of reality in general. So, philosophies that do not satisfy these human demands ... will not be accepted; and, hence, the question of their truth or falsity will be beside the point. (Murphy 1990, p. 35.)

It is one of James's most fundamental metaphilosophical convictions that individual satisfaction and temperament are relevant in philosophy. They are relevant even in metaphysics, and especially in metaphysics. The human temperament involved cannot be irrelevant to the way the person in question thinks the world is. (See James 1907, ch. 1.) James thought (particularly in his writings on the problem of religious faith) that the world can be a "rational" world for man only if it fulfills (some of) our ultimate human needs. Otherwise, the world would be an alien place for us, impossible to live in. Only philosophies rendering the world in some sense "familiar", "in harmony" with our deepest needs and hopes, could be humanly accepted. This requirement is determined by human nature: our nature as men ultimately determines what kind of philosophical accounts of the world and ourselves as parts of it can be seriously defended. This determination is one element of the inevitable normativity of man's being in the world.

This Jamesian position may seem to be too close to "wishful thinking". It must not be dismissed too easily, however. Generally speaking, what is philosophically important in pragmatism, in my view, is that it satisfies (or at least may satisfy) a great number of our natural, vital "human demands".[33] In a sense, it succeeds in doing this on a metaphilosophical level. This is, then, a pragmatic defense of pragmatism. In the end, I cannot think of any other consistent way of "defending" pragmatism.

I have illuminated the pragmatist's un-Rortyan need for metaphysics by commenting upon two deep metaphysical issues. One might say that these two, i.e., the issue of realism (which plays a major role both in Rorty's critique of traditional philosophy and in my counter-arguments) and the issue of human nature (which is, of course, intimately related to Rorty's relaxed, physicalistic conception of man), are tied to each other by the Kantian idea of *transcendental philosophy*. Having argued that the pragmatist must tolerate metaphysics in general and metaphysical reflection on the nature of man in particular, I now claim that a commitment to transcendental philosophy is also pragmatically required. It is also one of our "human demands". The pragmatist cannot (again, contrary to what Rorty and others have claimed) just give up the transcendental project. In Kant's first *Critique*, transcendental philosophy meant, roughly, the reflection on the necessary conditions of the possibility of cognitive experience of an objective world. It was, essentially, philosophical reflection on the "epistemic conditions" of human experiential representation of objects or objective reality.[34] Later, pragmatists and many others have given up the Kantian project of finding and legitimizing some static, ahistorical, immutable, and *a priori* given conditions of human experience. Here, I of course sympathize with the attacks on *such* "transcendental principles". But the transcendental project itself is as inevitable as ever. The problem of accounting for the possibility of human experience of the world cannot just be dropped along with a particular aprioristic version of it.[35] Rorty has not shown us that we could get rid of Kant.

The pragmatist who follows Quine, Goodman, Rorty, Putnam, and other key figures of the neopragmatist turn by abandoning such sharp Kantian distinctions as analytic vs. synthetic and *a priori* vs. *a posteriori*, can still engage in transcendental reflection. This reflection aims at a philosophical conception of the "epistemic conditions" of there being an objective world for us (with no assumption of any sharp contrast between "epistemic" and "pragmatic"). These conditions must be understood in an historically relativized, dynamical way. There is no return to Kantian apriorism, but the pragmatist is still, in a sense, continuing the Kantian project. The idea of epistemic-pragmatic conditions, on which the possibility of representing objects of the real world is based, is part of the central Kantian question of man. In reflecting (transcendentally) on the issue of realism, for instance, one is, by trying to characterize the epistemic conditions of human experience, *ipso facto* reflecting on the most inclusive question of philosophy: what is man? The same question is also invoked in the Kantian reflection on the proper use of human reason – in particular, in the Transcendental Dialectic, where the task is to show how reason inevitably arrives at metaphysical illusions and how they can be avoided.

The anthropocentric orientation of pragmatism should make us suspicious of the idea that philosophical problems could ever be illuminatingly discussed – let alone "resolved" or "dissolved" – in total abstraction from a philosophical reflection on what it is for us, as members of the human species, to reflect on them in the first place. But this is, again, very different from saying that the problems are not real or genuine problems. We have seen that the problem of human nature, the key issue of philosophical anthropology, looms behind all important philosophical topics.[36] We might even say that such special branches of philosophy as philosophy of science, of art, of religion, social philosophy, and so forth, are subordinated to philosophical anthropology. Philosophers working in these areas are not just concerned with what science or art or religion or society is; they are above all concerned with how we, as human beings, should think about these aspects of our life.

Presumably, there might be beings who would not feel the need to engage in this kind of philosophizing. In particular, there might be beings with no ontology, beings who, in a Rorty-like fashion, would not regard their actions or linguistic expressions as committing themselves to any views about anything. In short, there might be a form of life without any notion of existence (and, *a fortiori*, without any notion of human existence).[37] My claim is that we, as men, would not easily understand such a form of life – even though we might, as some of us seem to do, pretend we could. Our practice includes ontological or metaphysical practice. However, we might have to *try* to learn about such a form of life. Rorty perhaps would like us to do so. But, as he has stressed himself, *we have to start from where we are*. There is no other place to start from. *We* cannot just drop philosophical reflection on the problem of human existence.

5. Conclusion

I am not in the grip of the illusion that I should have produced a thoroughly convincing argument for the relevance of such philosophical problems as the issue of realism and the problem of human nature against Rortyan "pragmatists" and "post-Philosophers". Rorty has, in the end, stepped beyond rational argumentation. If the critic emphasizes, say, the importance of the problem of human nature, the Rortyan can always respond that she is in the grip of the old metaphysical and epistemological tradition which she should give up. This kind of claim is beyond argumentation in precisely the same sense as the creationist's absurd claim that God created the universe in such a way that all evidence we find about its history make us mistakenly believe that it already existed billions of years ago, even though "in reality" it was created only some thousands of years ago (with some rather misleading documents to "test" our faith, perhaps). But such claims do not need any serious refutation.

However, I do hope that I have been convincing enough in my claim that some argument of the sort developed in this paper must be confronted by Rortyan thinkers in order for them to keep rational discussion going. Otherwise, no edifying conversation can take place.

My negative conclusion is, then, that Rorty's "pragmatism" (along with such views as anti-representationalism and non-reductive physicalism closely related to it) should be rejected. I have given plenty of reasons for this, and I have only very briefly touched the issues of truth and reference. There is, however, also a positive conclusion: metaphysics is (*pace* Rorty) necessary for the pragmatist, too. In particular, the pragmatist, picturing man (naturalistically but non-reductively) as an active being trying to solve various problems she faces in the environment in which she lives, makes a commitment to a philosophical picture of man. She cannot avoid engaging in philosophical anthropology. Even Rorty, I suspect, cannot consistently avoid *some* kind of normative conception of man.[38] The deep irony of his position lies in the fact that he attempts to confine our philosophical (not "Philosophical") interests to our contingently human sphere but ultimately finds this contingent humanity philosophically (as well as Philosophically) trivial and uninteresting. We should be interested in our human condition!

This is not to suggest that any traditional, essentialistic theory of humanity should be accepted. There is no Platonic "Form of Man"; nor should we hope that man's essence could be easily captured by such Aristotelean definitions as "rational animal" or "political animal". Our conception of humanity must be much more flexible, informed both by all available empirical knowledge of man and by the critique of Western metaphysics of man that we have now witnessed for some time. I hope it has become clear that even an anti-essentialist pragmatist (such as James) is able to reflect on the problem of human nature and can even base her other philosophical views on a certain conception of human nature.[39]

I have no definition of man to offer. My goals have been much more modest, albeit somewhat more general. Rortyan pragmatism is one of the key obstacles that contemporary philosophers interested in such traditional areas of philosophy as philosophical anthropology (or metaphysics in general) must face. By showing that Rorty, too, must base his views on certain philosophical statements and that some of these statements are problematic in many ways, I have tried to show that metaphysical study of human nature is a legitimate and respectable part of philosophy. It is, at least for the pragmatist, perhaps even the most important part. I think that this is something that the classical pragmatists – James in particular – never denied. Still, Rorty's work is worth pursuing. It has stimulated some important defenses of traditional philosophy, and the debate seems to be getting even busier. As pragmatists have always urged, the value of anything lies in its fruits.

Biography

Sami Pihlström, Ph.D., was born in Helsinki, Finland, in 1969. He defended his doctoral dissertation *Structuring the World: The Issue of Realism and the Nature of Ontological Problems in Classical and Contemporary Pragmatism (Acta Philosophica Fennica,* vol. 59). The Philosophical Society of Finland, Helsinki, 1996) at the University of Helsinki in May, 1996. At the present, he continues his work on the tradition of pragmatism in Helsinki.

Notes

1. I have dealt with the topic of this paper in some Finnish publications of mine, especially in 'Richard Rortyn "postfilosofia" ja realismin ongelma' ('Richard Rorty's "Post-Philosophy" and the Issue of Realism', *Tiede & Edistys* 3/1993). I also discuss these issues at length in my Ph.D. dissertation (Pihlstrøm 1996). Some passages of that work are incorporated, with changes, to this paper. I am grateful to many persons for important critical suggestions – in particular, to Vittorio Hösle, Ingvar Johansson, Simo Knuuttila, Jonas Nilsson, and Pär Sundström for the discussions we had during the Odense symposium. I also wish to thank Ilkka Niiniluoto and Heikki Kannisto for many helpful conversations. Finally, I wish to express my gratitude to the Chancellor of the University of Helsinki for financial support for my participation in the symposium. (Terminological note: the word 'man' in phrases like "the nature of man" and "the problem of man" is, of course, by no means intended as sexistic.)
2. See his seminal paper on NOA (1984) and many subsequent papers.

3. This attitude is based on his eliminatively naturalistic picture of man. See Stich (1990).
4. See e.g. Horwich (1990). Cf. also Quine (1990) and Kirkham (1992, ch. 10).
5. This term is adopted from Shakespeare's play *Measure for Measure*. See Rorty (1980, pp. 42-43).
6. See Rorty (1991, pp. 124-125) and the essay 'Unfamiliar Noises: Hesse and Davidson on Metaphor' in the same volume.
7. Davidson himself has expressed his key anti-representationalist point as follows (see also his 1989, pp. 165-166): "Nothing, ... no *thing*, makes sentences and theories true: not experience, not surface irritations, not the world, can make a sentence true. *That* experience takes a certain course, that our skin is warmed or punctured, that the universe is finite, these facts, if we like to talk that way, make sentences and theories true. But this point is put better without mention of facts. The sentence 'My skin is warm' is true if and only if my skin is warm. Here there is no reference to a fact, a world, an experience, or a piece of evidence." (Davidson 1984, p. 194.)
8. For Hilary Putnam's well-known critique of metaphysical realism and defense of internal realism, see his (1981), (1983), (1987), and (1990). Despite many similarities, Putnam's and Rorty's versions of neopragmatism are, in important ways, in sharp opposition, as we shall see.
9. This attitude might also be described as "deconstructive". Cf. Derrida's (1987) treatment of the pervasiveness of "metaphysical humanism" in Western thought.
10. The question of whether philosophy should come to an "end" or whether it should be "transformed" is discussed from various metaphilosophical standpoints in Bayes *et al.* (1987).
11. Cf. Wittgenstein (1953, § 133) and related remarks in the *Philosophical Investigations*.
12. For Rorty's most recent statements about the future of philosophy (and about the relevance of its past), see his (1995a, b). Both papers can be found in Saatkamp (1995), which also contains many critical comments on Rorty's work as well as his responses.
13. One radical post-Philosophical and even post-Derridean suggestion in this direction is Mark C. Taylor's and Esa Saarinen's (1994) "media philosophy", which is supposed to take us beyond literary academic culture, directly to the electric media age. Needless to say, I hope my arguments against Rorty apply to this radically pragmatist, postmodern idea also.
14. For Putnam's controversial criticisms of causal theories of reference, see his (1983), (1990), (1992), and (1994).
15. See the essay 'Why Reason Can't Be Naturalized' in Putnam (1983, pp. 229-247), esp. p. 246. The same essay is reprinted in Baynes *et al.* (1987), and its general theme constantly reappears in Putnam's recent work (1992, 1994). For a related criticism of Rorty's extreme naturalism, see Hance (1995).
16. It is an entirely different question whether it could be the case that nothing at all existed.
17. See especially his 'Solidarity or Objectivity?' in Rorty (1991, pp. 21-34).
18. Rorty has made some quite puzzling comments on Peirce, both positive and negative (see Haack 1993, pp. 418-424). Typically, however, he claims that Peirce has been "overpraised" at the cost of James and Dewey, who were much more original thinkers; Peirce's "contribution to pragmatism was merely to have given it a name, and to have stimulated James", in Rorty's view (1982, pp. 160-161).
19. See also Stuhr's (1992) and Rosenberg's (1993) related arguments. Stuhr (as well as

many other scholars) pays attention to Rorty's misreading and misuse of Dewey. Haack's most sustained critique of Rorty (and Stich as well) is put forward in her (1995). But see also Rorty's replies in Saatkamp's volume.

20. Niiniluoto (1984) has also remarked against Rorty that "edifying philosophy" needs results from "systematic philosophy": Rorty himself relies on Quine's, Sellars's, and Davidson's systematic arguments. Rorty could respond by claiming that the time has come to drop the "ladder" of systematic philosophy. But why should *we*, say, "we philosophers" or "we 20th century intellectuals", simply drop this ladder? Rorty has not argued convincingly enough that we have finally reached the top of the ladder of systematic philosophy. And if he did produce such arguments, he would be doing Philosophy.

21. Here Putnam has (as he admits himself) been influenced by McDowell's (1994) criticisms of Quine, Davidson, and Rorty. Furthermore, Conant is right, in my view, in saying that the fundamental difference between Rorty and Putnam lies in the fact that Rorty thinks it is possible to "without further ado just ... cut oneself free from certain philosophical controversies", while Putnam rejects this view and urges that we can gain something "by carefully examining the structure of such controversies". In this respect, there is a remarkable parallel between Rorty and Carnap. (Conant 1994, p. lxviii; cf. also Putnam 1990, p. 20.)

22. It is, of course, impossible to discuss Putnam's views in detail here.

23. See also Holówka (1990) and Devitt (1991, ch. 11); cf. Rorty (1980, pp. 276, 345). Farrell (1995) argues, however, that there are serious problems involved in the attempt to read Rorty as a realist.

24. Machan (1993) also points out that in discussing "Rorty's position" we are indeed discussing a "determinate reality", i.e., "the determinate reality of Rorty's own writings". This seems to take Rorty again into a self-reflective paradox. The reality of Rorty's position is one which we are thinking and talking about, and it is distinct from this thinking and talking (pp. 124-125). On a Rortyan account, we could not even debate on whether Rorty is right or wrong. Moreover, Moser (1994) shows that, while Rorty's pragmatism is supposed to go "beyond" realism and idealism (or ontological anti-realism), it nevertheless needs both of these presuppositions, which are, fatally, in opposition to each other.

25. My argument does not depend on any specific account of "the ontology of philosophical problems". They could be thought to be reducible to human mental states or even to the physical world.

26. See also Kim (1980, pp. 596-597), Gallagher (1984, p. 115), and Tolland (1991, pp. 148-149).

27. I might here briefly refer to a few additional critical replies to Rorty's metaphilosophy. Manning (1992) asks why a traditional "Philosopher" could not be a pragmatist. In his view, Rorty, in criticizing the correspondence theory of truth, self-refutingly and paradoxically "gives us Philosophical reasons to show us that we should not make philosophical arguments!" (p. 357). Nelson (1995) similarly argues that Rorty incoherently tries to persuade us to accept his own philosophical truth (about traditional philosophy, inquiry, etc.). Migotti (1995) draws attention to this same Rortyan dilemma: has Rorty given us argumentative reasons for rejecting traditional philosophy (thereby betraying his own post-Philosophical project), or is he just saying that he does not want to go on with metaphysics and epistemology? For broader, book-length discussions of Rorty (which also deal with the self-reflective challenge to his

metaphilosophical views), see Prado (1987), Nielsen (1991), Hall (1994), and Vaden House (1994). It is impossible to discuss these interpretations further here.

28. Some philosophers have argued that Wittgenstein made even a more radical case against traditional philosophy than Rorty, that is, suggested that we should abandon both "philosophy" and "Philosophy" in Rorty's sense (see Williams 1986, pp. 21-22; Nielsen 1991, pp. 92-93). On Putnam's alternative interpretation of Wittgenstein, there is no evidence for this, however (see Conant 1990). What Rorty and his followers do, it seems to me, is to banalize Wittgenstein's respect for the hopelessness of solving philosophical problems. For Putnam's most sustained discussion of Wittgenstein, see his (1995).

29. James (1911, ch. 3) himself pays particular attention to "the problem of being", the "darkest" question in all philosophy, which is the ancient problem of why or whence there is something rather than nothing. James's view of our abilities to find an answer here is pessimistic. So, the recognition of the value of metaphysics need not lead us to adopt a too optimistic prediction of the "solvability" of metaphysical problems.

30. In the last pages of the first *Critique*, Kant (1781/1787, A 838-840 = B 866-868) distinguishes between the *Schulbegriff*, which sees philosophy as a kind of scientific (or scholastic) enterprise aiming at solutions of systematic and well-defined problems (in short, something like what is today called analytic philosophy), and the *Weltbegriff*, a notion of philosophy as an intellectual activity serving original human purposes by, for example, reflecting on what can be called the "eternal questions" of mankind. The Jamesian "problem of being" (see previous note) would also belong to the *Weltbegriff* of philosophy. Conant (1990) argues, alluding to Kant, that the *Schulbegriff* without the *Weltbegriff* is blind, whereas the *Weltbegriff* without the *Schulbegriff* is empty.

31. Similar remarks occur in essays collected in *The Will to Believe* (1897), and elsewhere. In a footnote to *The Meaning of Truth* (1909, p. 103), in which he takes back his previous view that, if there were no future, the dispute between theism and materialism would be pragmatically empty, James writes: "... *framed as we are,* our egoism craves above all things inward sympathy and recognition, love and admiration" (my emphasis). He goes on to say that, because of this fact of our constitution, the godless universe of materialism would not "work" for us any more than an "automatic sweetheart" (a soulless maiden indistinguishable from a real one) would.

32. Dooley (1974) provides an account of James's philosophy as essentially a doctrine of *humanism*. Man is conceived of by James as the centre of all things; his theory of man unites, according to Dooley, all other aspects of his philosophy. See also Seigfried's (1990) reading of James, according to which James's basic concern is an examination of the human condition, i.e., a "concrete analysis of being human", which includes a critique of (intellectualistic) rationality, an emphasis on temporality (and thus on the notion of the future), a teleological conception of the nature of human experience, and an emphasis on the role of feeling in cognition (p. 45). According to Seigfried, this analysis is "found throughout his writings but not systematically developed in any one place" (p. 48). It is compatible with the Jamesian picture of man to think that man in a sense makes up his own nature; i.e., there is no ready-made human nature in advance of its concrete realizations (cf. Rorty 1991, p. 213). If *this* is all that Rorty wants to say, then the Jamesian pragmatist can follow him. But we still have an issue of (man-made) human nature in this case.

33. Cf. Seigfried's (1990, p. 323) remark on James: "The only reason for investigating activity and causality is to help us understand the course and meaning of life. The pragmatic stance is that we seek to know, not for its own sake, but to enable us to live

better." Seigfried observes that "James struggled to harmonize all our deepest human needs" (p. 254).
34. The term "epistemic conditions" is taken from Allison's (1983) influential defense of Kant's transcendental idealism.
35. Arguably, James also misrepresented Kant and Kantian philosophy in this respect. He was more of a Kantian than he himself recognized (cf. e.g. Bird 1986, pp. 5-6). At least he struggled with essentially Kantian problems. Cf. here also Pihlstrøm (1997).
36. From this point of view, Charles Taylor's project of a "clarification of the conditions of intentionality" – a species of philosophical anthropology – is highly relevant. See e.g. his (1987).
37. Cf. Quine's (1990, p. 28) observation that our notion of "ontological commitment" is, in a sense, "parochial".
38. What I have in mind is, in particular, the thesis that "our glory is in our participation in fallible and transitory human projects" (Rorty 1982, p. 166). The passage in which this phrase occurs was quoted more fully in section 2 above. Rorty (1991, p. 39) also says that "pragmatists would like to drop the idea that human beings are responsible to a nonhuman power" (in science, for instance). Isn't this a picture of humanity? Moreover, is Rorty giving us the essence of man by saying that "human beings are centerless networks of beliefs and desires" (*ibid.*, p. 191)? See also Levisohn's (1993) perceptive suggestion that, in defending "solidarity" over "objectivity", Rorty relies on his own ethical intuition and on a view of "what is and what is not fundamental to human nature" (p. 58).
39. James (1897) sometimes refers to his philosophy of religion as remarks on the "natural history" of the human mind. Similarly, Wittgenstein (1969) thought that he was discussing the natural history of human forms of life.

Bibliography

Allison, Henry E. (1983) *Kant's Transcendental Idealism: An Interpretation and Defense*, Yale University Press, New Haven & London.
Baynes, Kenneth, Bohman, James & McCarthy, Thomas (1987) (eds.) *After Philosophy: End or Transformation?*, The MIT Press, Cambridge, Mass. & London.
Bird, Graham (1986) *William James*, Routledge & Kegan Paul, London.
Conant, James (1990) 'Introduction', in Putnam (1990), pp. XV-LXXIV.
Conant, James (1994) 'Introduction', in Putnam (1994), pp. XI-LXXVI.
Davidson, Donald (1984) *Inquiries into Truth and Interpretation*, Clarendon Press, Oxford.
Davidson, Donald (1989) 'The Myth of the Subjective', in M. Krausz (ed.), *Relativism: Interpretation and Confrontation*, University of Notre Dame Press, Notre Dame, pp. 159-172.
Derrida, Jacques (1987) 'The Ends of Man', in Baynes *et al.* (1987), pp. 125-158.
Devitt, Michael (1991) *Realism and Truth*, 2nd ed., Basil Blackwell, Oxford & Cambridge (1st ed. 1984).
Dooley, Patrick Kiaran (1974) *Pragmatism as Humanism: The Philosophy of William James*, Nelson-Hall, Chicago.
Farrell, Frank B. (1995) 'Rorty & Antirealism', in Saatkamp (1995), pp. 154-188.
Fine, Arthur (1984) 'The Natural Ontological Attitude', in J. Leplin (ed.), *Scientific Realism*, University of California Press, Berkeley & Los Angeles, pp. 83-107.

Gallagher, Kenneth T. (1984) 'Rorty on Objectivity, Truth, and Social Consensus', *International Philosophical Quarterly* 24, 111-124.

Haack, Susan (1993) 'Philosophy/philosophy, an Untenable Dualism', *Transactions of the Charles S. Peirce Society* 29, 411-426.

Haack, Susan (1995) 'Vulgar Pragmatism: An Unedifying Prospect', in Saatkamp (1995), pp. 126-147.

Hall, David L. (1994) *Richard Rorty: Prophet and Poet of the New Pragmatism*, State University of New York Press, Albany.

Hance, Allen (1995) 'Pragmatism as Naturalized Hegelianism: Overcoming Transcendental Philosophy?', in Saatkamp (1995), pp. 100-121.

Holówka, Jacek (1990) 'Philosophy and the Mirage of Hermeneutics', in A. Malachowski (ed.), *Reading Rorty: Critical Responses to Philosophy and the Mirror of Nature (and Beyond)*, Basil Blackwell, Oxford.

Horwich, Paul (1990) *Truth*, Basil Blackwell, Oxford.

James, William (1897) *The Will to Believe and Other Essays in Popular Philosophy*, Harvard University Press, Cambridge, Mass. & London, 1979.

James, William (1902) *The Varieties of Religious Experience: A Study in Human Nature*, New American Library, New York, 1958.

James, William (1907) *Pragmatism: A New Name for Some Old Ways of Thinking*, Harvard University Press, Cambridge, Mass. & London, 1975.

James, William (1909) *The Meaning of Truth: A Sequel to* Pragmatism, Harvard University Press, Cambridge, Mass. & London, 1978.

James, William (1911) *Some Problems in Philosophy*, Harvard University Press, Cambridge, Mass. & London, 1979.

Kane, Robert (1993) 'The Ends of Metaphysics', *International Philosophical Quarterly* 33, 413-428.

Kant, Immanuel (1781/1787) *Kritik der reinen Vernunft*, ed. by Raymund Schmidt, Verlag von Felix Meiner, Leipzig, 1990.

Kim, Jaegwon (1980) 'Rorty on the Possibility of Philosophy', *The Journal of Philosophy* 77, 588-597.

Kirkham, Richard L. (1992) *Theories of Truth: A Critical Introduction*, The MIT Press, Cambridge, Mass. & London, 1995.

Levisohn, Jon A. (1993) 'On Richard Rorty's Ethical Anti-Foundationalism', *The Harvard Review of Philosophy* 3 (1), 48-58.

Machan, Tibor R. (1993) 'Some Reflections on Richard Rorty's Philosophy', *Metaphilosophy* 24, 123-135.

Manning, Richard N. (1992) 'Pragmatism and the Quest for Truth', *Metaphilosophy* 23, 350-362.

Margolis, Joseph (1986) *Pragmatism without Foundations: Reconciling Realism and Relativism*, Blackwell, Oxford.

McDowell, John (1994) *Mind and World*, Harvard University Press, Cambridge, Mass. & London.

Meyers, Robert G. (1971) 'Meaning and Metaphysics in James', in D. Olin (ed.), *William James: Pragmatism, in focus*, Routledge, London & New York, 1992, pp. 143-155.

Migotti, Mark (1995) 'Peirce's First Rule of Reason and the Bad Faith of Rortian Post-Philosophy', *Transactions of the Charles S. Peirce Society* 31, 89-136.

Moser, Paul K. (1994) 'Beyond Realism and Idealism', *Philosophia* 23, 271-288.

Murphy, John P. (1990) *Pragmatism From Peirce to Davidson*, Westview Press, Boulder.

Nelson, John O. (1995) 'Pragmatism According to Rorty: A Disaster Area', *Journal of Philosophical Research* 20, 349-366.
Nielsen, Kai (1991) *After the Demise of the Tradition: Rorty, Critical Theory, and the Fate of Philosophy*, Westview Press, Boulder.
Niiniluoto, Ilkka (1984) *Is Science Progressive?*, D. Reidel, Dordrecht.
Pihlstrøm, Sami (1996) *Structuring the World: The Issue of Realism and the Nature of Ontological Problems in Classical and Contemporary Pragmatism,* Acta Philosophica Fennica 59, The Philosophical Society of Finland, Helsinki.
Pihlstrøm, Sami (1997) 'The prospects of Transcendental Pragmatism: Reconciling Kant and James', *Philosophy Today* 41:3 (forthcoming).
Prado, C. G. (1987) *The Limits of Pragmatism*, Humanities Press International, Atlantic Highlands.
Putnam, Hilary (1981) *Reason, Truth and History*, Cambridge University Press, Cambridge.
Putnam, Hilary (1983) *Realism and Reason*, Cambridge University Press, Cambridge.
Putnam, Hilary (1987) *The Many Faces of Realism*, Open Court, La Salle, Ill.
Putnam, Hilary (1990) *Realism with a Human Face*, ed. by James Conant, Harvard University Press, Cambridge, Mass.
Putnam, Hilary (1992) *Renewing Philosophy*, Harvard University Press, Cambridge, Mass.
Putnam, Hilary (1994) *Words and Life*, ed. by James Conant, Harvard University Press, Cambridge, Mass.
Putnam, Hilary (1995) *Pragmatism: An Open Question*, Blackwell, Oxford.
Quine, W. V. (1990) *Pursuit of Truth*, Harvard University Press, Cambridge, Mass. & London, 2nd ed., 1992.
Rorty, Richard (1980) *Philosophy and the Mirror of Nature*, Basil Blackwell, Oxford, 1989.
Rorty, Richard (1982) *Consequences of Pragmatism*, The Harvester Press, Brighton.
Rorty, Richard (1989) *Contingency, Irony, and Solidarity*, Cambridge University Press, Cambridge.
Rorty, Richard (1991) *Objectivity, Relativism, and Truth*, Cambridge University Press, Cambridge.
Rorty, Richard (1992) 'Putnam on Truth', *Philosophy and Phenomenological Research* 52, 415-418.
Rorty, Richard (1993) 'Putnam and the Relativist Menace', *The Journal of Philosophy* 90, 443-461.
Rorty, Richard (1995a) 'Dewey between Hegel and Darwin', in Saatkamp (1995), pp. 1-15.
Rorty, Richard (1995b) 'Philosophy and the Future', in Saatkamp (1995), pp. 197-205.
Rosenberg, Jay F. (1993) 'Raiders of the Last Distinction: Richard Rorty and the Search for the Last Dichotomy', *Philosophy and Phenomenological Research* 53, 195-214.
Saatkamp, Henry J., Jr. (1995) (ed.) *Rorty & Pragmatism: The Philosopher Responds to His Critics*, Vanderbilt University Press, Nashville & London.
Seigfried, Charlene Haddock (1990) *William James's Radical Reconstruction of Philosophy*, State University of New York Press, Albany.
Stich, Stephen (1990) *The Fragmentation of Reason: Preface to a Pragmatic Theory of Cognitive Evaluation*, The MIT Press, Cambridge, Mass. & London.
Stuhr, John J. (1992) 'Dewey's Reconstruction of Metaphysics', *Transactions of the Charles S. Peirce Society* 28, 161-176.
Taylor, Charles (1987) 'Overcoming Epistemology', in Baynes *et al.* (1987), pp. 464 - 488.
Taylor, Mark C. & Saarinen, Esa (1994) *Imagologies: Media Philosophy*, Routledge, London & New York.

Tolland, Anders (1991) *Epistemological Relativism and Relativistic Epistemology: Richard Rorty and the Possibility of a Philosophical Theory of Knowledge*, Acta Universitatis Gothoburgensis, Göteborg.

Vaden House, D. (1994) *Without God or His Doubles: Realism, Relativism and Rorty*, E. J. Brill, Leiden.

Williams, Michael (1986) 'The Elimination of Metaphysics', in G. Macdonald & C. Wright (eds.), *Fact, Science and Morality: Essays on A. J. Ayer's* Language, Truth and Logic, Basil Blackwell, Oxford, pp. 9-25.

Wittgenstein, Ludwig (1953) *Philosophical Investigations*, translated by G.E.M. Anscombe, Basil Blackwell, Oxford.

Wittgenstein, Ludwig (1969) *On Certainty*, ed. by G.E.M. Anscombe & G.H. von Wright, translated by D. Paul & G.E.M. Anscombe, Basil Blackwell, Oxford.

Toni Rønnow-Rasmussen

Moral Realists and Moral Experts*

Abstract
On the face of it, moral realism seems to make room for moral experts with more ease than moral irrealism. If there is something to be known, we may suspect variation in knowledge among people. Focusing notably on Jonathan Dancy's recent views, I outline why this first impression should give way to a more sceptical attitude. Suggesting that when we commend someone for being an expert, we express in part our trust in that other experts in the relevant field would reach the same conclusions were they in similar circumstances. Dancy's particularistic account of moral reasoning has difficulties in meeting the intersubjectivity condition which appears to be necessary for expertise in general. The notion of moral expertise seems therefore not easily available to at least some versions of moral realism. But if there are no moral experts, then the idea that people endorse different moral opinions – which I think they do as a matter of fact – suggests that realism about moral matters after all is not the correct position to take.

The need for experts is increasing in today's societies. This seems at least to hold true of a great many subjects. Is it true of ethics? The number of ethical commitees that have been created during the last few years in many countries at least suggests that there are people who want others to come up with answers or guidelines to our ethical questions. Perhaps we should take this as an indication that some of us are ready to treat others as if they were experts on moral issues. But what does it take to be a moral expert?

Some decades ago an influential position among moral philosophers was that we should give up the idea of moral expertise. Moral philosophers had at least no special claim, it was said, to the title "moral expert". One reason for this aversion to moral expertise is well known – the idea that moral judgements were considered as nothing but expressions of people's emotions or desires made many conclude that reason has no part to play in the formation of moral judgements. Our moral opinions are as good or as bad as anyone else's. Therefore, no one could claim to be an expert in these areas.

Recently Richard Fumerton (1990) has maintained that philosophers can make no claim to be "experts" on moral issues. Admitting that philosophers can be "handy to have around", since they are good at analysing arguments, he still thinks that such "argumentative" skills do not define the concept of a moral expert. It tells us rather what a good philosopher is.[1]

Now, I do think that even a non-cognitivist could speak of better or worse moral opinions. However, whether or not we would see it as desirable to defend a notion of a moral expertise such that even a non-cognitivist would be able to call himself a "moral expert", it is important to keep this notion of expertise apart from the kind of experts we would expect to find in areas where truth was looked for. Our non-cognitivist "expert" would be someone who knew his/her metaethics, who could give us sound arguments for his/her normative positions, and who at the same time had more than average knowledge of the facts of the case under consideration, etc. (cf. Singer 1972).[2] Be that as it may, I will not say anything more here about non-cognitivism. Instead, I will confine myself to bringing a kind of cognitivist theory into focus that recently has been defended notably by Jonathan Dancy, and which seems at first sight to pave the way for moral experts. I will refer to this kind of theory as *moral realism*. It is a theory that contains the following tenet: (i) Moral properties are (non-natural) *sui generis* properties. Its advocates in addition make the claims (ii) there are moral facts (i.e. there are at least some entities that have moral properties) and that (iii) some of our moral judgements are true (in a realistic sense). In fine, the kind of theory which I have in mind suggests that moral qualities exist *in rerum natura*.

On the face of it, moral realism as outlined above does seem to be able to make a case for moral experts. If there is something to be known, we may suspect variation in knowledge among people. In what follows I will try to outline why I think this first impression should give way to a more sceptical attitude. However, before examining below the views of especially Jonathan Dancy, let me bring attention to one or two general features concerning our notion of expertise that I take to be less polemic than other ones.

First, if there are experts, there are non-experts. Not everyone can be an expert. Call this the condition of exclusiveness. Now, it seems reasonable not to extend the notion of expert to just any subject matter where truth is looked for. But whether or not I am correct about this, it is clear, I think, that we should not limit our use of "expert" merely to areas of professions (such as medicine, physics, carpentry).

I also take it that we will allow our experts now and then to give us the wrong answers to our questions. Expertise is no guarantee for infallibility. Notwithstanding, to recognize someone as an expert is to believe that he or she will more often than ourselves, *qua* non-experts, answer our questions correctly, and that the reason for this is that we believe they have what we do not have, namely, expertise. Otherwise it is difficult to see why we would call such a person an expert in the first place!

Given that there are different kinds of knowledge, we should also be alert to the possibility that there can be different kinds of expertise.[3] For instance, I may believe that Tom's answers, *qua* astronomer, about, say, the stars are trustworthy as well as I have been able to judge over the years, by the way he has repaired his various cars, that he is an excellent mechanic. Moreover, I have come to believe that he is able to distinguish between 25 different grades of brown (which I cannot see for my own eyes but which I believe he has learned as the son of a furmaker). Presumably he could be considered an expert in all three areas. Still, they involve at least in part different kinds of knowledge.[4] Happily enough, moral realists such as Dancy (1993) and McNaughton (1988) have made it sufficiently clear that they think that we "observe" or "discern" moral properties.[5] Although it is far from clear just how much we should understand by this, it should give us some clue to what we might expect from a moral expert who is a realist.

Moral realists do not have to endorse the idea that there are moral experts. David O. Brink,[6] for instance, maintains in fact that there is a grain of truth in the idea that we are all "roughly equally knowledgeable about moral facts" (Brink 1989, p. 96). His explanation for this is that since we all have to deal with moral issues some of the time, we will "grasp the subject". But, as he implicitly seems to be admitting further on, this point only establishes that people try to answer moral questions in a way they do not do with questions about, say, physics or chemistry. It does not show that among us there is a group of people, who in contrast to many of us, can give us the correct answer to our moral questions. Still he does recognize such people, whom he characterizes as persons who have "more moral insight and experience and have thought more about complex moral problems and so are morally more sensitive" (ibid. p. 96). Moreover, Brink thinks it is rational to expect to find these experts among "intelligent, well informed people who deal on a regular basis with complex moral problems, and who have thought about these problems in a systematic way". Other differences apart, Brink's view shows here some affinity with Sidgwick's view. Sidgwick too spoke of "experts", this "body of persons on whose moral judgement [the reader] is prepared to rely", and he thought that these persons were to be found among "those persons whom we take to represent Common sense" (Sidgwick, 1907, p. 343). However, Sidgwick also made it clear that there was unfinished business to attend too: "'I ought certainly to have discussed further how we are to ascertain the 'experts' on whose consensus we are to rely'" (loc.cit. Notice the use of inverted commas).[7] Brink on his part is convinced that he has located some of these members – that is, he maintains that "Insofar as there has been moral expertise, moral philosophers (or at least some among them) must be *among* the moral experts" (Brink 1989, p. 97).[8]

Another realist who seemingly opposes the idea of there being moral experts is David McNaughton. But on close examination, and as it seems, in stark contrast to Brink (and to some extent Singer), his aversion is directed rather towards the thought that we identify the "professional moral philosopher" (1988, p. 204) with the moral expert *simpliciter*. His reason for this has to do with his position as a *particularist* – the theory that says, in fine, that each situation has to be considered on its merits. Nevertheless, like Brink he does seem to think that there is a "way of seeing, a way of being sensitive to the moral facts" that opens the door for moral expertise.

Sturgeon (1986) is another relevant writer. He suggests, for instance, that there is a connection between virtue and moral insight (op.cit., p. 72). Also, his text lends at least some support to the idea that moral experts would have to be morally admirable persons. How strong the connection is considered to be, will in part depend on the stand we take on the internalists/externalists issue. Furthermore, it is clear that it would be to strain the connection too much if we let "being a morally admirable person" be a sufficient condition for moral expertise.

Another feature of expertise in general is that it comes in degrees. Brink, for instance, thinks this to be true also of moral expertise (Brink 1989, p. 97). Now, it seems likely that what Brink has in mind is that among experts in a field X, there can be someone who has more expertise than the other experts in field X. Actually there is a quality/quantity dimension to our notion of expertise. And if there is a "quantity" aspect to the matter, it seems likely that we can agree to Brink's idea, and say that (at least some kinds of) expertise do come in degrees. For instance, we may consider two surgeons as experts on a certain operation. However, since one of them has performed twice as many operations as the other one he could be considered "more" expert. Still, experience does not always relate to expertise in this way.

What about moral experts of a realist kind? Would there be room for similar variation, and for similar reasons? Can there be moral experts on, say, abortion that are maladroit on euthanasia, etc.? Is the number of occasions on which we have "observed" moral properties a merit in qualifying as a "moral expert"? Is the doctor who has performed a great number of abortions more of an expert on the ethical aspects of this issue, than a layman on surgical matters? People in general and moral philosophers in specific have, I suspect, rather firm beliefs about these matters (one way or the other). However, what interests me here is what a moral realist would say. Of course, he or she can lean back on a notion of moral expertise (such as was suggested in the introduction) that would be compatible with one that an irrealist/non-cognitivist might want to use. However, this would be tantamount to a drawback for the realists, who accuse irrealists of not being able to escape the suspicion that moral irrealism equals moral scepticism. If realists "fall back" on a notion of expert that a moral irrealist could accept, the sting has been removed from the "be-aware-of-the-moral-scepticist" argument. However, before looking into the views espoused by Jonathan Dancy, something more must be said about the notion of an "expert".

Now, if I am to acknowledge, say, Tom as an expert, it cannot in the long run be merely because I take his word for it. That Tom proclaims himself as an expert is *sans phrase* no reason for accepting that he is an expert. Something more is required. Above I mentioned that Tom must most of the time give (or be believed to be able to give) us answers to our questions that we consider correct (or, say, find somehow clarifying or useful). But here we should be careful, since it would be a mistake to allow mystics, gurus and others, who claim to have special gifts for reaching truth, to be experts. Whatever we think of the epistemic status of the opinions of this latter group, nothing would be gained, as far as I can see, by lumping these together with the experts. On the other hand, we do not want our notion of expert to be such that only those are entitled to call themselves experts who have a kind of knowledge that I, *qua* non-expert, could acquire. I am sure that there are things believed by experts in some fields that I simply have not the ability or intelligence to reach, no matter how hard I tried. But that should not impede me from sincerely calling someone an expert. Of course, this is far from all there is to the matter. Our trust or reliance that Tom is more often right in some field X than we are, must be coupled with the further belief that Tom's knowledge concerning X is at least at the level of the *best* persons in the field X.

The above expression raises the question of how we should understand "best person in the field X". Even if we put aside the idea that being an expert in one kind of field not necessarily means the same as being an expert in another field, there are, of course, various ways in which we could understand this expression. For one thing, we should differentiate between a commendatory and a neutral, descriptive use of the term. That is why I considered "best" in the first place, since it is one of the most often used terms for commending. However, nothing much hinges on whether we choose this or some other value term – as long as it carries a clear commendative force.[9]

The evaluative component of "expert" can basically be brought into play in the following way: When a person *a* sincerely says of a person *b* that s/he is an expert in field X, then

> (i) *a* expresses a non-cognitive state, viz., his/her trust in *b*'s answers concerning field X because of his/her belief that *b* is a member (or would be accepted as a member by other members) of the group of best persons in the field X – a group which *b* for some reason trusts gives, more often than non-members, correct (clarifying) answers to questions concerning field X, and/or
>
> (ii) *a* expresses a non-cognitive state, viz., his/her trust in *b*'s answers concerning field X because of his/her belief that *b* is a member (or would be accepted as a member by other members) of the group that *people* in general consider to be the best persons in the field X, and because of his/her belief that there is no stronger reason not to trust the choice of best group, regarding field X, made by people in general.

The non-commendatory sense of "expert" is used when a person *b* is considered an expert in field X because we believe that s/he is a member (or would be accepted as a member by the other members) of the group that people in general consider to be best persons in the field.

Now, lest I should be accused of beating about the bush, let me be bold and say that the above suggests that some kind of intersubjectivity condition appears to be necessary for expertise in general – one, moreover which I suspect moral realists will have difficulties in meeting. In broad terms, it is only against a background of "best people in the field" that a person's claim to knowledge is considered as constituting expertise, and, again, there would be no group to speak of, if it were not the case that the members of this group assumed that the process or method used by one member also was open to the other members.[10] Admittedly, this is not very informative. It is, for instance, reasonable to expect that "intersubjective" means different things depending on what field of knowledge we are considering. That a belief or hypothesis is intersubjectively testable will presumable mean something different to a historian than to a biologist (cf. Hermerén 1972).

Still, since we are in fact considering theories that stress that we do in fact "observe" or "discern" moral properties we are not totally in the dark. Thus, if a moral realist *a*, *qua* expert, observes or discerns a moral value in circumstances S, we should not be surprised if this property will so to speak pass non-experts by. However, we should also feel confident, it seems, that this would not be the case with the group of experts to which *a* belongs. If expert *b* is placed in similar circumstances as *a* we should expect *b* to see what *a* saw.

Let us now look more closely at the view espoused by Jonathan Dancy, as it is expressed in his recent work *Moral Reasons*. The book is rich in ideas, some of which I have had, I must confess, difficulties in following all the way. Needless to say I will not try to give a full account of his theory but confine myself to some parts that I find noteworthy, and which can be said to throw some light on whether moral realists are in a better position than, say, non-cognitivists, with regard to the issue of moral experts. These parts are in need of some unravelling, and I will therefore begin to outline the main ideas. Let me also at the outset make it clear that Dancy nowhere explicitly comments on the matter of moral experts.

Besides the fact that Dancy's book is a recent contribution to the cognitivist/non-cognitivist issue, there is a another reason why Dancy's view deserves to be scrutinized: He regards his own theory as a successor to intuitionism (Dancy 1993, p. ix) – the theory that at least some of us have an intuitive access to what are the moral facts. This opens for the possibility that his theory has solved some of the problems that (rightly or wrongly, were said to) besiege intuitionists. Intuitionists have sometimes, for instance, been accused of not meeting some kind of intersubjectivity condition. The reason, as Michael Smith (1994, p. 25) has recently argued, is their failure to give us a satisfactory account of how we come by knowledge of the relations between the moral properties and the natural ones. Does Dancy's theory fare any better on this matter? I think not – as will emerge later on. In the meantime let me outline the general traits of his theory.

Dancy considers moral properties to be *sui generis*.[11] Interestingly enough, he also advocates, in contrast to, for instance, Brink, a kind of internalism. What complicates the picture is his attempt to offer us an alternative to the standard Humean idea of motivation. Dancy tries his hand at an explanation of action that rejects the traditional view that belief and desire are distinct existences. I do not think Dancy's account of this matter is convincing but I will not further comment on it here (cf. Crisp 1993, Arrington 1994).

Dancy considers moral properties to be what he calls "resultant properties" – they can result from other moral properties – as for instance, when an action is wrong because it is unkind (Dancy 1993, p. 74) – as well as from natural properties. Nevertheless, in what follows I will for the sake of simplicity concentrate only on the latter case, since it seems to raise the more fundamental questions.

To begin with, Dancy warns his readers against what he calls some "abuses" of resultance. Hume, according to Dancy, committed one of these when he asked his readers whether or not they could discern the property of viciousness – a so-called resultant property – from the properties from which it results. Hume concluded that since there was no such discernible property, there was no such property as viciousness in the object. But to require this of the reader is to misunderstand, according to Dancy, what a resultant property is. So what is it? Dancy tells us that it is not a property "by the side of those properties from which it results" (Dancy 1993, p. 75). Rather, a resultant property seems to consist in the natural properties of the case, and the way that these properties, or at least some of these, relate to each other.

The second abuse concerns what he refers to as the epistemology of resultance. Thus, it consists in, as he puts it,

> assuming that those who lack the concept of some particular resultant property can acquire it from others by noticing the base properties present when the resultant property is attributed to different objects, and working from there (Dancy 1993, p. 76).

Dancy maintains that we may expect that the one who lacks a certain moral concept will be able to discern each property in the resultance base. However, it would be wrong to assume that the "shape taken by the resultance base is one which must be discernible by those who lack the concept" (Dancy 1993, p. 76). In other words, if Jane says that x is good, and another person, say Jim, says that he does not understand why Jane considers x to be good, which is what I take to be an adequate response of one who lacks the concept of goodness, we may take it that on Dancy's account Jane and Jim may hold the same beliefs about the natural properties of x. What differs here is that Jane but not Jim has a concept of goodness such that he is able to discern the "structured shape" of this so-called *resultance base* of natural properties.

The notions of "resultance base" and "shape" are crucial to Dancy's account (cf. Dancy 1993, p.114). To start with, what we learn from Dancy is that the resultance base should not be considered as a "flat list of properties, but as a structured shape in which those properties are placed here" (Dancy 1993, p. 74).[12] However, as will be clear in a moment, it becomes evident when we read on that Dancy considers it to be a mistake to identify the resultance base with an exhaustive description of the natural properties of the case under consideration. Let me already at this point ascribe the following *preliminary* thesis to Dancy:

(T1) The (resultant) moral property M of situation S consists in the resultance base N – where 'N' refers to a subset of S's natural properties and how these natural properties of the subset N relate to each other, viz., their so-called structured shape.

With regard to the third kind of case, Dancy says the following:

> The third abuse of resultance is the expectation that moral principles can be extracted from individual cases of resultance. We might hope that, given an example of a wrong action, which we understand well enough to be able to specify its resultance base, we can immediately get from this the moral principle that all actions that match that specification are wrong. (Dancy 1993, p. 76)

Now, since the above passage touches on a key idea in Dancy's book, namely, his particularism and the attack which he launches against the universalizability principle, I will briefly comment on why I think Dancy fails to establish his point that it would be an abuse to extract a principle from a particular case.[13] However, to begin with a caveat is in place. Although Dancy describes himself as a particularist, and attacks what he calls generalism, I agree entirely with van Roojen's recent comment that it is difficult to find "a canonical statement of either" (van Roojen 1995, p. 119).[14] Of course, this makes it difficult to assess Dancy's arguments. Still, given Dancy's (adherence to John McDowell's) characterization of particularism – "particularism [...] is the claim that we neither need nor can see the search for an 'evaluative outlook which one can endorse as rational as the search for a set of principles'" (Dancy 1993, p. 56 s.f. Cf. McNaughton 1988)[15] – I will proceed as if Dancy's arguments were set out to show that moral principles are of little or no use. I will do so by considering two standard ways of formulating principles. This will help me bring out what I take to be Dancy's arguments.

Suppose we try to extract a principle from a certain case. Presumably, the principle could take, say, the following form:

(P1:) *For all persons, if person x is relevantly similar to person a then x ought to do act Ω* (where the relevancy concerns the set of natural properties of *a* from which the extraction is done).

Now, why would the extraction of P1 be a sort of abuse? And why would this insight give us a reason to avoid using principles in moral reasoning? If Dancy's point is merely that it would be an example of "fast reasoning" to conclude that what holds for a particular situation must hold for other situations that are not exactly similar to the original one (see for instance Dancy 1993, p. 77), he has a point, but not one that is either controversial or sufficient for making the use of moral principles in moral reasoning into something unwanted, and much less into something describable as an abuse. Surely we can apply a principle such as P1 until we run into a situation that contains countervailing properties in addition to the properties that made us say that a ought to do Ω.[16] The role of prima facie principles or rules of thumb has not been questioned by establishing that what holds in one case not necessarily hold in general (even for cases that are to a great extent similar to the original one).

Dancy has a further reason for opposing the use of principles in moral reasoning. His second reason is, as far as I can see, directed towards principles that are not formulated in terms of relevant similarity. Let us therefore rephrase P1:

(P2:) *For all persons, if person x is exactly similar to person a, with regard to universal qualities, then x ought to do act Ω* (where a universal quality is one that is describable without reference to individuals).

The objection that Dancy raises here is that such a principle will "coincide with the supervenience base, i.e. it will cease to exclude any of the natural properties" (1993, p. 81). To reach such a principle, he thinks, will be a "trivializing result" (loc.cit):

> One thing we should notice on the way is that the moral principles generated by thoughts about universalizability are becoming progressively less use, since as the universalizability base grows the number of actions relevantly similar to the first diminishes correspondingly. (Dancy 1993, p. 81)

Thus, the objection to P2 should now be clear: Since the principle is formulated in terms of exact similarity (with regard to universal qualities) the principle will only apply, I assume, to one actual case, viz., the one from which it is extracted. And this, it is argued, trivializes the principle. But Dancy fails to take into consideration the use such principles can have when we apply them to hypothetical situations in which the roles of the actual persons are reversed. The morally important question "What if I were in his or her shoes?" has made many a person, I suspect, change their first moral opinion with regard to a situation. The fact that we assume that there will be no two qualitatively identical cases is in itself no reason to disqualify moral principles. For instance, the use which R. M. Hare's so-called "critical principles" play in his theory, does not derive from the fact that they are general principles.[17] On the contrary, these critical principles are to such a degree specific that we have good reason to think that they will apply only to the actual case under consideration. This does not prevent these principles from having an important role to play, since they also apply to hypothetical situations.

Dancy would have a point if he could show us that the fact that the two situations, say, S1 and S2, differed only with regard to the numerical identity of the individuals involved, had a bearing on the matter of whether the moral principle P that applies to S1 also applies to S2. However, as far as I can judge he is not ready to allow numerical identity to have any moral relevance. Consider for instance the following passage:

> What we get out of supervenience is the truth that any object exactly similar to this one in natural respects must share the moral properties that the first one has. (Dancy 1993, p. 78)

Dancy speaks here of objects, but it seems safe to assume that he would include here even situations, acts and persons. Let us therefore ascribe the following thesis to Dancy, and let us call it SUP:

SUP: For any acts (object, situation or person) S1 and S2, if S2 is exactly similar to S1 in natural respects, S2 must share the moral properties that S1 has.

Now, Dancy's reasons for attacking the use of principles in moral reasoning are for the above reasons not convincing. Moreover, as far as I can see, SUP runs into trouble with (T1):

(T1) The (resultant) moral property M of situation S, consists in the resultance base N – where 'N' refers to a subset of S's natural properties and how these natural properties of the subset N relate to each other, viz., their so-called structured shape.

On face value, either SUP or (T1) has to go. That is, a situation S1 may be similar to S2 in natural respects, but whereas the natural properties of S1 form a certain structured shape, say, F1, the natural properties of S2 form another shape, F2. Given SUP it would still be true that if S1 had the moral property M, so would S2. However, on (T1) this would not be true *without further qualifications*.[18] But it is difficult to see just how Dancy will adjust SUP or (T1). The problem, as I see it, lies in the notion of the so-called "structured shape"; being, as I take it, a complex of properties, it refers in no obvious way to a natural property (or for that matter any property at all).

Let us next consider in somewhat more detail what Dancy has to say about shape. He begins by dividing "the properties of a situation" (Dancy 1993, p. 112) into two groups – those that are and those that are not relevant to the question of what one should do. The relevant ones are what he calls "salient" properties. He explains this notion, and the relevance it has for his idea of "shape" as follows:

> To see a feature as salient is to see it as making a difference to what one should do in the case before one. Since there are normally several different salient features, related to each other in various ways, a full view of the circumstances, will not only see each feature for what it is but will also see how they are related to each other. Such a view will grasp the *shape* of the circumstances. (Dancy 1993, p. 112)

In speaking of what sometimes is called "thin properties", Dancy actually goes on to "identify" such properties with the "shape of the circumstances – what it is about them which calls for just this action" (Dancy 1993, p. 115). We can therefore reformulate (T1):

(T2) The thin moral property M of situation S is identical to the shape of the resultance base of S.

In some places it seems as if Dancy thinks that thin properties are "constituted" by the shape of the thick properties. However, it is unclear whether he actually thinks this is always true. Whether or not, the idea that we must somehow have thick concepts in order to have thin ones seems to me counter-intuitive, and I will therefore assume that Dancy does not endorse such an idea.

The idea that situations somehow have a shape raises the further question whether they have more than one shape. Dancy actually gives an affirmative answer (p. 250). In that case Dancy must somehow argue that there is a correct shape in order not to fall in the hands of some form of moral relativism. It must here be recalled that as far as T1 and T2 are concerned there is nothing that explicitly rules out the idea that a situation has as many shapes as there are viewers, and that there are, in consequence, as many moral properties as there are people involved.

Consider for instance the following passage:

> When we come to give a description of the situation, the various saliences (i.e. the shape of the situation) make a difference to how we should go about it. It is not as if it doesn't matter where we start among the myriad properties here present. *There is a right and a wrong place to start – many wrong places, in fact.* (Dancy 1993, p. 112. My italics.)

Unfortunately Dancy does not explain further just how we should understand what is a right place to start. What we are told is that the description of the case should be seen as a "form of narrative" that can have "the vices and virtues of narrative; features can be mentioned in the wrong order, and important relations without which the story does not make sense can be omitted, distorted or misplaced" (Dancy 1993, p.113). The properties of the case are said to "have a shape which the order in which they are mentioned (the narrative structure of the description) is intended to reveal." (loc.cit). But is there *one* story to tell? Is there an exhaustive story? Would it not be possible to think that two persons who, although they started from the (right?) same place, ended up discussing where to end the story? Is there a natural end to the story?

Whether or not Dancy thinks there is a right story to be told, these questions must be burdensome for anyone who wishes to make moral experts into narrators who reveal a hidden structure.

However, let us move on to the four-stage analysis of value, which Dancy offers as a promising view on value. The stages involved are the following:

(1) The resultance base (more precisely, the shape of the resultance base)
(2) The value.
(3) The disposition to elicit a (merited) response.
(4) The occurrence of the response. (cf. Dancy 1993, p. 159)

The idea behind this analysis seems to be the following: When I experience that a certain situation has a certain value, I experience the situation in a special way, namely, as one that calls for a certain response. This can be seen, according to Dancy as a "disposition in the case to extract a merited response from us" (Dancy 1993, p. 161).[19] But we must, according to Dancy, still differentiate between stages (2) and (3). We should not just see value as a disposition to elicit a response in us. Rather, Dancy's view seems to be the following. Value is present in the object as a disposition, distinct from both the shape of the resultance base and from the "experience it is a disposition to cause" (Dancy 1993, p. 159). Stage 3, he says, "exists in virtue of (results from) stage 2" (Dancy 1993, p. 160). Moreover, such a four-stage analysis of value applies also, he thinks, to colours.[20]

Now, like Dancy I am prone to consider colour as a phenomenal quality that is not identical to any primary qualities in the object. However, in contrast to Dancy, I find the use of indexical terms such as "here" or "there" about such phenomenal qualities dubious (references to time are, I suspect, an exception). Thus, when Dancy maintains that "the disposition to cause a certain experience exists in virtue of the phenomenal property *in the object*" (Dancy 1993, p. 159, my italics), I am in want of an argument that could convince me that the place to locate the phenomenal quality was *in* the object, situation, or act rather than somewhere else.[21] As far as I can see, Dancy assumes that once we admit the existence of phenomenal qualities, it makes sense to speak of these as if they were *in* objects. But an additional piece of reasoning is required here.[22]

I started this paper by addressing the question whether moral realists are in a better position than irrealists to give us an idea of what a moral expert is. The matter is one that in the long run deserves to be taken seriously by moral realists. If there are no moral experts, to the effect that we are more or less equally able to gain moral knowledge, then the idea that people endorse different moral opinions – which I think they do as a matter of fact – suggests that realism about moral matters after all is not the correct position to take. On the other hand, suppose only some persons are experts on moral matters. In such a case the non-experts need some kind of reassurance that the kind of knowledge attained by these experts is not too private, too mystical. That is, if we are to acknowledge these as moral experts we need to believe in something more than that they think they have the answer. My suggestion has been that we should at least expect that the "best" people in the relevant field, placed in similar circumstances, should reach the same moral conclusions. Which people? Which kind of competence should they be said to have? Are we talking here about actual agreement on the moral facts of the case or do we merely have in mind agreement in principle? These and other questions still await an answer. Above I merely discussed some of the views of one moral realist. Dancy may or may not agree in thinking that there could be moral experts. Again, whether or not we are to say that his particularistic, narrative account of moral "reasoning" paves the way for moral experts depends on our answer to questions of the following sort: Is it reasonable to expect that agreement will be reached regarding which criteria to use to single out the "right" point of departure – when we are to start (or, for that sake, when we are to end) the narration? Dancy's point that a situation can have more than one shape endangers the very prospect of reaching such agreement. If a situation can have more than one shape there will not be only one point of departure. Personally I doubt, given the underlying metaphysical assumptions, that such agreement will be reached. Moreover, I strongly suspect that the people who would in fact come forward as a candidate for membership in a moral "best group" would express such divagating views on moral issues that the very prospect of setting up such a group seems already at the outset doomed to failure.

Biography

Toni Rønnow-Rasmussen was born in 1956. He is a Doctor of Philosophy and presently working as Assistent Professor at Lund University. He has previously published *Logic, Facts and Representation; An Examination of R. M. Hare's Moral Philosophy* (1993).

Notes

* I am indebted to Dan Egonsson, Wlodek Rabinowicz and Ingmar Persson for valuable comments.
1. How do, say, administrators decide whom to hire as moral expert? Do they, as Fumerton asks, "make up their minds that they want a nonrelativist, objectivist, actual consequence rule utilitarian, or do they just keep their fingers crossed and hope that the philosopher they hire doesn't think within the framework of a mistaken metaethical theory?" (Fumerton 1990, p. 6). Cf. Furberg 1989.
2. Singer's expert is one who first gathers information. His/her next step is to assess it and bring it together with whatever moral views s/he holds. During this process s/he should be aware that personal desires do not lead to bias in his/her deliberations. See especially p. 116.
3. I suspect that many of what might be considered as candidates for being ethical expertise committees, include people from (various) religious communities. Does this indicate that people in general are in fact inclined to think that religious persons are experts on moral issues? To some extent I believe so. However, I do not think it is because people necessarily think that religious persons have a special religious sense to see what is right or wrong. Rather, what seems to count here is the belief that religious persons tend to be not only interested in solving their own and other people's moral problems but they also make claims to the effect that they do know how to solve these problems.
4. I owe Wlodek Rabinowicz the example of the mechanic who has "know how". Actually, I am not sure what to say about Tom's special gift or skill in distinguishing between different shades of brown. Perhaps it is just another case of know how? On this matter (and on competence in general) I have found much of intererest in Rolf, Ekstedt, Barnett (1993).

5. McNaugthon, for instance, says: "moral observation is not to be thought of as in a special category of its own, quite unlike any other kinds of observation. The belief that moral properties cannot be detected by ordinary methods of observation may, perhaps, be traced to an unduly restrictive view of what can be observed." (op.cit. p. 56). McNaughton seems to mean that we need a more generous theory of perception. Cf. Platts (1988) who denies that "we detect the moral aspects of a situation by means of some *special faculty* of the mind, the intuition. We detect moral aspects in the same way we detect (nearly all) other aspects: by looking and seeing" (op.cit., p. 285). References to the idea that we see moral properties are abundant in Dancy (1993); see for instance pp. 70, 115.
6. A caveat: Brink should not be regarded as a realist in the same sense as, say, McNaughton and Dancy. Brink, for instance, is best characterized as some kind of a naturalist. Cf. Darwall, S, Gibbard, A & Railton, P. (1992).
7. Walker (1994) made me aware of this passage in Sidgwick. Recall also Williams's (1985) characterization of Sidgwick as a "government house utilitarian".
8. Unfortunately it is not clear just how we should interpret the proviso "or at least some among them". It would be reasonable to draw the conclusion that if moral properties were *sui generis*, then we would have good (if not conclusive) reasons to rule out irrealists from the group of expertise.
9. The expression "commendative force" is used in a generical sense, referring to one of a number of attitudes (such as, for instance, trust, discussed in (i) and (ii)).
10. In one sense there could be a group by luck. Assume that the members all made claims that as a matter of fact coincided with each other. Suppose we also believed that the methods used were idiosyncratic in the sense, say, that they arrived at their claims in virtue of having experiences of "inner visions". The presence of a belief among us, non-experts, to the effect that there actually is such a group would, I take it, to a great extent depend on whether these members actually gave us the same answers. Still, even if such a group did survive for a time, the fact that we believed that it was merely by luck they reached similar beliefs, would be an obstacle to trusting their answers. And if there is no trust in the methods employed by the "experts", we will not consider them as experts. The role of the intersubjectivity condition is in part to exclude luck from having any role. Moreover, this suggests a way of drawing the demarcation line between mystics and experts in the sense outlined above, viz., whereas a mystic is conceived of as a mediator, an expert is not someone who relies on luck or on being given that which constitutes his or her expertise.
11. See also Smith (1994, p. 3), who also ascribes to Dancy the claim that moral properties are *sui generis*.
12. What is unclear here is whether or not Dancy actually believes that we somehow ever conceive acts, persons and situations as a "flat list of properties"? My own suspicion is that we do not.
13. For a more detailed examination of arguments against the principle of universalizability, see Rønnow-Rasmussen (1993).
14. Van Roojen (1995, p. 119) adds "Some formulations seem merely epistemic: 'the behaviour of a reason [...] in a new case cannot be predicted from its behaviour elsewhere' (p. 60). At other points (pp. 92, 104), particularism seems to entail the non-existence of any general moral truths".
15. McNaughton says, for instance: "Moral particularism takes the view that moral principles are at best useless, and at worst a hindrance, in trying to find out which is the right action" (McNaughton 1988, p. 190).

16. Actually, Dancy seems himself on p. 67 to allow some such role to moral principles. He also considers Ross's idea of prima facie duties. But his reasons for opposing this idea have to do with Ross's position as a cognitivist.
17. In his appendix on Hare's later views, Dancy actually seems to open the door for this role. See for instance p. 260.
18. Dancy returns in several place to the importance of the shape. For instance, he says that we should start "from the idea that the resultance base, in the particular case, has a certain shape; the interrelationships of the various properties are important" (p. 76). When Dancy discusses the relationship between "thin properties" (such as goodness and badness, rightness and wrongness), and the resultance base, he maintains that "[…] the identity is between the shape of the resultance base and the thin moral property, not between the thick and the thin properties" (p. 116). See also what I later on call T2.
19. Cf. the following passage: "The experience of value is the experience of a situation as calling for a certain response, and we can see this as a disposition in the case to extract a merited response from us" (p. 161).
20. At the end (p. 162) it becomes clear that he regards the analysis as better suited to colour than to value.
21. See Carlson (1987) who compares "Nagel's neorealism" with Moore's *Principia Ethica*. Both of these writers, it is argued, regard goodness, for instance, as an "object of thought, not a property of objects" (p. 45).
22. For some reason Dancy does not discuss Harman's argument that values are explanatorily redundant. This is all the more strange considering that he apparently thinks that they are not! For an attempt to meet, for instance, Harman's objection that moral beliefs do not have the same link to testing as do scientific explanations, see Sturgeon (1986).

Bibliography

Arrington, Robert L. (1994). "Review of Jonathan Dancy's *Moral Reason*, Philosophy 69, nr. 267, pp. 114-116.

Brink, David O. (1989). *Moral Realism and the Foundations of Ethics,* Cambridge: Cambridge UP.

Carlson, George R. (1987). "Moore and the New Realism", *Philosophical Papers*, XVI, nr 1, pp. 41-52.

Crisp, Roger (1993). "Motivation, Universality and the Good: a critical notice of Jonathan Dancy, Moral Reasons", *Ratio* VI, nr 2, pp. 181-190.

Dancy, Jonathan (1993). *Moral Reasons*, Oxford UK & Cambridge USA:Blackwell.

Darwall, Stephen; Gibbard, Allan & Railton, P. (1992). 'Toward Fin de siècle Ethics: Some trends.' *The Philosophical Review*, vol. 101 (1, January) pp. 1115-189.

Fumerton, Richard A. (1990). *Reason and Morality: A Defense of the Egocentric Perspective,* Ithaca and London: Cornell UP.

Furberg, Mats (1989) "Är Akademisk Etik Komisk?" in ed. Claes Åberg, *Cum grano salis: essays dedicated to Dick A. R. Haglund.*

Hare, Richard M. (1981). *Moral Thinking: Its Levels, Method and Point,* Oxford UK: Clarendon Press.

Hermerén, Göran (1972). *Värdering och Objektivitet*, Lund: Studentlitteratur.
McNaughton, David (1988). *Moral Vision; An Introduction to Ethics*, Oxford UK: Basil Blackwell.
Platts, M. (1988). "Moral Reality". In Sayre-McCord, G, ed., *Moral Realism,* Ithaca and London, Cornell UP.
Rolf, Bertil; Ekstedt, Eskil; Barnett, Ronald (1993). *Kvalitet och kunskapsprocess i högre utbildning*, Nora, Nya Doxa.
Rønnow-Rasmussen, T (1993). *Logic, Facts and Representation: An examination of R M Hare's Moral Philosophy*, Lund: Lund University Press.
Sidgewick, H. (1901). *The Metods of Ethics,* Hackett Publ. Company, seventh edition.
Singer, Peter (1972). "Moral Experts" *Analysis,* vol. 32 no 4, pp. 115-117.
Smith, Michael (1994). *The Moral Problem*, Oxford UK: Blackwell.
Sturgeon, Nicholas, L. (1986). "Harman on moral explanations of natural facts", *Southern Journal of Philosophy*, vol., XXIV, Supplement, pp. 69-78.
van Roojen, Mark (1995). "Review of *Moral Reasons* by Jonathan Dancy" *The Philosophical Quarterly*, pp. 118-120.
Walker, Margaret Urban (1995). "Where Do Moral Theories Come From?" *The Philosophical Forum,* vol. XXXVI, no. 3, pp. 242-257.
Williams, B. (1985). *Ethics and the Limits of Philosophy,* London: Fontana Press/Collins.

Pär Sundström

Historicism and the Study of Human Nature *or* does Philosophical Anthropology have a Subject Matter?

Abstract
In my paper I discuss the possibility of a philosophical anthropology. The question is discussed in the light of historicist ideas to the effect that human agency is a cultural product, and that therefore the study of human nature may be problematic. I discuss three versions of such historicism – moderate historicism, radical historicism and Charles Taylor's version of historicism. My main line of argument is that historicist considerations can challenge certain theories *of human nature, but not* theorizing *in general on the subject. I grant that human agency may be realized in qualitatively different forms in different cultures, and that we therefore run the constant risk of confusing a local realization of humanity with humanity as such. I am even prepared to grant that human agency is so tied to culture that it can be described only in terms peculiar to one society or other. But I argue that such assumptions do not contradict a general philosophical anthropological ambition. On the contrary, such assumptions are sustainable only if human nature has certain qualities. Philosophical anthropological theorizing would be pointless only if there was no human nature at all to inquire into. But then, I argue, a historicism going such extremes is indefensible.*

I

In this paper I shall discuss the possibility of a philosophical anthropology. More specifically, I shall discuss whether the field has at all a subject matter; whether, in other words, there is a ubiquitous nature of human agency. If there is not, then philosophical anthropologists find themselves at a dead end.

The background and continuous point of reference for my discussion is a strand of modern thought in which the notion of a human nature is looked upon with suspicion, or is even outrightly rejected. I shall refer to this strand with the term "historicism."

In its most general form, historicism is defined by the idea that we ought to mistrust references to so-called "human nature." We (whoever "we" are) take one form of life to be "natural." But as we look at other cultures, past and contemporary, we find that the forms of human life vary in striking fashion. In fact, it may look as if it is of the very nature of humanity to have no nature. And from the standpoint of historicism, this question is not of merely scientific, or philosophical interest. Misguided beliefs about human nature have political implications. They mislead us into identifying a current manifestation of humanity with humanity as such. As a consequence, they arrest political imagination as well as political activity.

I believe that historicism contains important elements of truth. But I shall claim that the truths of historicism do not contradict a general philosophical anthropological ambition. Historicist considerations can challenge certain *theories* of human nature, namely theories that allow too little room for human plasticity. But historicist considerations do not undercut philosophical anthropological *theorizing* as such. Indeed, I am going to suggest that historicism itself contains one philosophical anthropological assumption or other.

These would have been my last words on the matter were it not for a disturbing version of historicism suggested by Charles Taylor. According to Taylor, the human nature can be described only in the language of one culture or another. In a sense, therefore, theories of human nature will necessarily fail to capture their subject matter. Paradoxical as this may seem, I believe Taylor's position is consistent, and I shall try to show what is and what is not contestable in it.

Before turning to defend my claims, I want to point to an ambiguity in the notion of a human nature. In discussing human nature, we may have in mind the biological constants of human agents. "Human nature" in this case means "human biology." But we may also have in mind features of our existence without which we would not be human at all; without which we would be *merely* biological organisms. In this paper, I am concerned with the latter meaning.

II Moderate historicism

In this section, I am going to outline what I take to be at least possibly true in historicism. This possibly true view I shall call *moderate historicism*.

My main purpose, however, is to evaluate the implications of moderate historicism for the enterprise of philosophical anthropology. I shall argue that whether true or not, there is nothing in moderate historicism that contradicts a philosophical anthropological ambition.

Historicism, I said above, is defined by the idea that we ought to mistrust references to human nature. Now of course, all theorizing is fallible, and hence all fields of study should be met with a certain amount of skepticism. But we may have reasons to be especially concerned about references to human nature. In the field of philosophical anthropology, it may be claimed, we are liable to make a peculiar kind of mistake. This kind of mistake is, by now, fairly familiar. Consider the following account.

> Whenever we are inclined to say something about the nature of human agency, we ought to remind ourselves about examples from the history of social thought, such as Aristotle's theory of natural slaves. To Aristotle, it appeared as if some people were born slaves. We believe today that he was mistaken in this. A reasonable hypothesis about the nature of his mistake, is that Aristotle was in the grip of an ideology, more specifically the ideology that people are naturally apt for specific social positions. In reconstructing the circumstances of Aristotle's theory, we find this ideology showing up in several places.
>
> First, the ideology probably affected Aristotle's perception of social life. But second, it conceivably contributed to shape the very object of his perception, i.e. the slaves, in the first place. To the extent that the ideology was wide-spread, the slaves must have taken themselves to be born for their social position. Possibly, they had a self-esteem and self-understanding such that their very emotions and motivations approached that of the supposed natural slaves. They may have regarded feelings like humility and modesty to be the true fulfilment of life, and experienced obedience to authority to be a demand grounded in the very nature of things. Slavery then appeared to be something flowing from the inner nature of agents themselves rather than something arbitrarily imposed upon people. And then – and this is the third place where the ideology shows up – it is probable that Aristotle's ideologically laden perception of an ideologically shaped object contributed to consolidate the ideological shape of the object. By confirming the ideas that originally shaped both the perception and the perceived, it preserved the vicious circle of which it was itself a part.
>
> This historical example tells of a theoretical mistake. Aristotle had a false belief about the nature of some human agents. But the mistake

was also related, in an intricate way, to political matters. It originated in ideology, and it turned out to preserve an ideology.

The message to us of this example is to mistrust references to so-called "human nature." Aristotle was unaware of the contingency, as well as the ideological underpinnings, of the social practises he observed. And as *he* was inclined to – wrongly – take *his* society with its to *him* invisible ideology, to be "natural," so is any thinker of human nature.

Whether this story is actually true or not, I believe that it is a story of what *might* have happened, and that its message therefore should be taken seriously. This belief is not essential to my main argument, though. The point I am really interested in making is that even granting that the story says something important about the predicament of philosophical anthropology, it implies nothing that would make the enterprise as such impossible or morally questionable.In order to see this, let us take a look at the two related cornerstones of the story.

One cornerstone is that human life takes many forms. In social contexts other than our own, people have taken certain features to be inescapable parts of human life. Since these features are not parts of our life, we know that they are not inescapable. Similarly, features that we take to be inescapable may be known by others to be not so. Now this may be true, but what follows from this? It follows that it is going to be an elaborate task to *confirm* theses of philosophical anthropology. It will certainly not be acceptable to just seize upon whatever appears natural to us. It does *not* follow, though, that there *are* no inescapable or universal features of human life.

In fact, it seems to me that there are determinate limits to what can be disproven about human nature by means of examples of cultural diversity. Examples of cultural diversity can disprove specific *theories* of human nature. They can show that we have drawn the line between what is perennial and what is changing in human life in the wrong place. But they cannot show that there is no such line to be drawn.[1] The reason is that philosophical anthropological theories can, trivially, admit of more or less plasticity in human nature. So, if X is shown not to be a perennial feature of human life, then Y may be, and if Y is not either, then Z may be, and so on. For example, if a certain motivational content (say, material welfare for oneself) is not a perennial feature of human life, then the structure of motivation (say, long-term rational calculation) may still be, and if the structure is not perennial either, then a more abstract structure (say, some deliberation or other) may be.

Let us turn to the other cornerstone of the story told above. This cornerstone consists in the assumption that the activities of human agents are partly products of social influence, or self-understanding, or both. Again, this may well be true. It would then follow that we should be especially careful when theorizing in the domain of philosophical anthropology. In trying to single out what in human beings is universal and what is local, we are, by hypothesis, dealing with a subject matter that is, at least potentially, shaped by ideas about these things. But it would not follow that there is no human nature to study. On the contrary, the claim that human agents are parly shaped by their social circumstances *is* an assumption regarding the nature of human agency.

Notice that the anthropological assumption about the mouldability of the individual is a necessary condition of the coherence of the moderate historicist story. Unless this assumption was true, the objects of Aristotle's perception could not have been shaped by ideology, nor could Aristotle's theory have its alleged political consequences. The ideological illusion of natural slaves is possible only if human agents are susceptible to the influence of ideology.

I conclude that moderate historicism does not challenge the general enterprise of philosophical anthropology. A philosophical anthropologist may well grant that many theories (perhaps even all existing theories) confuse local realizations of human nature with human nature as such. He or she may also grant that such mistakes are pregnant with practical implications of moral significance. In fact, I have suggested that a philosophical anthropological standpoint is not only *compatible with*, but even *required by*, such a historicist outlook. It is *because* human nature have certain characteristics that there are reasons to scrutinize the subject critically from both a scientific and a moral point of view.

Radical historicism

The general enterprise of philosophical anthropology can accomodate both the idea that human nature is highly determinate and that it is highly indeterminate. This suggests that only a historicism in which the very idea of a human nature if denied can challenge the enterprise as such. Such historicism I shall call *radical historicism*.

Radical historicism faces an immediate problem. Human agents of different cultures have a by and large common biology. Now, in the strict sense it is conceivable (or so it may seem) that even though we share a biology, there is no common core to our humanity. But this can be so, it seems, only if our biology sets no limits to the development of our humanity. For suppose that biology sets limits to our humanity. Then it will be true to say that it belongs to human agency to be realized within those limits. So, as far as our humanity goes, biology can at best be a necessary requirement for its occurring at all. *How* it is realized must be, from the point of view of biology, a wholly open question. Radical historicism will have to show, in other words, that human agency is through and through a product of culture.

Possible as this may seem, I doubt that the idea makes sense. In order to evaluate the position, however, we should consider in greater detail what it presupposes.

For any foreseeable future it will be true to say that human beings characteristically walk upright, have prerequisites of articulate speech, and possess highly flexible hands. But it may be claimed that such features of our biological nature have nothing to do with our human features. True, there is *some* connection between our biological set-up and our human traits. For example, we express our thoughts in articulate speech, and our motivations are translated into bodily action. But perhaps this connection is but *contingent*. It so happens that we express ourselves through a body with those and those characteristics. But our bodily set-up could be wholly different while our desires, emotions, motivations and cognitions remained the same. And then radical historicism may be true. While the outer shell of human agency is biologically determined, its inner essentials are – without residue – products of historical circumstances.

Let me repeat that the completeness of historical explanation is essential here. A philosophical anthropologist need not be contradicted by claims to the effect that human agency is partly, or even largely, a product of historical circumstances. Such claims challenge certain theories of human nature, but not theorizing about human nature in general. On the contrary, the claim that human agency is largely a historical product *is* a claim about human nature.

If, on the other hand, human agency is without residue a cultural product, and cultures moreover differ widely, it is probably futile to search for perennial features of human agency. But then it is precisely the claim to the completeness of historical explanation which seems to me indefensible. In fact, I think radical historicism is self-defeating. Let us consider.

The first thing to notice is that a radical historicism, even if it was true, could hardly sustain the kind of moral point that has accompanied our previous historicist considerations. The point has been that references to "human nature" may mislead us into thinking that changeable social injustices are grounded in the nature of things, and are thus not changeable. Thereby, ideas about human nature may, whether intended or not, arrest political action.

Why do I claim that radical historicism, if true, would fail to sustain such a point? Because the judgment that a social phenomenon, such as the institution of slavery, is unjust does not make sense unless the institution frustrates some significant human needs. If slavery in no way constituted an obstacle to human growth and fulfilment, it is difficult to see what could be bad about it. But now, radical historicism is defined by the claim that there are no given human needs. Cultures may produce significant needs. But then different cultures can produce different significant needs. Following radical historicism they do. By hypothesis, there are no cross-cultural significant needs in human life. Love and charity can be better than slavery and torture only for historically local reasons. There is no ground for holding that the former conform to needs belonging to human agents as such, in a way that the latter do not.

This consequence of radical historicism should enable us to appreciate the extremes to which the position takes us. But we may not want to reject the position on this ground alone. For in the strict sense, cultural relativity of moral values is conceivable.

There are, however, at least two, to my mind insurmountable difficulties with the view that human agents are through and through products of culture.

First difficulty: *The view implies that human agency is an odd, spontaneous creation out of nothing, rather than a cultural product.* The argument rests on the fact that if biological nature has nothing to do with human agency, then there is nothing upon which cultural forces can act to shape agency. Consider an example. We subject a new-born infant to severe torture. What will happen? The infant's body will be damaged. But what will happen to the infant as a person? What traits will this infant develop? As far as I can see, it follows from the radical historicism that anything may happen. The infant may come to develop like other infants, or it may come to differ from them; it may come to develop an integrated personality, or a fragmented one; it may come to feel harmonious, or tormented. The reason is that there is nothing – apart from an empty, neutral shell – upon which our torture acts. There are no human needs which we either frustrate or satisfy when we torture the infant. There is nothing there which we either help to grow or inhibit. As far as human agency is concerned, cultural forces work – literally – upon nothing. Now, to begin with, it is metaphysically odd that something – human agency – comes out of nothing. And even if we grant this oddity, it still makes no sense to say that this something has been *shaped* by culture. Shaping appears to presuppose that there is something there – an X – which will assume one shape if it is treated in one way, and another shape if it is treated differently. When there is no such

X, we have no more reason to say that agency is a cultural product than to say that agency is spontaneously created out of nothing.

And of course, if human agency is not a cultural product, then radical historicism is false. Following this argument then, the position is self-defeating.

Second difficulty: *The view resists all conceivable specifications of itself.* Here goes the argument. The claim is that human agency is without residue a product of culture. Now, we should like to know just what this is supposed to mean. *How* do cultural forces produce agency? But it seems that no answer to this question could even be compatible with the claim. It cannot be the case, for example, that it is the pattern of social interaction in a culture that shape agency; nor that it is the interactions with inanimate nature; nor, again, that it is the conceptual system of a culture. Why? Because these are all statements about what belongs to human agency as such. And this presumably goes for every conceivable specification of the claim. If any specification is true, then it is true to say that it belongs to human agency to be shaped by such and such.

In effect, it is difficult to say what the relation of "production," alleged to hold between culture and agent, is supposed to amount to. On the one hand, the formulation seems to promise an explanation of the latter in terms of the former. But on the other hand, it seems that the hypothesis does not allow us to replace "production" with any more specific term.[2]

I think the two difficulties point in the same direction. Something must be added to radical historicism for the hypothesis even to make sense. But the candidates for addition, would all introduce a philosophical anthropological assumption into the account, and thus make it inconsistent.

I conclude therefore, that historicism, insofar as it goes to the extreme of denying philosophical anthropology its subject matter, is not defensible.

Taylor's version of historicism

The message so far is fairly straightforward. The enterprise of philosophical anthropology does not conflict with a historicist caution regarding the theoretical and moral perils of theorizing about human nature. Furthermore, if I am correct, it is difficult even to make sense of the idea that philosophical anthropological theorizing should be futile.

This could have been my last word on the matter were it not for a qualification regarding the possiblility of philosophical anthropology suggested by Charles Taylor.[3] Taylor does not question that there is a transhistorical human nature. The historicism he proposes can be regarded, therefore, as a form of moderate historicism. It puts in question theories of, rather than theorizing in, philosophical anthropology. However, Taylor's version of historicism differs from moderate historicism as this was presented above. There we considered the possibilities that some, or perhaps even all existing, theories of human agency could be false. But Taylor goes, at least in one sense, further. He questions the possibility of at all formulating true propositions about the human nature. I suspect, he says, "that no satisfactory general formula can be found to characterize the ubiquitous underlying nature of a self-interpreting animal [such as man is]."[4] In other words, it may be that all attempts – past, present and future –, to formulate the nature of human agency will necessarily fail to capture their subject matter.

In what follows, I shall try to clarify, and show what may, and may not, be contestable in this idea.

It may appear paradoxical – but perhaps, by now, not suprising – that Taylor's historicism is intimately connected with a certain view of the nature of human agency. It is necessary to briefly consider this view.

Taylor's view is that it belongs to human agency to take stand on the qualitative worth of one's existence. Human agents judge their own being in terms of whether it is, for instance, noble or base, fulfilling or not fulfilling, virtuous or vicious, cool or not cool. What a human agent is, is a matter of concern to the agent. As a consequence, a human agent is a peculiar kind of "thing." Human agents are partly constituted by what they take themselves to be. We cannot give an exhaustive description of a human agent without mentioning the agent's own self-description. For example, in describing the desires of an agent, it will not be sufficient to describe their objects, strengths and frequencies. Following Taylor's account, any such description would be incomplete unless it included the agent's own evaluation as to the *worth* of the desires; whether the actions to which the desires incline the agent are taken to be, e.g., noble or base, cool or not cool.

Let us condense this view into the claim that it belongs to human agency to be situated in a moral space, that is, in a space of questions about the qualitative worth of one's existence.

It is not my intention to evaluate Taylor's philosophical anthropological thesis here. Instead, I am interested in Taylor's meta-theses; what he claims about his claim. Taylor says that he has identified something "inescapable and hence universal" about human agency. At the same time, though, he apparently claims only local validity for his formulations. "The language of the self in moral space is a quintessentially modern language," he tells us.[5] This sounds paradoxical, but as I shall try to make clear, it is not incoherent. The meta-thesis in short, is that a universal feature of human agency has been described in the language of one of its historical realizations. Taylor is going to claim, moreover, that this is the best we can do.

To begin to make sense of this, let us clarify what may be quintessentially modern about the account of the self in moral space. Taylor has mentioned at least two characteristically modern traits of the account. First, it is connected to "our post-Romantic understanding of individual differences as well as to the importance we give to expression in each person's discovery of his or her moral horizon."[6] This modern sense of identity, Taylor claims, would have been incomprehensible to our forebears of a couple of centuries ago. They, or many of them at any rate, would have found the idea reprehensible if not incomprehensible that I have to scrutinize myself in search of the good, since the good for me need not be identical to the good for you. Second, Taylor holds that even arguing the very point of the self in moral space makes sense only within modern philosophy. As we conceive of it, the self can be thought of as inhabiting a neutral world. Compare this with, e.g., a platonic world-view. According to Plato, the self – or rather, "the soul" – consisted of three parts, one of which, the rational, was defined by its ability to grasp an objectively existing moral order. On this view, moral space is *conceptually* inseparable from the soul. Taylor suggests, therefore, that "one could perhaps not get Plato to see what issue you were raising with the language of the self in moral space."[7]

In this way, a claim about a transhistorical feature of human agency is articulated in a modern language. The idea is that there is something in common to human agents. But this common feature is realized differently in different cultures. And in order to describe the feature, we have borrowed the language of its modern realization.

As we have seen, Taylor insists that there are instances which are distorted if described in this language. To people of other cultures, our modern language may appear misguided, perhaps reprehensible, and perhaps even unintelligible. This does not mean that they are not situated in moral space. Instead, it means that both moral space and situatedness within moral space mean something entirely different to them.

Why then, has Taylor used a distorting expression? This question takes us to the heart of Taylor's historicism. The reason is that we can do no better than that! He seems to think that the predicament is inescapable. Whenever we want to formulate truths about the nature of human agency, it is inevitable both (1) that we borrow the language of one of its cultural realizations, and (2) that we thereby distort some other cultural realization of human agency. And it is as a consequence of these two facts that no satisfactory formula can, allegedly, be found to characterize the ubiquitous nature of human agency.

Is this true? I do not know, but I shall make an attempt to single out what is contestable and what is not contestable in Taylor's account. As far as I can judge, there is, once we grant Taylor's philosophical anthropology, a convincing argument for claim (1). The argument for claim (2) is, though, less convincing.

Here goes the argument for claim (1). It belongs to human agency, according to Taylor, to judge whether existence is, e.g., noble or base, cool or not cool. We expressed this above by saying that human agents are partly constituted by what they take themselves to be. Now it seems to me reasonable to assume the following. First, agents can take such a stand on their existence *at all* by virtue of *at all* having a language. Judging about one's existence seems to presuppose one moral vocabulary or other. Second, *how* agents take a stand on their existence – that is, what discriminations they make, and what kind of justifications they employ for their valuational judgments – will correspond to the categories available in the language they use. An agent possessing the category of coolness will make discriminations that an agent lacking this category will not make. And an agent with a moral vocabulary including an objectively existing moral order will take a somewhat different kind of stand on his or her existence than an agent who relates his moral terms to innate, physiological needs.

Given Taylor's view then, the relation between language and human agency is highly intimate. *That* human agents are situated in moral space depends upon them having a language. And the *character* of the moral space as well as of the situatedness within it will correspond to the character of the moral vocubulary.

If this is correct, it follows, I think, that the feature of being situated in ethical space can be articulated only by borrowing the language of one of its realizations. There is no such thing as "simply" being situated in moral space. This situatedness *exists* only as realized within one moral vocabulary or other.

So far, the argument seems to me to be in good shape. It is possible to dispute Taylor's philosophical anthropological thesis, of course, but given the thesis, the rest appear to follow.

But the fact – if it is a fact – that we need to borrow the language of some particular realization does not in itself imply that philosophical anthropological theories fail to capture their subject matter. If this was all, we could borrow the language of one realization in order to describe what is common to them all.

But now Taylor has claimed something more. Claim (2) above says that when we do borrow the language of some realization of human agency, there is always some other realization that we thereby distort. As a consequence, we can*not* describe what is common to them all in the language of one realization. What is the argument for this claim?

Taylor tells us that the terms that define moral spaces and situate agents within them, vary in striking fashion. As we look through history we often find moral spaces so different as to be incommensurable. It is impossible, therefore, to define a common set of terms in which all different outlooks can be undistortively stated.[8]

The claim, in other words, seems to rely upon an observation regarding the diversity of moral vocabularies. Moral vocabularies are so diverse that for each vocabulary there will always be another vocabulary such that there is no set of common terms in which the two can be undistortively stated.

I find it difficult to judge about this argument. I am not even sure that I have a clear grasp of what it would take to establish whether there is, or is not, a common set of terms in which to undistortively state two different moral vocabularies. This argument seems to me to be the weakest point in Taylor's account.

Unable to judge about its truth-value, it seems to me reasonably clear what Taylor's version of historicism consists in. Let me summarize. Following the version, philosophical anthropological theories are impossible in one specific sense. It is impossible to formulate what is common to human agents. The reason for this is that human agency is necessarily realized within one moral vocabulary or other, and the existing vocabularies are incommensurable. Hence, no description of human agency is possible outside of moral vocabularies. And no one vocabulary will do justice to all manifestations of humanity.

III

I have tried to evaluate the implications for the enterprise of philosophical anthropology of the (sometimes) alleged historicity of human existence. I have granted that human agency may be realized in qualitatively different forms in different societies, and that we therefore run the constant risk of confusing a local manifestation of humanity with humanity as such. Indeed, it may even be that it is in principle impossible to find a satisfactory formula to describe what is common to human agents. But none of these possibilities show philosophical anthropological *theorizing* to be a futile occupation. On the contrary, I think, these are possibilities at all only if human nature have certain qualities.

Philosophical anthropological theorizing would be pointless only if there was no human nature to inquire into at all. But a historicism going such extremes is, I have argued, indefensible.

Biography

Born in 1966. Ph.D. student in Theoretical Philosophy at Umeå University, Sweden. In my current work, I focus on topics in philosophical anthropology, in particular questions regarding the structure of human motivation and human action.

Notes

1. We may have to make some reservation for this point. As I shall try to show in the discussion of Taylor's historicism, a claim about cultural diversity, in conjunction with a specific hypothesis about the nature of human agency, imply that we cannot find a satisfactory formulation of what is perennial and what is changing in human life, *even if* we are convinced that the distinction is real.
2. The argument may appear to simply exploit the idea that radical historicism consists of the incompatible claims that (1) there are no transcultural features of human agency, because (2) human agency is without residue a product of culture. (These are incompatible since the truth of (1) implies the falsity of (2) and vice versa.) But that is not exactly my point. I do not think such an argument should worry a defender of radical historicism too much. The radical historicist could simply reformulate his claim, saying that there is one and only one transcultural feature of human agency, namely that it is without residue a product of culture. My argument is that in order to make concrete sense of the last clause, it seems inevitable to assume that something or other is true of human agency as such.
3. What follows is an attempt to make sense of scattered remarks made by Taylor. Taylor has not, to my knowledge, given any extended, systematic presentation of his views on the matter.
4. *Sources of the Self: The Making of the Modern Identity* (Cambridge, Mass: Harvard University Press, 1989), p. 112.
5. "Reply to commentators" in *Philosophy and Phenomenological Research*, vol. LIV, no. 1, Marsch 1994, p. 208.
6. *Sources of the Self*, p. 28.
7. "Reply to commentators", 208.
8. "The dialogical self" in *The Interpretive Turn: Philosophy, Science, Culture*, ed. David R. Hiley et al. (Ithaca: Cornell University Press, 1991), p. 306.

Merete Sørensen

Environmental Ethics and/or Environmental Aesthetics?

Abstract
In our antropocentric culture many people have learnt to accept extremely low ethical standards for the treatment of non-human organisms. A great part of those people strive, however, to cope with very high aesthetic standards in their use of animals, live as well as dead, plants and artifacts. Seemingly a conflict between their ethical and aesthetic perspectives.

By focusing aesthetically on some of our, ethically regarded, low standard practices towards non-human organisms I want to raise the question, if it be more realistic and fruitful to interpret this conflict as a conflict within aesthetics, between a surface and a full aesthetic perspective, opening for the possibility of a parallelity between aesthetic and ethical perspectives on nature.

I want to bring up some actual questions from the borderland between ethics and aesthetics of nature. My assumptions are

(1) ethical and aesthetic aspects of our relationship to non-human nature are closely interconnected and interdependent
(2) awareness of this interdependence
 (i) is a fruitful, perhaps even a necessary, condition for expanding the ethical field beyond the boundary of sentient beings and letting it comprehend non-sentient organisms, too
 (ii) might help us in developing adequate ethical concepts to guide our attitudes to biotechnological operations recently made possible, esp. in cases, where what is, intuitively, perceived as ethically problematic transcends traditional ethical argumentation.

My main interest is environmental ethics. Below I shall, however, as a consequence of the presumed interconnection between ethical and aesthetic dimensions of our relationship to non-human nature, attempt to focus (exclusively) on aesthetic aspects of this relationship. Another reason for this one-dimensional focus is, that we live in a culture, where it is more legitimate to point at aesthetic aspects and appeal to aesthetic emotions than to ethical ones, when non-human objects are concerned. I shall concentrate on the field of sentient beings, partly because the mentioned interconnection apparently can most clearly be demonstrated within this field; partly because convincing documentation for the interdependence of aesthetic and ethical aspects in the field of sentient beings seemingly represents the strongest evidence for the ethical relevance of aesthetic considerations in the field of non-sentient organisms.

Instead of using rational argumentation I shall attempt to appeal to the aesthetic judgement via exemplification. I hope, that the chosen examples sufficiently clearly demonstrate the relevance of applying the aesthetic judgement to them. Looking at our concrete daily life, the parallelity of aesthetic and ethical aspects in our practical relations to non-human creatures might not seem evident at all. Apparently, a lot of ambiguities, even opposites, are expressed, not least due to today's degrading way of treating great parts of the non-human organisms, who give to us products of high aesthetic quality, f.ex. the trapping of wild animals or caging of former wild animals in order to use their fur for most beautiful coats.

The interesting question is, if such ambiguities or opposites necessarily must be expressed as conflicts between ethical and aesthetic dimensions, or if they instead, perhaps more simply and adequately, can be interpreted as conflicts within aesthetics, more precisely as conflicts between superficial and deeper aesthetic perspectives, respectively.

It is a fact, that to many people in Western countries, aesthetic considerations play a great role in their daily life concerning dress, furnitures, cars, paintings, music and preparation of their meals. It is remarquable, however, that most of these people, even the most intelligent and reflective among them, do not care or care much less about the aesthetic aspects of the (treatment of the) raw materials basic to their consumption; especially about the treatment of the fields, trees and animals, whose products they so proudly wear and so diligently prepare in their kitchen. At least they give priority to aesthetic qualities directly perceivable by the senses. So, in practice they accept – or rather abstract from their knowledge about – herbicides on the plants and confinement of the domestic animals in monotonous concrete stables without windows, lighted by neon light up to 24 hours a day, smelling of ammonia and filled with a constant, monotonous noise from the ventilation plant, necessitating the farmer to protect his nose and ears, when these products can be seen as means for expanding their possibilities of aesthetic in- and expression on the surface. What counts is, partly the resulting, measurable qualities of the products, detatched from their origine, partly the creative human contribution to the meal, dress etc. – In other words, apparently, most people can easily abstract from extremely low aesthetic qualities, attached to the origine of a product, when only the directly perceivable qualities of the resulting product are satisfying as basis for the human enjoyment and creativity.

This discrepancy in aesthetic judgement, due to the priority given to the human contribution, becomes still more evident, when the comparison is not between two phases of the life of organisms, but between organic and artificial products. It is, for example, mirrored in the fact, that whereas most educated people would judge anyone who would think of cutting off a corner of his oil painting or of his architect designed furniture in order to make it fit to the form of the room, a barbarian, they stoicly accept the amputation of tails and teeth, horns and peeks of their future pork, beef and chicken, that means the amputation of the designs of Nature, in order to make those adapt to a system of production, which gives to humans a great variety of consumer goods (– and possibilities of selfexpression).

To me the following (from my point of view rhetoric) questions are raised: Can the former mentioned, high aesthetic (surface) standards be seen as an extenuating circumstance for the latter, or does the latter lower standards concerning the origine of the products put the former into a caricaturing relief? Is it a sound intuition which makes this broad spectrum of aesthetic sensitivity question, what I call the aesthetic integrity of the person, and indicate an inadequate use of his/her mental ressources?

Today a way of adapting Nature's designs to our system of production much more refined than the upper mentioned cuts off is rapidly developing, namely that of genetic engineering. Below, I shall limit myself to looking at genetically modified animals, the so-called transgenic animals. In that case the operations are not carried out on screaming youngs, but on quiet, patient, microscopic, fertilized eggs, the operator using sophisticated motoric skills in ultra hygienic laboratories, without violence, blood, sweat and tears. – Apparently an operation aesthetically most satisfying. Nevertheless, I find an aesthetically based critique concerning the practise of genetic engineering on animals crucial, not least ethically crucial. My reason for this is, that a trendsetting, narrowly ethical argumentation fails to grasp any problematic aspects in applying this advanced technology on animals, provided, that unintended side effects can be eliminated. It is namely a remarquable fact, that the successful process of genetically modifying animals transcends the traditional animal protection and animal welfare considerations, on which the animal protection legislation is founded. For this operation takes place at the level of fertilized egg, long time before the development of the nerve system, that means before the development of the sensitivity to pain. Accordingly, if no unintended, painful side effects occur, no welfare problems seem to be connected with the process of shaping transgenic animals, and therefore, according to prominent utilitarian animal ethicists, the sentienists, no ethical problems, either. Along this line the Danish Ethical Council Concerning Animals characteristically states, that in assessing the ethical defensibility of making transgenic animals, whether genetically modified disease models, organ donors or so-called bioreactors, "the decisive factor is, from an ethical point of view, the potential suffering of the animals, and not the method by which they are created." (Statement Corcerning Animal Experimentation, 22. 9. 1992)

Because my intuition does not at all feel reassured by this elimination of the importance of the method, but finds, that the engineering of the genes of the animals, making our genetic change be transferred to coming generations, rather might represent one further, radical step on our path of animal degradation, I want to look at the process in an aesthetic perspective.

The upper mentioned priority given to the human contribution to organicly based products seems to have led to an (temporary?) extreme in the fact, that patents can be and have been granted to genetically modified animals, even to mammals. Thereby is demonstrated the assessment, that the primary status of such animals is that of an artefact. That means, that the human contribution is judged more important than the original organic equipment of the animal. But whereas it was a characteristic trait of the upper mentioned preparations on basis of the non-human organisms, that these should be improved, at least on the surface, according to human aesthetic standards, the aesthetic standards can be compromised with, even on the surface (although perhaps only on a longer sight, that means at a later stage in the development of the organism), when (commercially important) patents are concerned. For it is remarquable, that the first patented mammal was the so-called oncomouse, i.e. a mouse genetically modified to spontaneously develop breast cancer after 90 days, the patent being granted to Harvard University in 1988.

To this it can be objected, that the relevant alternative to the oncomouse is not a healthy, genetically unmodified mouse, but a mouse subject to a conventional transfer of (growing) pieces of cancer tumours below the skin, that means subject to a much more obvious, inharmonious and invalidating handicap. Compared to this mouse, the handicap of the transgenic oncomouse is much less marked.

I do not accept this objection. Whether the conventional operations on experimental animals used in the cancer research can be judged as more or less aesthetically revolting than that of genetic engineering, the fact, that the first radical, human fingerprint on non-human mammals which was estimated sufficiently drastic to make the animal an object of patenting, was the transfer of a most feared human disease, cannot be eliminated. Furthermore, the awareness, that our society through generations has accepted and made itself depending on degrading animal experimentation, should rather make us still more critically question the defensibility of making transgenic experimental animals, because it seems likely, that the habituation to degrading animal experimentation has blurred our critical sense. – I shall, however, leave the discussion of aesthetic defensibility of transgenic experimental animals (disease models), letting the possibility be open, that no aesthetic defence is possible, because transfer of cancer to a healthy genome simply is aesthetically degrading in itself.

Instead I find it more challenging to apply the question of aesthetic acceptability of a genetic modification of animals to an operation, which, apparently, has neither painful nor obvious aesthetically degrading consequences for the animal. I want to question the aesthetic defensibility of the transgenic bioreactors, that means animals who are genetically modified to produce pharmacies in their milk, blood or eggs, for instance the Scottish sheep who produce the hemophelia drug factor IX in their milk, and who are already or will soon become commercially utilized.

These sheep, apparently, do not suffer at all as a consequence of the genetic change – on the contrary, because of the expensive content of their milk they are taken better care of than most of their cousins within conventional husbandry. According to conventional welfare parametres, they have no welfare problems – and according to prominent animal ethicists, we have no ethical problems in constructing them.

Because analytically satisfying, ethical terms do not, to my estimation, grasp the the essentially new (ethical) aspects of this advanced technology, I want once more to turn into an aesthetic perspective, in the hope of thereby bringing in factors fruitful for this discussion. I shall limit myself to looking at one aesthetic question connected to bioreactors: The transgression of the species boundary. This problem is specific for genetic engineering not least in cases, where it is the boundary to humans that has been transcended. The question is, whether respect for the species boundary is an authentic aesthetic value. At least it can be claimed, that the possibility of blurring the species boundary has made us aware of the respect of the species boundary as a potential value. And, not least, made us aware of the actual fragility of this potential value, due to the growing threat from the expanding commercial interests in exploiting the possibilities of species boundary transcending bioreactors.

This threat, inevitably, sharpens our imagination: We cannot help reviewing the map of the multitude of living species, focusing on the context of the network of extremely fine, fragile boundary contoures. Nor can we (psychologically) help admiring this magnificent network – provided, that commercial or professional interests have not blurred our emotions.

A characteristic trait of this value is, that it is a common, inter-human value, which is entrusted to the care of the genetic engineers. They administrate it, respectfully or disrespectfully, on behalf of all humanity: The destroyed contoures of the boundary network cannot be rebuilt. And even if the boundaries are not completely destroyed, but only blurred (only a few genes out of 100.000 are changed or transferred), the aesthetic loss might be great, because it might be the very sharpness of the boundary network, which gives the aesthetic treat – perhaps a treat indispensable for mobilizing the energy necessary for a whole-hearted defense of the species boundaries...

The great question is: Do there exist considerations weighty enough to defend the blurring transgression of these boundaries? If so, do the present and planned transgenic products represent such ones? Who should bear the burden of argument?

Reply to this question transcends this paper. Here, I shall finish by reflecting on the question of Human Design or Nature's Design. This question is interesting and challenging in different respects, as far as it concerns a real alternative, that means, as far as a richly differentiated non-human nature, authentic to a high degree, exists and is open to us. In other words, as far as Human Design can be seen as an alternative to, ideally, as an enrichment of Nature's Design. In cases, where nature becomes so degraded, that Human Design turns into a substitute for Nature's Design, Human Design will presumably loose a great part of its attraction, too.

I have striven to limit myself to an aesthetic perspective. Inside my head, however, the aesthetic aspects cannot be separated from the ethical dimensions. Accordingly, my writing has been accompanied by a parallel ethical discussion, functioning as either an inspirator or a corrective. I have in no way tried to silence it. Rather, it has strengthened my assumptions, turning them into the conviction, that when, in analyzing certain situations, conflicts occur between aesthetic and ethical dimensions of our relationship to non-human nature, at least one of these dimensions has not been adequately grasped.

Biography

Born 1952. MA in Philosophy.

Tommi Vehkavaara

A Metaontology and the Metaphysics of *Différance*

A Hermeneutical Interpretation of *Différance*
and its relation to metaphysics

Abstract
The purpose of this paper is to tear something positive out form Derrida's 'pseudoconcept' différance by asking what its influence is in human understanding. By taking temporality and contextuality seriously we find that meanings and identities cannot be realistically identified. All the ontologics are 'idealistic', because they are based on idealised entities – at least some différences are always forgotten or regarded marginal. However, we are constantly using concepts as if they were properly identified. The presented explanation is that we as human beings get power by using idealisations. Différent ontologies and metaphysics are constituted according to our interests, and that is the reason and the cause of their existence in human practice. Ontologies and theories are necessary and useful for us, but their interest-relatedness restricts their applicability – their unbounded use must be criticised. Now, différance *can be interpreted to form a general frame of reference, a metaontology, that refers only to different metaphysics. In this metaontology we can place différent metaphysical systems (or entities) at différent kinds of metaphysical levels. The more idealised the ontological beings are the more concrete metaphysical level is in question. As a metaontology,* différance *can work as a medium of legitimation for certain non-standard approaches (especially for evolutionary epistemology). On the other hand,* différance *can, as a metaphysics, also motivate the study of non-standardisable changes.*

1. Introduction

Jacques Derrida has introduced an artificial term "*différance*" in his criticism against 'the western metaphysics of presence'.[1] The issue in this paper is what the 'metaphysics' of *différance* contains, even if this might sound self-refuting for those who already are familiar with Derrida's texts. It is true that Derrida's own use of the word "*différance*" contains a direct attack against any metaphysical thinking, but the term "*différance*" can nevertheless be seen as 'representing' something alternative (or even superior) to traditional metaphysical conceptions. Therefore, the discussion about *différance* belongs to the metaphysical field and as a term, *différance* is metaphysical at least in this weak sense.[2] Even for Derrida all philosophies have certain metaphysical contents, including his own. He does not really claim to try to get rid of metaphysics (because he thinks it is impossible), but he just tries to keep himself at its limits,[3] where it might be possible to ask really new questions. However, *différance* does not contain most of the traditional concepts of metaphysics.

This paper is not a scholarly presentation of Derrida's philosophy. Rather, it tries to present one, hopefully useful, interpretation about *différance*. Moreover, this interpretation is consciously abusing Derrida's texts and perhaps even raping his deepest intentions instead of searching for some authentic or original interpretation. Nevertheless all this kind of activity is just *différance* at work.[4] This interpretation may be characterised as 'hermeneutical', because it is trying to tear something positive out from *différance* – what its influence is in human understanding. Therefore, we will examine how *différance,* metaphysics and sciences can be considered together, what their mutual relationships are. However, first we must introduce *différance* by deconstructing the concepts of meaning and identity.

2. Time and the Act of Interpretation: From Meaning to the Process of Reshaping Meaning

The background of *différance* lies in French structuralism as well as in its phenomenological critique. In structuralistic thinking the meaning of a sign has been seen as a rigid, at least in principle identifiable, ideal object. In fact, meaning is an essential part of the sign, the signified (*signifié*), which means that if the meaning of a sign changes, the identity of the *whole sign* changes.[5] *Différance* attacks this notion – in fact, it attacks any such conception of meaning that presumes that a meaning has an identity. By doing this, *différance* can be said to create an alternative metaphysics that has neither ontology nor epistemology, although the reasoning for this alternative can be found to be pragmatic (and thus epistemic). As we will see, this kind of metaphysics is far from what has traditionally been called metaphysics, because it is absurd to deal with most of the traditional metaphysical problems within *différance* (or they can be dissolved as trivial ones).

The central point in this paper is to emphasise the significance of the *act* or *process* of interpretation. The following two remarks characterise the frame of reference:

1. When we are trying to define or clarify the concept of meaning from the point of view of the act of interpretation, we have to notice that every act is happening at certain time. Moreover, this time is not some *point* of time, but an *interval of time* – acts of interpretations are processes that are not just *in time*, but they also *take some time*.
2. Acts of interpretation are never impersonal – there is always an agent who is interpreting or giving meanings and who always has a certain (historically developed) context within which (s)he is interpreting. When we talk about a meaning, we have to ask what it is for the interpreter.

Whenever we make the common assumption that the meaning of a sign could have an identity, we must first ask – if we keep in mind these remarks – in what circumstances could this meaning be identified. Can we say that there can be found contexts similar enough, where the agent (of interpretation) can repeatedly find the sign to have the identical meaning? We are forced to argue that without any idealisations this is impossible.

It should be quite clear that different persons (or agents) have always different contexts, because they are as themselves the results of different unique historical processes (as well as their contexts are too). However, even one person (or agent) cannot have an identical context in the different acts of interpretations, because the acts of interpretations (of a certain person) are *ordered in time*. In every pair of interpretations the context of the later interpretation differs from the context of the former interpretation. For the context of the former interpretation, the later interpretation does not exist, but the former interpretation is always structuring the context of the later interpretation. Thus, the context of the later interpretation includes some *traces* from the former interpretation and these traces will produce contextual difference in every case. Traces can be direct conscious remembrances or, at least, they are drawn into unconsciousness – traces from earlier interpretations are always reshaping the (unconscious) structures of meaning.[6]

If the significance of time is to be taken seriously, the meaning of a sign is reshaped towards an unidentifiable and flexible pseudo-object, that is constantly differing and changing from one interpretation to another. This process of differing or 'the flow of reshaping meaning' has been described by the term "*différance*". Because of *différance,* we can no longer properly speak about meanings: every time when somebody thinks or says that something means this or that, this same act of giving meaning changes this meaning. As a result, there are no identifiable objects to which the *concept* of meaning could refer. Its extension is empty, and not just actually empty but empty in principle. In a sense, meaning as a concept refuses to exist 'really' – all its possible extensions have to be (in a strong sense) *idealised*.[7] This is the core of the conception of meaning in the metaphysics of *différance*.

What have we left at hand? If we accept this kind of argumentation, the concept of meaning seems to lose its content. However, despite all this we can still talk about this or that having the *same* meaning. We must just keep in mind that there are always at least some differences between interpretations. *Sameness* does not have to mean identity, if we do not *idealise* the influence of temporality. This kind of sameness, that can be characterised as evident connections between different interpretations, is itself produced by *différance* through spatio-temporal differing.[8] Even though every interpretation is in a sense creating a new meaning (or in fact, a new *sign*), this new meaning is in many ways associated with earlier interpretations. The traces of earlier interpretations are usually quite easy to read from the new sign (meaning). Moreover, these connections between interpretations or signs are in many cases so evident, that we become too easily blind to the differences or we just regard them as marginal. (And therefore, some traditional idealist could conclude that the 'illusion' of the existence of self-identical ideal objects called meanings appears.) One of the main motives for discussion about *différance* is to take seriously those differences that have usually been either forgotten or regarded marginal.[9]

From this point of view, *différance* can be seen as a radical generalisation of the hermeneutic circle. It is a generalisation, because for *différance* interpretation is not tied to conscious interpretation – when one is perceiving or acknowledging a sign or a difference, this perception does not have to be conscious to be influential or significant. Brainwashing and certain forms of propaganda and advertising are common examples of this. On the other hand, in the general case there is no convergence of meaning in *différance*. That the movement of *différance* is also the process of *differing* can, for instance, be interpreted as the *adaptation* of a sign (or meaning) to the changing context – no end (not even hypothetical) is needed.[10]

3. The Metaphysical Consequences of the Conception of Meaning in *Différance*

The conception of meaning in *différance* seems to be the result of a certain aim, that could be defined as *subjective realism*. The content of this metaphysical attitude is to give as realistic a picture as is possible about the world appearing to *us* (or, to 'generalised me'). Because of its realistic intention this picture must also include how the world is appearing to us.[11] Therefore we have to pay attention to those various idealisations (concerning, for instance, temporality) that must be made for the sake of understanding and communication. In this sense we can say that the metaphysics of *différance* is just trying to be (subjectively) realistic by denying the existence of meaning (as an *object*).

Although *différance* has so far been connected here purely with the concept of meaning, it gives an alternative to the whole ontological way of thinking. What happened to the concept of meaning – it lost its content by losing its objects – is generalisable to epistemology as well: If we follow the attitude of subjective realism, the situation in epistemology will become analogous to what we said about the concept of meaning. Because we cannot define the meaning of a sign without ignoring the influence of temporality, we cannot either define, recognise, or even name any 'existing object'. In every recognition there remains just the *trace* of 'the original object', which is no more identically similar to 'the original' – the original exists no more (for us), there remains only an imperfect *copy*. This changing character of perception or any other act of knowing also holds for other (causal) influences of an assumed object, no matter whether they are consciously cognised or not. Every event or phenomenon is always temporally and spatially unique, and so are its influences too. Thus, the identity of any object of knowing is the same kind of idealisation as the self-identical meaning of a sign. Objects never appear twice to us as identically similar (even indirectly), which is due to differences in space and time. Our assumed ability to identify objects seems to be an idealised form of our experience.[12]

Now we can ask whether we need ontology (as we earlier asked whether we need the concept of meaning). If our ability to identify objects is already ideal(ised), then why should we assume the existence of objects that are independent from this ability? The possibility for ontological thinking is undeniable, but from the point of view of subjective realism we have to ask what is the reason for this kind of thinking. Most of the answers to this question can probably be reduced to the view according to which either the independent existence of things, the nature of the *Geist*, the existence of subject, or some other variation like these is just *the best explanation* for various similarities between different appearances (in our experience). Ontology is needed because *we*, as human beings, want to explain – *we want to know*, take control over the appearing and mysterious world. Thus, while we think or talk about the objects independent from us, we actually tie them to our actual purposes. Ontology cannot be 'objective', it is a *method*. It is a choice for looking at what is stable and idealisable instead of looking at change and differences.[13] This preference is certainly no more objective than the aim towards 'subjective realism'. The demarcation line between ontological and subjective realism lies at the point where the question: "What are the ontologies for?" is no longer considered relevant. For subjective realism, the issue is not our knowledge about assumed ontological objects but our *ability* to construe and identify them.

Thus, the metaphysics of *différance* is metaphysics only in the sense that it forms a sort of alternative to what has traditionally been called metaphysics – there is no general ontology. Because the extension of any ontological object is actually empty, the content of the concept of the ontological object vanishes. In fact, there remains no need for the concept of the ontological object (or thing). Correspondingly, there is no need for epistemology either (at least not *ontological* epistemology). *Différance* does not form any metaphysical system, because it does not contain or use traditional metaphysical concepts and because it concerns traditional metaphysical problems being mostly irrelevant – *différance* is too general a term to be included in any genuine metaphysics.[14]

So far the argument might be classified as a phenomenological critique of the structuralistic notions of meaning and sign. Although the point of view has been that of an individual, it must be noticed that the critique of the concept of identity concerns also the self-identity of the experiencing and interpreting subject. In the metaphysics of *différance* the experiencing subject has no privileged ontological position – the self-identity of subject or *self* is the same kind of idealisation as the self-identity of any 'outer object'. When every interpretation is differing from others and meaning appears as an endless process, then also the experiences from the identity of the interpreting subject (*I, me, self*) become part of this 'play of differences and traces'. Familiar self-sceptical questions represent *différance* in this respect: How could I possibly know who I am? Doesn't my notion of my identity rest only on certain continuities in my memory and environment? Doesn't my experience of my identity depend much on the feeling of how well I can understand what there is to me, in me, and around me?

4. The Relation between the Metaphysics of *Différance* and Science

Because the metaphysical attitude behind *différance* pays attention to the idealisations that are made for the sake of understanding and communication, the metaphysics of *différance* may seem to be classified as belonging to traditional idealistic metaphysics. The existence of meaning (as an object) and the self-identity of all things including experiencing subjects is denied, which may make this impression even stronger. Every (scientific) theory, definition, or hypothesis is always 'idealistic', even and especially those with 'realistic' ontology, because the assumed existence of stable or identifiable objects of realistic ontology presumes the same kind of idealisations as the definable concept of meaning.

However, aiming towards subjective realism cannot be the 'highest purpose', because its practical value is mostly critical: with it we cannot do or even say very much. Theories and definitions are, like many other idealisations, certainly necessary for human life and culture, but they are ultimately constructed for more or less practical purposes, usually one way or another, for power and control.[15] This does not mean that they would necessarily contain something wrong or immoral, but rather that they can only draw a partial picture about the world (because of their special view). It is perhaps too much to say that because of their ideal character, theories, definitions and things should never be considered apart from the special interests that they are constituted for. However, the critical point in the metaphysics of *différance* is that we should never forget these interests. A good example is Davidsonian semantics, which is clearly build for mechanical translation from one language into another and because of that purpose it so anxiously tries to idealise away the mutual incoherence of languages.[16] (The same could be said about Chomskyan grammar.) Their descriptions of language can never be realistic or impartial, because these descriptions are not *just* descriptions but they are *for translation*. Therefore they are necessarily idealistic and partial.

Thus, the practical necessity or usefulness of ontologies or of (scientific) theories is not denied, even though their unbounded and objectivistic (metaphysical) use is criticised. In this respect it makes no difference whether these ontologies and theories are intuitive or scientific – or products of religious, political, or artistic thinking. As far as some ontology or epistemology is dealt with only methodically, with clear consciousness about its restrictions, there are no controversies with the metaphysics of *différance*.[17] But whenever some metaphysical conceptions are widened to establish an all-including system of basic principles, when there is a belief in its ultimate justifiableness – as a practice or general attitude often is in scientific realism, or more broadly, in the scientific world-view – then controversies will arise.

The metaphysics of *différance* does not form an alternative only for realistic metaphysics but for subjectivist metaphysics too (including major parts of phenomenological tradition) by deconstructing the self-identity of experiencing subject. As in the case of science, this does not mean that the self-identity of subject becomes totally destroyed but is just shown to be ideal. That is, we accept 'the fact' that a conscious subject is not able to have a perfect control over the flow of meaning, *différance*, even if (s)he is anxiously trying to have this control. The metaphysics of *différance* is probably compatible with the idea according to which it is the identity-consciousness of the human subject which is most important, at least for the sake of ones mental health.

5. The Use and the Legitimation of the Metaphysics of *Différance*

But if all the metaphysical conceptions and attitudes have, according to the metaphysics of *différance*, some constitutive (more or less) practical interests, then what are the interests of the metaphysics of *différance* – what is its deconstruction of metaphysics for? We need some preliminary work before we can answer this question.

5.1. *Différance* as a Metaontology: Metaphysical Levels

Différance cannot as such be used as a methodology in any special act of interpretation;[18] something more is needed. (For instance, in the previous chapter we gave the explanation according to which our common 'idealistic' use of language is a medium of power.) *Différance* as such cannot give much, if any, practical tools for understanding, because it does not give any useful concept of meaning. Through its conception of meaning, *différance* can, at its best, produce only a highly abstract, holistic and 'almost-nothing-saying' view to the world – its best possibility as such is to form a general frame of reference for different metaphysics. In this sense, *différance* can be seen as a term, that is enclosing different ontologies, theories, and definitions within itself by showing their proper place and use. This suggests that *différance* can be interpreted as a 'metaontological' but at the same time self-referential pseudoconcept; a point where we can judge other metaphysics as well as that ongoing process of judging.

Différance is metaontological, because it is in a way before any genuine ontology or metaphysics. Different ontologies are products of *différance* – the process of differing is needed before differences can be defined, before the world can be divided into pieces.[19] Since this can be done in numerous different ways, the limitations of different ontologies can be viewed from the metaphysics of *différance*. However, because *différance* is itself metaphysics, at least in a weak sense, it is at the same time in its own scope. The twofold character of *différance*, metaontological and metaphysical, makes it self-referential.

What then could *différance* interpreted as a 'metaontology' contain? Different ontologies or metaphysics do not necessarily exclude each other but some of them are mutually compatible. One sort of compatibility appears as a hierarchy of metaphysical levels with respect to the abstractness and concreteness of ontological beings. The metaontology can thus be described in a hierarchical form. In this hierarchy some ontologies with a certain kind of ontological abstractness may have several exemplifications or 'applications' at more concrete metaphysical levels. Different metaphysical *systems* may be placed at three metaphysical levels: at the level of 'concrete ontologies', at the level of 'abstract ontologies', and at the level of 'epistemic metaphysics'.[20] However, in extreme concreteness there is a naive, incoherent, historical, and flexible 'common sense', that has always worked as a historical source for 'more sophisticated' metaphysics. Consequently in extreme abstractness there is *différance* itself, as a non-understandable and all-enclosing pseudoconcept.[21] The criterion for division and naming of metaphysical levels as well as placing concrete examples of them is naturally a quite arbitrary, or at least uncomplicated, operation. Therefore, the particular division in figure 1 serves only as an example or sketch and even then it is just preliminary.

The abstractness or concreteness of ontologies is not at the level of theories or notions. Even though there are theories and notions (especially in exact sciences), which are very difficult to understand and in this sense 'abstract', the abstractness of this kind does not necessarily correspond with their ontological abstractness, because their ontology may still be quite concrete. The concreteness of ontology means only that there is given some specific division of the world (or of some phenomenon) in it. Therefore in concrete ontologies it is of no matter how weird or unintuitive the beings are.

Abstract ontologies do not give any *specific* division, but introduce the *form* of the dividing the world. The ontology of classical first order predicate logic serves as a good example of an abstract ontology: It does not tell exactly how the world should be divided, but whenever it is divided (according to it), it gives the form of this division. There is always a group of static individuals that have certain properties and mutual relations. Abstract ontologies are also produced within special sciences. A good example is Richard Dawkins' *replicator*-ontology that has been idealised from the more concrete (but also more problematical) gene-ontology in the theory of natural selection.[22]

The next step to the more abstract direction is the level of 'epistemic metaphysics'. In metaphysics, which are called 'epistemic', the central point of view is either that of the interpreting and experiencing subject or that of unconscious structures (in us), that are constantly restricting and modifying our way of acting and knowing. Ontology is more or less antirealistic or relativistic but still the experiencing or already structured subject is at least implicitly held stable or permanent. The last transition has already been described in previous chapters: *Différance* is deconstructing both the experiencing subject and the identity of sign (and meaning) by taking temporality (and spatiality) seriously. However, this deconstruction is not destruction, because *différance* also gathers all the other levels together and sets various metaphysics to the proper levels at the same time as it sets itself to the extreme abstractness.[23]

Here we find *différance* again and a crucial question rises: Is the metaphysics of *différance* necessarily effecting only by means of genuine metaphysics or can it possibly give something supplementary that cannot be reached through ordinary metaphysical means? There is no easy answer to this question, but what follows is one trial of a positive answer.

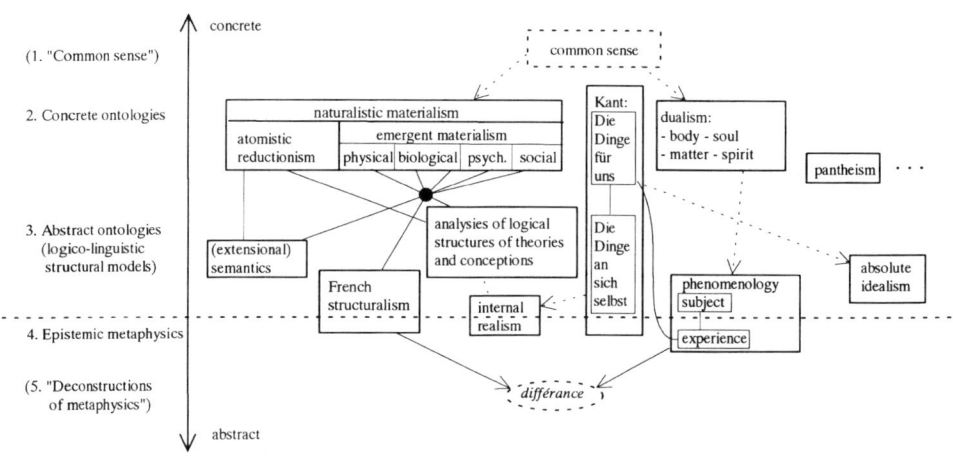

Figure 1: Différance *as a metaontology.*[24]

5.2. Motive: *Différance* and Evolutionary Epistemology

The significance of *différance* presented in this paper is twofold: *Différance* as a *metaontology* can work as a medium for the legitimation of certain non-standard approaches of study, which does not necessarily seem to increase our power over the world at all. These approaches are more interested in changes and processes as such rather than (re)construing them by using idealised and standardised stable units. This interest in non-standardisable changes is also inspired by *différance*, or by the *metaphysics* of *différance*.[25] The special case that is behind this particular paper is the so-called *evolutionary epistemology* (EE).

EE has as its central idea the handling of evolution, and especially the concept of natural selection, in terms of knowledge processes – adaptation to the environment means gathering and storing up knowledge from the environment.[26] Still, the discussion about EE seems to have become increasingly marginal and it has partly turned to areas that do not seem to have much general interest. There are probably two reasons for the marginality of this discussion. One is the concentration on genes in evolutionary theorising and the other is the dominance of self-sufficient scientific realism, or more generally, the domination of a restrictive logico-analytical conceptual scheme in the philosophy of science.

EE is roughly divided into two 'programs': the 'genuine' evolutionary epistemology that studies genetic constraints in human and animal knowledge, and the other, philosophical branch that concentrates mostly on producing evolutionary models for progress in scientific knowledge.[27] The first program is more biological than philosophical and the issue within it is rather to search for relatively stable universals than to understand the nature of change. While EE as a biological program is on 'the level of concrete ontologies', the scope of EE as a model for scientific change has been set too narrowly to allow any wider influence in spite of its more abstract ontology. In addition, the discussion could be characterised as highly speculative in both branches.

However, EE might at least potentially have some 'conceptual power' in both the positive and critical senses concerning 'the metaphysics of change', but it is often frustrating to discuss it at the level of abstraction associated with contemporary evolutionary discussion. If we consider 'the metaphysics of change' without trying to analyse it only by means of naturalistic ontology, the ideas of EE are at their best when they are dealt with on the level of epistemic metaphysics.[28] This does not mean that they have no influences at more concrete metaphysical levels, but only if its core is on a relatively abstract level, can EE successfully be defended against substantial criticism. Some of the consequences of EE (perhaps the most important ones) are purely conceptual – for instance, the idea of a structural knowledge[29] is extending the concept of knowledge far beyond the standard notion about 'a knowledge as a true justified belief'. As such, knowledge can be seen as a unit of natural selection, but only if we are speaking at a quite abstract metaphysical level. Genes are only one concrete exemplification of structural knowledge – it is possible that there are also other (more or less concrete) structures (social, linguistic, psychological, etc.) that may be said to contain some structural knowledge produced by natural selection.[30] The problem is, that whenever one is talking about natural selection, the first association is to relate natural selection with genes and speciation. Natural selection is mistakenly held as a theory *only* at the level of concrete ontologies, while it could (and should) be considered at more abstract metaphysical levels too. The proper motive for foregoing metaontological hierarchy and the whole discussion about *différance* is, that they could clarify these kinds of problems, emphasise the kind of importance of abstract metaphysics and, most of all, legitimate this kind of non-standard discussion by breaking the narrow-minded monopoly of concrete ontologies and their insufficient approach to the nature of change.

Remarks:[31]

1. It may sound self-refuting to make claims about the inappropriateness of the concepts of meaning and identity, because such a claim has to use these concepts itself. However, of course these concepts have conventional uses in different languages and in order to discuss their metaphysical status we are naturally forced to use these concepts. We have to use the language we share in order to communicate. (This fact is evidently forgotten by some philosophers.) In this paper I am not denying the possibility (or necessity) of using concepts like identity, meaning, object, etc. but I am just referring to their inappropriate metaphysical or ontological status. I am not concerned with whether we are using such concepts, but with the sense in which we should use them.
2. It is justifiable to wonder if it is possible to dilute completely all the concrete implications of the metaphysics of *différance*. It could be thought that because it is often practically necessary to use 'theoretically unjustified' concepts like identity, meaning and object, then why should we care about 'the fact' that these concepts are constituted by human interests. Why could we not also idealise this interest-relatedness away, if we are at all events bound to use the concepts as already idealised?[32]

However, the status of power or interest-relatedness is not equal with that of temporal ordering, for instance. We have shown the non-identifiableness of certain conceptions, but on the other hand we are actually using them as if they were identifiable. Now, 'the will to power' is a *solution* to this dilemma. It is an *explanation* about why we actually need these idealisations – we get power through them. Certainly, to express this conjecture (which as such is nevertheless 'quite natural') means to be transferred to a more concrete level in the metaontological hierarchy, but this is the price for saying something.[33] Moreover, the interest-relatedness is not just an explanation, it is also a *justification* for these idealisations. *It is a cause and a reason* – and a guide to a better self-understanding. Now we can see that if we idealise this interest-relatedness away, we have to search for another explanation, or at least we have to justify the use of these idealisations by other means.

Biography

Tommi Vehkavaara (born 4.9. 1965 in Tampere) Master of Science, 5.2. 1992 at the University of Jyväskylä. Researcher of philosophy at the University of Tampere. Preparing the dissertation on 'Structural knowledge and the metaphysics of changes – A dynamic epistemology in terms of evolution and power'.

Notes

1. 'Pseudoconcepts' of *différance* and *trace* are discussed in Derrida's article "La Différance" [1968], but their proper use and context are better exposed in Derrida [1967a, 1967b, 1967c], where 'the western metaphysics of presence' is deconstructed.
2. "For us, differance remains as a metaphysical name; (…)" (Derrida [1968], p. 158).
3. Derrida [1972], pp. 6, 12. In this respect Derrida can be compared with Wittgenstein.
4. Even if somebody holds that this kind of 'consciously-made-possible-misunderstanding' is immoral, the defence can refer to Derrida's own text, where he claims to try to *write* without meaning to say anything (Derrida [1972], p. 14). If we accept the conception of meaning that is included in *différance*, there will be no original or authentic meaning to refer to – and this must hold for Derrida's texts as well.
5. See Saussure [1916], pp. 108-109 (page numbers are in accordance with the standard pagination adopted since the second edition in 1922).
6. There has recently been some new research concerning the logic of meaning as a process (Oesch & Rantala [forthcoming]).

7. 'Identifiable meanings' are ideal in two senses: Firstly, they exist only in our (structures of) understanding – they have no 'independent material existence'. Secondly, these 'ideal objects' cannot be identified unless their mutual ordering in time (and their temporality in general) is not idealised away.
8. Derrida [1972], p. 9.
9. In this paper only temporal ordering is concerned as a motive for *différance*. However, spatial ordering and differing have as central consequences for *différance* as temporality, even though they are not concerned here (unlike in Derrida's texts).
10. Surprisingly, it is possible to find an analogy between the Darwinist conception of evolution and *différance*: In Darwinism the *genes, organisms* or *species* are adapting to an ever-changing *environment*, similarly as *meaning* is adapting to ever-changing *context* in the metaphysics of *différance*. However, the concept of adaptation is dangerous, if it is applied too carelessly – all the changes cannot be interpreted as adaptations. The idiotism of Voltaire's Dr. Pangloss must be avoided. See Gould & Lewontin [1979] and Lewontin [1978, 1979, 1982].
11. The idea is about the same as in Husserlian phenomenology (which is also its intellectual ancestor through Derrida [1967b]). Because of its epistemic character subjective realism as metaphysical attitude is clearly related with traditional idealism as well as with radical empirism (and positivism!) It could be also called *epistemic realism*, because the ontological units are not considered 'from the God's eye point of view', but from the point of view of the human subject. However in addition to its relatives, subjective realism emphasises realism especially with respect to concepts and practice through which the world is appearing to us. Subjective realism can be contrasted with *ontological realism*, in which some linguistic, logical, psychological, or physical structure is (often implicitly) taken as a basic 'a priori' system, which cannot be overcome within the same system.
12. The phrase "our experience" should be interpreted here in a wide sense. Experience refers here also to 'inner experience' and 'the object' of experience can be a mental state or even the whole experiencing subject as well as any 'outer object' (or 'the Other').
13. The choice for ontological thinking does not properly exclude the possibility of looking at changes, but whenever changes are researched, what is seen (and looked for) is just what has remained stable. Concepts of natural law and causation are good examples of this.
14. The point here is not to claim the impossibility of, say, realist ontology. Rather, the point is to introduce an alternative that is more general and less restrictive than traditional metaphysics – an alternative that fulfills all (or at least the most of) those reasons that recommend ontological thinking.
15. Even basic research can be said to be constructed for power although in quite an indirect way. So called 'theoretical interest' may start to seem 'practical' (although apparently less practical than pure technical interest), if we consider the researcher's personal motives; why (s)he has such an interest. Of course, the conception of power is referred to here in very general sense – probably its closest well-known relative is Foucault's conception about *power/knowledge*. Here the conception of power can be characterised generally as an *ability to do something*. For instance, any genuine increase of knowledge about the world can also be seen as the increase of our power. The better we understand relations between the world and us, the better we are capable of doing what *can be done* – we have more resources to manipulate the world the way we like. It could be maintained that this is the ultimate justification (and perhaps also a source of satisfaction) in any research based on 'theoretical' interest. This bond

between power, knowledge, and potential action is not restricted only to conscious knowledge and action, but is generalisable over unconscious fields also. On the status of power see remark 2 at the end of this paper.

16. This can be seen for instance in the article "On the Very Idea of a Conceptual Scheme" (1974), pp. 183-198 in Davidson [1984]. Notice, that only Davidson's *metaphysical* conclusions (or presuppositions) about the nature of languages are criticised here.
17. For instance Saussure was clearly aware of the methodical and idealised character of his theory of linguistic signs (Saussure [1916], pp. 150-151). However, the practice has not always been the same as the theory later in French structuralism.
18. Derrida [1983], pp. 70-71.
19. Derrid a[1968], pp. 153-154.
20. Three levels seem to be a minimum amount of levels. Of course, the division could be more detailed or more dimensions could be added. For instance, there are also other ways to different ontologies to be compatible but just hierarchical. One is the attitude of instrumentalist, relativist, or pragmatist, where different ontologies are valued as theoretically equal but the criterion of choice is pragmatic, non-constant and common sensical 'better appropriateness'.
21. Here neither *différance* nor common sense can be considered as 'systems'. Whenever we are using them as 'coherentisised', we are in fact introducing a 'system' or 'metaphysics' that is placed at some metaphysical level *between* these two – like all the other metaphysical systems and notions used by sciences, philosophy, religions, etc.
22. The concept of replicator has been abstracted from the concept of gene by picking a few, but for natural selection sufficient, properties of genes and defining the term 'replicator' by these properties. Even though the whole operation was made to emphasise the status of genes in natural selection, it also has other consequences. According to Dawkins the concept of replicator is applicable not only to genes, but also to *memes*, that can work as units in sociocultural evolution. This is one way that abstract ontologies become legitimised. By shifting the ontology of natural selection to a more abstract level Dawkins made also an effort to widen the scope of this kind of theory of natural selection. (Dawkins [1976,1978]) On memes (and critics of Dawkins) see also Hull [1981, 1982]. Mutually incompatible theories or notions at one level can be compatible with some theory at a more abstract level. So, the more abstract a metaphysics is, the more general, at least potentially, theories and notions are and they are applicable to more phenomena.
23. There are many features of this metaontology that cannot be discussed in detail here: For instance, the more abstract the metaphysics of a theory is, the less it can say about the world. Also its application, outside the apparent discourse of this theory, is less direct (and usually less probable too). Even though at the level of 'epistemic metaphysics' different sorts of antirealistic attitude are common they are not necessary. The realism-antirealism dichotomy does not match exactly with the ontological concreteness-abstractness -'axis'.
24. If this figure does not seem to enlighten the mutual relationships of metaphysical levels, it should not be considered any longer. Its only purpose is to concretise the metaphysical levels of the metaontology.
25. If the 'necessary' power relation behind this interest has to be defined, it may rise from the anxiety that ontological thinking is not enough anymore – the characters of the world it necessarily forgets have at last become relevant. In this way, as a source of analogy, it is possible that the metaphysics of *différance* can increase our power.

26. A classical formulation of the kind of EE referred to here is Campbell [1974].
27. Callebaut & Pinxten [1987b], p. 4.
28. A good example of evolutionary analysis at this level is a kind of *dialectical* interpretation of evolution that is discussed in Levins & Lewontin [1985] (although this does not itself belong to EE). In EE a fruitful approach can be found for example in Plotkin [1987], although it is based on research at a more concrete metaphysical level, see Plotkin & Odling-Smee [1979, 981, 1982].
29. Structural knowledge can be characterised as (usually unconscious) environmental information that has been stored up in some kind of structure. These structures can be physical, as genetic structures, but they can as well be mental or cultural. Even though there is correspondence between a knowledge and the world, there is no sense to talk about the truth (or truthfulness) of structural knowledge in general. Structural knowledge is characteristically non-propositional (like genetic information) and it corresponds only with past world – it is always (more or less) out of its time. Even though no other change happens in the environment, the environment is changed at least by this process of knowledge-storing itself. Therefore, a kind of *uncertainty principle* (analogous to the quantum mechanical *Heisenberg's uncertainty principle*) can be said to hold for structural knowledge (and probably for all knowledge). If Dawkins' conception of meme is reasonable at all, memes might form an exemplification of 'socio-structural knowledge'. This would need some further study, but the conception of 'socio-structural knowledge' is apparently at more abstract metaphysical level than memes are.
30. Because structural knowledge is here almost synonymous with adaptation, the same reservations about its too eager use have to be taken into account. See the note 10.
31. These remarks arise from the discussion after my presentation in Odense in 13.8. 1995, although some of the corrections have been made straight into the text (especially in chapters 3 and 4). I cannot unfortunately answer all comments, but these two seem to be the most crucial. I am grateful to all the participants of the workshop led by associate professor Søren Harnow Klausen (from the University of Odense).
32. I am indebted to professor Ingvar Johansson (from the University of Umeå) for this problem. Even though I could not give an answer to it satisfactorily in the discussion, it made me study the status of idealisations more carefully. I am grateful to him for this question and I hope that I understood his question correctly and that the following answer is complete enough.
33. Unlike Derrida (Derrida [1972] p. 14), I do not have any motive for trying to say nothing. Surely, it is possible to keep talking only at 'the level of deconstruction'. However, if we stay purely at that level, meaning will appear as a 'totally uncontrollable flow' and we cannot have any clue about what are the 'real' effects of our words. Because we are not usually holding forth on 'the most abstract level', we are capable to control that 'flow of meaning', even though this control is always only partial control.

Bibliography

Callebaut, Werner & Pinxten, Rik (eds.) [1987a] *Evolutionary Epistemology. A Multiparadigm Program,* D.Reidel; Dordrecht.

Callebaut, Werner & Pinxten, Rik [1987b] "Evolutionary Epistemology Today: Converging Views from Philosophy, the Natural and the Social Sciences", in Callebaut & Pinxten [1987a], pp. 3-55.

Campbell, Donald T. [1974] "Evolutionary Epistemology", for instance in Plotkin [1982], pp. 73-108.

Davidson, Donald [1984] *Inquiries into Truth and Interpretation*, Oxford University Press; Oxford 1991.

Dawkins, Richard [1976] *The Selfish Gene*, Oxford University Press; New York 1978 "Replicator Selection and the Extended Phenotype", *Zeitschrift für Tierpsychologie* 47, pp. 61-76.

Derrida, Jacques [1967a] *Of Grammatology,* (*De la grammatologie*, transl. Gayatri Spivak), The Johns Hopkins University Press; Baltimore and London 1974.

Derrida, Jacques [1967b] *Speech and Phenomena And Other Essays on Husserl's Theory of Signs,* (*La Voix et le Phénomène,* transl. David B. Allison), Northwestern University Press; Evanston 1973.

Derrida, Jacques [1967c] *Writing and Difference,* (*L'écriture et la différence,* transl. Alan Bass), Routledge & Kegan, Paul; London 1978.

Derrida, Jacques [1968] "Differance", ("La différance", transl. David B. Allison), in Derrida [1967b], pp. 129-160.

Derrida, Jacques [1972] *Positions,* (transl. Alan Bass) The University of Chicago; Chicago 1981.

Derrida, Jacques [1983] "Kirje japanilaiselle ystävälle", ("Lettre à un ami japonais", transl. Mauri Pasanen) *Synteesi* 3/1985, pp. 68-72.

Gould, Stephen Jay & Lewontin, Richard [1979] "The spandrels of San Marco and the Panglossian paradigm: a critique of the adaptionist programme", *Proceedings of the Royal Society of London* B 205, pp. 581-598.

Hull, David L. [1981] "Units of Evolution: A Metaphysical Essay", in Jensen & Harré [1981], pp. 23-44 1982 "The Naked Meme", in Plotkin [1982], pp. 273-327.

Jensen, Uffe & Harré, Rom (ed.) [1981] *The Philosophy of Evolution,* St. Martin's Press; New York.

Levins, Richard & Lewontin, Richard [1985] *The Dialectical Biologist*, Harvard University Press; Cambridge (Mass.).

Lewontin, Richard C. [1978] "Adaptation", *Scientific American,* 293(3), pp. 156-169.

Lewontin, Richard C. [1979] "Sociobiology as an Adaptationist Program", *Behavioral Science* 24(1), pp. 5-14.

Lewontin, Richard C. [1982] "Organism and Environment", in Plotkin [1982], pp. 151-170.

Oesch, Erna & Rantala, Veikko [forthcoming] "Interpretation, Reception, and Aesthetic Experience".

Plotkin, Henry C. (ed.) [1982] *Learning, Development, and Culture: Essays in Evolutionary Epistemology,* John Wiley & Sons; New York.

Plotkin, Henry C. [1987] "Evolutionary Epistemology and the Synthesis of Biological and Social Science", in Callebaut & Pinxten [1987a], pp. 75-96.

Plotkin, H. C. & Odling-Smee, F. J. [1979] "Learning, Change, and Evolution: An Enquiry into the Teleonomy of Learning", *Advances in the Study of Behavior,* 10, pp. 1-41.

Plotkin, H. C. & Odling-Smee, F. J. [1981] "A multiple-level model of evolution and its implications for sociobiology", *The Behavioral and Brain Sciences,* 4(2), pp. 225-268.

Plotkin, H. C. & Odling-Smee, F. J. [1982] "Learning in the Context of a Hierarchy of Knowledge Gaining Process", in Plotkin [1982], pp. 443-471.

Saussure, Ferdinand de [1916] *Course in General Linguistics*, (*Cours de linguistique générale*, eds. Charles Bally & Albert Sechehaye, transl. Roy Harris), Duckworth; London 1983.

Peter Wolsing
Nature and Life Practice in the Epistemology of the Young Hegel

Abstract
In his early work Hegel presents a philosophical diagnosis of modern consciousness and its way of understanding and acting in the world. Accounting for the main views in his "Difference treatise" I argue that Hegel theoretically anticipates some of the practical problems of late modernity's relation to nature. What Hegel considers the dualism between a powerful subjectivity and a oppressed objectivity from Descartes up to Fichte has a striking parallel in the manipulating and exploiting features of the activities of modern science and technology towards nature. Accounting for some aspects of Hegel's critique of Fichte's concept of nature (inner nature and social life) I use Hegel to suggest that both an oppressive and an unrestrained relationship to nature can be traced back to the intellectual level. As an alternative to abstract understanding Hegel develops a concept of concrete reason which considers nature potentially ideal. The visions he develops from that intuition corresponds convincingly with experiences of our century: the necessity of integrating inner nature to achieve the wholeness of the personality (psychoanalysis); and the free development of life as a necessary condition of a whole and stable society.

In this paper I will present an outline of one of the early writings of Hegel, namely "The Difference between Fichte's and Schelling's Systems of Philosophy". This work is commonly ignored among Hegel scholars as it belongs to his early production which mainly consists of short essays or fragmentaric pieces that comment on the philosophical research of his days. And indeed this work ("Difference-treatise") is no exception to that. It is purely programmatic, offers no detailed treatment of any particular philosophical problem and furthermore it is a defence of a position held by another philosopher, namely his college Schelling.

Still Hegel here presents a problem which ought to be of current interest to our time. It not only concerns the epistemology of his time but even seems to anticipate and describe a far more serious situation, namely the appearing problems in late modernity's problematic relation to nature. In this paper I intend to sketch the view of the treatise and suggest that Hegel in this treatise draws a very accurate picture of the situation and problem mentioned. The exposition will aim at hinting that Hegel has some interesting points as to the nature and origine of its conflict, the main one being the argument that philosophy is that very practise that is able to and is obliged to present a conceptual diagnosis of essential problems of the life practise of the age and that such a critical analysis – as it proceeds – forms the vision of an ideal human life.

The task which Hegels imposes on himself in his "Difference treatise" is – as the title suggests – to defend his college and friend Schelling against a tendency to neglect the peculiarity of his philosophical system. In a survey over the philosophy of the age the influential philosopher Reinhold almost identified Schellings system with Fichtes arguing that Schelling has not – as intended – surpassed Fichtes position. In his treatise Hegel defends Schelling and tries to stress the differences in a comparative account of the systems of his two colleges emphazising the originality of Schellings concept of Nature. The task which Hegel imposes on himself is then to account in details for the epistemological and practical consequenses of taking – as Schelling does it – one's philosophical point of departure in an intuition of Nature as the basic source of all conscious life. In order to unfold that idea Hegel confronts it with the opposite position, namely with Fichtes philosophy which systematically sets human subjectivity as the centre for all experience and rational action. The exposition then runs as a critique of the view that sets subjectivity as the counterpart to life (Fichte). The basis is Schellings view on nature as the basis of all life including human subjectivity.

But in a wider context Hegel's enterprise also invokes interest due to the philosophical tradition in which it places itself. Indeed he is strongly influence by Schelling who was the younger pioneer of the time. But still, in a prosaic reflection of the philosophical conquests of Schelling Hegel attempts to show that serious progress is now being made in the cartesian tradition to overcome the dualism which philosophy has struggled with from Descartes' "cogito" up to Kant's and Fichte's concept of transcendental subjectivity.

But also as a source to an understanding of Hegel's own philosophy this early treatise is important. Hegel's commonly known stressing of the ethically actualized individuality (the basis of the "Philosophy of Right") instead of the "isolated" subjectivity of Kant and Fichte is here presented in its epistemological aspect. His critique of cartesian dualism not only expresses his interest in theoretical philosophy but is motivated by an interest in the social and spiritual conditions of his age, – a concern that lies behind his enterprise of the whole "Difference treatise". In this short paper I intend to give proof of this point of view: The view that Hegel's main task is only an epistemological one trying to overcome the dualism of his predecessors *theoretically* is too narrow. There is a distinctly practical aspect of his dialectic, a pronounced interest in matters of life practise. The general orientation towards human reality and history in Hegel's mature system is indeed commonly known. But I will argue that already the "Difference treatise" in a very clear way shows the inner connexion between epistemology and life practise as Hegel thought it – say in his "Philosophy of Right".

Hegel was not the first to introduce the practical aspect of understanding, in fact within the german philosophical tradition Fichte already did that, considering transcendental subjectivity not only an apperception as in Kant but an act. Kant indeed suggests that practical reason is prior to theoretical but not untill in Fichte this idea becomes fundamental to a philosophical system. In short, the consequence of Fichte's step meant that practical reason as a conscious act sets reality as it is, leaving it to theoretical reason only to reflect what already has been constituted by this act. Knowledge then becomes the theoretical attitude that accompanies the originally practical engagement in the world.

In that step from Kant to Fichte Hegel saw an important progress in the philosophical tradition because it contributed to seeing the concrete, that is, the living relations between man and nature and the social relations as the proper background to philosophy's otherwise abstract reflections concerning the nature of subjectivity, of being and of knowledge, action etc. In Hegel's eyes, however, the problem in Fichte is that after all he does not admit that practical relations as historical facts can be essential. Though practical in its origin Fichte's concept of reason is not "loosened" from the ideality of subjectivity. It remains a kind of practical, that is moral, vision which cannot see itself reconciled with empirical reality. The latter namely is partly characterized by what Hegel calls opposition, difference and aimlessnes. And that creates a vehement problem when the intrinsic nature of reason is to actualize itself. The resulting collision between subjectivity and objectivity, between the moral vision of the good life and actual life as both good and bad is what Hegel tempts to show as the result of a fichtean philosophy which takes abstract subjectivity as its point of departure.

The fundamental problem, Hegel argues, is that in order to transform, so to speak, the abstract intuition of selfconsciousness into reality – which is absolutely necessary for it to become a truth – the "I" (that has the vision) has to find itself in shapes of that reality. It is here that Hegel sees the essential merit of Schelling's philosophy of nature: Or if the "I" should be able to actualize itself as a part of nature in the widest sense of this term it must be shown philosophically that nature – in Hegel's terminology both outer and inner nature as well as society – , that nature itself is potentially rational. The age needs – in Hegel's words – a new concept of nature which can liberate it from the role it has played up till now as "pure matter" only suitable for being formed by the intellect and by the enterprises of a self-centered human being. – That way of speaking indeed sounds emotional and may not be proper for a philosophical treatise but in fact Hegel uses expressions like that only to tell us what ought to be the basic motive of philosophical thinking. He speaks about nature having become *maltreated* by the systems of Kant and Fichte and about a need for a philosophy that can provide us with a *reconcilliation* with nature.

Now, if as a hypothesis we assume that we are such subjectivities as the fichtean one creating images of nature that reflects our practical engagements which forms it for the satisfaction of our selfconscious purposes, – how then must we on a philosophical level understand nature to change this attitude in order to accomplish this socalled reconcilliation with nature in practical life? Though basically interested in practical matters Hegel nevertheless insists that philosophical contemplation is necessary because it alone can develop the change in our way of thinking which is the very basis of a change in practical attitudes. In relation to Fichte he considers the anthropocentric attitude and suppressing relationship to nature to be rooted in what he calls "understanding" ("Verstand"). The character of understanding is essentially a determining activity, that means that its very nature is to identify something. Now, Hegel's point is that the act of determining can never be brought to an end because it is blind to the essential feature of the world as a living self-developping whole. Understanding as a determining activity in a way makes its object "stiffen". Consequently, claiming its power in an endless effort to determine nature understanding nevertheless is condemned to create the limits to its own activity. The light it sheds on the world in the progress of science is accompanied by an inherent shadow, the "thing in itself", the essence behind. It is furthermore Hegel's view that the character of this kind of thinking also reveals itself in the philosophical tradition, f.x. in the dualisms between body and soul, freedom and necessety and faith and knowledge. Hegel's point is here that the socalled metaphysical aspect of these antagonisms are in principle not inaccessible to reason. They only appear as "a beyond" to the shape of it called understanding.

So Fichte's understanding turns out to be insufficient as to theoretical knowledge. It does not succeed in getting rid of the Kantian "thing in itself". But at a practical level it is even worse; here it becomes the very source of oppression both in individuality's relation to himself and in the state's relation to its citizens. As to the first aspect – man's relation to his inner nature – what presents itself to the intellect seems to be chaotic impulses, inclinations and emotions. Why is that? Because these natural qualities disturbes the steady and self-transparent being-for-itself of selfconsciousness. And being principally a determining activity man's relation to his own nature can only be an oppressive one.

Now Hegel's scheme allows for an alternative attitude. From the point of view of *reason (Vernunft)* – as opposed to that of *understanding* – he argues the other way around: inner life is ideal in itself (in Hegel's words: nature is potential reason), – that means that it promotes by nature the growth of the human personality. But it presents itself as chaotic and threatening to selfconsciousness only because the latter makes a threatening , that is determining, attack on it. If, on the contrary, man's relation to himself is seen from the perspective of reason, the inner natural powers turn out to be the opposite, namely indispensable instances of self-actualization. What is needed is to turn the activity of determining into an active awareness of the inner nature's own presentation of its inherent reason. Identifying us with that process we should gradually discover ourselves in it – not as abstract selfconsciousness but as concrete and living individuals.

As to the aspect of social life Hegel's treatise not only deals critically with Fichte's political philosophy but speaks with anxiety about the miserable condition that modern society finds itself in. The object of his critique is both the almost totalitarian state that Fichte constructs and the atomized, individualistic society that he witnesses in his age. It is easy to see that the one presupposes the other. Hegel suggests that the fichtean state is almost the logical answer to the anarchistic tendencies of the modern individualistic society: If people cannot controle themselves the authorities must do it for them. As a construction of understanding social life in Fichtes philosophy becomes essentially a determined one. Being principly the maintainer of freedom against the anarchism of natural human life the exercise of state power in as many human relations as possible must be the only way to actualize freedom. But paradoxically what should be the realm of freedom now turns out to be a police state: the more controle the more freedom. As a critique Hegel uses the reduction ad absurdum. The theory falsifies itself. From the point of view of reason Hegel can argue that the omnipotence of the totalitarian state is always only an apparent power. Its sneaking into every area of society cannot be interpreted as an expression of power but as its impotence. Here again the nature of "understanding" shows itself. As state controle increases the potential opposition does as well. In order to grasp every aspect of reality (here in the literal sense) understanding only pushes the indeterminate in front of it, here in the shape of the unpredictable in social life which is therefore the potential threat to the state. Hegel's point is here that unity in social life cannot be actualized on the premisses of a totalitarian state power just as man on his part does not develop into a real harmonious whole individuality on the basis of abstract subjectivity alone.

However, in this treatise Hegel do not elaborate his alternative views on the nature of man and society in details. They confine themselves to short hints beside his detailed critical remarks to the subjective idealism in the philosophy of his time. For instance he suggests his vision of "…the noble community in which laws can be replaced by manners and customs, the excesses of unsatisfied life by holy pleasures, and in which the crimes of the oppressed power can be rendered superfluous by possible work for noble subjects" (Hegel. Werke in zwanzig Bänden, Frankfurt am Main 1970, vol. 2: page 84).

What Hegel says here – almost prophetically anticipating the miserable experiences of mankind in our century – is that laws and state controle are not the means to put down crime and excess. On the contrary these are sometimes "logical" responses to the oppression of human nature. Hegel's point is that it is understanding that creates the distance to nature and among men, a distance which leads to various kinds of oppression. It is precisely understanding – an imperfect shape of reason – that creates the monster that it endeavors to put down. If nature is exclusively treated as "pure matter to be modified by an external power" its potential reason will react in a correspondingly destructive way. And contrary, if that part of nature which Hegel here calls social life is considered potentially ideal the basis for a union of mankind is present. For if life is entrusted to itself it will manifest the pulse of freedom which it has in itself, namely a productive interaction of both differentiation and association. That kind of life, in Hegel's words, will further the consciousness that contradictions presuppose union and that only the unity which can endure its own differentiation is a true, that is, a real one.

Though the "Difference treatise" is in a sense not a complete work I find it important for several reasons. First it states Hegel's view on the relationship between epistemology and life world in a way that in many respects is more clear than in his "Philosophy of Right". The young Hegel connects theoretical philosophy with social philosophy in that he lets such concepts as subjectivity, dualism, nature etc. be expressions of a the spiritual state of man in a certain age. The basic problem of theoretical philosophy, dualism, then is a problem that should be solved exactly because it reflects unbearable tensions in individual and social life. The concept "Entzweiung" which Hegel uses frequently both relates to philosophical dualism and tensions in human life. Philosophy then serves life in that its meaning is to begin from the engagement in the life of one's time. On the other hand it can contribute to that life: philosophical thinking according to Hegel has the concepts to make us able to survey and diagnose the age and insisting to overcome "Entzweiung" it may produce insights and fruitful visions for life.

The present treatise invokes interest because it is an attempt to come to terms with an urgent problem of modernity, namely the "oppressed" nature. By analyzing this complex practical mater in philosophical terms and by placing it within a certain philosophical tradition and way of thinking Hegel, in my opinion, not only succeeds in presenting an interesting diagnosis of the core of modernity but furthermore he drives philosophical thinking to a spiritual level where it might become a source of visions which can contribute to solving problems of practical life.

Hegel's critical but also constructive philosophical analysis of man's relation to himself, his analysis of modern social life as well as his explanation of the atomized and totalitarian society speak for themselves. Nature might indeed be the riddle of modernity and this embarrasment the basis of its crisis.

Biography

Born in 1963. MA in philosophy and indian philology. Currently working on a Ph.D.-thesis.

Bibliography

G. W. F. Hegel: "Differenz des Fichteschen und Schellingschen Systems der Philosophie" in Werke in Zwanzig Bänden, Suhrkamp, Frankfurt am Main 1970, bd. 2.
Georg Henrik von Wright: "Vetenskapen och förnuftet", 1986.
Peter Wolsing: "Intellekt og natur" i Philosophia årg. 19, nr. 3-4, Århus 1990, s. 52-70.